Stories From the Well
by
Tracy Medling

House of Walker Publishing

Permissions:

Library of Congress Control Number: 2015934546
Copyright © Stories from the Well/Tracy Medling
Cover design by: Bethany Brohinsky
Art work by: Alicia Smith
ISBN: 978-0-9834762-4-5

Table of Contents

Special Thanks

To my husband, Steve:

Thank you for loving me and caring for me through some pretty intense times over the past 32 years. There are days when it surprises me that we have made it this far considering our challenges. Thank you for not giving up. I love you!

To my mothers,

Rachel Etchells and Estelle Medling:

Thank you for being my models of growth, tenacity, determination, and faith despite everything you endured. Thank you for showing me that surrendering to God is not defeat, but the only way to victory over frustration for things we cannot change – but He can. Thank you for your love, your confidence and your heart. I will see both of you in Heaven someday!

To Carol, Judy, Deb, and Lynn.

You are women I have been privileged to call my best friends – and so much more! From raising our children while trying to retain our sanity, to exploring true faith and learning to depend on God for everything, I am blessed to know you all. I will forever be grateful for your presence in my life.

To Loring and David

Your help in editing was invaluable to me. Thank you both for "polishing the stone", to bring more clarity and to reveal the beauty from the rocks in my collection.

To Alicia and Bethany

Your talents and abilities to take the picture from my head and create the cover of my life story is amazing. Thank you so much for sharing your gifts with me for this project!

To Michelle

You will always have my gratitude and thanks for enabling me to publish the life-lessons I have learned - and am still learning! - for the purpose of helping others navigate their own journeys through life. Your encouragement, expertise and patient perseverance with me through this process is very much appreciated! Your friendship is a gift I value.

May God's Blessings and Limitless Grace Abound toward all of you!

Dedication

I dedicate this book to Jesus Christ - my Savior and so much more.

Thank You for meeting me at the well, continually and gently freeing me from condemnation and fear. Thank You for showing me how "precious and multiplied Your thoughts and intentions are toward me", especially when I've felt so completely valueless and unworthy of Your gentle affection and unconditional Love. You are the lifter of my head and I want to praise You with everything in me forever, for everything You've done, are doing and continue to do in my heart and in those I hold dearest to me.

My greatest regret in life is not running after You sooner and discovering how truly wonderful You are and enjoying You, before my ignorance of Your Grace adversely impacted other people and our time together.

Thank You for removing every trace of shame and for promising that You are still completing Your work in us all. I cannot imagine my life without You!

In gratitude, I offer this book to those who want to meet the Man Who told me everything I ever did – and made it possible for me to smile about it!

Stories from the Well

One Woman's Journey After Meeting
"The Man Who Told Me Everything I Ever Did"

Introduction

In the Bible's book of John, Chapter 4, a wonderful story is told. Less than 2 thousand years ago, a dusty, thirsty man, a carpenter by trade, had what looked like an "accidental" meeting at a well with a woman no one else in the little Samaritan town of Sychar wanted to associate with. As she approached the well in the heat of the day, far from others' watchful eyes, she realized she was not alone. Not in the mood for conversation, she busied herself with the task at hand - drawing the water she needed for her daily use at home. He broke the uneasy silence as He asked her for a drink. She was wary of this Jewish man, as she reminded Him that "Jews do not associate with the Samaritans".[1] Jesus challenged her perceptions of the meeting and told her He could give her a drink that would forever satisfy her deepest need. Her wariness gave way to curiosity as she pointed out the obvious – that He had nothing to draw with and the well was deep. How could He possibly give her water? He explained what He offered her was not natural water that required her continual return to this hole in the ground, but an encounter that would result in "a spring of water welling up to eternal life"[2] within her.

This conversation was getting a little too intense for her liking and she changed the subject to flattery and distraction, bringing up the differences in their religious beliefs. That, she thought, should end this pretty quickly and she could then return home as she had planned. But He took a detour through the barriers she erected, revealing that He knew everything about her, in sharpest detail. He followed that up with a declaration she could not escape: those who truly want to worship God must "worship the Father in spirit and in truth (reality)".[3] Her interest was piqued as the shell she had spent years enclosing her heart behind began to crack. Could this be...? Her breath caught in her chest as she dared to think that maybe, was it possible...? Could she really have stumbled on the greatest hope of her broken heart, the answer to her outcast state in life? "I know that Messiah (called Christ) is coming. When He comes, He will explain everything to us."[4] Her trickle of hope became a geyser of freedom as He plainly told her: "I...am He".[5] In just a few moments, she was changed from a guilt-ridden, secretive outcast to the first joyfully unashamed Samaritan evangelist, running back to town to share the freedom of heart she received from this "chance" meeting.

So it can be with all of us.

This book is my heart sharing. They are the stories from my life – past, present and still unfolding. It is a display of God's gentle guidance, of closed and opened doors, and of encouragement along each step of a sometimes bitter path. Each one of these experiences has helped to shape the person I am becoming. The chapters of this book address issues and encounters I have had in my own life. I have lived to see the other side of each one of them with increasing degrees of victory - because of Jesus.

Like the woman at that well in Samaria, who ran back to town and was unashamed to shout out to the people she had been avoiding moments before, "Come, see a Man Who has told me everything that I ever did!",[6] I offer stories from my life and the lessons He is teaching me along the way. This life is a process, not an event. Each encounter and experience discloses more of who we are in relation to our greatest hope. And like the Samaritan woman, I have gone from wariness, to curiosity, to being a joyful recipient of this living water that continually finds new ways to quench my ever-thirsty and sometimes way-ward heart - given to me from a very loving and compassionate God.

I offer analogies and illustrations in the many different ways He is helping me navigate this process of life — sometimes as Daddy, sometimes as Captain, sometimes as a cheerleader, sometimes as supply sergeant - His repertoire is endless in its variety. Sometimes He interacts directly with me and sometimes He takes alternate routes through the tender care of other people. He is so many things in my everyday life. He is my redeemer, my ever-present help in time of need, the best friend I could ever have - past, present and future. He is the lifter of my head when I am tempted to hang it in shame. He is the shield against the fiery darts that want to consume my efforts when I struggle ineffectively to win various battles on my own. And when my own efforts prove once again to be vastly insufficient for the task at hand, He gently reminds me that I am trying to fix things myself instead of seeking His solutions. He invites me once again to get reconnected with Him as my source of loving guidance and instruction, without berating me or chiding me for my failures.

He promises… "Come to me, all you who are weary and burdened, and I will give you rest".[7]

His invitation is purposeful and omniscient — He knows everything about us and loves us deeply in spite of our waywardness, far beyond our ability to understand. He already knows all of our baggage. He knows the pieces of our past that have shaped and led us to where we are now. If allowed by each of us, He will use and arrange these shattered pieces to create the perfect stained glass window of who we were thoughtfully and intentionally created to be. He reaches out to dispel the lies that make us shy away from Him and tells us clearly: "Therefore [there is] now no condemnation...for those who are in Christ Jesus...for the law of the spirit of life, [which is] in Christ Jesus,... has freed me from the law of sin and death"...and nothing "else in all creation will be able to separate us from the love of God which is in Christ Jesus our Lord"[8] when we accept His gift for ourselves!

He reassures us that His plans for us are "plans to prosper you and not to harm you, plans to give you hope and a future."[9]

He calls and invites us to lay down our blinders and pride when He says to us "In rest and repentance is your salvation; in quietness and trust is your strength."[10] And when we resist this path, He lets us "ride off on (our own) horses" of self-provision and self-determination until we feel like a flagpole on a hill,[11] exposed to the elements and weary from the battle, before gently reminding us that this was never His intention for us. He holds out His hand and lifts His voice to tell us He is waiting for us, to bless us and restore us and heal us and He "will rise up to show you compassion..." He is leaning forward to hear the slightest whisper of a prayer from our hearts reaching out for His grace. He promises that if we give Him a chance, He will deliver "His victory...favor...love...peace...joy... and His matchless, unbroken companionship"[12] and mercy to all who call on Him! He calls to the depths of your heart: "Whether you turn to the right or to the left, your ears will hear a voice behind you, saying, 'This is the way; walk in it'."[13]

I want you to understand that I am still very much a work in progress. I am not some expert that has gotten this all right and now am telling other people how to do life. I still get frustrated; I still battle inside myself when I slip back into not relying on God's grace for my strength. I want to reflect the words of Paul in Philippians 3:12-14 that say, "not that I have now attained [this ideal], or have already been made perfect,"... "but one thing I do...forgetting what lies behind" - both the good I have been able to do in Christ's enablement and regrets over things I wish I had done differently on my own - "I press on toward the goal". I am thankful for the hope He freely gives and am determined to take hold of everything that Jesus' death on the cross provided for me. I am learning to enjoy the priceless gift of peacefully resting in God's will for me every day!

In the process of this sharing, I bring up teachers and resources I have benefited from along the way - vessels that Jesus has used to draw water for me from His well, people who have been used by God to contribute to my story. I reference friends, family, publications and acquaintances that reflect our common humanity and share how they have won victories over similar struggles. I recommend some of their books throughout my writing (in addition to the footnotes giving them due credit) as resources for your journey. Some are sign posts providing direction; some illustrate boundaries that should not be crossed, others are lamp posts that help to shed light on the correct path for our lives. All have been useful and my heart "overflows in many [cries of] thanksgiving to God."[14]

The people referenced have been valuable to me, fulfilling their roles in the body of Christ; for them I am very grateful. When I recommend books and teachings for your edification and spiritual education, if their "flavor" of worship or teaching is not something you are used to, that's okay too. We all come from different experiences and challenges. Jesus clearly told us, "I have other sheep"[15] in sheepfolds (denominations, belief systems, experiences) that are not our own. Instead of getting caught up in the details that we don't agree on right now, I encourage you to consider the different perspectives they offer and submit it to Jesus. Pray that the Holy Spirit would thresh out the husks and feed you the kernels of truth He personally wrapped up specifically in these teachings for you. He will teach you everything you need to know and show you what to discard. For now, while we engage in debate and share ideas with one another, we may have to agree to disagree in some areas, as we continue to relate as brothers and sisters. When we ultimately get to heaven, He will reveal where we each strayed in our understanding.

When used in reference to what I am explaining, I have used several translations of the Bible. Passages from the Amplified Bible are designated by (amp). This version includes details taken from the original Greek and Hebrew meanings in [brackets] and (parentheses) to broaden our understanding of the translation. Where otherwise noted I have also used references from the New International Version (NIV), for ease of reading and to keep the flow moving smoothly, and the New King James version (NKJV) for familiarity for most people who began with and are still using King James (KJV). I've also used a couple from the English Standard Version (ESV) for the specific words that version uses. I encourage you to look up these scriptures in the translation you usually use or are more familiar with to see the differences and subtleties between them.

Now let us go together to the well, God's well of truth, knowledge and love. The only well that can permanently quench the deepest thirst of our souls!

Come! Meet a Man who told me everything I ever did!

[1] John 4:9, NIV

[2] ibid v. 14

[3] John 4 23, amp

[4] John 4:25, NIV

[5] John 4:26, amp

[6] ibid, v. 29

[7] Matt. 11:28, NIV

[8] Rom. 8:1, 2, 39, amp

[9] Jer. 29:11, NIV

[10] Isa. 30:15, NIV

[11] ibid, vv. 16-17

[12] ibid, v 18

[13] ibid, v 21

[14] 2 Cor. 9:12, amp

[15] John 10:16, NIV

Chapter 1

Daddy God or Fire and Brimstone?

"I keep asking that the God of our Lord Jesus Christ, the
glorious Father, may give you the Spirit of wisdom and
revelation, so that you may know him better."
Ephesians 1:17 (NIV)
"See what great love the Father has lavished on us,
that we should be called children of God! And that is what
we are!"
1 John 3:1a (NIV)

Before the rest of this will make any sense to you, there is
one thing that really has to be settled in your heart and in
your head. What do you think of when the term "God"
comes to mind?

We are told God is this eternal entity that tells us to love
our enemies, to trust Him (even in the hard times) and to
put no other gods before Him. Is this a realistic
expectation? In the Gospels, Jesus invites us to follow
Him, to believe Him and rest in His Peace. Throughout the
Bible, His written Word reveals God as a tender shepherd
Who tells us "He is the rewarder of those who earnestly
and diligently seek Him [out]."[1] But how can that coincide
with another attribute of God, His justice? His "perfect
justice" in regards to the cities of Sodom and Gomorrah is
legendary. How can both be true at the same time? Is He
what some perceive as a supernatural fire and brimstone-
throwing dictator, or is He really the God that Jesus
tenderly called "Abba! Father!"[2] while preparing for the
most trying ordeal of His earthly life? The Aramaic
translation of "Abba" indicates a warm, loving

endearment, a tender "Daddy!" Is that how we feel about Him?

We are told that God is our "Heavenly Father" and if we submit to His way of living we will see a promised happy, never-ending, life-after-death when time ceases and the Son of God ushers in eternity in light and peace "...for all who have longed for His appearing".[3] But when it comes right down to it, is *our* perception of God something that draws us toward Him? Do we *long for His appearing*? Or are we just trying to stay under the radar until we die attempting to avoid hell?

The Bible tells us that once we accept the gift of God's atonement for us in the person of Jesus Christ, then we are all members of one family in Him. A big part of our understanding of that "family" situation is framed by our own family experiences, and many of these have not been pleasant memories.

Some of us have had Dads who have been harsh in their discipline, punishing and rarely showing appreciation for the good we do. Others are distant and not available, unwilling or unable to show love or provide purposeful training, while some are affectionate and tender, and sometimes over-indulgent. Still others are seemingly silent partners of strong-willed wives who run the show.

Our perception of God can get distorted if we take our experiences with our physical earth-bound Dads, each with their own pain, weaknesses, and flaws... and transpose them onto our concept of Who God is. No matter how good they are or how much we love them, our

Dads are human beings with their own baggage to carry. God doesn't have those emotional handicaps.

If our experiences with our earthly Dads were not pleasant, it is not uncommon for us to develop a mental picture of God as an all-knowing, all-seeing distant administrator, who watches over each of us on earth, and like some kind of eternal arcade game, plays Whack-A-Mole, with us as the poor mole! It can feel like He exists solely to hammer us down when we reach a pre-determined threshold of violations against an ever-expanding list of do's and don'ts.

Although I would never have admitted to this perspective earlier, this is how I viewed God for most of my life. It didn't matter that I heard how loving and protective He is. It didn't matter how many times He had proven His care over me in so many different ways. I took for granted much of the good I received from Him and endured difficulties as perceived *whacks* on the head (most of them consequences for my own poor choices). I feared that at any time I could be the recipient of His unyielding retribution. *(whack!)*

I never really thought about the discrepancy in these ideas, but let it continue just off to one side of my awareness. The confusion of this dichotomy kept me from actively seeking a more personal connection with Him for a long time. But it's hard to continue believing lies when there is so much evidence – both written and in my own experiences – to refute them!

When I started reading the Bible for myself and began to challenge those false perceptions, my pre-conceived ideas gave way to a completely different view of God. He has used many different situations to reach my heart and reveal Himself more clearly to me. Even now, He daily opens up my awareness to other lies I inadvertently believe that can create distance between us. As He shines His light on each one, He helps me disprove and discard them all.

He not only tells me He is my Heavenly Father and Jesus is my brother, He calls me precious throughout the Bible and tells me that all my tears are "saved by Him in a bottle".[4] He promises that one day He will personally wipe them all away. That doesn't sound at all like that whack-a-mole God I envisioned earlier! Accepting this new perspective was hard for me because it was so foreign to my physical experiences up to that point.

Accountability for your own choices, tempered with merciful and patient instruction for the future is far different from unyielding retribution. Is God a harsh disciplinarian or a loving, tender, caring Daddy God? How did I bridge the gap and reconcile these two very different concepts?

I needed to see where the confusion started. A line from Lewis Carroll's classic book, "*Alice's Adventures in Wonderland*," directs Alice to "start at the beginning and when you get to the end, stop."[5] Where is "the beginning" in reference to where we are right now? Our experiences are all so varied, how can we begin on common ground?

Common Ground in Shared Pain

If you are reading this, you have either already made the decision to accept that God has a plan for you and have begun to follow Him… or you may have chosen not to take that road yet for any number of reasons. Maybe you think the process of just accepting that "Jesus loves me", must be too simple an answer. What difference could that possibly make in our lives?

We benefit immensely by examining the foundation of the things we believe and taking a fresh look at *why* we feel the way we feel. If we are holding back, maybe we should explore why we've hesitated to rely on God up to this point. Did you grow up in a home where God was never talked about? What difference does it make, really? Have you ever been in contact with anyone whose faith was a big part of their life? Were their actions proof of a Greater Love? Or very different from what they talked about? You've gotten this far in your life without believing in Him and figure "Why start now?" Or maybe it's something deeper than that.

No matter where we come from or what we do in life, we've experienced pain. Sometimes we feel like we've been singled out to suffer while others seem to have it so easy. Does anyone really care? We put on a good face for the public, no time to deal with all that anyway; we have to keep putting one foot in front of the other, right? But there comes a time when all that pain can no longer be ignored. The hurt we feel reaches a tipping point and we can't go on without being healed. The deepest cry from our hearts searches for reasons: "Why?" …and not knowing the answer just makes us angry.

Pain and disappointment are universal, but some experiences are more damaging than others. Perhaps we need someone to blame for not coming to our rescue. Is it possible that personal pain and disappointment are clouding our perceptions and giving us reasons to doubt the concept of a loving God who cares tenderly and deeply for us, personally? After all, He's God isn't He? He should have been there; He could have stopped "it" from happening. Sometimes we decide to reject Him for not being big enough or effective enough, gentle enough or powerful enough. We might consider all the ways that we think He should have, could have and *didn't* intervene; we hold back and wonder why He permitted these things to happen in our lives. Is God *worthy* of our trust?

At this point in my life, with everything I have been through, jumped into, fell into, *been pushed into*, run away from, embraced and cried over, I can tell you the answer unequivocally is Absolutely, Yes He is! I don't know all the why's and I can't explain the reasons why individual situations and world events that tear people in pieces are allowed to happen, but I can tell you from personal experience that God alone is the only One Who can take every bit of pain, loss, rejection, embarrassment, guilt, shame, foolishness, rebellion, hatred, selfishness and every other negative thing we have ever experienced or inflicted on anyone else and change it into something He can use to help us - and then help us help someone else.

Please hear me! We need to understand that all the events in our lives have come together in precise timing and purpose to make us the people we are today. Just as the ingredients in a cake need to be mixed together to produce the delicious result everyone can enjoy, the difficult times in our lives are blended together, in just the right ratio, with the sweet and wonderful times to create who we are becoming.

Eggs for example, if eaten raw are not appetizing at all. But when added to the other ingredients in the cake and then baked in a hot oven, they all interact with each other to make it rise into something light and delicious. Without the eggs, the cake comes out flat and dense; without the heat, it just sits there like goo, not becoming what it was intended to be. No one volunteers for the ovens in life, or enjoys hardship in the moment, but we have been created for eternal purpose that cannot reach full impact without the internal strength that experiencing difficulty allows each of us to develop.

We all have regrets in one form or another. Some of us can pick out one or two specific things that everything bad in our lives seem to hinge on. We think of that thing as the turning point – the reason why everything else after that "went to hell" in our lives. Maybe it's a lost relationship. Maybe it's a bad decision. Maybe it was something someone else did to us. Whatever it is, we look back on that thing and measure the rest of our lives from that point. Sometimes we suppose that if we were able to eliminate that one thing, then it would rectify the difficult issues we are now dealing with and we would be better for it.

Science-fiction alone will tell you that's not possible. The problem with altering one detail of that past is that when one thing changes, everything else around it also changes. Every action has its own set of reactions. We can't eliminate one situation without losing the other things it triggered. We can't predict what these situations will produce or the chain reactions that follow, but God does.

And the good news is He cares about those reactions and their multiplied effects on us. We have pain. We've had hard things impact us. That's reality. Eliminating them from our past is not possible. But we can become willing to do something positive with the things we learn in the difficult times. We should not allow the pain we've gone through so far to become a wedge that separates us from the only answer to the whys in our life.

God knows everything we've been through. He is the only One Who can calm our frustration over what we think *could have been* "if only...". He helps us to follow through with the incredible purpose we exist on this planet to fulfill – not as so many of us have been taught, "in spite of it all" – but by *using* every bit of it.

This is the practical application of the term omniscient, or all-knowing. Like the perfect chess master, God can see and incorporate not only our own actions and reactions in any given situation, but the outcome of everyone else's actions and reactions and how each one will play out in tandem with one another into infinity. He knows how each situation will impact our character and the perseverance we develop as a result. The truth is some of our most difficult situations in life are the very things that shape our compassion and empathy for others. The comfort we have received in our difficulties uniquely equips us to encourage others who are faced with similar painful trials later on.[6]

Nobody wants to go through hard circumstances, but relying on God and accepting that He not only knows what we're going through, but tenderly cares for us through each one, is the key to successfully navigating through painful times. He can turn them from obstacles into opportunities.

I recently heard a song by Selah titled, "Unredeemed". It says in part that when "anything is shattered and laid before the Lord, just watch and see, it will not be unredeemed"[7]. Romans 8:28 tells us God can and does use all things, no matter how horrible it feels at the time, for good if we love Him.

Reaching toward God and His Word as *the* answer will empower every part of us to be victorious, even when all we can see are the obstacles. We've built walls around our hearts for years to shield ourselves from pain. Along the way, we discover we have become prisoners inside those walls and don't know how to get out. God is the only one who can dismantle them and lead us to freedom. He longs to respond to our anguished cries of, "WHY!?" with gentleness, truth and compassion.

I've had many battles in my life with "Why". He has met me in each one and brought me out to the other side. The biggest of these battles involved regret and guilt that seemed to have no chance of resolution. He was gentle, taking one step at a time, at different points in my life, carefully and patiently putting the necessary tools and opportunities in place at just the right times. But even with that done, He needed to correct a pretty major misconception for it to have its intended impact.

In a Bible study I was doing in 2010 by Linda Cochrane called *"Forgiven and Set Free,"* I was being directed to look at the attributes of God. At first I thought, " None of this is new information... yeah, yeah, God is Love... I'll skim over this part and get to what I really need in the next chapter." But the pain I was experiencing at the time prompted me to keep reading anyway. I didn't want to miss something that was tucked into the middle of what I thought I already knew. I was so grateful that I did! Somewhere between "His Relationship with Us" and "His Love for Us" in chapter 2, I got a wonderful mind-picture that shows how God sees us - and how He loves us in a way that never occurred to me before. I would not have applied those Truths to my own guilt, so He gave me some outside help – from inside my own house. Gretta may help me explain.

Gretta's Story

We received our dog, Gretta, from a rescue situation. My husband Steve's cousin found her abandoned, took her in and cleaned her up, but then discovered very quickly he couldn't keep her. His cat would not allow it! We *adopted* her, fed and took care of her, unaware of the details of her background. A week or so later Steve picked up a newspaper, tucking it under his arm to carry it into another room. When Gretta saw him with the rolled up paper, she immediately shook with fear, squatted down on the floor and peed. Watching him with her chin touching the floor, her brown eyes looked up at him in terror as she anticipated what she had grown to expect from whoever had abandoned her.

In her fear and brokenness, she made a mess all over the floor. However, Steve's response was far from punishing.

He got down on the floor with her, talking softly and reassuring her over and over that he would never do anything to hurt her. He petted her, took her face gently in his hands and comforted her until she stopped shaking. While he was soothing Gretta, I cleaned up the mess on the floor, and then we gently bathed her. It wasn't that we weren't upset about the puddle near her shaking body, but our anger was directed where it should have been in the first place – toward her previous cruel owner, who had obviously trained her through his own actions toward her to expect such abuse.

It tore at our hearts to think for a second that she would anticipate that kind of treatment from us. Steve said something like, "If I ever get my hands on the guy who did this to you...!"

When God brought that memory to mind during the Bible study, I understood the connection He was trying to make in my heart: this is *exactly* how God sees us! (Only God doesn't call us dogs, He calls us His sheep. More on that later...) God has compassion for the errant sinner knowing that we are fearful and broken, while maintaining His justified anger at the sin. When we cower before Him guilty and ashamed of our messes, thinking He will strike at us at any minute, He has deep compassion for our misunderstanding.

Far from demanding we beg for a few treats or kind attention, His attitude toward us is tender and reassuring. He loves us more deeply than we are capable of knowing and lavishes us with His Grace. Simultaneously, He has intense hatred for our real enemy, who uses other hurt and heart-sick people to beat us down and convince us that God is like the cruel, abusive people we've come in contact with. God does not play "whack a mole" on us, but invites us to come to Him so He can clean up those messes. He shows us how much He loves us, how much compassion He feels about the things that have happened to us when we had a different master and binds up our broken hearts.[8]

Unlike Steve who doesn't know who our dog's previous master was, God knows exactly who *owned* us before, what he's done to mess us up and where the blame lies for our misunderstanding of God's intentions toward us. Like Jesus, looking down at Jerusalem with tear-filled eyes, heart-broken at her continued refusals to accept Him in Luke 13:34, He calls to us as well. He longs to gather His people under His wings, but we cower, afraid or rebellious, avoiding the Love we so desperately need.

He tells us the blessings He intends for us to enjoy. He gives us the power to make choices. He tells us that some of those choices will bring us and those around us more pain and others will bring joy. There are natural and logical consequences when we choose the pain in spite of His warnings. But even when we choose unwisely, He still longs for us to come to Him for help.

God wants us to see His true intentions. He wants us to run *toward* Him for shelter – not cower in a corner waiting for the proverbial newspaper beating. When we make messes, He cleans us up and comforts us, encouraging us to keep walking with Him in the covering He provides for us. I had never put those two concepts together before – it was His personal illustration! What a cool way for God to explain how He loves us!

Another misconception was also dismantled in this illustration. As dog owners, we sometimes believe that the way to train them not to make messes in the house is to rub their noses in it before putting them outside to "teach them a lesson". People who specialize in canine instruction have shared many stories of dogs that have been taught this way – and learned to *rub their own* noses in it and then beg to go outside for their punishment! Talk about negative reinforcement!

But haven't we all seen this demonstrated in our own lives? Isn't this why religion has negative connotations for some people? Legalism around the rules of do's and don'ts – and feeling rejected by people when we don't live up to them – is a perfect example of this. After being "beaten up" by other people and having them "rub our noses" in the messes we've made, we often begin to self-punish, rubbing our own noses in the shame and guilt we feel with no way of escaping the regret. Many people react to this situation by throwing out the rules. If there is no absolute right and wrong, then there's no reason for guilt or punishment, right?

But throwing away the boundaries for acceptable behavior is not the solution. There **is** right and wrong. Certain things will result in harmful consequences no matter how much we defend them or rationalize them. But God has the perfect remedy for legalism. When we "make messes", breaking the rules, He meets our regret and acknowledgement of our wrongs with Grace.

God truly does not "rub our noses in it" when we make messes in our own life. He is not waiting for us to come to Him so He can gloat over us or wave His finger in our faces – He wants to heal us and correct our misunderstanding. He wants to teach us the right way to live our lives so that blessings follow us and flow through us to others. When we do break the rules, and suffer the consequences of those infractions, He patiently instructs us again. This is Grace. Far from gloating, He responds to our offenses with compassionate instruction. He comforts us, teaches us, makes us feel safe and provides for our every need, while maintaining the boundaries we are told not to cross.

James 1:5 tells us "If any of you is deficient in wisdom let him ask of the giving God [Who gives] to everyone liberally and ungrudgingly, without reproach or faultfinding, and it will be given him." - and He tells us we are to "arm ourselves with the same thought and purpose" – [having the mind of Christ]."⁹

Instead of rubbing one another's noses in our messes, we are to acknowledge the infractions and ask God – and one another – for help in cleaning it up. And He does, without reproach or a grudging attitude. It is we humans who have a hard time with this idea. After all, if we "let others off the hook", doesn't that just encourage them to keep doing it? I don't know. How have you responded to people who have given you a break when you really messed up? Do you become determined to hurt them again? Or are you grateful for their understanding and try to do better?

Even if someone does do wrong again and again, and we don't specifically do anything to "pay them back", it doesn't mean they get "away with it". Eventually people's harmful actions result in painful consequences. It's not wishful thinking or simply a possibility – it's a promise.

Unlike the sentiment Steve expressed toward Gretta's previous owner, as individuals, we will never have the ability to make others "pay for" the hurt they inflict.

When we realize that the reason some people hurt others is because they themselves are hurting, we may be able to find added compassion for them. Sometimes people who are wounded are not trying to hurt us, they are just not yet capable of doing anything else. Grace is the perfect solution for this!

That is not to say that evil does not exist – it does. And those who have been hardened by it have done absolutely horrible things. Consequences for these actions can and must be enforced (the judicial system of our government and international enforcement agencies were instituted for this purpose). But enforcing justice is not the same thing as individual retaliation or vengeance.

We are in fact warned NOT to take matters into our own hands. God's Word is clear that the entity responsible for evil in our world will receive "payback" (for all eternity!) for the heart-breaking results of his twisted leading and the deceptive lures he used to batter us. There is no doubt of that - rest assured, He will! ("Vengeance is mine, I will repay (requite), says the Lord."[10])

And although this assurance can give us comfort in our painful times, we must be wary of gleefully anticipating God's vengeance toward other people. Justice is good and keeps order in society, but seeking retaliation makes us more broken. We receive compassion and Grace for our sins. We need to remember that God also applies this compassionate, patient instruction toward those who hurt us.

After His assurance of making things right, He calls us to pray for our enemies, just as Jesus prayed as He endured the cross for the people who hung him there! He totally understood they were deceived and He had compassion for them as well, asking His Father to forgive them. He is the God of second chances, after all.

However, although His patience with us is long, there is a point of no return. Each of us will eventually find ourselves at a cross-road of decision, just like the thieves hanging on their own crosses near Jesus. One made his decision quickly. He acknowledged his own guilt, accepted Jesus' forgiveness and was told that his place was reserved in paradise. The other continued to rail at Jesus for not getting him off his cross, with no acknowledgement or remorse for anything he'd done wrong. He did not receive the same assurance.

In God's Grace we are individually given this same opportunity We can start today with a clean slate by accepting His forgiveness. We can choose to give others this same opportunity by forgiving the emotional "debts" they owe us. Or we can simply keep railing against the pain. Which will you choose?

Once we allow God to change our errant perceptions of Him and reveal to us His true nature, we realize there are lots of other impressions and opinions we've believed that no longer make sense. Changing long-held attitudes can be a tough journey to start. But great understanding can come from taking a look at some important concepts. There is a proverb that states "a journey of a thousand miles begins with a single step". We all start at step one.

AA (Alcoholics Anonymous) and other 12 step programs begin by acknowledging that our lives have become painfully unmanageable in our own strength. Most of us can assent to that fact. In one way or another, there are things that have happened to us or to the people we love that we have no control over – and we prove that time and time again by trying to fix problems ourselves with little positive result.

Now consider the possibility that a "power greater than ourselves" can do whatever is necessary to positively influence any negative situation and "restore us to sanity"[11]. AA's "12 Steps" assign the name for this entity: "the God of our understanding" or our "Higher Power" and encourages us to begin to let Him help us *before* we have fully figured out for ourselves what He looks like. After seeing the track record of success for hundreds of thousands of people who have used these 12 steps and been able to kick decades of habitual and destructive behaviors and live productive, happy lives, most people will concede that this simple act of acknowledging a higher power has merit. So let's start there.

We can go a step further and also concede that if these programs have such a good track record, then the principles these programs employ can effectively apply to other conditions we have experienced and not solely to alcoholism or addiction.

We begin by accepting that there is something more powerful than we are. We acknowledge that after years of banging our heads against the walls of self-will and unavoidable circumstances, we are not in control. Obstacles in our lives may have included other people, inborn and acquired tendencies toward self-destruction or situations and things we cannot control no matter how hard we try. No matter what culture, country or background we come from, we can acknowledge a "God of our understanding" who _can_ control what we cannot.

Whether some believe it is a collective consciousness, a punishing dictator, or an ethereal Santa Claus, the starting place can be agreeing that it isn't us.

Once we come to the point of acknowledging the existence of a "higher power" then we can make progress toward resolving the pain that has been accumulating and adversely affecting our choices and our lives. Our previous attempts have been disastrous on several levels. We have been ruled by whims and desires and have tried to substitute a variety of remedies that promise so much more than they have been able to deliver. So why not try this "God of our understanding?"

When we begin to seek help, the harsh concepts of God we may have held previously are challenged. Why would this follow? If we acknowledge God has the power to do what we cannot, and we are looking to Him for healing or relief from the pain we see as bad, then the God of our understanding must be good. This new perspective challenges our previous "whack-a-mole" concepts of God and leads to new understanding of His character – soon we find we have replaced avoidance with hope-filled connection. How can we cultivate this new hope?

Your Dream Dad?

Put aside your ideas of what God has meant to you in the past for a moment - think instead of your ultimate *dream Dad*. What does he look like? How does he act toward you? What strengths would you admire in him? I will share what my dream Dad looks like as you add to what you imagine yours to be.

Mine loves me completely, no matter what I do. He comforts me when I am so sad that I just want someone to make the pain stop. He is forgiving, not throwing in my face the things I am ashamed of as soon as I do them. He is compassionate and knows what I am going through. He understands that the misguided things I have done seemed to me like the only logical options I had at the time to get the results I thought I wanted. He doesn't laugh at me when I see for myself later it was the wrong choice and produced the wrong result – like he warned me it would beforehand. He is powerful enough to protect me and defends me even when I'm wrong, just because I am his child. He punishes those who intentionally enjoy hurting me, but also shows me when I have assumed hurtful intent from others that is not there. He is faithful to correct and discipline me, but doesn't enjoy administering punishment. He prefers to be with me rather than getting too busy with "things that have to be done." He gives me everything I need - even if I don't know I need it. He has a twinkle in his eye when he surprises me with something special just to show his love for me. He brags about me to other people. He doesn't complain about my shortcomings to others. He wants what is best for me and knows what that is.

I could go on for a while listing all the things I can envision my perfect Dad to be like. In my mind, these attributes and character qualities are also all the things I wish I was, and hope I am becoming, for my own children and grandchildren. As I spend more time with God, getting to know Him, reading the Bible, hearing from other people who spend time with Him, I am finding out that He is all these things and more. He tells us He wants to be our best friend. He wants to be our God and He wants us to be His people.

But so what? How can just accepting that He wants to be my friend and God, truly be the thing we've longed for this whole time? Part of the problem is that, although God is omniscient (all-knowing) He doesn't appeal to us through our cognition. He is certainly intelligent, wise and discerning in all things. He is the one who put the principles of the universe in mathematical precision together, from molecules to galaxies, exactly the way it needs to be for life to exist. He is the logician behind all logic, but He doesn't *think* His way into our heads. He appeals to us through our hearts – to the core of who we are – from the core of Who He is. That core is love - and love often does not make logical sense.

What is logical about how much you love *your* children? Does it make sense that when they hurt over something that you know as an adult is not going to really make a difference to them a year from now, you still try to comfort them? Does it make sense that when they are heart-broken over a first boy-friend or girl-friend's betrayal you want to rip the little twit's heart out for what he or she did to your baby girl or baby boy? It would be an unreasonable response to be sure, but it is an honest reaction to want to defend and vindicate the ones we love.

Does it make sense that you'd rather die than accept some doctor telling you there's nothing you can do for a loved one and that you just have to accept medical facts without seeking a miracle cure? Does it make sense to do half the things you've already done to try, in your very limited power, to relay certain concepts and then struggle to get your kids to understand something, when they just don't seem to get it? Can I submit to you that each of these feelings is felt much more intensely - and multiplied many times over for each one of us - by the One Whose blueprints we are fashioned after?

I have truly come to believe that we *are* made in God's image, which means we reflect the heart and characteristics of the prototype. No matter what we've been through, He is the original. He has been there, done that. He also deals with kids who think they know better, who do exactly the opposite of what you suggested they do and then get mad at you when it blows up in their faces. He's been screamed at for things He didn't do, cared for His "kids", cleaned them up, had to deal with consequences He didn't deserve and still He continues to love, feed, heal, reach out to us, and expose His heart to our fickle emotions and loyalties. He loves us anyway, forever. He understands all of it and wants to call us His own. That's what He came for.

"For we do not have a High Priest who is unable to understand and sympathize and have a shared feeling with our weaknesses and infirmities and liability to the assaults of temptation, but One who has been tempted in every respect as we are, yet without sinning."[12]

He personally identified with us so that we would be able to identify with Him. Just as our kids benefit from the things we teach them and warn them about ahead of time, God dearly wants to do that for us. So what? If we ask this eternal dream Dad to come into our hearts and guide us, how is that supposed to help anything?

We simply can't see enough of His thought process to make the choices and decisions that will turn out best for us on our own. But He can guide us. The Bible tells us that His thoughts are higher than our thoughts and His ways are above our ways.[13] It doesn't make sense to us that He would want anything to do with us after some of the things we've done and the damage we carry in our hearts. It doesn't make sense that such powerful help is ours for the asking, even after we've dumped on Him and spurned His intentions for us for so long. But it really is that simple and that amazing. His love toward us is beyond our highest hope. Look for Him, He wants to be found! "I love those who love me and those who seek me early and diligently shall find me"[14] "Seek and you shall find, knock and the door will be opened to you, ask and it will be given to you."[15]

I AM

All we ever have to do at any age is accept what He is offering each and every one of us and believe that He loves us. But with much of life under our belts we get hardened and it seems too simple to reach out with child-like faith to the great "I AM". I am? I am what?

When God sent Moses to Egypt to rescue the Israelites from slavery, He offered proof that He really did send this former sheep-herder to rescue them with this declaration: "Tell them… 'I AM' has sent me to you"![16]

What in the world was that supposed to mean? There is a part of basic sentence structure missing here. I had a very detail-oriented 8th grade English teacher; I can still diagram a sentence 39 years later! "I" is a pronoun denoting the subject of the sentence. "Am" is a verb, a form of "to be" that is supposed to lead to an object or activity. How can you put a period after "I AM" and have it be a complete sentence? It works because **He** is complete. At any given time, you can fill in the space after "I AM" with what you dearly and most desperately need Him to be at that moment: I AM your redeemer, I AM your strength, I AM your help in times of trouble, I AM your defender, I AM your provision. God doesn't need to add an object in His sentence, because it's a declaration. *You* are His object, the target of His loving action and intention. And though it might seem a little ego-centric on the surface of it, He told us in His word that *your ultimate perfection* is the precious motivation He has for everything He does. The more we look *to* Him for our answers, the more we look *like* Him in our character. He is everything you need Him to be and more. This is why He relates His feelings and position to us, as a loving father to His children.

Because life has been tough, because we have all experienced much disappointment, because we've struggled so much… this simple concept may not inspire instant confidence. Over the years the things and people we have put our faith in have let us down and we are disillusioned and wary of professed ideas of God's mercy and grace toward us. We find it hard to apply tender traits toward God as a loving father. Like the third servant in the story of the talents in Matthew 25, we may view God as a "harsh man" and have no desire to know Him personally, and we "bury our talent in the ground".

We may still anticipate Him as judgmental and vindictive. We can sometimes be unaware that we have lots of help coming to that conclusion! Disastrous things happen and God is blamed. Questions arise in our minds that, if God is all-powerful, how could He allow this to happen? Even insurance companies, in an attempt to limit their liability, describe all manner of destructive occurrences as "acts of God"!

When the idea is introduced that we could get to know God personally and allow Him to be a guiding light, a source of joy and peace in a world of pain and disappointment, we are doubtful that anything could be that big *and* that good. We let our hope get swallowed up. We don't want another let down. People make choices based on all kinds of weak emotional reasoning; fear, greed, self-gratification, the need for a quick-fix to resolve an immediate issue, without even thinking of asking for God's direction or input. When it doesn't work out right, we rail against God for not allowing it to be fixed.[17]

Please hear my heart! God is not some distant voyeur getting His kicks by watching us struggle. He is not a vindictive or uncaring boss that makes rules so He can write us up for not meeting company standards. He's not some eternal bully with a magnifying glass reveling over ants He can burn on the sidewalk! Whatever negative experiences you've had with people in your lifetime, associating that pain, rejection and isolation with the real God of the universe is simply not valid - nothing could be further from the truth!

I heard Christian speaker Beth Moore say with a joyful intensity and fervor, "God is *not* just a big version of us!" When we attribute the anger, the impatience, the pain, the self-defense, the distrust (and a host of other emotions we build up over time) to God, we just make Him bigger than us with all that pent up misguided emotion on steroids! We set up road blocks in our minds to

24

experiencing the most incredible, passionate and all-encompassing love we can ever know! If we have any hope of finding out what all the fuss is about, we need to determine who we are deciding to reject or choosing to follow. It will be the most important decision you will ever make.

There are so many preconceived notions floating around about God that it becomes a hunt to find reliable sources in a world filled with fallible and hurting people. Some of us, even though we believe in God, can be very poor envoys of a most amazing grace! Our pain distorts His reflection in us, and He gets the blame. Misinformation and the suppositions we believe can also twist our view of Him!

I am just one person, but I want to share how I transitioned from the "whack-a-mole" concept of God I had, to experiencing confidence in His extraordinarily tender care for me personally, and for everyone else on earth. My experiences on this journey are entwined with the ultimate autobiography on the subject of God - the Bible. See if you can identify with any of these examples:

Flawed AND Favored!

In the beginning of my search, there were some things in the Bible that seemed to contradict each other. Things that seemed to be mutually exclusive were not easy for me to reconcile. All through the Old Testament, the wrath of God seems poured out and the holiness of God is held up as the unapproachable standard that we are told we can never reach on our own. God is separate, a great and terrible power to be feared and obeyed - or else.

The flood destroys the face of the whole earth as described in Genesis, chapters 6 & 7. The earth swallows up people in Numbers 16:32. Fire and brimstone come down from heaven and wipe out entire cities in Genesis 19. Fire comes down and consumes animal sacrifices and "the man of God kills all of the priests (of Baal) with a sword" in 1 Kings, chapter 18. Jerusalem itself is wiped out because of the people's continued disobedience after centuries of prophets telling them that they needed to change. People are warned over and over again that God is not someone to be trifled with; when the hammer of divine punishment comes down, there are heavy duty consequences!

Yet there are many times when God seems to choose some people for special attention and favor, even when it doesn't seem to me that they deserve it. Intertwined and documented for our consideration, time after time, God's deference, mercy and tender care are demonstrated toward certain people who, like us, keep messing up. This condition of man is nothing new. We sin... and God keeps coming to our aid and helping us.

Noah and his family of 7 are spared from the flood, safe in the ark God had Noah build. This man who is described as "just and righteous" in Genesis 6:9 is shielded from the anger God releases on the rest of the planet in chapters 7 & 8. After months and months cooped up in a boat with hundreds of animals, Noah finally sets foot on dry ground again. Knowing he would be fearful of a repeat performance, God makes a promise to the aging prophet-turned-zookeeper and puts a rainbow in the sky as a symbol of the "everlasting covenant" between God and man that He would never again use water to destroy the earth.[18] But then, a few short verses later, Noah gets drunk and ends up cursing one of his sons. Despite his human missteps, long after his death, God still holds Noah up as a faithful man.[19]

Another of God's favored people is Abraham. God promises that Abraham will be the "Father of many nations" after telling him to set off for a place He will later show him.[20] After leaving his father's family compound in Haran, Abraham shows a serious problem with self-preservation. Not once, but twice on his way there[21], Abraham tells the kings of two different places (and gets his wife to confirm it) that she is really his sister and not his wife. (half true; they were half-siblings having different mothers, but they were also married) He does this because he is afraid they will have him killed in order to steal his wife, due to her amazing beauty. Based on this lie, the kings offer him all kinds of gifts and take her to be part of their harems! God intervenes immediately with dreams and horrible consequences and keeps Sarah from becoming defiled like this.

I thought, after the first time at least, that Abraham would learn his lesson, or that God would be a little more upset with *him* than He was! Instead, God inflicts judgment on both the kings *and their people*. God even tells the second king to have Abraham pray *for him* so that the plague they are going through will stop! They end up sending Abraham away from their cities a VERY rich man.

Now let me get this straight: Abraham, acting in fear, lied to kings and endangered his wife to save his own neck. He worried about something that hadn't even happened, yet

God still held him up hundreds of years later as the father of many nations and the main example of living by faith in Hebrews 11! Of course he was not commended for these episodes of fear, lying and deception, but for the way he kept following God, living his life day after day in courage, hospitality and trust, as spoken about all through the book of Genesis. God blessed him, as flawed as he was. And he's not alone...

Abraham's grandson Jacob cheats his twin brother out of the first-born's blessing and birth right, necessitating his escape to another country (never seeing his mom again) to avoid his brother's revenge. Several years later, after being cheated himself by his wives' father, he leaves there to return home in Genesis 30-32. Long before anyone ever *thought* of the word karma, Jesus told us "in accordance with the measure you [use to] deal out to others, it will be dealt out again to you."[22] He ought to know, He set the principle in place before any of us came to be! Jacob is undeniable proof of this principle. His swindling and cheating actions toward his brother are repaid to him in spades by his father- and brothers-in-law. But it is also the crucible that teaches him the rewards God gives for devotion and obedience. When he leaves his father-in-law to return to his childhood home, he willingly gives credit to God for his new life of favor.

Jacob is rich beyond measure with all kinds of livestock and a huge family in the providence of God. On the way home, he hears his twice-cheated brother is coming to meet him. His first reaction to the news is fear. He supposes evil intention on his brother's part and prays to God for help. He sends the whole family ahead of him with gifts to appease his brother, while he goes through mental gymnastics about what is about to happen when they meet one another for the first time in years. He meets that night with "The Angel of the Lord"[23] who Bible scholars say is the pre-incarnate Jesus. And how does he interact during this meeting? He gets in a wrestling match and says he won't let the angel go until he gets a blessing from Him – and HE GETS IT! He's limpin' - but he's blessed!

That's some presumption there! Far from being vindictive and punitive, God <u>rewards</u> Jacob's boldness and tenacity! God changes Jacob's name (which means swindler, supplanter and grasper) to Israel which means "contender with God". God's favor surrounds him as he comes face-to-face Esau. His much-dreaded meeting with his brother goes very well and they reconcile wonderfully.

Several generations later, God deposes the first king He installed over the nation of Israel for disobedience. King Saul began to sacrifice offerings before the people, which only the priests were allowed to do. The boy that God chooses as Saul's replacement, the youngest son in a *really* dysfunctional family, is trained in the court of his predecessor.

Young David becomes the beloved friend of the king's son Jonathan, and a mighty warrior in battle – you know, the whole David and Goliath thing. Despite his meteoric rise to fame and favor, (or maybe because of it), he becomes the one who commits the most infamous act of adultery the world has ever heard of. If that wasn't bad enough, King David follows up his adultery with Bathsheba by murdering her innocent and honorable husband. As a consequence of his un-repented sin, their "love child" dies.

But what does God say when He discusses David's place in history? Instead of perpetual punishment for the shame this act brought to David's track record, God later blesses their second son Solomon, through the prophet Nathan, actually calling him Jedidiah, which means "loved of the Lord."[24] In Acts 13:22, God continues to call David "a man after His own heart" and in Hebrews 11, lists David as a prime example of faith and victory. God did not withhold His loving favor from David, even after such sinful acts.

Yes, there absolutely were painful consequences for these people's actions, but God still granted them favor, healing, honor and blessing, holding them up as examples for us. Even after dozens of failures, they are highlighted in the lineage of Jesus and all commended in the book of Hebrews for their faith and relationship with the Lord!

With my mind steeped in legalism and calling out, "Tilt! Tilt! Tilt!" for the seeming contradiction, God granted special favor and deliverances to them and many others, even after their disobedience. So why do we so often jump to erroneous conclusions of being "God-forsaken" when we fail?

This mindset was very hard for me to grasp personally. As the oldest daughter in a family of five children with a very authoritarian father, I saw the hammer come down for numerous infractions. When consequences for actions were laid out, the message behind those consequences focused a critical eye on the wrong, but little, if any acknowledgement of the right I'd done. It became a (learned!) personality trait that I am still fighting to overcome. I found I am not alone in this tendency.

Little Black Dots

Flash forward to the late 1990's, long after my leaving home. At a training exercise for work, we were shown a large white screen with a single small black dot in the middle. The moderator asked us all what we saw. Everyone – without fail – said "a black dot". When prompted further, "what else do you see?" some of us just stared blankly at the screen and said "nothing". Eventually the moderator pointed out there was a large field of white on the screen, and the point was made that as managers, we need to remember to include the large white field of good, compliant, admirable and beneficial qualities in our employees when we need to bring correction for little black dots of non-compliance. That was a new perspective I had never applied in that way to viewing situations and people in my sphere of influence.

We NEED to remember while dealing with other people not to minimize the good attributes, contributions and aspects of their past behavior and to let those good attributes modify our initial response to their short-comings and slip-ups. There is a BIG white field of good things to soften the little black dots. Let us show that kind of perspective and mercy to others, like God does when He looks at us.

God doesn't ignore the fact that we sin; He requires us to confess it to Him. But He confirms to us that He completely removes it from the picture when we confess our faults[25], and He tells us how He can see us this way: "The LORD is compassionate and gracious, slow to anger, abounding in love. He will not always accuse, nor will He harbor His anger forever. He does not treat us as our sins deserve or repay us according to our iniquities. For as high as the heavens are above the earth, so great is His love for those who fear Him; as far as the east is from the west, so far has He removed our transgressions from us. As a father has compassion on his children, so the LORD has compassion on those who fear Him; for He knows how we are formed, He remembers that we are dust."[26]

In my roles as parent, spouse, sibling, employer, and friend this has become an important differentiation I am still learning. Acknowledging the efforts toward compliance and obedience and correcting the things that are not where they should be, are two compatible and cooperative actions with the same goal. They should not be viewed as exclusive from one another. In trying to teach and share this, I have learned that this is the difference between punishment and discipline.

Punishment is a punitive reaction to the black dots with no other purpose than retaliation for the offense. True discipline is the instruction to do right with the purpose of teaching the desired path. It uses rewards for adherence to the good, consequences for the wrongs and exhibits confident assurance that you believe in the other person's ability and desire to do the right thing. It gives knowledge and understanding of the choices presented and attempts to teach the eventual consequences in both directions with motivation to choose the desired course of action.

God clearly uses the word discipline – not punishment – when talking about how He deals with His children in Proverbs 3:12 and Hebrews 12:10, "in love" and "for our good" – not in anger and retaliation.

This is how these two very real and present attributes of God – holiness and justice - can both be true at the same time. Far-from-holy, imperfect people *can and do* receive the mercy and undeserved favor of God. He is still true to

His own nature, as the Bible says He inexorably is. It says "God lives in inapproachable light", but it also says we can "come boldly to the throne of Grace." The penalty for the black dots all over our lives is something that the Grace of God deals with in a very different way than most of us have come to expect.

Heading to the Fridge

I was reading a Bible study by Beth Moore called "Living Beyond Yourself – Exploring the Fruit of the Spirit" and it made a reference about the "approachability" of God. It said to read Ephesians 2:18 and to circle whether God is approachable or distant. When I read the verse, I got this really cool impression that was not really in the words I read, but revealed itself to my heart in a continually unfolding wave of details.

When you go to someone's house you don't know well by yourself, you stand at the closed door, knock and wait for someone to yell "come in" or open the door for you. But when you visit the house of someone that you know really well, you feel much more comfortable just going in. It's more natural, not formal or forced, just an approachability that feels routine, friendly and you don't really think anything of it. I was thinking about the teens that have come into our house through the years when the whole troop just walks in and goes for the fridge. "Hi Mom!" or "Hi Dad!" is heard before they even cross the threshold, followed frequently by "Howya doin'?" and "Whatcha up to?" Conversations, give and take, flow naturally with no discomfort and no hesitancy.

THAT is how God's word says we can approach God _**in Christ**_ - not being afraid or formal, not using big lofty words or feeling like an outsider, not timidly hoping to be noticed, but like one of those teens walking in the door and heading for the fridge with Jesus as the big brother, hanging out and sharing time together.

This is so totally different from the impression we had of God before the fulfillment of our Promised Redeemer's arrival in the Gospels! Jesus Himself said He had not come "to undo or do away with the Law and the Prophets", but "to complete and fulfill them."[27] So doesn't that mean the Law with all its regulations is still in place and we are still living under the hair-trigger of retribution when we mess up time after time after time? Aren't we living in the shadow of a giant _whack-a-mole_ kind of God who is just waiting for His opportunity to hammer us down? Isn't He insisting on our blind obedience while knowing that we can never reach the impossible goal, slamming us down again in some cosmic, sadistic arcade game? No! No! A thousand times and to eternity – NO!

With all the evidence that kept building up in my search that proved His measureless grace and favor to flawed people just like me, it just didn't make sense that I could still see Him like that! I just hadn't taken the time to logically think it through before. I discovered that living life with all its distractions, responsibilities and demands doesn't _accidently_ leave much time for finding out and stumbling on confirmation of God's goodness. You have to set time aside every day to _find_ the truth and purposefully acknowledge the good things that are happening. That can be difficult with the constant bombardment of misrepresentation, accusation, and deceit we are hit with on a daily basis.

If God is this distant, condemning and demanding overlord, picking and tossing aside what and who He doesn't like, *why not* make up gods of our own that seem a little more agreeable? *Why not* get the warm fuzzies in something we have some illusion of control over and blow off this tyrannical joy-killer who seems to only be interested in spoiling our fun? If no one is good enough, why bother trying? With beliefs like that, is it any wonder some people choose to avoid the subject? Who would want to cultivate a relationship with an all-powerful antagonizer who doesn't ever forget anything you do wrong and keeps throwing it in your face at every opportunity?

Purposeful Accuser

One pivotal thing we need to understand is that this is not an accidental characterization of God – there's a reason why many people think of God in these terms. We are told that lie every day of our lives in various ways by someone the Bible calls "the accuser". In the same way we don't just stumble over a beneficial relationship with a loving God, the accusations of Him being an all-powerful bully don't just come out of thin air either. It takes time for satan to continuously repeat the lies he wants us to accept as fact. Yes, I know. I just crossed another line.

For a lot of people, as soon as you say anything about the devil, satan, whatever you call him, you get an internal – or even visible - eye-roll. They seem to be thinking, "Oh great, here we go again with that 'evil presence' stuff." The walls go up and the next few sentences bounce off and are disregarded as some kind of "spook talk." By ignoring or discounting the overwhelming evidence of its existence, evil is able to attain its goals unhindered by scrutiny. We need to remove this cloak of invisibility in order to diffuse its effectiveness. This is not a new concept. The battle between unseen benefit and maleficent opposition is a universal theme throughout history.

Since the beginning of everything – whether we choose to ascribe to Judeo-Christian tenants or not – there has been a war going on in our hearts and in our world. It is an ideological war to be sure, but in its essence, it is a war between good and evil. From Grimm's Fairy Tales to Star Wars, Lord of the Rings and the Chronicles of Narnia to the real-life battles for possession of land, dominion of ideas and ways of life, the personal desires we battle in our minds reflect the manifestations of two very different sides battling for domination on this beautiful and sometimes violently assaulted globe. Both physical and unseen forces interact, opposing one another for control and victory on every level from cosmic to microscopic. As we become aware of the good, so too we must recognize the presence and effect of the evil opposition around us, if we are to be prepared for the battles we engage in every day of our lives.

If you take the time to really think it through, anyone can readily acknowledge the presence of evil in the world. Adolf Hitler is the quickest example of evil to come to mind for most people. And with the recent happenings in the Middle East, ISIS is an obvious current illustration of remorseless, aggressive malevolence for this generation. Unfortunately there are many other examples of people who have done, and *enjoy* doing things so heinous and twisted against others, against animals, against life itself, that there truly is no other completely encompassing explanation besides the presence of evil. We are told about it all over the world.

This certain knowledge is told again and again in myths and legends, in screenplays and skits. It seems every story has a villain. No place on earth is devoid of the belief of the ongoing battle between good and evil. They are continuously at odds with one another; it is acknowledged in every culture for a reason. Evil exists. But merely accepting the existence of both good and evil is not enough, there's more.

A military maxim declares: know your enemy. Even if we are certain that evil exists, sometimes we have trouble personalizing it. We need to understand evil is not just some disjointed nebulous force for wrong. Not random chance or disconnected "bad", but *very* personal – *and purposeful*. The Bible describes it as being "like a lion roaring [in fierce hunger] seeking someone to seize upon and devour."[28] It is designated with a male pronoun – he. He is a being who feeds on and instigates destruction, death and pain. And just like a pride of lions, he does not work alone but has helpers. He displays evidence of strategy and team work in taking down his prey. We need to know this to defeat him.

One of the strategies of evil is to deny his own existence to those he is trying to destroy to diffuse suspicion. In this way he can become not just a silent enemy, but a non-existent one. This strategy is not without merit. If we can blow off the idea of evil, then we are much more easily defeated. And if we can blow off the idea of evil, we can also be manipulated into denying the goodness and care of God as well.

Keith Green, a contemporary Christian songwriter who lived during the height of what I refer to as "hippie time" in the 1970's, was an amazing man who clearly saw this concept. He wrote and sang an insightful, all-be-it sarcastic, song about how much easier it is for the devil to get a foothold in our lives because, "No one Believes in Me Anymore".

Oh, my job keeps getting easier
As time keeps slipping away
I can imitate the brightest light
And make your night look just like day
I put some truth in every lie
To tickle itching ears
You know I'm drawing people just like flies
'Cause they like what they hear
I'm gaining power by the hour
they're falling by the score
You know, it's getting very simple now
'Cause no one believes in me anymore
Oh, 'heaven's just a state of mind'
My books read on your shelf
And have you heard that 'God is dead'
I made that one up myself!
They dabble in their magic spells
They get their fortunes read
You know they heard the truth
But turned away and followed me instead
I used to have to sneak around
But now they just open their doors
You know, no one's watching for my tricks
Because no one believes in me anymore
Everyone likes a winner
With my help, you're guaranteed to win!

And hey man, you ain't no sinner, No!
You've 'got the truth within'
And as your life slips by
You believe the lie that you did it on your own
But don't worry
I'll be there to help you share our dark eternal home
Oh, my job keeps getting easier
As day slips into day
The magazines, the newspapers
Print every word I say
This world is just my spinning top
It's all like child's-play
You know, I dream that it will never stop
But I know it's not that way
Still my work goes on and on
Always stronger than before
I'm gonna make it dark before the dawn
Since no one believes in me anymore
Well now I used to have to sneak around
But now they just open their doors
You know, no one watches for my tricks
Since no one believes in me anymore
Well I'm gaining power by the hour
They're falling by the score!
You know, it's getting very easy now
Since no one believes in me anymore
No one believes in me anymore
No one believes in me anymore![29]

If becoming aware of this kind of trickery and deception motivates you to root it out into the open, you are wise. If you allow fear of the battle to deceive you into denying the existence of evil, you are missing an incredible truth. Yes, evil is powerful. Yes, it is scary to think that something bigger than us enjoys inflicting pain, destruction and harm, even on the most innocent and helpless. But denying his existence does not protect us from his hurtful intentions.

We need to understand there is a personified evil in the world just as certainly as there is a gracious and loving God. But we are *not* helpless before evil's schemes. Knowledge of his existence equips us to succeed in the battle against him. We are empowered by our indwelling God so that, in His strength, we can defeat the evil. We do not need to cower before him, give into his threats or believe his tempting - but empty - promises.

I went to a conference recently where the speaker pointed out that this is in no way a "fair fight" – in fact there is no contest! He said, "It's like Bambi versus Godzilla – and satan is Bambi!" (as he made a splat sound, reminding us of a cartoon from 1969). We have an ally in Christ whose power and love toward us is unmatched by any other. No matter how small we feel sometimes, we can all the more trust in God's surpassing power, whose excellent might makes evil look pitifully inadequate.

Satan has no power over us that we do not willingly cede to him. He can be tricky, so we need to know how to spot him when he slinks onto the scene with his tool box.
In addition to just acknowledging the presence of both good and evil, we need to be aware of their individual characters – their different modes of operation. We've taken a brief look at God's character, what is His antithesis? What are the "tricks of the trade" so to speak, the enemy uses to undermine our victory? The biggest strategy the devil uses is deception, but as I mentioned previously, he also pairs that up with another weapon that

many times sneaks out right under our own noses: accusation.

Accusation All Around

The Bible uses the term "the accuser of the brethren"[30] to describe this enemy of our souls. This is an important moniker to comprehend. When we understand it, our armor against it gets stronger and more effective. In multiple teachings I have heard Jimmy Evans (pastor and founder of *Marriage Today*) talk about the 5 ways satan accuses in our lives: he accuses God to us, us to God, us to ourselves, us to others and others to us.[31] It is a simple tactic, but its effectiveness is clear to see. Satan uses accusation strategically in his attempts to destroy each of us. He instigates these attacks both individually and collectively, by dividing us and baiting us to take offense in all our relationships.

The devil accuses God to us. Way back in the garden he began accusing God to Eve telling her that God was holding out on her. Then he questioned God's motives for keeping something from her. He paired that with the deception that God wasn't really keeping her from death, but keeping her from being god-like. The tactic worked with instant and horrific results...and he's still using it today. He accuses God to each of us with help from the media, self-justifying desires and outright lies. "Safe" sex, pornography, alcoholism, food addictions, abortion, homosexuality, murder, and unforgiveness, are just some of the boundaries that God tells us in His tremendous love for us not to cross *for our own good*. These boundaries are constantly railed against as everything from harmless indulgences to victimless crimes and are presented as inherent "rights" that need to be defended against all opposition! God flat out tells us He has "set before us life and death...choose life that you and your descendants may live."[32] When we choose truth over the deception, we live the abundant life we are meant to live! When we listen to the enemy of our souls, we fulfill *his* plan for our lives. And his plan is not pleasant. He is intent on perpetuating one thing – pain. Satan "comes only in order to steal and kill and destroy. I [Jesus] came that they may have and enjoy life, and have it in abundance (to the full, till it overflows)."[33] Succumbing to the accusations the devil aims at God leaves us disillusioned and hopeless instead of joyful.

The devil also accuses us to God. After we fall for the deception and go against the good plan God has for us, the devil points his condemning finger in our direction, turns to God and says "see I told you they were no good! Why do you waste your time on these weak-willed sinners?" Job chapter 1 is a perfect illustration of these behind-the-scenes accusations. Sometimes these finger-pointing sessions come against those who ARE following the right paths and doing their best to seek God in their lives! Whether these accusations are based on us giving into temptation or just his envious taunting doesn't matter, he is hell-bent on dividing us from our relationship with God. But he doesn't stop accusing there.

As he breathes out his accusations of us to God, he sneers at us as well. *He accuses us to ourselves* in the form of condemnation and temptation toward shame. The very things he tempted us to do in the first place are the things he throws up in our faces as he accuses us *to us:* "You'll never amount to anything", "You did it *again*!", "Why can't you ever do anything right?" He points to failure after failure and tries to dig out the ground from under us making our footing unstable. That is why we need a relationship with God. He is the solid rock we can stand on – the truth we learn, follow and believe in that gives us sure footing. If we are trying to stand on our own efforts and abilities, the ground will give way underneath us every time! But whether satan's efforts work at first or not, he keeps trying, because he isn't finished yet....

He accuses others to us just as vehemently, trying to get us to be a part of tearing other people down for their failed efforts and infractions against us. The verbal abuse many of us have engaged in – and been victims of - is a perfect representation of this reality. He wants us to partner with him to dig out *their* foundation and stability. And in our painful reactions to perceived betrayal, *he simultaneously accuses us to others*. Suggesting to their hearts that our motives were selfish, that we "did something on purpose" to hurt them or cheat them or embarrass them, etc... we continue blaming and being blamed, while the deception continues.

If we fail to see the danger of these attacks, we walk this life blinded by the resulting pain and the deception that produces more hardship. There is purpose in this antagonism. The goal of these accusations is division and strife: to divide us from one another and to divide us from God. We self-insulate, put up walls and lose our joy and the encouragement that we could be giving each other.

In dividing us from God (in the vertical relationship) and setting strife and offense between us (in the horizontal relationships), he segregates us and singles us out, "culling us from the herd," to make easy work of us later when he chooses to finish us off. We can become demoralized, frustrated, helpless and wounded.

Deception

Without active acknowledgement of a personified evil and understanding our enemy's tactics, we fall prey to the biggest deception of all. If there is no evil, there is no good, and everything we go through is just people hurting people or random chance and fate. If we *do* acknowledge the presence of evil and of good, then deception is used to maximize the one and minimize the other.

One version of this lie says that evil really isn't that all that bad and good is impotent to stop it. If we are not careful, we begin thinking all the pain deep in our hearts is due to intentionally hurtful people around us and the unreachable God who lets it all happen.

But that's *not* reality; there *is* an unseen realm and the battle for our hearts is very real. The choice is ours whether we will acknowledge and address it head-on, or succumb blindly to its results. We are warned: "For we are not wrestling with flesh and blood [contending only with physical opponents], but against the despotisms, against the powers, against [the master spirits who are] the world rulers of this present darkness, against the spirit forces of wickedness in the heavenly (supernatural) sphere."[34] This statement is *not* meant to deflate us or throw us into hopeless resignation to the powerful enemy we face. Far from making us helpless, this knowledge launches us far beyond a struggling status quo or settling for a stalemate toward surpassing victory over it!

It is with this certain knowledge of God's grace that we are given the weapons we need to defeat the enemy and win the battles we encounter. Even though we are living "flesh and blood" lives, the weapons we use are "not physical [weapons of flesh and blood], but they are mighty before God for the overthrow and destruction of strongholds."[35] Not for just getting by or limping over the finish line but for the complete destruction of the obstacles that try to tie us up in knots and hold us captive. God has ALWAYS been in the business of setting captives free. The weapons we are given are waiting for us to draw them from an unlimited arsenal, given to us by a very loving, tender-hearted Father.

The price He paid to accomplish our redemption and equip us for victory proves His care for us beyond any doubt. He compassionately weeps over your distress and leans in close, waiting to hear your slightest call to arms. He comes to your rescue, gives you the powerful weapons you need to win the battle, and mends your broken heart, loving you with everything He is and protecting you under His wings![36]

That is the call of salvation! That is the *fulfillment* of the Law that shows the boundaries of "the knowledge of good and evil" – the fruit He told Adam all those years ago not to touch! Jesus warned us that "all who draw the sword will die by the sword"[37], but the cry of His heart is "the just... shall live by his faith."[38]

"Come to Me, all you who labor and are heavy-laden and overburdened, and I will cause you to rest. [I will ease and relieve and refresh your souls.]"[39] Just come? That can't be it, can it? Don't we have to DO something? Live a certain place, travel to a distant land, go to church every day – or at least every week? Don't we have hoops we need to jump through to "make it," or *earn* Gods favor? No. That is another deception we get stuck in.

Believe

It's not a matter of 'do'; it's a matter of 'be'- believe. "For God so loved the world that He gave His only begotten Son, that *whoever believes in Him* should not perish but have everlasting life"[40] (emphasis mine). Most people have heard that line, but what about the next one – "For God did not send His Son into the world in order to judge (to reject, to condemn, to pass sentence on) the world, but that the world might find salvation and be made safe and sound through Him."[41] This doesn't sound like that whack-a-mole God I used to avoid!

I mean, seriously, I have done lots of things to help other people when they've needed a hand; I usually *want* to help others! But, as a Mom, I *never once* thought of sacrificing one of my children (not even on one of their bad days!) in an agonizing and torturous death to free someone else from the consequences of their life-destroying choices! And if I am honest about it, *I never will*! That kind of love is beyond my ability to give. But it's not beyond God's.

He did exactly that, for you and for me. He loved us so much He put away His eternal glory and put Himself through a terrestrial life cycle as a human being. He began his human life in the womb of Mary, a willing, engaged but not-yet-married, devout, Jewish, teenage girl, and gave her and her betrothed, a young, honorable, hard-working earthly dad, the task of raising him. As a helpless baby, He grew up hungry at times, cold at times, but a life noted here and there with promises of great things to come. As he grew and began learning his earthly trade, He was also learning to be a God-pleasing son. When He grew up, He used His connection with His Heavenly Father to provide for others: healing, feeding, encouraging and teaching about the deepest love they could ever know.

And he wasn't some timid push-over afraid to rock the boat when necessary. He wasn't afraid of calling people out. He did not allow Himself to be held back by religious convention or personal co-dependence. If something needed to be said, He said it. His motivation for everything He did and said was presenting and magnifying God's glory. If others accepted what He said and allowed His instruction to draw them close to God, He celebrated. If they hardened their hearts and refused to accept His correction, He knew it was their choice - and their loss. But He allowed them to make that choice.

He never rejected a repentant sinner. He always showed them forgiveness and restoration. He was angry with those who condemned others' sin while refusing to address their own. The religious leaders were responsible for educating the people, protecting them, and providing for their needs. He was incensed by their pride and self-indulgence at the expense of the people they were supposed to lead to God – people He called His "sheep". He knew He was stepping on their toes. He didn't shirk from the responsibility to tell them what they needed to do, even if they were not going to accept it.

Knowing everything that would happen in response ahead of time, He called the teachers of The Law hypocrites and vipers, not because of any personal offense to Him, but to snap them out of their stale status quo mindsets. These were not displays of prideful anger on His part. He was righteously upset over arrogant "shepherds" who used their position to elevate themselves.   He did not avoid the truth to save His reputation with powerful people who were taking advantage of their status in the community.

He challenged them to change what they were doing, exchange their superior attitudes and disdain for the people for a role of servant leadership. This was not what they expected. Some took advantage of the opportunity to come to him and ask questions. The rest plotted to put Him to death. None of it surprised Him. He knew their hearts. But He didn't let that hold Him back.

He flat-out told the Roman occupier/ruler at His trial that the only power Pilate could use over Him, was given to him from heaven. And He was fine with that. He was where He was supposed to be – and He knew it. He forgave the people who spit on Him, pulled out His beard, stripped Him naked and hung Him by nails on a wooden cross. He did all of this in love. The deepest, purest, most perfect love ever known. While they were laughing and jeering at Him to save Himself, He was doing what needed to be done to save them from a destruction they couldn't imagine, literally asking His Father to forgive them, because they didn't know what they were doing.[42]

We still don't.

During a sermon our pastor told us some things about the crucifixion that had never occurred to me. Due to the modesty of most people, and out of reverence for Christ, the depictions we see of Jesus on the cross show Him with a loin cloth on. That wasn't how they did things back then. Part of the agony of that method of torturous death was also the embarrassment of being naked. In addition to the physical pain of the whippings that peeled off sheets of skin exposing His bones, His face marred beyond recognition and being jeered at like some kind of murderous freak, Jesus was completely naked. In Isaiah, chapter 53, God prompted a prophet hundreds of years before His earthly birth to foretell every detail of the ordeal. He knew it was going to happen! He knew it all! That was why Gethsemane was so torturous for Him! That was why He "sweated great drops of blood."[43] He knew what was coming, all of it. Jesus knew He would have to be separated from His continual, intimate contact with His Daddy Abba Father for His purpose to be fulfilled - for our redemption! He would be forsaken so we would never have to feel that agony.

Jesus, God in human form, died horribly, on purpose, giving up His own Spirit in a public spectacle. Those who each carried out their part never knew they were instruments in fulfilling God's redemptive plan for all of us! From the occupiers, to the religious leaders, to each person in the mob crying for His death, each one had a part in the salvation process to be fulfilled. And Jesus didn't wait long for that fulfillment to begin. Immediately after His bodily death, one of the battle-hardened soldiers, seeing the blood and water pouring from His side believed – right then and there. At the resurrection, it became dozens, after His ascension into heaven, it was hundreds. Because of first-hand experience with the Holy Spirit at Pentecost, it became thousands. Now multiplied millions believe in His love for them. All over the world, Jesus' sacrifice 2,000 years ago sustains and empowers others who daily experience His care and healing in the most dire circumstances imaginable. But we still have trouble seeing Jehovah God as the loving, tender-hearted parent who sacrificed His own son for us!

Because of what Jesus went through, at the direction of God the Father, we are not just forgiven, we are adopted. Jesus is not merely called the Son of God but the "Only *Begotten* Son" of God. Why make the differentiation? God doesn't waste words. If He makes a difference or reference to something, it is important. Jesus took lots of opportunity while He was here to tell us why. Jesus is not the only son God has. He has many sons – and daughters. As soon as we believe that what God did He did specifically for us, we become God's children. Jesus is our brother and we become heirs with Him of our heavenly Father's loving parentage. Jesus is "begotten", "the firstborn among many brethren"; we are adopted, grafted into the original, and gifted with all the rights and privileges of sonship in Christ. And make no mistake; Jehovah, Yahweh, God the Father is the best Father we can ever have!

He is better than human Dads who teach us baseball and coach our games or become scout leaders. He is better than Dads who teach us to play an instrument or work a computer or plow a field or care for their families by their day-in and day-out dedication. God is the greatest Dad. God is not suffering from the character flaws some of our earthly dads struggle with of vindictiveness, laziness, drunkenness, retaliation and vice toward His children. He's not a hard-hearted task-master, a distant kill-joy, or a vindictive bully.

But that's the point, isn't it? If denying His existence doesn't work, the accuser attempts to interject doubt on the goodness and love God has toward us. He incessantly attacks fathers. Fatherhood is a threat to satan because our Dads form our earliest concepts of the character of God. If he can distort those concepts by messing with our dads, you know he will! Satan wants us to view God in derogatory terms so we don't trust Him, so we don't turn to the only One Whose Love can defeat his schemes against us. He has to distort our perceptions of God to isolate us.

One of the troubles we have in recognizing those distortions are not all his attacks are direct. This starts at a very early age, in ways so stealthy we miss it sometimes. From advertising that demeans parents as being stupid or clueless for not getting their kids this product or that, to programming that shows – and glorifies! – Dads who are abusive, foul-mouthed and dismissive, he has lots of help fostering this misconception. If we don't make the effort to expose these schemes for what they are, they infiltrate our perceptions of God.

God's feelings toward His children are much different.

When the Bible talks about how God feels about us, it uses words like "delight", "rejoicing" and "compassionate". He is a powerful defender, a forgiving benefactor and a tender Father. Why do we so often miss that part? Read these slowly, thoughtfully and *treasure* what He says about you!

Zephaniah 3:17: "The Lord your God is in the midst of you, a Mighty One, a Savior [Who saves]! He will rejoice over you with joy; He will rest [in silent satisfaction] and in His love He will be silent and make no mention [of past sins, or even recall them]; He will exult over you with singing."

Hosea 11:3-4 "Yet I taught Ephraim to walk, taking them by their arms or taking them up in My arms, but they did not know that I healed them. I drew them with cords of a man (the NIV calls it "cords of human kindness"), with bands of love, and I was to them as one who lifts up and eases the yoke over their cheeks, and I bent down to them and gently laid food before them."

He delights over us with singing; He tenderly heals our pain, whether inflicted by others or the pits we run into on our own. He gently comes to feed us the "food that is needful for us."[44] At first it is milk and easily digested truth, as we begin with baby stages: "I am the Lord your God, Who brought you up out of the land of Egypt. Open your mouth wide and I will fill it."[45] Our only job as babes in Christ is to be willing to receive it from Him.

Then, as we progress in our walk with Him, He gives us more complex things to digest – combinations of trials and triumphs to encourage us and build up our spiritual muscles to insure that we grow.

"He delivers the afflicted in their affliction and opens their ears [to His voice] in adversity."[46] "And though the Lord gives you the bread of adversity and the water of affliction, yet your Teacher will not hide Himself any more, but your eyes will constantly behold your Teacher"[47] and He "never forsakes us nor leaves us!"[48]

Getting to know Him and the heart He really has toward us is such an encouragement and anchor against some of the experiences and other people that (more than any other time in my life) have been tearing at my heart. At times I can feel like an outsider, like I am waiting on the other side of a locked door with no one to let me in! But I don't need to stay there. "See what [an incredible] quality of love the Father has given us, that we should [be permitted to] be named and called and counted the children of God! And so we are!"[49]

I can tell you from personal experience how tenderly and carefully God meets us exactly where we are, no matter what we think of Him at the time.

Big Shoulders

While I was still in "whack-a-mole" mode, my dad was diagnosed with stomach cancer. After he went through an exploratory surgery that determined the tumor was inoperable, the diagnosis came back that without chemo (which my dad refused to consider due to my grandfather's experience with it years before) he had 3 – 6 months to live. This happened just four months after I lost my mom in a car accident. I was 26 years old. I had two small children and a big chip on my shoulder.

I had lots of church experiences up to this point, in several different denominations. I believed in God, I knew right from wrong, and I knew I was tipping the scales on the wrong side of things repeatedly. I was trying to make up for it as best I knew how. I had recently begun going back to church, got my kids involved in Sunday School, said my night time prayers with them and started going to Al-Anon meetings. When my dad got his diagnosis, I was completely angry at God.

I remember standing in a room all by myself looking up at the ceiling and the accusations were flying through my head. God had "taken my mom away" in the car accident, leaving my 13 year-old sister (and the rest of us siblings) "without a mom" for all the important things that were coming up. He "could have stopped it"; He "could have healed her". I had "gone back to church", I was "trying to be good", what more did He want from me!? I lifted a balled up fist to the ceiling and screamed at God: "You PROMISED! You said you'd never give us anything we can't handle! Well, cut me open and look inside cuz I CAN'T HANDLE THIS! I CAN'T bury both my parents in the same year! DO SOMETHING!"

There was no reverence, no "Thee's" and Thou's" just raw pain. I was a tiny little girl, in a grown woman's body, crying out in complete heartache to her Whack-a-Mole idea of God for action. Not asking, but demanding that God be faithful to my perceptions of His promises, regardless of my own failings. It wasn't flowery, it wasn't nice, but it was probably the most honest conversation I'd had with Him in a long time.

I say conversation, because I got His answer.

A few days later, after weeks of not being able to keep anything down, my dad made this amazing recovery. He not only kept down the Jell-O and lighter stuff, he was able to eat real food without pain. The doctor couldn't explain it. The tumor was still there. All kinds of blood vessels and other factors still made it inoperable. But within days he had the feeding tube removed, he was walking around and he got to go home. A week later he was eating a full spaghetti dinner with all the fixings my brother had made for him.

We went all kinds of places with the kids – the aquarium, museums, etc. He helped us refurbish a wreck of a house. I got a year and a half of reconciliation time with my dad, learning and initiating emotional boundaries and establishing accountability in our relationship we'd never had before – something I never got to do with my mom.

Around the one and a half year mark, the physical toll on his body began to show itself more directly. He got tired more easily, started losing weight and got more irritable with the increasing pain levels. I'd had an additional year in church, my own daily devotion and prayer time with God, made baby steps of encouragement, instruction and getting a better understanding of a very small part of what God was doing in my little world.

When we had to admit Dad to the cancer unit of a local hospital, I felt defeated. But I was in a much better place spiritually than I had been earlier. This time when I sat down to have my "heart-to-heart" with God I was tearful and resigned to what was happening, just asking for help. "I don't know if I can do this God. I finally got all that junk between us dealt with. I don't want to lose him."

What I got back as a response to this request was a very tender, very personal thought from my Daddy God. That thought was a single sentence that began with Him calling me by name, and with that one sentence came all the background understanding for what it meant: "Tracy, even Lazarus died the second time."

The peace of mind that followed that sentence assured me that, yes, this time the answer to my prayer was not natural healing, but an end of my dad's physical suffering. And that was okay. Just like Jesus had raised Lazarus from the dead and returned him to his grieving sisters for all Jerusalem to see back then, he'd given my dad and all us kids a second chance to spend some time together, not adding grief upon grief over the loss of my mother so soon before.

But also like Lazarus' sisters had to grieve again for their brother's second death after Jesus' crucifixion, we would be grieving the loss of my dad this time. But this grief was tempered with a greater appreciation for the extra time we had with him and the fact that he was no longer suffering the ravages of this awful disease. He was now enjoying the promise of life after death because of his belief in Jesus' death and resurrection.

The peace that came with that one statement was so comforting! "Tracy, even Lazarus died the second time." It was the first time I can remember God calling me by name. Is has not been the last. Knowing without a doubt that you are tenderly loved and compassionately cared for even when you're angry, belligerent, screaming and in pain, makes it a whole lot easier to discard deceptive ideas of distance and rebuke and lean in to the Answer to your deepest longings! Don't be afraid to be real with Him. He has BIG shoulders. He can take our fear, our anger, our pain, and our false impressions. In return, He gives us Grace - and relationship. He is my Daddy and I am His daughter. Sometimes His answer is yes, sometimes it's no. But there is no doubt He Loves me. He has proven it more times that I can count.

I want more than my previous misconceptions from my relationship with God today! I want to run in the door, knowing that I can flop on the couch any time I want to. I want to KNOW that I am completely welcomed and can have goofy, fun times and heart-felt, serious conversations with my heavenly "Dad" about anything I am going through. I want to *be* that kind of person myself toward other people. I had become so frustrated and so resentful toward so many things. It seemed that everything I was angry and upset about just lead to something else I could criticize. I don't want to be like that anymore.

I would LOVE to be known eternally like the descriptions of some of the godly people in the Bible! Like Enoch, "walked with God"[50], Noah, "a man who walked in [habitual] fellowship with God"[51], Abraham "the Friend" of God[52], David, "A man after God's own heart"! Seeing God in these terms is not a feeling of disrespect or irreverence – it's how He *calls us to approach Him*!

So as I share some of the things He has helped me through - as we share at this well - let us begin with this first step, this first understanding: Jehovah God, Our Heavenly Father, the God of the Universe, the All Powerful One is tenderly, deeply and extravagantly in love with you! He is good and He calls us to His throne by way of the only door – the cross of His Son Jesus Christ, by Whom we cry "Abba! Father!"[53] He has the ultimate open-door policy and has everything awesome, every good and perfect gift, stocked up and waiting for us to come on over. He encourages us to come often, anytime, with his kid Jesus and spend some time hangin' out together!

Our Daddy God. He is better than Ozzie Nelson, Danny Thomas, Gandhi, Nelson Mandela, Billy Graham and Bill Gates all rolled into one. He is the wisest, most compassionate, life-loving, freedom-fighting, faithful and richest Dad in the world. He has used a wide variety of situations and experiences to show me His matchless love for me – and I've only scratched the surface! So now that you've met my Heavenly Dad, c'mon! Let's go! I'll race you to the kitchen!

Footnotes

[1] Heb. 11:6 amp

[2] Mark 14:36 NIV 1984

[3] 2 Tim. 4:8 NIV 1984

[4] Ps. 56:8 amp

[5] "Alice's Adventures in Wonderland", by Lewis Carroll, MacMillan and Company publishers London 1865

[6] 2 Cor. 1:3-7 NIV 1984

[7] "Unredeemed" Brian David Petak/Tony Wood/Chad Cates ©2006 Growth Spurt Music (ASCAP) (admin. by Music Services)/New Spring Publishing (ASCAP)/Row J Seat 9 Songs (ASCAP)/Upper Cates Music (ASCAP). All rights for the world on behalf of Row J Seat 9 Songs and Upper Cates Music administered by New Spring Publishing. All rights reserved. Used by permission

[8] Ps. 147:3, Isa. 61:1 NIV 1984

[9] 1 Pet. 4:1 amp

[10] Rom. 12:19b amp

[11] "The Courage to Change" Al Anon Family Group Headquarters, Inc. 1992 Steps 1 – 3, page 367

[12] Heb. 4:15 amp

[13] Isa. 55:9 NIV 1984

[14] Prov. 8:17 amp

[15] Luke 11:9 NIV 1984

[16] Exo. 3:15 NIV 1984

[17] Prov. 19:3 NIV 1984

[18] Gen. 9:15 NIV 1984

[19] Heb. 11:7 amp

[20] Gen. 17:4 amp

[21] Gen. 12, 20 NIV 1984

[22] Matt. 7:2 amp

[23] 2 Sam. 11, 12 NIV 1984

[24] 2 Sam. 12:25 NIV 1984

[25] 1 John 1:9 NIV 1984

[26] Ps. 103:8-14 NIV 1984

[27] Matt. 5:17 amp

[28] 1 Pet. 5:8 amp

[29] 4"No one Believes in me Anymore (Satan's Boast)" Words and Music by Keith Green and Melody Green copyright © 1977 EMI April Music Inc. Copyright Renewed All Rights Administered by Sony/ATV Music Publishing LLC, 424 Church Street, Suite 1200, Nashville TN 37219 International Copyright Secured All Rights Reserved *Reprinted by Permission of Hal Leonard Corporation*

[30] Rev. 12:10 amp

[31] "How to Build an Emotionally Healthy Marriage", by Jimmy Evans, www.MarriageToday.org

[32] Deut. 30:19 amp

[33] John 10:10 amp

[34] Eph. 6:12 amp

[35] 2 Cor. 10:3-4 amp

[36] Ps. 91 amp

[37] Matt. 26:52

[38] Hab. 2:4, Rom. 1:17, Gal 3:11 amp

[39] Matt. 11:28 amp

[40] John 3:16 amp

[41] John 3:17 amp

[42] Luke 23 amp

[43] Luke 22:44 NIV 1984

[44] Prov. 30:8

[45] Ps. 81:10 amp

[46] Job 36:15 amp

[47] Isa. 30:20 amp

[48] Heb. 13:5 NIV 1984

[49] 1 John 3:1a amp

[50] Gen. 5:24 NIV 1984

[51] Gen. 6:9b amp

[52] James 2:23 amp

[53] Gal. 4:6 amp

Suggested Resources:

"Keith Green the Ministry Years Vol 1 & 2" CD's by Keith Green

"Evidence that Demands a Verdict" by Josh McDowell

"The Case For Christ" by Lee Strobel

"Healing the Father Fracture" by Gregory Dickow

"Restoring Fellowship With The Father" by Joyce Meyer

Chapter 2

The Power of Choices

"I call heaven and earth to witness this day against you
that I have set before you life and death, the blessings and
the curses; therefore choose life, that you and your
descendants may live."
Deuteronomy 30:19

When I first became aware of a local event called *40 Days for Life*, I was a 44-year-old grandmother of two. One of my grandchildren was running out in the open where I could see him, and the second grandchild was eating, moving and developing certain unique characteristics that we would soon see in a few short months. She was a girl with the most beautiful blue eyes and grin, easily startled by loud noises and capable of some incredibly urgent screams just for not getting what she wanted at the moment. (She is carrying on a three-generation tradition, after all!) And as I began to write this, my third grandchild (my second granddaughter) was moving and growing in utero, seemingly doing gymnastics (or was it water ballet?) usually while my daughter-in-law was trying to sleep. She was not due for another two months, but she was absolutely making her presence felt. She was promising to be a very active little girl! My grandchildren, Jason, Emily, and Natalee are the second generation of personal victory in my life. My children are the first... but they were almost not born.

Several years ago, during that local *40 Days for Life* campaign, I was given the opportunity to share my experience publically for the first time. This nation-wide event is a time for prayer, education and outreach to help people understand the importance of defending life both personally and in the public arena. It incorporates a 40-day time period in which people all over the country organize local activities ranging from round-the-clock prayer vigils, walking in front of abortion clinics to pro-life rallies and educational events. The activities are all coordinated with Pro-Life organizations and abortion alternative pregnancy resource centers such as Birth Right, Care Net and many churches. The articles of conduct the participants agree to in conjunction with these events mandate supportive and non-violent interaction with everyone they come in contact with, no matter what the setting or provocation.

I was invited to speak, along with other women and pro-life organization representatives, to all the students attending my former high school during a school-wide assembly for the 2007 *40 Days for Life* campaign. All the girls in the school got involved; some made posters, another created not one, but two powerful and creative PowerPoint slide presentations set to music, others wrote letters and poetry. They were all so energetic and passionate about their choice for life. It was wonderful and I was honored to be asked to be a part of it. But it was not without pain. My part in this event was not one of clinical facts on human development. It was not one of a conscience-free idealist who has always followed that path of defending life as the gift and miracle it is. I was the messenger of warning - and of hope. My part was to try and tell of the personal decision I made 28 years before this event: my decision to have an abortion while I was attending this very high school. I would be sharing the before and after, the road that brought me to a pit of fear and regret at a very young age, and the consequences that were far more costly than I could have imagined. But I also came to share the hope of true freedom in God's grace and forgiveness that lifted me out of that pit and healed my heart.

I wanted to be a lighthouse of sorts, warning the girls away from rocks of pain and shame. I wanted them to hear from one who had very definitely experienced the dark side of certain choices. Choices related to dating, personal integrity and self-respect. It was an admonition not based on rules, but on the love of Someone who cares for them more tenderly than any other relationship they could ever have. Jesus has healed me, and like the leper who is now free from his curse, I wanted to run back and tell others how amazing His love truly is! His love - and staying within some basic boundaries founded on that love - would never put them in the position to make this particular choice. I prayed that I could explain the deception that led to my abortion. I wanted to convey the pressure and fears I experienced when I was faced with that choice up close and personally. I prayed that my sharing would keep even one of these girls from making that same painful choice someday. My hope was to empower them from putting themselves in a position that could lead to "having to" make that choice in the first place. As I spoke that day, there was no condemnation in their eyes, no judgment, just the embrace of compassion.

Every Choice Matters

It is vital for everyone to understand that while it may not be fair, it may not be politically correct, and it may not be comfortable to acknowledge personal responsibility and the reality that everything you do impacts not only yourself, but other people around you, it is true, nonetheless. <u>Every</u> choice you make affects others - without exception. Even something as silly as what kind of sandwich you have for lunch, not only affects your own body chemistry but how much of that sandwich meat is left for the next person who wants that kind of sandwich. The stakes and results of the impact vary, but the truth is this: *every choice matters.*

Proverbs 10:17 states, "He who heeds instruction is not only himself in the way of life, but also is a way of life for others. And he who neglects or refuses reproof not only himself goes astray but also causes to err and is a path toward ruin for others." This principle clearly states that our choices – good or bad, beneficial or detrimental – affect not only us, but those around us – including those we've never seen. Whether we like it or not, we are all interconnected and our choices can lift others out of pits of depression and discouragement, or they can drop us and other people into degradation and futility. What we say and what we do matters. The instruction and correction of which we avail ourselves will affect our decisions. We need to heed instruction; we need to keep learning and let the things we learn increase our discernment and understanding. What we study, learn and pray for will impact our decisions for the better in our immediate circumstances and in this world around us.

The person I became in my mid-teens was not "heeding instruction" and I was repeatedly "refusing and neglecting reproof" more often than not. If I did consider the possibility of unfavorable outcomes, I figured I would just deal with it later. I was overconfident in my ability to turn things to my favor. But I didn't see it that way at the time. I tended to point fingers of blame toward other people and situations I didn't like as the reason that I did and said things. As a result I made poor decisions — both in behavior and in companionship.

Proverbs 27:17 says, "Iron sharpens iron; so a man sharpens the countenance of his friend [to show rage or worthy purpose]." Make no mistake; our decisions *are* our own responsibility. We need to take ownership of the consequences of what we do. But our ability to stick to those decisions is often impacted by the people we associate with. The people we choose to be companions with can support us and encourage us to stay on the right course, or they can promote rebellion and turn us away from sound judgment. Instead of making choices of companionship, actions and goals that were in agreement with what I knew to be right, I chose what *felt* best or gave the quickest, easiest solution to what I wanted at the time irrespective of future consequences.

Proverbs 12:26 shows us the application of this truth: "The righteous man is a guide to his neighbor, but the way of the wicked causes others to go astray." We need to decide the direction of our path in advance. Will we be companions of those who hold us to a right standard of moral character? Or companions of those who encourage us to do things and make choices that destroy our lives and the lives of those we love the most? Will we be an encouragement and "spur one another on toward love and good deeds"[1]? Or will we be "a path of ruin"? We are clearly warned, "Do not be misled: 'Bad company corrupts good character.'"[2]. This is a lesson I learned the hard way, much later than I needed to.

I'm not saying that *no one* tried to deter me from the self-destructive path I was on, but there were plenty of other people who encouraged my rebellious attitudes, rewarded or condoned bad behavior and fed my self-pity. I selfishly thought that I shouldn't have to go through so many hard circumstances because of *other people's* choices. Those who encouraged my bad behavior were the people I gravitated toward, the ones I listened to. The choices I made for myself as a result of this mindset were far more detrimental than anything *anyone else* had done to me! I was actively helping my worst enemy destroy my life.

I was on a bad track physically, mentally, emotionally and spiritually back then. I was the oldest of five children, still reeling from my parents' divorce, deeply upset at the consequences I was living with because of other people's choices - although I couldn't express it that way then. I was upset over having to take responsibility for things I had no control over. Like many misguided young adults, I wanted to start living so that the consequences I was living with were from *my own* choices and decisions. The maxim, "be careful what you wish for, you might just get it" was soon to come into play – and I was completely unprepared for the results!

I left home shortly after my 16th birthday. The state's emancipation laws gave me more rights than I was mature enough to handle and prevented my mother from forcing my return. This was only the beginning of a chain of choices that brought me more pain than I could have anticipated.

I continued going to school like nothing in the world was wrong, moving in with my boyfriend who promised a ring and a wedding. (It is a misnomer to call him my "boyfriend": he was seven years older than I was - a grown man of 23 with a full-time job, but it's easier to use that term.) I discovered less than a year later that I was expecting a baby.

I was not aware that he was not willing to be a father. In my mind (and in "pillow talk" during more intimate moments) we had already decided that we were going to get married after I finished high school, and of course to me that meant having children. I was devastated to learn that his solution to my unexpected pregnancy was abortion, which he demanded on condition of my staying in his house. I was not ready for that kind of ultimatum and it scared and confused me.

The only "crisis pregnancy" organization I knew about at the time was Planned Parenthood. The wording of the name sounds nobler than it is. Yes, they provided free (or less expensive) birth control, and with my limited means that was important back then, but there was a dark side hidden from the much-publicized propaganda that I knew little about - yet.

I had not heard of Birth Right, Care Net, Operation Rescue or a host of other pro-life organizations that offer factual information on fetal development, support, encouragement and resources that answer the financial, emotional and spiritual questions young women face during an unexpected pregnancy. The knowledge they offer gives options for a completely different set of choices that I could have made back then, much to my dismay later in life.

During this decision-making process I was living a double life. Hard-studying, parochial school girl during the day with concerns about grades, peer pressure, and fitting in (thank goodness the uniforms took care of the "what-to-wear" worries!), and at night I was the focus of a grown man's adult affections, *"playing house"*, taking on the role of a wife without any of the commitment and documentation that would offer legal protections. There was no personal security beyond the emotions we both felt at the moment. I ignored the facts that I didn't want to see and rejected those who tried to point them out to me. It seemed for a while that I had the best of both worlds. But that was a lie. Living outside the boundaries of Biblical morality was taking more from me than I knew. Now I was facing decisions I never wanted to make – and I didn't use the resources available at the time to make the right choices.

Deliberations

My thought processes at 16 were at best, severely jumbled. I decided that I *had* to go through with the abortion. If I didn't, I wouldn't be allowed to continue living with the man who told me he loved me and was going to marry me. I had been given a pre-engagement ring with a small diamond chip in it the second week we were "dating", when I had given my virginity to him. My mother was newly divorced on State assistance and still raising my three youngest brother and sisters. She did not have the means to support two more. My relationship with her was still pretty rocky and this was more than she could handle; she advised abortion as well. My father advised against it, but his job and the child support he was already paying meant he had no means of financially supporting us either. I thought if I chose to go through with the pregnancy and keep the baby I would be on my own. My dad was living in a cold-water flat and could barely support himself at the time.

I was the oldest of five and knew the work that was involved in caring for a baby. Each time a new baby brother or sister had arrived since I was 9, the crib was put in my room. I knew up-close and personal about 2 am feedings and being up all night with a sick child and then heading off to school. I had no illusions when it came to that part of baby care. People all around me were talking about not "ruining the rest of my life by limiting my options" so early, with "so much more of my life ahead of me" before I settled down.

When adoption was posed as a possible alternative to abortion, I flat-out refused to consider it. I had heard about how many women so desperately wanted a baby and were unable to, for various reasons. I knew I was emotionally at a disadvantage. Two parents could give a more stable and secure home than I was capable of then, but I would not consider that option. I reasoned (this is the thing that still makes me cringe as a justification for it all) that if I went through with the pregnancy and gave the baby up for adoption, I would spend the rest of my life wondering where he or she was. What if I did find them and the adoptive parents wouldn't let me see him or her? I would be devastated. I couldn't bear that!

I wish to God that I had gone the rest of the way through that thought – "I would rather kill my own child than to let someone else give him, or her, a happy life". (Adoption is a much different proposition than my dread led me to believe. Adoption options where the biological mom gets to choose or have some input as to who the adoptive parents are, have visitation, and a host of other provisions are available today that were never seriously considered before. Adoption is redemption in so many ways for all parties involved! I was not educated on the subject, so I was going by "what-if" fears instead of facts).

I believe that if I had followed that train of thought to its logical conclusion that I would have chosen differently back then, but I know from experience that I am capable of some pretty messed up choices in the panic and heat of the moment, and I will never know for sure.

That is one reason I am so humbled and grateful for God's grace and why I try not to be judgmental of other people when their choices seem so obviously harmful in hindsight. That is the true application of "There, but for the grace of God, go I." We all need to develop the humility that comes from truly knowing that we too are capable of horrific decisions, given sufficient incentive. None of us can say what we would do in all situations, especially when we are young with so few experiences and so little wisdom built up.

Young people don't have the benefit of past experience to be able to look back and compare previous mistakes with present circumstances and say – "Oh no! I am NOT doing that again! I remember what happened the last time this came up..." That is the real reason children need parents and older, godly counsel to help think through the consequences of possible choices in the deliberation stage and point out the flaws in their hormone- and youth-compromised logic!

Often, wise counselors can see the outcomes of our choices before we have to experience the pain of those consequences for ourselves. That is a major reason I believe in parental consent and notification. Very often, what a young woman fears in the middle of a difficult situation is far from the broader reality. Older, wiser and sometimes cooler heads can bring clarity. I know now that each one of my reasons for having the abortion was based on fear and ignorance. Financial stability, previous plans and misinformation, while compelling reasons for changing your own behaviors, are *not legitimate considerations for terminating a pregnancy.* There are many other options that address these factors.

My first child paid the ultimate price for my short-sighted, fear-induced ignorance and my subsequent rejection of God's plan for life.

The day I went to the local Planned Parenthood clinic, the baby's father wouldn't come with me. I didn't have my driver's license yet. A girlfriend and mutual guy-friend I knew brought me to the clinic and waited in the car for me. We were tearful about the situation, but going through with it enabled me to maintain my current living arrangements. I was blinded by all the what-ifs of dread and doom, and not looking forward in hope to any of the good possibilities of not having the abortion.

I went in and had their pre-procedure chat. While we were talking, she said something to the effect of it being "a lump of cells about this big." I sneered and said that I already knew that was a lie. She sat up a little straighter, leaned forward a little more and told me if I was having any doubts about this that I could stop and not go through with it. I was so upset about the whole thing that I didn't realize I was being given a second chance to back out of the worst decision of my life.

I burst into tears and said, "No, you don't understand! My boyfriend will throw me out if I don't do this!" I shut the tears off and determined that this was what I needed to do. (I wasn't sure how far my baby's development had progressed, but I knew it wasn't just a bunch of random cells. I have thought many times in retrospect if only they had had an ultra-sound machine there for me to see...!)

I kept saying, "I have no other choice." That was a lie. I had lots of choices! In reality, as I look back without the burden of the *victim mentality*, I made lots of bad decisions all along the way that eventually required me to choose between life and death for my baby. I was not considering her at all in my deliberations. I was completely self-absorbed in my own panic. Ultimately, I was not willing to experience the fearful (supposed) outcomes of continuing with the pregnancy.

We All Fall Down

The pain involved in the abortion procedure was worse than any period I had ever had – and that is saying quite a bit! I usually went through three days of being doubled over with menstrual cramps, headaches and nausea that kept me home from school. This was way worse. I cried almost the whole time, but the pain I was in was not all physical. I felt no relief; no one could make me feel better afterward. I laid down on a cot in a room with several other women, sipping orange juice and vomiting for more than an hour. During that time, I watched other women come in and go out of the same clinic. I was stunned by the ones who came in and practically danced out of the room afterward. No tears, no vomiting and seemingly no adverse effects.

I actually found myself judging them for their lack of regret and distress! How could I have felt superior to them because I was taking it so badly and they were not? We had just gone through the same procedure! How was I judging them when I too had just allowed someone to kill my child for pay? I still don't know the answer to that one. In the midst of the worst choices of my life, I found something else to be self-righteous about!

When I got to the car, I was still crying and told my friends how horrible it was. I wished I had never agreed to it, but it was too late. They helped me back to the apartment and after a little while, left me there to rest. When my boyfriend got back from work, we talked. I told him in graphic detail everything that had happened while I was there. I wanted him to know how much I was hurting. I told him about the pain, the sounds, the thoughts running through my head, and all my regret. Part of me wanted to hurt him as much as I was hurting. I blamed him; in my head it became his choice and I absolved myself for any part I had in the decision-making process. He held me and told me that if he had known how bad it was going to be, he would never have insisted that I go through with it. His regret seemed to mirror my own and I couldn't stay angry with him about it in light of our complete inability to change the facts at that point.

We cried together and I stayed with him, still attending the same Catholic high school, still living in my own misguided and ungodly choices. I knew this was not the best situation for either of us, but it was easier than changing my path (for now).

The following year, still not changing the actions that got me pregnant in the first place, I became pregnant with our second child. I told my boyfriend I was "late", truly anticipating that this time we would get married and begin our family. I had been taking birth control pills the whole time, even though they induced horrible migraine headaches. But it does say right on the flyers that come with them that they are not 100% effective. I was stunned when his answer was a short and to the point, "You know what to do."

I went from almost happily nervous to furious. "WHAT?! You told me the last time that if you only knew how horrible it was that you would never have made me do it and now you're telling me to do it again!?" I remember screaming, "I will NOT kill another one of my babies for you!" (I had somehow reacquired the responsibility for my first child's death and forgiveness gave way to deflected blame and self-hatred for what I had done. I was determined not go to down that road again.) I was right over the top – and fear was not anywhere near the picture. "You're right! I DO know what to do! I'm leaving!" and with a few obscene gestures causing white knuckles to be held high in the air, I started packing my stuff and getting out of "his" apartment.

I called the girlfriend who had taken me to Planned Parenthood the year before and told her what happened. She let me move in with her, trading babysitting services for room and board. She was in her mid-to-late twenties and had a two year old by this time and a full-time job. We figured we would cross the appropriate bridges when we came to them, but I was not going to have another abortion.

A few days later when the dust settled a little, I was getting scared again thinking of how I was going to be able to go through with all this. I looked at the pack of birth control pills I had been taking that had gotten thrown in with all my other things while I was packing. I wondered: if I took one, would it "fix" the "problem"? I took one (or was it two?) and went on with whatever I was doing at the time trying unsuccessfully to push the conflict I was in out of my mind.

Later I couldn't escape the thoughts bombarding me about what I had just done. It was too late to throw up the pill. I cried and started to pray and apologize for giving in to the fear. "God, I am so sorry! Please forgive me! I am scared and I shouldn't have done that. Please save the baby, please help the baby be healthy and help me figure out how to do this the right way!" I resolved to go through the pregnancy and care for my little one the best I could with all the help I could get. A couple days later I started to bleed – hard. I was filled with remorse. I felt so ashamed! I don't know if taking that pill could have caused the miscarriage, but the torturous thoughts I've had over the years have *never* depended on facts.

Don't Get Stuck in Semantics

In the current debate as to whether to call the "morning after" or "emergency contraception pills" abortion pills or not, understand that what you call them is a moot point. Human hormone levels differ from one person to the next and hormone supplements like birth control pills differ in strength and intensity. Every person's body is different and therefore responds differently to medications and alterations in these hormones – hence the need for different strengths. There are too many variables in play to give absolute answers to questions that would apply equally to every person. Because of these differences, pharmaceutical companies and doctors cannot say with any veracity that contraceptive pills won't cause a miscarriage if taken by a pregnant woman. Thus the debate continues between the terms contraception (*preventing* conception) and abortifacient (abortion *inducing*) drugs.

Some may claim that contraceptive pills prevent fertilization but not implantation once cell division and growth begin. Products presented as "morning after" pills, which most people understand are just a stronger level of the same hormones as birth control pills, more dramatically alter the body's levels of these hormones than those marketed as contraceptives. But if they are taken after the sperm and the egg have contacted one another, the effect of these pills is to destabilize the hormonal shift that happens in the early stages of pregnancy to aid implantation and instead forces the shedding of the uterine lining – whether or not the developing embryo has already established "roots" in that lining. RU 486 pills make use of this fact with tragic results. Many women have experienced hemorrhaging and other complications following their use – in addition to the untimely loss of their children. Some have died.

With only one exception in all of history, the only way to avoid pregnancy is to prevent sperm from contacting the egg. The fact is once the sperm meets the egg, life has begun. All the physical characteristics that baby will have are wrapped up tightly in the unique DNA configuration of that child and it is only a matter of maturation before we will be able to see what is already encoded in each of his or her developing cells. Growth is not possible without life. Changes in the mother's hormone levels after conception do not keep the baby from growing.

Whether the baby has started to develop and is prevented from implanting into the wall of the mother's uterus, or whether the baby is released from the uterus after implantation has already occurred, the effect is still the same: it is still abortion by pill.

Recently, I was reassured that the hormone level of the birth control pills I had at the time would not have been strong enough to cause a "spontaneous abortion." Due to the factors involved and the gestational development that had already been reached by the time I took them, I really don't know for sure. After all these years, it really is irrelevant. My intent at the time, no matter how momentary it was, was cause enough for decades of guilt and shame.

I went to the doctor's office crying and desperate for them to do something to save my baby. One of the doctors looked at me and impatiently said "What are you crying for? Everything is going to be fine." I half growled back, "Everything is NOT fine! I am losing my baby!" A pregnant 17-year-old staying with a friend, no income, education or job, was now miscarrying. I knew it wasn't the best situation to bring a baby into, but even in the uncertainty of my living arrangements, I didn't want to lose the life I was carrying. "Fine"? I guess it all depends on your point of view.

I lost my second baby.

Depressed, remorseful and grief-stricken over the loss, I was having a really hard time living inside my own head. But to be honest about it, I was also somewhat relieved. I felt similar to when a close relative dies after struggling with a debilitating disease. You're sad they are gone, but grateful they are not suffering any more. But in my context, the emotional undercurrent contains no nobility whatsoever. I was grateful I was not conflicted anymore about where I would be and what I would be doing. But the feelings of relief over not knowing how I would provide for my child were overshadowed with all kinds of self-recrimination and guilt over "forcing" a miscarriage. I stuffed these feelings down deep and continued on the same behavioral track I'd been on.

I was so completely self-absorbed and clueless! I was trying to sort out my feelings. I was a mess. I needed to figure out what to do with my life. School was going to be starting up again and I needed to get there every day without a driver's license. When the baby's father found out that I had miscarried, he told me I could move back to his place. It was walking distance from school. I went back to him. (Can you say the word stupid?) I understand now that it all had to do with the emotional connection we had as a result of him being the one I gave my virginity to. I understand he was the one I trusted with my provision and protection after I left home. Like the prodigal son, I was sure that life had to be better out there than dealing with my own broken family and refused to consider that as an option – yet. I justified it all again. He wasn't all bad. He had good qualities. But seriously, how many times do I have to get burned before I stay away from the stove?

[Note: During the "40 Days" assembly, when I shared with the girls that I had gone back to him after the miscarriage,

I saw looks of unbelief and flashes here and there of disdain – good! I made the right point. I want to help other girls avoid making the same self-destructive choices in their own lives. No other person on the planet is worth the kind of choices I made back then! But I was looking for comfort and stability without responsibility. It is ironic that I would choose to try to fill a "wife" role, but not want to retain the far-easier role of "daughter" and "sister" in my own family. The role I chose then had far more responsibility than the roles I walked away from!]

Hard Lessons

I finished up my junior year at the same Catholic high school *and* I was now in wedding planning mode. While "negotiating" my return after the miscarriage, my boyfriend had given me an engagement ring with a bigger diamond in it and was now openly promising marriage immediately after graduation. I wasn't quiet about my living arrangements and showed off my new ring between classes and at afterschool activities. I was excited about the anticipated wedding and quickly getting closer to my senior year. I was looking forward to the white graduation gown, class ring and yearbook, all the while thinking about wedding plans. I was even talking about having my boyfriend take me to the senior prom.

It's ironic that the thing I was looking most forward to was an intra-school tradition called being a "big sister." This is when a senior takes on an in-coming freshman as a "little sister", as someone to show around the school, getting her comfortable with her new surroundings and mentoring her. I fondly remember my own big sister from my time as a freshman. She was a beautiful Philippine girl with long dark hair, a wonderful accent, a singing voice that I admired greatly and had been the lead in all the school musicals. She was my hero and a source of encouragement and stability in the messy first year of high school and my parents' divorce. I was looking forward to being that type of helpful mentor and I saw nothing wrong with the dichotomy of the school's Catholic teachings and my personal lifestyle.

I was having my cake and eating it too, or so I thought. Some of the sisters at the school had several behind the scenes discussions concerning the influence a senior would have on underclassmen who saw a supposed role model "living in sin" and still being allowed to attend their school. On the last day of my junior year, one of the sisters came up to me and informed me of their decision and shook me to my core. I was not going to be allowed back for my senior year. I was crushed and panicked. I vowed to move out of my boyfriend's house and to "do it right." I would move in with my dad. I would do anything I needed to, to keep going to that school. I was openly begging them to let me stay. After all, "hadn't I endured all the underclassmen years and had kept my grades up, even after the divorce of my parents? Yes, I understood I was in their private school on full scholarship, but I had worked really hard and *deserved* all the perks of being a senior at that school!" With all the pain, pressure and struggling that had been going on in my life; my school had been the only anchor of stability and normalcy that I knew and I desperately needed it.

No one at the school knew about my abortion or the miscarriage. They weren't using that as an argument for my leaving and I obviously didn't bring it up. I had thrown myself whole-heartedly into everything good at the school. I had been excitedly involved in the musicals, helped with cleaning classrooms after the school year ended, even participated in concerts with the choir at a nearby women's prison for Christmas. I didn't want to give all that up! A saddened face tried to explain to me: "Tracy, you've had two years to change your ways." They had moral responsibilities to other students and parents who sent their girls to this school for parochial education that included religious instruction. They had to enforce certain boundaries. It was a matter of institutional and moral integrity. Sometimes the choices we make close doors that we can't open, even if we begin to do things the right way. That was one of the doors.

I flipped out. I switched from deep sadness and pleading with them to change their minds (vowing changes I truly believed I would make given the fork in the road I now faced) to yelling angrily that they were out of touch and clueless about "real life". I decided *they* were the ones who had the problem and I took on a self-righteous attitude (again). I was the second biggest loser due to the choices I made and my refusal to change during my underclassman years. Now I was faced with the loss of so many milestones I had so dearly looked forward to: the senior prom, the class trip, the formal graduation in the brand new auditorium. I angrily blamed the loss on others' "antiquated religious beliefs" rather than taking responsibility for the consequences of my own self-destructive choices and disappointment.

I defiantly made arrangements for night school and got the remaining credit I needed for history and my fourth year of

English. I graduated in December, six months earlier than my classmates, by attending night school at the local adult education program. Taking a "licking my wounds" attitude and consoling myself with early graduation, I now had my day time free from class schedules. Routine activity and daily expectations were gone. I was adrift, making it harder to feel any purpose for my life.

And I still stayed on that broken path of self-reliance that made my heart bleed! I reasoned that if I wasn't going to be able to go to the school anyway, why should I move in with my Dad? I stayed in the house with my boyfriend for another year.

Several years later, while visiting the school and talking with one of the other sisters about the events of that year, she told me I could have appealed the decision. But it was too late. It was already done. And that lesson was one hard-learned truth I have carried forward to other things in my life. It was painful to learn, but looking back on it now I can see that it was a valuable lesson, a turning point that I needed to understand to escape the behavioral rut I was in.

True Love

Those who love us, *truly* love us, will sometimes need to make difficult choices that teach us and enforce hard consequences when we are younger. When we fight against their correction, their steadfastness in discipline attests loudly that their main concern is for our growth and ultimate good character. I couldn't or wouldn't see it at the time, but these sisters, who were trying to teach me the right path to follow, loved me far more than I knew. In staying with my boyfriend, I thought I was choosing love over religious intolerance. I was wrong. I was choosing my own lust and others' acceptance of my wrong choices over true Love and concern for my ultimate welfare.

I have since experienced times when I have been the one who tearfully enforced consequences I did not want to stick by; it is a hard position to be in. I now understand how hard it was for them to stand by their commitment. And although there are times I wonder how it would have felt to experience all those precious milestones, I am very grateful for their decision today.

The longer we wait to learn (and later offer) that kind of love in enforcing those painful lessons, the more painful the lesson has to be to get the same message across to our ever-thickening hearts and heads. Some people never have someone love them so tenderly and deeply that they are willing to take another's pain onto themselves. Sound familiar? Parents all over the world have said, "This hurts me more than it hurts you." As kids we never believe that, but when we become parents we feel it personally. Parents feel pain over some of their children's choices; just like our Heavenly Father feels pain when we make choices against His instructions for safety and good living.

That, in essence, is the difference between human love and God's love for us. Human love can be a gushy feeling that ebbs and flows and passes based on circumstances, but God's love is a *decision* He makes in his perfectness. Called "agape" love in Greek, it means to do and say the right things for the ultimate good of the other person no matter what the personal cost to the giver. *That's* how

God loves *us*. His love for us is perfect, permanent and freely given, not earned nor held back due to our daily failures.

Chris Rice sings a song that says in part, "Sometimes love has to drive a nail into its own hand."[3] Jesus did that. Jesus took our punishment on Himself to create *The Way* out of a no-choice-but-death situation, to offer us eternal life with Him. Today He is accused of intolerance, of exclusivity, of being out-dated and hopelessly out-of-touch with reality. Nothing could be further from the truth! He took on unbelievable pain and suffering to give me and you the opportunity to learn lessons from our *temporary consequences* that will save us from the very *permanent consequence* of separation from Him in hell. These opportunities are filled with Grace so we can discover God's free gift of salvation and eternal life. "For God so loved the world that He gave his one and only Son, that whoever believes in Him shall not perish but have eternal life."[4]

I was so blessed at the time to have someone so in touch with Jesus (the ultimate lover of my soul) that they were willing to endure the pain from the hurtful words and blinding tears of my rage to teach me this lesson. It would be many years before I fully realized what it was, but God's timing is perfect! Sometimes our choices force others to make decisions they would rather not make. We wrongly choose and choose and choose again. Then we get the consequences of those choices. We reap according to what we sow, we harvest what we plant and we cannot blame it on others. (Well, we *can*, but it doesn't change the real accountability for our choices.)

Acknowledging that lesson is the beginning of growth, maturity and real change in us. We need to choose differently, repeatedly! And *then* we get the *good* consequences, the rewards, for our self-discipline and wise but sometimes difficult decisions. I am truly fortunate to have had people in my life who loved me like that. My prayer now is that I can love others in the same way, even if it frequently hurts and is misunderstood. This lesson has stayed with me like a beautiful and *pointed* jewel that has gained many more polished facets of realization to reflect that beauty through some painful cuts of my life. But I wasn't ready then to admit any of that yet – I needed more unpleasant consequences to steer me right.

Another Wake-up Call

Shortly after I completed my high school credits at the adult education program, I turned 18 and decided college was the next step. My intention was to better myself and to be able to provide my own support, instead of being solely dependent on others for the things I needed. But now the disappointment I felt over not being able to finish high school with my fellow classmates was coupled with broken wedding promises. I pressed my boyfriend for a wedding date. I pointed out the engagement ring he had given me as proof of our joint intention all along and cried over the things I had "given up for him." He said it was "just a ring" and he wasn't ready for marriage. Even though I had willingly continued in this relationship through all the ups and downs we'd been through, I felt used. Because of my involvement with this man, I lost the whole senior year of high school experiences and everything that went with it. Now the wedding I thought I had chosen over those rights of passage in my life, turned out to be a disappointing mirage. I felt betrayed. That's when, amid all the other things that were happening in my life, things took another dramatic turn.

I moved in with my Dad in his cold-water flat and tried to stay away from my ex-boyfriend, fighting against all the previous feelings I had for him. I swung back and forth for a while, alternately dating other guys and then trying to make up with my "ex". It was an emotional roller-coaster. But I was beginning to see through the fog, and realize that I had more options than I thought for my life in general.

The college I attended was a local community college that allowed me to live at home and still take courses during the day, avoiding many of the expenses of campus living. I worked hard and got involved with some very colorful people in the drama club and school newspaper. They were out-going, supportive and lived in some pretty unconventional ways.

It was not anything I had been acquainted with nor seen growing up in a Catholic high school and small mill town setting. I made life-long friends there, but my moral behavior tanked even farther. I still had some standards, but little by little I surrendered more of what I should have been holding on to. Even if I was not willing to do things myself, I reasoned back then that I "had no right to judge others" for what I knew to be wrong. Tolerance was the watch-word and personal moral standards were thought to be an "uneducated" perspective needing enlightened correction.

I love the people I met in college. A couple of them helped me through some of the darkest days of my life. Even though many years have gone by, I still get to see some of them. They are dear to my heart and I miss seeing the ones I've lost contact with. I have fond memories of the time we spent together, even though some of the situations we put ourselves in hurt each of us in different ways.

I now know the difference between judgment and discernment. There is an important distinction that must be made: acknowledging that there are right and wrong choices and standing by those beliefs is not synonymous with condemnation and rejection of people. It's about agreeing that some choices bring peaceful and beneficial results and others bring pain, regret and harm to yourself and others. Judging people and passing sentence on them creates division and distance, but discerning between right and wrong actions, and then making beneficial decisions based on proven moral principles is critical to having a life worth living! It is possible to disagree with someone's decisions, perspectives and choices and still love them unreservedly! I did not understand the difference at that time in my life.

In retrospect, I've learned so much more about how God sees us. He loves us so deeply, we simply can't fathom it. God is absolutely perfect, yet He has unwavering compassion for our pain and the broken places in our hearts, even when some of those situations are the direct result of our own choices. He has a wonderful ability and passionate desire to use any difficulty to help us turn to Him and guide us in the right direction.

I understand now that He wants so much for us to give Him the chance to heal us! But He abides by our choices in that area too. He doesn't force Himself on us. He sends people into our lives to help us, He works in our hearts, softening our rough edges and breaking off pieces of the hardened shells we build around our hurts. He pokes and prompts us with His voice of conscience and sometimes knocks us off our horses of self-determination to get our attention. He is not a distant bystander in the process, but we have to choose to accept His help.

If we truly want to experience life the way we are meant to, we do well to yield to God's perspective and let Him show us His safety zones for living our lives under His protection. We are ultimately happier if we learn and respect His boundaries. Remember, fences not only keep good things in, they can also keep *bad* things out! Staying within godly limits protects us from harm. Realizing we will frequently fail in our efforts does not negate this truth. Thankfully God has gates installed in the fences, so to speak, so when we do choose to wander from the yard, we always have the ability to come back in! Like a child who gets mad and runs away from home for the afternoon, we can run back home to waiting, open arms!

I took many chances and put myself in positions that make me shudder when I think about all of the adverse possibilities. I repeatedly avoided accountability for my own choices. And as a first-born girl with an over-developed sense of responsibility, that was extremely hard to do! I was always at war with my conscience. I was trying to get connection and acceptance in detrimental relationships. I did not like the direction these new experiences were taking my life and the changes I saw in who I was becoming. I was manipulative, angry, and lied to get my way with little or no remorse. And I justified it all by deflecting blame to others. I was cynical most of the time and missed the easy laughter my loss of innocence had taken from me. Eventually, I started to make choices that were not at odds with my own conscience. It was a start in the right direction.

There are times when I consider the many possibilities of what more could have happened if God had not faithfully protected me back then. These thoughts simultaneously bring feelings of both deep regret and intense gratitude. I foolishly acted like I was in control of everything around me. I was not. Solomon said: "a man's mind plans his way, but the Lord directs his steps and makes them sure."[5] Even in the sorry state I was in, God continued working in my heart and directing me in the way He wanted me to go. Make no mistake; I still made some really bad choices during this point in my life. There are consequences for my actions that I am keenly aware still affect my life today, many years later. But it could have been so much worse had God not shielded me from some things while I walked blindly down some of those paths He'd clearly told me to avoid! Promiscuity is not a right or a virtue – it's Russian roulette! Don't let anyone tell you differently!

Redemption and Grace are powerful allies and Jesus is faithfully stubborn in His tenacity and persistence to keep who and what belong to Him – and that includes me (and you!)

New Beginning

I met the man who is now my husband while I was living with my boyfriend during the summer I turned 16. He was good friends with someone else we both knew and we spoke briefly on the rare occasions we saw one another. He didn't know what was going on with me because our conversations were mostly small talk about weather and local events, or parties we had gone to. I knew his Mom from the local Town Hall and whenever I saw her I would ask her to tell Steve that I said "Hi!" That was the extent of our relationship.

One night, while I was still trying to "ride the reconciliation rollercoaster" with my ex-boyfriend, we decided it would help rekindle our relationship by going to a local Knights of Columbus fund-raiser dance in our community around Mardi Gras. Maybe some dancing, fun and loud music would help. Things were not going well between us that night. There was no "rekindling", just icy walls and hurt feelings. I saw Steve when we walked in and we started talking. We considered each other just friends, but hadn't seen one another for a long time and wanted to catch up. My boyfriend decided it was more than that and got ticked off. Steve tried to smooth out the situation to no avail. Women sometimes use the tactic of "shutting off" their partners when they're upset about something. My boyfriend decided to shut me off by not dancing as punishment for my "indiscretion." It was finally obvious to me that night the relationship between us was not going to change for the better.

I decided to make the best of the surroundings by continuing my conversation with Steve. We talked about all kinds of things, but kept the conversation light and friendly. He was funny and interesting. He was into hiking, hang gliding and was taking flying lessons. He had a full-time job building submarines in a shipyard nearby and was an avid reader. When my ex-boyfriend repeatedly refused to dance, and I resorted to moving around in my chair to the music, Steve asked me if I would dance with him. Of course! (But only the fast dances. I was, after all, there with someone else.) Steve's Mom and Dad were both there, along with a lot of other people we knew in town. We wanted to make sure everything remained innocent and casual, we just danced and talked.

When some people asked Steve about his new "girlfriend", he quickly corrected their misconception.

He was hesitant to ask me out and I was clueless that he wanted to. But my conversation with Steve and my boyfriend's reaction to it that night helped me settle a few things. It became clear that the possessiveness without real commitment, the repeated refusals to marry (accompanied by all the "benefits" of that arrangement) and his jealousy over harmless conversations with other men were just not working. It all came to a head and I decided (again) to try to do things right. A week later I moved back in with my Dad. Steve and I began dating very shortly after. It was four months before my 19th birthday.

I wanted to live right. But old habits die hard and right ways of thinking take time without encouragement and support. (I know that's an excuse, but there it is.) In truth, within three months Steve and I were living together. We justified it by pointing to my Dad's apartment and complaining about its size and facilities. We were in love.

We defended our decisions and supported one another in them.

Most of the people around us were of the same mind-set we were, a form of "situational ethics." Sure it's wrong, but you have good reasons for what you're doing and it is socially acceptable. Anyone who used the term "living in sin" was marginalized and ignored. We had our own plan. We would get married after I graduated college. In the meantime we got to know one another better. We went to family functions on both sides of the family (preferring his because of my rocky relationship with my mother) but never hesitated to take my younger brother and sisters out for day trips, vacations to Vermont and other activities.

I told Steve about my abortion and miscarriage. We used birth control pills to "prevent untimely reoccurrences". (Why I would trust their effectiveness after all this I don't know - and I was still getting migraines.) I am so glad that God is patient and gracious! We both knew His standard of marriage before living together and having sex, but disregarded it as "old-fashioned." We ignored God in our relationship. He just wasn't part of our lives at that point, or so we thought. God still loved us and protected us from some of the horrible circumstances that other people in similar situations have had to deal with. I can't explain the Grace that we were benefiting from, and taking for granted the whole time. But God was still working in our hearts little by little, drawing us closer to Him - and we were changing.

My relationship with Steve was very different from the one I had previously. I was grateful for his unselfish care and concern for me. He was, and continues to be, a man of character and sacrificial protection and provision for me, even in the face of some hefty obstacles. No relationship is perfect, but he is my hero in a lot of ways and that has deepened over the years.

Steve and I were married two weeks after my college graduation. When I got pregnant a year later, there was no doubt we would keep the baby. We were nervous, but looking forward to it. When I started bleeding and lost my third child, I was heart-broken. Steve consoled me while I shuddered with tears. I was afraid the miscarriage was my fault and that somehow my body was damaged after two D & C's (one for the abortion and one done after the "pill-induced" miscarriage to "prevent infection"). I feared I would lose every baby I carried. After all, I now had lost two of my children following the abortion. Would this continue forever?

The doctors assured me that there was no residual damage from the abortion (of course!) and we sought genetic counseling. We had blood tests to see if there was a genetic reason for the miscarriages; all tests were negative. I would find out much later that I have a genetic mutation called MTHFR, a condition I inherited from both my parents. One of the side effects of this amino acid "swap" in the DNA chain is the propensity toward miscarriages and migraines. The choices I made when I was younger including the foods I ate and the vitamins I took, just made it worse. I didn't find out until I was 51. It seems that pre-methylated B vitamins would have helped with many of the symptoms of this genetic mutation.*
(*see www.MTHFR.net for more info) A little late to find this out now! But following some of the protocols associated with this diagnosis is helping with other aspects of this condition.

What I did find out during the doctor's investigation was I had severe endometriosis. My uterus was "fractured" and pieces of it were independently having their own cycles of enlarging and then trying to discard the excess tissue. With no outlet for these free-floating pieces, they swelled and then shrunk back to pre-menses size as the hormone cycle ebbed and flowed. This condition caused extreme pain every month that no over-the-counter pill could relieve. It also made it a lot harder for my body to carry my babies. I had no idea that endometriosis could adversely affect a pregnancy, but felt the painful effects of this truth nonetheless. No one knows whether this condition was initiated or aggravated by the abortion procedure. We had no "before" picture or baseline to go by, but we do know it got worse over time. [By the time I was in my late 40's, the pain was so bad that I opted for a hysterectomy. It wasn't until they went inside that they found many of these pieces had adhered themselves to my internal organs and needed to be carefully scraped off to remove them.]

We comforted one another with the idea that we just weren't emotionally or financially ready to begin our family yet. When we can't understand something, sometimes we simplify our perspective to enable us to shrug it off. We tell ourselves, in times of disappointment and self-consolation, that it was just "not meant to be."

Truth Hurts Before It Sets You Free

During this time, we were watching lots of science programs and came upon the public TV program Nova. We watched it all the time. While watching "The Miracle of Life" episode, we saw a fiber optic camera's view of a baby's growth from conception through birth. The program documents each stage of development, showing when the heart starts beating (two weeks in utero - before you even know you're "late"!), when the arm buds have finger bones visible through translucent skin, when the eyelids form, and so on, right up to the day the baby is born.

I wanted to see it. I wanted to know. But something that should have been just an awe-inspiring wonder was intensely painful. The unexpected thing about the focus of this pain was I was not applying these weekly developmental milestones to my grief over my recent miscarriage, but to my earlier pregnancy at age 16. I started doing the math: between 12 to 16 weeks …. I saw in living color and movement right in front of me: everything was already formed! An ultrasound would even have been able to tell me whether it was a boy or a girl at that point! Basically, the only things left to develop on my first baby at the time of my abortion were hair, lungs and fingerprints – and tripling in size.

My husband held me and comforted me while my soul was racked with guilt. He was dealing with his own grief over our lost child and I was nearly hysterical, rocking back and forth sobbing over the undeniable evidence of what really happened several years earlier. It's not that I wasn't awe-struck over the sheer amazement of the intricate balance and details involved in fetal development, I absolutely was. But it brought fresh heartache to the grief of two miscarriages and compounded it over the guilt of my decision to abort. People tried to be helpful over the years, telling me time would lessen my pain over this loss. That was not what I was experiencing at all!

Much later I would find out why. In several of Jimmy Evans' teachings from Marriage Today (www.marriagetoday.com), he relates the differences in physical healing and emotional healing. He points out the old cliché "time heals all wounds" may be valid for physical injury, but not for our souls. Our bodies are created with built-in repair systems like our lymphatic system, digestive tract and renal system. So physical bodies, given time and rest, can attack disease, collect and eliminate bodily waste and initiate repairs. "Emotional and mental wounds don't heal like physical wounds. In the case of physical wounds, there is an immediate attempt by the body to heal itself. After a period of time, we are healed 'naturally'. However, our inner wounds aren't that way. The scars of our soul don't heal until we have allowed them to."[6]

"Allowing them to" involves submitting our emotional and spiritual wounds to God as our Great Physician. Using love, truth and forgiveness, He heals the breaches and dissipates the scars till we are no longer crippled by the past. Healing is accomplished through a purposeful partnership, not a passive layover. Expecting emotional healing simply by waiting for it over time is futile. When we are emotionally damaged, time is our enemy. God warns us in Hebrews 12:15: "See to it that no one falls short of the grace of God and that no bitter root grows up to cause trouble and defile many."

Time makes emotional wounds fester and breeds bitterness. It twists our perceptions, in essence "spreading the infection" to other areas in our lives and to other people. Self-defense mechanisms like denial, transference, repression and distraction can briefly mitigate some emotional pain and act as a temporary buffer, until we can deal with it directly at a more opportune time.

But if we don't take the time to truly heal with God's truth and grace, the grief smolders just under the surface. The pain can act like an inner time bomb that goes off at the strangest moments, triggered by the least expected incident. It will not be ignored indefinitely. When it finally rears its ugly head, it can be unbelievably crippling. I was discovering this the hard way.

From the time I was 16, through everything that was happening up to this point, I couldn't look at another baby without crying. When out in public and seeing a mother holding an infant, I would ache inside and turn away. If it was someone I knew who offered to let me hold their child, it was intensely painful. Sometimes I could hold my emotions together, be polite and even enjoy it for a little while. I would let them know how happy I was for them and look into their children's little faces. But when I was alone later, I would be so self-condemned and I didn't want to be in the same room with myself! This went on for years, with some episodes more intense than others. (Some of you have experienced what I am talking about.)

My shame and guilt were relentless and were doing more damage than I knew. They actually kept me from the relief I so desperately needed. I was so legalistic and had seen that character flaw in so many people in my life that it became how I saw God too, as a stern, demanding, punisher instead of an open-armed, something-special-for-My-little-girl, wipe-your-tears-on-My-shoulder kind of God that He really is. I guess for me that was the difference between conditional and unconditional love – the difference I saw between my dad and my grandfathers.

My dad's affection seemed to be based on what I did or didn't do. When I did well, he was proud of me; when I didn't do what he wanted, the hammer came down hard. But my perception of my relationship with my grandfathers was very different. I never doubted that my Grandpa and my Pepiere loved me unconditionally - no matter what I did or didn't do. I viewed God in the same light as my Dad up to this point, instead of my Grandfathers, and that detrimentally impacted my faith.

I was, and am, so grateful for my husband! He loved me through all the difficult times, forgave me my outbursts, and never gave up on me. He was always comforting and supportive, even while he was going through his own issues and grief. He was part of my healing - a model of what a man is supposed to be for his wife in so many ways! And even though I did not recognize it at the time, God's love and comfort was expressed through Steve as a balm on my wounds until I got to the place where I could finally relinquish all of it to God for complete healing!

Steve and I waited several months before *planning* our next baby. By this time in my life, I had made an inner vow that I would make sure my children all knew they were planned and would have no chance at all to believe, like I had, that they were "accidents."

When I discovered I was pregnant again, I was thrilled and hopeful. When we had gotten three months into this pregnancy I started bleeding again. I begged and pleaded with God to save my baby. I didn't want Him to "punish me for my abortion by taking away another one." People I talked to before this had told me "God doesn't work that way." I pointed to David and Bathsheba's first child[7] and used it as proof that "yes, He could!" I didn't want false comfort, but I also didn't want to feel condemned. I didn't want to lose my baby because I had messed up so badly earlier in my life. I prayed for the thousandth time for God to forgive me for what I had done and to please let this one live. I still had (and have) so much to learn about the love of God! He met me where I was at the time (He always does), and although I thought I had no right to expect otherwise, the bleeding stopped a couple days later. Except for gestational diabetes necessitating a change in my diet, the pregnancy proceeded normally after that.

My daughter was born in October, healthy, complete, and with a full head of hair. We love her dearly and are blessed to have her in our lives. I am forever grateful that God doesn't depend on our misconceptions of who He is for how He responds to us as we grow in our very limited understanding of Him. He is love. He is tender and caring toward His children. Sometimes we go through hard things. And sometimes there seems to be no reason for the heartache we experience, but He "never leaves us nor forsakes us."[8]

A few months later, enjoying every day of her life, we found out we were expecting again. Four of our cousins and friends had overlapping pregnancies that year. We were all thrilled. Three months in I started bleeding again.

This time was bad. I knew exactly how developed everything was. We rushed to the ER. I passed out in the examination room waiting for someone to come in. There was no call cord or button in the room and I was hemorrhaging. My husband yelled for help and I came to with an IV being jammed into the back of my hand. I miscarried. The compounding grief for yet another loss was unbelievable. But it was different somehow this time. It seemed misplaced, but it was a little easier for me to deal with this loss. I had my little girl at home who needed me to care for her and it helped distract me through some of my grief. Maybe it also helped me bond closer to her, I don't know. But I know it hit Steve a lot harder this time. I got to stay home with our daughter while he went to work, thinking about what would have happened if...

A few days later I went out for the mail. Not thinking anything of it, I opened a card addressed to both of us. It was all white with swirling script letters sending condolences on our loss. I burst into tears and threw the card across the room like it was on fire. I didn't even know who signed it. All kinds of things were running through my head. *Who would do something like that*?

When Steve got home from work, he couldn't understand a word I was saying through my tears, and had no idea what was wrong with me. I pointed to it (still on the floor) from across the room. He picked it up and read it and his face softened as he tried to explain. It was a heart-felt expression of compassion from a dear older man that Steve worked with and his wife. As Steve held me in the kitchen, tears pouring down my face again, he began *apologizing* for the guy. He told me, "Tracy, if he had any idea you would react this way, I am sure he would never have sent the card. He was trying to let us know they felt bad for us."

In trying to deal with his own loss, Steve had confided in Walt at work, so he could be strong for me at home. Walt and his wife were reaching out to comfort both of us. I felt better about it then. It hadn't been some cruel joke. It was a tender acknowledgment of our loss. Only then was I able to accept the true intention the card was sent with. I hadn't intended to be cynical; it just hit me from far out of left field! I never thought about sending anyone a sympathy card for a miscarriage before. Didn't most people just put it behind them and go on?

I have no idea what their personal story was concerning children. Nor did I know if they had ever dealt with this situation themselves, but they will always be remembered fondly for reaching out to us in the middle of that emotional black hole I was in. I still have the card.

Over the next few weeks, friends and relatives started coming out of the woodwork to tell us about their own losses. You don't know how many other people miscarry (or how many times) even in your own family until something like this happens. There was unspoken comfort in the hugs I got from women who knew the depth of my pain, without me having to say a word.

My husband didn't want to try again. He didn't want to risk losing me and having our little girl grow up without her mom. That never even occurred to me. I took a different tack. I consoled myself in the loss with the determination that in four more months... (Did I mention I was stubborn?) We waited the required time the doctors had suggested after the miscarriage and I told Steve I wanted to try one more time. We did. My usual first trimester spotting terrified us, but cleared after several days. Another round of gestational diabetes, but a normal – albeit shortened – pregnancy followed.

Our son was born one month prematurely. We named him after my husband's Dad. The fact that he had 4 more weeks to go meant he had some additional hurdles to cross. It was hard to watch the hospital staff do everything they had to do for him, but it was harder to be home. I stayed at the hospital and Steve stayed home with Jennifer. We went through a week of additional medical intervention due to jaundice. A lot of prayer and time under the lights stabilized him so we could bring him home permanently. The thought that we could have lost both of them made them more precious to us in many ways. We couldn't take them for granted. We were done. We had two beautiful children - a boy and a girl, both healthy and both doing well. We agreed that we were not going to go through those risks again.

A New Perspective

Through all these years of beating myself up over my abortion, God revealed several key points that helped change my heart and mind toward His character and my faith. God tells us that His "thoughts toward us are precious" and "vast are the sum of them."[9] I understood that more clearly now as a mother.

That had been a foreign concept to me before this. I thought God did not particularly care for, or think about me, unless I was begging Him to save me from something. Then didn't He just back up again (like the song) and watch me from a distance?

On the contrary, He says in Jeremiah 1:5, "Before I formed you in the womb, I knew you and approved of you." Not only did God make me Himself inside my mother's body (as He does with each child everywhere in the world), but He *knows* everything about me and *loves* me and *approves* of me! Just as He approves of you.

He may not be thrilled with some of the things I do – in fact, I know some of my actions hurt Him deeply – but I know now He never stops loving me and *approves of me as His little girl*. That was a huge gift to my wounded soul!

He tells us that even when we *feel* like He has abandoned us and we *feel* lower than ashes, "God's mercies are new every morning" and "His compassions never fail."[10] Every morning, every day, He gives us a clean slate to work with. Yes, we need to confess our sins and repent from the wrong we've done, but He's not sitting there with an ever-increasing list of things we have to make up for and dig ourselves out from under before He will consent to help us when we call out to Him. He rises quickly to show us mercy and come to our aid. The Psalms speak beautifully to this truth.

He's completely aware of our limitations. He says, "He remembers that we are dust"[11] and He "knows the heart of man".[12] He knows we aren't perfect, not even close! He knows we are capable of some pretty hurtful and outright horrible things. But He also knows how hard we try sometimes to get it right and He meets us wherever we are when we turn to Him for help.

As I took this all in, certain facts began to emerge and set me free. Even though God is the Ultimate Father, He is very different from our earthly Dads in some very important ways. Yes, He disciplines us. But not like human parents. He doesn't have a temper tantrum and hit us out of a lack of self-control, guilt or embarrassment. He trains us "for our certain good"[13] in ways that He can see far in advance that will allow us to grow up to be the people He created us to be.

Do you remember your Mom's secret weapon as you got older? "I'm not angry with you – I'm just disappointed." It was an emotional hand-grenade! It worked with even more effectiveness and less effort than physical punishment or external threats.

But God doesn't even go there with us. He <u>can't</u> be disappointed in us. He KNOWS what we are going to do before we are faced with any situation. He tells us what choices He wants us to make. He tells us some of the consequences ahead of time. He blesses us with so many beautiful and beneficial experiences along the way to encourage us to stay within His boundaries. He grieves over some of our choices, to be sure. But He lets us make those choices, after giving us direction and multiplied opportunities to choose well.

When we choose incorrectly, He shows us our error and leads us to repentance. He *does* let painful circumstances happen to both teach us to avoid destructive choices and to direct us toward right living.[14] He reaches out to restore us and sets us back on the path when we turn to Him after the fall. He draws us to Him for what we need and offers Himself to us with open arms every time. He keeps knocking at the doors of our hearts. Sometimes He uses blessings and sometimes He uses hardships to motivate and empower us. But He always reaches out in Grace for our every need – if we only use our spiritual eyes to see it!

There are so many ways He corrected my understanding of His character and His heart toward me. He closed the gap between us in great love and lifted me out of so many pits and problems – a lot of them of my own making – that I have long ago lost track. I have learned more about His heart than I knew back then. I still have a long way to go. I am daily looking forward to the journey and to the adventures He has in store for me to complete the process.

***

During my speech, I tried to fit in everything I could, sharing most of my story with the girls and the sisters who were in the room that day. I told them I understand now how God warns us in Romans 1:21 that our "senseless minds are darkened" and we "become futile in our thinking" when we don't follow His way of living. I had been insistent upon making choices that I knew were opposed to His path, and it began "to seem right to me"[15] as I heaped up friends and other people around me that "satisfied my own liking and fostered the errors I held."[16] I shared the pain and rejection I felt at that time in my life. But I also shared how God assured me of His forgiveness by repeating His truth to my guilt-ridden heart that, "There is now therefore no condemnation for those who are in Christ Jesus."[17] I shared how He worked in my heart to rebuild me as a new vessel - "reshaping my clay" for His purpose.[18]

If I allowed Him to, He could use my past as a warning and an encouragement to others. The mess I made could be redeemed, becoming a *mess*age of hope. The test I had failed could become a *test*imony and beacon of truth to keep other girls on the path I had repeatedly strayed from. The horrible turns in my life were not based on a single choice in a clinic one afternoon. It was a series of decisions that put me in places I should never have allowed myself to go. I didn't have to experience those heart-breaking situations, but now that I had, I didn't have to stay in a continual state of self-condemnation. I could allow Jesus to redeem those experiences to help me grow and to tell others. Jesus could use them to bring trustworthy and experienced advice to other generations, one life or one group at a time.

There are so many options before a pregnancy occurs to keep from having to make decisions that end someone else's life! There are also many options after the pregnancy begins. Pregnancy Resource Centers (PRC's) like Birth Right and Care Net help prospective parents with counseling and resources for their next few big decisions. Ultrasound machines prove what some people try to hide from scared, unknowing girls – the **_life_** they are carrying!

PRC's provide baby clothes, formula, diapers and many other baby supplies that are donated by others for the expected needs of these new Moms and Dads. The staff in these facilities (many of whom are volunteers) provide counseling, education, loving support and encouragement - all free of charge - so new parents are not left feeling alone in the struggles of unexpected parenthood. They also share accurate information on adoption - a self-less, life-giving alternative when keeping the baby is not a viable option. Things are very different in the adoption process than most of us realize. And the future after adoption offers miraculous twists and opportunities that can delight hearts many years later.

In Marilyn Meberg's book, "I'd Rather Be Laughing", she tells the story of how her daughter Beth, whom they adopted when she was very young, had a reunion with her birth parents many years later and now has an on-going relationship with her biological family. Rebecca Kiessling's story and her current relationship with her birth mother is an amazing journey of reunion and advocacy like none I have ever heard! Check out her blog and other items on her website: http://www.rebeccakiessling.com/index.html Both Marilyn and Rebecca's stories are very personal examples of alternate possibilities I had not been open to earlier in my life because of base-less fears. Information is power. So is Perfect Love - it dismantles fear.

Pro-Choice or Pro-Life?

Even with all this information, some still say that "being 'pro-choice' is better than taking away other people's options." I find it ironic that some people who call themselves "pro-choice" adamantly ridicule people who believe in the preciousness of life. Life is a choice. Why are they opposed to *that* choice?

You can tell in a New York minute which side of the abortion issue people are on by how they express terms used for the respective sides of the debate. Those who favor killing pre-born infants call themselves "pro-choice", not pro-abortion or pro-death, while sneering at pro-life proponents calling them "anti-abortion activists" (like "anti-abortion" is something bad). It's no less than Orwellian "new speak." Changing what you call it doesn't change what it is.

Acknowledging what really happens in these procedures is crucial. Fetal development is very well demarcated for each week of growth. This information is easily accessible on the computer and clearly seen on ultrasound monitors all over the world. Interrupting this growth at any point in the process has the same end result: A beating heart within a living, moving, growing body is pulled apart in what is supposed to be the safest place on earth, a mother's womb. Regardless of the information she has at the time, regardless of the reason that is cited for "terminating the pregnancy", the facts of what takes place is the same. Even if the truth of this is not known for years afterward, the results follow a very common outcome. The child is gone and the heart of the mother is broken with regret and remorse when she comes to grips with the facts. Abortion is murder plain and simple, a murder for the sake of convenience, fear, or ignorance.

But thankfully, once this truth is acknowledged for those of us who chose this option, it doesn't have to stop there. Acceptance of this reality is merely the first step toward healing and restoration.

I made wrong choices earlier in my life. Some of them I have been able to rectify. I deeply regretted the ones I can do nothing about. But my inability to undo some of my choices doesn't mean I am without hope. God is a God of redemption, renewal and purpose. Calling abortion what it is is not about unending condemnation, it's an invitation to live in the freedom of forgiveness. Listen to women like Gianna Jessen, Claire Culwell, Abby Johnson and Jill Stanek. These women's experiences range from being survivors of botched abortions to being the ones who used to perform abortions. Listen to them tell their stories. Each of these women share what abortion means to them from personal experience. They stand side-by-side with determination and love to defend life. Why?

If that's what they've chosen and that's how they feel now, why should that translate into a fervor and passion to share this knowledge with those who don't – with those who ridicule and despise them for their stand? Because the relief and weightlessness that is experienced after carrying so great a burden and then realizing that you are free of that internal pressure is something that you want to shout from the rooftops! Ignorance is NOT bliss, it's an elephant that won't get off your chest and convinces you you're better off with it there. Being able to live life without its crushing weight is a cause for celebration of that truth at every opportunity! It's a truth that begs to be shared.

I am post-abortive and pro-life. This has elicited accusations of being a hypocrite. The hypocrisy tag is a double edged sword wielded by way too many people in error. It is not hypocrisy to tell others, "I have been where you are considering going, and I can tell you from personal experience, that's a ride you don't want to sign up for and these are all the reasons why..." Earlier in my life, I would have argued that hypocrisy would include someone who says "I would never personally have an abortion, but I would never stand in the way of someone else exercising the right to have one". Now I realize that statement is not one of hypocrisy, but of not fully understanding what they are defending. Caring, loving people don't knowingly allow friends and family to make decisions that will scar them emotionally, physically and mentally for decades if they have the opportunity to stop them ahead of time.

Rape, child abuse and attempted murder are traumatic events that some people have gone through that bring with them a host of consequences that are not immediately visible. In the aftermath of these events, the victims require physical, emotional and spiritual healing in order to come to be restored and come to a place of peace and well-being. Even someone who has never experienced the wounds associated with traumatic experiences like these would never defend the perpetrators' "right" to choose these acts. That would obviously be misguided.

The people who commit these actions on another person are rightfully prosecuted for exercising their power of choice in this way because their choices inflicted harm on another person. So why is abortion different? There is no difference in reality between these actions, only in the perception of whose rights are being violated and what consequences we are defending.

Now that I have experienced the consequences of my choice to abort my child, I can testify that these results are not something I would ever wish on someone else. I am able to stand and speak with educated perspective to warn those who simply don't get what they are defending as a right. You don't have to jump from a building without a parachute and die – or go through months or years of recuperation from the resultant injuries - to tell others not to jump from a building without a parachute. You beg them to listen to you and not to make the choice to jump. If you have survived the experience, and lived to warn others about the dangers, that is not being a hypocrite - that's being compassionate!

Contrariwise, if you have a friend who survived a horrible experience that was a "matter of choice" and you were contemplating doing the same thing, wouldn't you want them to warn you? What do you think your reaction would be if they didn't warn you about all the after-effects? Would you hail them as a hero who defended your right to damage or destroy your life or would you demand why they didn't warn you about the injuries you were about to face?

I would caution anyone who is tempted to throw the H word around so freely: be careful what you defend as a right and who you label a hypocrite without walking in the consequences of those "rights". If you open your heart to what's behind their impassioned pleas, you might just hear something that will change your perspective.

Many people defend this act under the language of "reproductive rights" or "reproductive freedom". Although the government has legalized this choice and society promotes abortion as a solution for unwanted pregnancy, it is not a "right". It's not reproductive and it's not freedom. Ask those living healed on the other side of that choice; they are emotionally free enough to tell you the truth.

If this choice has already been made in your life, and the remorse feels too great to bear, please don't remain stuck with the guilt and regret! Freedom from condemnation and self-recrimination is a blessed peace and joy that cannot be easily explained to those with no frame of reference, but I can absolutely testify it is a gift beyond measure for anyone who reaches out and grabs hold of it! It is yours for the asking! Contact a local Hopeline – 1-800-203-4673 is one 24-hour option for help on both sides of this choice – pre- and post-abortive. Contact a local Pregnancy Resource Center, Care Net facility or other pro-life organization for referrals. The way to this freedom is found by getting on God's path for your life. There are millions of people willing to help you find it, if you let them.

Forgiveness and Healing

God has put many special people and situations in my life that have advanced me beyond the crippling remorse and guilt, to the freedom and peace of mind concerning this issue and other circumstances in my life. By going back to my high school, visiting with these sisters, speaking to the students, I have been blessed by my relationship with them. Through them I have met other women who are associated with Birth Right and I have attended several pro-life "coffee houses" filled with music and laughter. Through the church I currently attend, I met others who work with the Care Net Pregnancy Centers. Through TV programming on PBS, Discovery Channel and other science venues, I have seen the undeniable progression of life in human embryology and witnessed the miracle of conception, development and birth from beginning to end. EWTN, TBN, Daystar and the internet have introduced me to Silent No More, Priests for Life, National Pro-Life Alliance, Operation Rescue, Americans United for Life, Rachel's Vineyard, Concerned Women for America and many other groups who defend life. These valuable groups educate about abortion and help women, along with their families, to heal after abortion has taken place. Together, though each one may have a different specific focus or a different area they work within, they are teaching and sharing God's love with a new generation about the truth of the preciousness of life.

No two people are the same, no two situations fit exactly for each person, but the commonalities can bring us together to defend life - life of the unborn and lives left scarred by the deaths of millions of pre-born children. There is help.

God knows all my children. He cradles them in His arms. Someday I will meet them all; I am now looking forward to that with anticipation instead of dread. I know undoubtedly that God forgave me the first time I asked Him to and is giving me His peace. But I've also come to understand that each of us travels a slightly different road toward that healing. I didn't always know this. Some women's paths to healing involved things that I did not need for my own - and vice-versa. That doesn't make one or the other wrong, just different. Don't get discouraged.

Listen to protectors of life, hold dear their friendship and share their love of Jesus. Be encouraged by their tenderness and passion for life. They can share the ways God helped them overcome their hurdles. Some of them may be just what you need; others will be something you should side-step, for very different reasons. That's ok. We're all individuals. For the guidance you need to pursue your own personal healing, go to the Source. God will lead you in all truth. He will let you know which specific path to follow, one designed just for you. It may be a different path for others, or it may just be a difference in timing. When you are feeling the release from your weight and want to share that gift with other hurting women, know that others may need more time or different pathways than you did. Give others the same respect and freedom you needed in your journey.

When Jesus healed several blind people in the gospels, He used different methods for each one; for one He simply declared it, for another He touched them, for another He made mud with spit, for another He told them to wash in a pool. For some the healing was instantaneous, for others it came in stages, like the man who said that first he saw men as trees and then after another touch from Jesus, he saw clearly.[20]

Each person was different. Each one was healed differently, but they were all healed. We can be completely healed too. Some pain is so deep we must pass through different levels to heal, step by step on the path. It's not that God isn't strong enough to do it all at once - He emphatically is. But He knows that we are more fragile in certain areas and He takes a tender and metered approach to make sure we are not overcome in the process.

So it was with me.

Healing in Layers

God took a lot of baby steps with me. He took the time to show me how precious I was to Him. He showed me that He made me on purpose, that I was not an accident; that He is always with me and will never leave me nor forsake me. He taught me that my worth to Him is not based on what I've done, but on the fact that He is My Father, and He loves me unconditionally. I've known these verses for years now. They have anchored my soul and given me a rock to stand on.

By the time I was in my mid-forties, I could do things I could not do before. Thankfully I could celebrate with women enjoying a new baby again and could volunteer in the church nursery. I could talk about my experience with selected people without breaking down in sobs. I still shed a few tears here and there, but I figured that was "normal" at that point.

I had made so many advances in attitudes and emotions since this journey began that I thought I was done. I thought, after all this time, the healing was completed. I was wrong. God was preparing me for the final release from the last of those chains.

***

In May of 2009, I attended a *Care Net* fundraising banquet at the University of Connecticut and had the opportunity to meet the local director of two *Care Net* facilities. The festivities of the evening were coming to a close and I wanted to let her know how much I appreciated what she said. Two weeks later I called her and set up a meeting. We talked for a while and she showed me a book. It was a post-abortion healing study written by Linda Cochrane called, "Forgiven and Set Free". "That's nice," I said. "but I don't need that anymore, I'm good. But I am glad you have a good resource to share with other people."

Pati told me about her own journey through the study and I thought afterward how powerful her testimony was, though I still had no intention of doing it myself. Being able to openly talk about how our individual experiences affected us is not "polite dinner conversation", but it brings a release no one can find any other way. I wanted to keep talking with her. We decided to meet again the following week.

At our next meeting, she asked me if I had prayed about doing the study and I said, "No, it never occurred to me to pray about it." She shrugged and laughed and said something about "at least I was being honest" about it...But something had changed. Between our two meetings, during one of my morning devotional times – I call them my "quiet times" - God simply declared: "Tracy, when you're done this study, you will be completely free." He hadn't tried to talk me into it. He didn't command me to do it. There was no threat involved. He simply and gently offered a solution to a deep desire for true freedom that I could not walk away from. Pati hadn't needed to convince me of anything; God changed my heart on the subject. There was no doubt I would do the study. We began the following Monday - and I will never be the same.

The study was set up so that participants would have a short reading and some questions to answer each day of the week, and then we would review the points that were brought up and apply them through specific activities when we met on Mondays. The readings came from different parts in the Bible, dealing with different aspects of the process: denial, anger, forgiveness, acceptance and healing. It is designed to be done in a group with several participants sharing what they learned apart during the week when they get together. But it can also be done one-on-one with a facilitator or by yourself. The opportunities this Bible study opened up to me involved some amazing realizations that rolled crushing weights off my heart.

Two weeks into reading it, when I got to the section on "God, Our Righteousness", I found some scriptures that I had read before about Jesus being the Righteous Branch and how He "did not come into this world to save the righteous."[21] Even though the material was familiar to me, in that moment it hit me like it never had before: that meant He had come to save the *unrighteous* – I knew without a doubt, with the focus on that part of my life that meant *me*. What happened next could be nothing less than the two-edged sword of the Spirit: "For the word of

God is alive and active. Sharper than any double-edged sword, it penetrates even to dividing soul and spirit, joints and marrow; it judges the thoughts and attitudes of the heart."[22]

It was such a strange feeling. It felt like I was dissecting my own thoughts, as if they belonged to someone else. There was no pain in it; just a sudden release from a blind spot I realized did not need to be there anymore. Before I knew what was happening, God faced me with the lies I had been *telling myself* for years, getting comfortable with them and accepting them as fact. This locked-off area in my mind had made the memories of my abortion experience feel nobler, easier to look back on, with less accountability.

I was faced with the bare truth of *my* choices, unvarnished and putrid. But now I was seeing it through different eyes. I had seen myself before as a victim of someone else's ultimatum. Now I was disconnected from the emotion of that time, looking at my own life in retrospect. Several things popped into my head with a new perspective for me – in a way I had never seen before.

The word sorrow came to mind, and I typed it in to Bible Gateway.com to find part of a verse. God gave me what I could not have anticipated – and more. I read verse after verse that spoke of His Grace for my sin: Ps 31:10, Ps 32:10, Ps 34:18, and then came Ps 51:17: "My sacrifice [the sacrifice acceptable] to God is a broken spirit; a broken and a contrite heart [broken down with **sorrow** for sin and humbly and thoroughly penitent], such, O God, You will not despise."

I knew I was sorry for what I had done, but I never thought about my sorrow and repentance being a *sacrifice* I could offer to God...

"I acknowledged my sin to You, and my iniquity I did not hide. I said, I will confess my transgressions to the Lord [**continually unfolding** the past till all is told]--then You [**instantly**] forgave me the guilt and iniquity of my sin. Selah [pause, and calmly think of that]!" [23](emphasis mine)

I *did* think about it. I had thought about it *a lot* – but never in this context. It was safe to confess the last, darkest secret.

The forgiveness I experienced in that moment was quicker than immediately, it was *pre-emptive*; it was back-pedaling to rush forward! God already knew, I wasn't telling Him anything He hadn't already seen. He had been there with me the whole time – even in that examination room during my abortion - and He still loved me deeply and completely. He was giving me the chance to show Him my deepest wound so He could "instantly" take it away after 32 years of me trying to hide it behind putrid bandages of self-help, legalism and denial.

I knew more than I let on about my baby's development before I aborted. I had told everyone (and finally began to believe it myself) that I really didn't know. I'd said it for years. But right in the front of my mind somehow, with the assurance that "Jesus did not come to save the righteous", I needed to be honest about the *whole* situation or I would still be trapped by these grave clothes stinking like a mummy and crawling with... (I don't know what!)

I purposely did NOT try to find out exactly how much of my baby was already formed at that point. I didn't *want* to know specifics because that wouldn't have fit in with my idea of "freedom" and being carefree, away from my responsibilities. I refused to find out specifics at the time, so I wouldn't be talked out of it. I knew my baby was more than just a lump of cells. I knew most of what I had later seen on TV. That's *why* I was hammered with guilt when I saw the truth of it in "The Miracle of Life" episode on NOVA. The act was already done, I couldn't undo it. That was why I had reacted so badly at the time. But enough time had gone by, by the time I saw the video, that I could "back claim" some kind of ignorance and continue lying to myself about my own part in it.

The truth of the matter was, I let my "boyfriend" push me in the direction that I wanted to go, and his ultimatum gave me the outlet for not accepting the blame for what I wanted to do but felt too guilty about doing on my own. Denial was a hiding place to protect my sanity until God had completed the rest of His healing to keep me from being overwhelmed by that ugly truth.

If I had tried to face that truth earlier in my life the self-reproach would have been too much for me. That thought would have sickened me to the point of ultimate despair. But in God's perfect timing and tender mercy, facing it now, God's grace was right there reminding me that "weeping may endure for a night, but joy comes in the morning."[24] I realized right then, by my admitting it, it lost its power on my heart! I cried – but not in pain. It was gratitude that because of everything He had done for me, I was no longer that person. I felt His instant comfort with no condemnation whatever - just like He promised.

120

I could have turned my back on the unpleasantness of it all, attempting to move on without taking care of this once and for all. That has always been an option. But nothing compares to this saving Truth. "Jesus *became* sin, so that I could *be* His righteousness."[25] He bore my shame on the cross *because He wanted to set me free*. No matter what I say or fail to say out loud to others, the Spirit of God living in me knows the truth in my heart.

It had been something that I didn't want to face. It had festered all this time, under the surface. But now I was FREE! God's promised assurance from that morning in my loft came true. The truth won't stay hidden in the light - but it can be redeemed. God has been faithful in His perseverance not to let me go and He keeps saying, "the old things have passed away... all things are made new"[26] and "His mercies are new every morning."[27]

The best explanation for this feeling came by way of a recent TV ad describing an insurance company's policy of a "vanishing deductible." A woman sitting on a bench becomes aware that a huge boulder is hanging over her head in a cargo net and she cringes below it, expecting it to crush her. She does NOT want to be there, but is afraid to move. Then, as the insurance man explains their program of reducing the deductible each year you don't have an accident, the boulder quickly shrinks in size until he tosses her this tiny little rock that she can easily deal with.

Before I was emotionally capable of acknowledging my own sin, Jesus, in His ultimate sacrifice for me, changed my perspective on my abortion from an enormous boulder I could never survive and lifted it off me so I wouldn't be crushed under the weight of it. He reduced it to a tiny pebble compared to the size of His Grace, and then He gifted me with a new Choice: the choice to relinquish that sin back to Him for my forgiveness and healing. I felt it. "For godly grief and the pain God is permitted to direct, produce a repentance that leads and contributes to salvation and deliverance from evil, and it never brings regret; but worldly grief (the hopeless **sorrow** that is characteristic of the pagan world) is deadly [breeding and ending in death]."[28] I had felt this "worldly grief" for 32 years, now I felt the joyful release of complete repentance. It was AMAZING!

In Jesus, the sin we have done is condemned while the spirit inside us is made alive and runs forward to Him! Don't miss this amazing opportunity! Don't exchange God's fulfillment, blessings, joy and protection for the false promises of acceptance, validation and "love" whispered in the dark – it's a lie that will cause more pain than you ever want to know!

I beg of you to learn from others, so that you do not have to personally experience the same kind of regret that I had to be healed from! Yes, the reason I am the person I am today is greatly influenced by what I have experienced along my journey. But believe me when I tell you it is much better to side-step some pathways than to walk down them.

But if you do – or did, like me – don't stay stuck in that lie. You can begin again, right where you are! You can know joy and peace and real love. God already provided the way out of that pit – forgiveness through Jesus Christ. New life comes from death – His for yours.

There are things I have experienced in the middle of this journey I am grateful for. I am grateful for the people I have met who have helped me in the healing process. I am grateful to know my husband knows my darkest moments and loves me dearly still. I am grateful that I can use my testimony to comfort someone else who can't yet express how deeply she hurts. I am grateful to be able to assure her that God's Grace is the only thing that can heal pain that profound. I don't just think so, I *know* it. I am grateful to be able to share that.

I have perspective now at 53 years old I never had before. I have the benefit of hindsight and see things much more clearly than I did at 17 and 18. Looking back at my mid-teens, the speed of my progression from innocently dating a boy in my youth group at 15, to the downward spiral my subsequent choices took me on was stunning!

One summer, I was refusing to French kiss a 15-year-old blonde kid with freckles and attending a youth retreat through my church, then by the next summer I was no longer a virgin and my Mom was threatening a 23-year-old with statutory rape charges if I wasn't back in my bedroom by nightfall. At a younger age I had dreams of my sweet-sixteen party with family and friends around for a huge celebration. In reality, I was grounded for my 16th birthday for ditching my brother at the swimming hole a week before, going to Ocean Beach with a bunch of older kids in some guy's van and coming home drunk for the first time in my life. Not how I dreamed the day would go, but I chose the path that got me there.

Please understand I am ***not*** bragging here. I am issuing a warning that enough seemingly "harmless" wrong choices in quick succession can dramatically alter your life, and leave you wondering how it all happened so fast. You have the power to choose – I beg of you to choose wisely!

Truly Free!

I was almost done with the post-abortion Bible study, *"Forgiven and Set Free."* I was hanging on every word when the breakthrough of a lifetime hit me about a chapter and a half from the end. The differences in the meanings of two words made all the difference in my understanding of God's Grace. Although I *had* accepted God's forgiveness, I was still somehow chained to residual guilt of that particular sin. I couldn't explain why. I didn't realize I was still trying to "make up for" it.

Prior to this breakthrough, my emotions still dragged me down, throwing me into debilitating regret at a moment's notice. They had become idols I unwittingly served. Fears, frustrations, resentments and doubts all had a part of discounting and de-valuing the grace and peace God repeatedly told me were already mine. But instead of enjoying God's gift of freedom, I had focused on the painful memories, thinking it was part of an essential penance for my abortion. Bowing to these memories drove my joy into the dirt every time. I found out that day, in a moment, that *I was choosing* my wounded emotions over God's sovereignty and loving instruction when I did that. I was needlessly carrying my guilt and regret forward by not releasing them. By accepting that I can't possibly atone for any of it, and acknowledging His atonement on my behalf, I was set free!

In verse after verse God revealed my final healing was being blocked by a twisted form of pride: my insistence in trying to pay my own debt! I didn't realize it was arrogance that kept me running in circles, refusing the simplicity of God's forgiveness and insisting I remain chained to the shame. In some kind of misplaced Christian piety, I was still trying to atone for not only the abortion, but for other things I was beating myself up over: my resentful relationship with my Mom, my unforgiving and dishonoring relationship with my Dad, my own self-condemnation over not being a perfect wife and Mom to my family. In effect I was punishing myself for all these things instead of accepting God's atonement... and I didn't have a clue that's what I was doing.

The chains were forever broken by understanding the difference between **atonement** and **restitution**. I knew the concept of Jesus' salvation for me in my *head* and had heard about it for a long time, but this dropped the understanding of it with an amazing thud the rest of the way to my *heart*!

When I read Numbers 5:5-8 and Leviticus 6:4-7, I finally saw the details I had been missing concerning the most amazing exchange of all time. It is offered by God for our deliverance, formerly carried out by human priests through physical animal sacrifices in the Old Testament and spiritually fulfilled in the New Testament in the person of Jesus Christ.

The exchange describes how the one who sinned presents a sacrifice of atonement for his guilt: a "male ram without blemish and of the proper value" to the priest. The priest sacrifices the lamb, presenting it to God for the atonement of the guilty one and they are forgiven. Period. That person is justified (so that I am "just-as-if-I'd" never sinned) - cleansing the conscience, knowing the truth of what He tells us: "...and he shall be forgiven for *anything* of *all* that he may have done by which he has become guilty."[29](emphasis mine)

The parallel between the Old and New Testament application for me at that moment was the most amazing epiphany of my life! The *atonement* (amends, punishment, payment) of all my sins is fully met in the Lamb. Only One sacrifice fits that description. Jesus is the Lamb, presented as the sacrifice for sin. Jesus is also the Priest.[30] He presented Himself 2000 years ago to God on my behalf for what I had not done yet, but in His omniscience, He knew about even then. He had seen into the future and knew I needed redemption for the taking of my child's life – and He sacrificed His Life for mine. Only Jesus Christ's atoning death on the cross is the "proper value" to cover the depravity of what I'd done. Nothing else would do the job.

Leviticus 6:7 clearly told me "Anything" and "all" that I had done to make me guilty was completely atoned for! His sacrifice completely covers my abortion, and any other sin any of us may have committed. Once we accept Jesus in our hearts as our personal savior, agreeing to accept His forgiveness based on the sacrifice He presented to His Father on our behalf... it's gone! That sacrifice for the "guilt offering" is complete in and of itself. It does not need augmentation or additions from me.

Jesus said, "I desire mercy not sacrifice, go and learn what this means."[31] Jesus said He "does not delight in sacrifices and sacrificial offerings"[32] from us. In fact, the only sacrifices He will accept from us are "a broken and contrite heart" over our sin[33] and "the sacrifice of praise."[34] Samuel told Saul, "Obedience is better than sacrifice and to heed is better than the fat of rams" but he doesn't stop there; he continues: "for rebellion is like the sin of divination and arrogance like the evil of idolatry."[35]

I was rebelling against God in my sin, but then I was being arrogant by thinking for a moment that I could do anything on my own to make up for what I'd done! When I insist on somehow adding my own guilt as part of the atonement, I block the process and continue to be hindered, burdened, and kept from God's release from my chains!

THAT'S what Paul is talking about when he said do not allow yourselves to be enslaved again in the yoke of slavery to sin! God doesn't keep us groveling - we keep going back there! We can choose at any time to confess it, accept His forgiveness, and then move on praising Him - frolicking in the glow of His Grace, delighting in the freedom from all of it in an instant, *if we choose to*!

The verses in Numbers Chapter 5 and Leviticus Chapter 6 awakened me to this truth. The atonement had already been made. But there was more. What happened to the second part of the requirement? Didn't I have to do something to "make up for" what I did, like we learned as kids? Those verses said something about *restitution* too. God's Old Testament requirement was for the value of what was stolen or defrauded plus 1/5 of that item's value to be paid for restitution (the act or fact of restoring something or repaying someone) to the person it was stolen from[36]. If the person who was wronged (or a close living relative) was not available to receive this repayment then "the restitution belongs to the Lord."[37]

Here I also discovered something I had missed before: The *atonement* of the "guilt offering" is a completely separate thing from the *restitution* that was to be made for any wrong that was done. I thought, "Ok, God help me with this. You completely atoned for my abortion and I no longer have to carry the guilt of that around with me. I am free. But I don't understand this restitution thing. What can I possibly give you to repay you for the life of my daughter? I know she is up in heaven with You, but how do I put a value on her earthly life and give something to You for cutting short her time here, by not allowing her to be born and grow up?" The incredible power of the next realization had me so excited I was almost jumping out of my skin! The author of "Forgiven and Set Free" had us read Revelation 12:11 in connection with this section and suddenly I was released to see the purpose God had woven into the pain I'd clung to for so many years. "...we overcome the evil one..." (The same evil one who used deception, fear and intimidation to tell me that abortion was my best and only option at the time.) "...by the Blood of the Lamb and the word of our testimony." The Blood of the Lamb paid the atonement penalty for my choice for death - and the word of my testimony is my restitution that acknowledges the value of her life! At that moment I was holding my restitution in my hand – the "proof" of my book, "The Power of Choices"! My "testimony", whether written or verbal, is one of the ways I make restitution AND overcome the evil one! I was so excited by this realization I wanted to cheer out loud!

As I said earlier, sometimes our understanding needs adjusting so we can see something in a new way. A verse that the Holy Spirit has recently corrected my perspective on is Luke 12:3: "Therefore whatever you have said in the dark shall be heard in the light, and what you have whispered in private rooms shall be proclaimed on the housetops." (ESV) For all my life, I took that verse as a threat. I was certain this meant that God was going to reveal every bad thing I'd ever said and humiliate me, so I should be very careful what I say behind closed doors – and I extended the meaning to include anything I'd ever done as well. In my mind I pictured a video montage of all the sinful, embarrassing and disgraceful things I'd ever done on full display in front of everyone as another way for God to punish me for my sin.

I will never forget the "aha!" moment I had just a few weeks ago: I was preparing for a song I was going to sing when that verse popped in to my head. Along with it came a new context: It's NOT God who "proclaims it from the rooftops" in punishment for our sins. That perspective is NOT consistent with God's assurances that Grace is more than sufficient and His forgiveness complete. So who else is left to proclaim it from the rooftops? It's *US*! We proclaim it (wait for it....) *as a victory cry*!

When we realize the true freedom God gifts us with when we fully submit ourselves, past choices, sins, warts and all to His Grace, we can't help but let others know the incredible joy that comes from the release from our various prisons! We confess (agree with Him) something is wrong, and He completely forgives and heals us. Once we realize the depth of that freedom for ourselves, we can't help shouting about it! WE run back and shout out to others how wonderful He is to be a Daddy God Who loves and cares tenderly for us because "I was a wretch", and now I am a forgiven and blessed daughter and heir of the King of Kings! I can joyfully shout from the rooftops anything and everything that was "done in secret" because I am free, and in doing so I "overcome the evil one" and dismantle the hold he tries to keep on some areas of my life by revealing *my own* previous secrets to others to dispel their power over me.

Now that I am on the other side of my healing, I have new ways of looking at many things. And the "aha! moments" are multiplying!

Two other verses God has given me a new understanding on are found in the book of Proverbs. Proverbs 24:11 says "Deliver those *who* are drawn toward death, And hold back those stumbling to the slaughter." Proverbs 31:8 says "Open your mouth for the speechless, In the cause of all *who are* appointed to die." (NKJV) God has shown me through my own healing that this admonition is not merely applicable to the pre-born children who are in jeopardy of being aborted, but to pre- and post-abortive mothers as well.

It was not something I considered earlier. As Christians, we can tend to make allowances for our own behavior, but are often legalistic and critical of other's faults. Like the situation with the woman "caught in the act of adultery", Jesus' admonition to the Pharisees and spectators that day to "He who is without sin among you, let him throw a stone at her first"[38] is somehow lost to our hearts. We have no difficulty seeing we need to defend helpless babies, but are often blinded to the desperation and fears that "draw" a woman "toward death" in the decision to abort.

Without Pregnancy Resource Centers to show pre-abortive mothers the truth of **all** her possible options in love, she often succumbs to those fears. Those who have not experienced the coercion toward abortion, the deception that promises to "fix the problem" so you can "get on with the rest of your life" need to operate in compassion toward those who are "stumbling toward the slaughter" and speak gently, with knowledge and wisdom, without reproach for the circumstances that brought her to this point.

If she cannot see past her fears and chooses abortion in spite of what you share with her, make sure she knows you are still a resource for her afterward. She will need you! Pray for her. If possible, reach out to her. Let her know you want her to come back to see you, no matter what she decides.

After the deed is done, she often becomes speechless in her pain hurting so deeply she cannot express it, stuffing it, denying it, trying to ignore it, and sometimes defiantly defending it as her only option at the time. Condemnation from someone who has never been in her shoes (or tried to talk her out of it) is the last thing that she needs.

I was so blessed by God to be granted a shield of protection on my healing journey that I did not encounter one person anywhere when I began hinting that abortion was something from my past that condemned me or made me feel additional shame. Everyone I ever spoke with was encouraging and helped me toward God's healing. Even one of the sisters from the parochial high school I attended hugged me and showed her compassion for me. Sadly, this has not been everyone's experience.

In speaking from church to church and in different opportunities I've had one-on-one, I found women most fear the condemnation of others for what she's done and those fears keep her bound by the guilt and regret. If they breach the silent divide, it is in hushed tones where no one they know can hear them so they can get out from under it even if only for a moment. "What will they think of me if they know...?" In sharing my testimony I can begin speaking for these speechless women who cannot speak for themselves, I can breach this divide for them. I can speak for those who suffer underneath the crushing weight of their past, rather than bring it out – even to otherwise trusted friends or family. I can share my secret to open the doors for them to share theirs.

When I share my story with others and I bring up that we "overcome the evil one by the blood of the Lamb and the word of our testimony"[39] I also bring up Genesis. The same evil one who drew us toward death and convinced us it was our only option is also the one who keeps us imprisoned with the shame afterward and tempts us to condemn others for what we think we would never do. If we stay silent, he wins. One day after another he holds us, beating us up and fulfilling his purpose. In fact, in Genesis God tells the serpent he will "bruise our heel"[40]. He has that ability. But the wonderful news for us is, God also promised the serpent in this same verse, the offspring of the woman will "crush your head"[41]! The reason this is wonderful news is God's promise refers to Jesus – He is the Offspring that crushes the serpent's head.

Every time I share my testimony, I partner with Jesus to overcome the evil one! He shed His blood – the blood of the Lamb shed for sin – and I open my mouth and speak.

I can't atone for my sin, Jesus already did that. But I can tell my story. I can share my relief with others who are still trying to carry around their own "ball and chain of (self) atonement"[42] by understanding the real "hammer and nails of restitution".[43] Like Linda Cochrane, who shared what God showed her in "Forgiven and Set Free", John Newton, the ex-slave-trader who wrote "Amazing Grace", and thousands of others who tell what God has done for them, I can share my life. In doing so, I not only acknowledge the life-value of my daughter who I chose to abort and my other three miscarried children I have not yet held in my arms - without guilt. I can *gladly* make restitution, giving time, effort, respect and my own testimony to others when I revel in the fact that He *instantly* forgave me. He put it all under the atoning blood sacrifice of Christ and removed it "as far as the east is from the west"[44], NEVER to hold it against me again! THAT is freedom! Listen to what God says on the subject – from His heart to yours:

"Therefore [there is] now no condemnation for those who are in Christ Jesus, who live [and] walk not after the dictates of the flesh, but after the dictates of the Spirit, for the law of the Spirit of life [which is] in Christ Jesus [the law of the new being] has freed me from the law of sin and of death. For God has done what the Law could not do, [its power] being weakened by the flesh [the entire nature of man without the Holy Spirit], sending His own Son in the guise of sinful flesh and as an offering for sin, [God] condemned sin in the flesh [subdued, overcame, deprived it of its power over all who would accept that sacrifice]."[45]

His mercies are new every day[46]. That is the real power of choices. Which will you choose; the ball and chain of self-atonement that you've carried unnecessarily for your own sin, or the free gift of a freshly wiped white-board every day given to you by your Daddy God? He knows you and loves you so dearly. He heals, I am proof. I am not alone and neither are you!

Since writing the first edition of my book, "The Power of Choices," I have gotten the training I needed to share "Forgiven and Set Free" with others, facilitating these 11-week classes through my local Care Net affiliated Pregnancy Resource Centers. I'm writing. I am speaking in schools, coffee houses, churches and anywhere else I can to share this amazing release from 32 years of post-abortion guilt that no longer has a hold on my heart. I am living in grace and new beginnings the life God prepared for me with a clean slate every morning, living in the power of better choices.

Let me offer you a perspective you may not have considered in quite this way before, a point of view that I told the girls that day in front of those sisters: *God is pro-choice*! God gives us free-will and has endowed us with the ability to choose. After two chapters of listing the blessings of doing things His way and the curses we bring upon ourselves if we do things against His instructions[47], He puts it plainly in one sentence: "I call heaven and earth to witness this day against you that I have set before you life and death, the blessings and the curses, therefore choose life that you and your descendants may live."[48] God is pro-life. God is also pro-choice! But there is a right choice and there is a wrong choice. As long as you are still alive and Jesus has not come back yet, it is not too late to make the right choice! The door is still open and it's an open book test. Choose life.

As a result of taking this opportunity to choose life and healing - even after making the choice for death so far ago in my past, God gave me the most precious gift of discovery. I will continue to shout it from the rooftops for as long as I am here on this planet: I am post-abortive, and I am no longer ashamed! Like Joseph declared in Genesis 50 – What the devil meant for evil, God meant for good, to save many. And I will glory in that opportunity to reach others with this knowledge with inexpressible joy! I pray that you find your opportunity as well. God Bless you!

Footnotes

[1] Heb. 10:24 (NIV 1984)

[2] 1 Cor. 15:33 (NIV 1984)

[3] "Sometimes Love" by Chris Rice © 1995 Clumsy Fly Music (Admin. by Word Music, LLC) All rights reserved. Used by permission.

[4] John 3:16 (NIV 1984)

[5] Prov. 16:9 (amp)

[6] "Freedom From Your Past" by Jimmy Evans and Ann Billington © 1994, 2006, 2009 p. 94

[7] 2 Sam. 11-12 (amp)

[8] Heb. 13:5 (NIV 1984)

[9] Ps. 139:17 (NIV 1984)

[10] Lam. 3:22-23 (amp)

[11] PS. 103:14 (NIV)

[12] Luke 6:45 (NIV 1984)

[13] Heb. 12:10 (amp)

[14] 2 Cor. 7:10 (amp)

[15] Prov. 14:12 (amp)

[16] 2 Tim. 2:3 (amp)

[17] Rom. 8:1 (NIV 1984)

[18] Jer. 18:8 (amp)

[19] "I'd Rather Be Laughing" by Marilyn Meberg, ©1998 W Publishing Group, div. of Thomas Nelson Inc., p. 33-45

[20] Mark 8:23-25 (amp)

[21] "Forgiven and Set Free" by Linda Cochrane, © 1986, 1991, 1996 Care Net, 1996 Baker Books, div. of Baker Publishing Group, p. 25

[22] Heb. 4:12 (NIV 1984)

[23] Ps. 32:5 (amp)

[24] Ps. 30:50 (NIV 1984)

[25] 2 Cor. 5:21 (NIV 1984)

[26] Rev 21:45 (amp)

[27] Lam. 3:23 (amp)

[28] 2 Cor. 7:10 (amp)

[29] Lev 6:7b (NIV 1984)

[30] Heb 10 (NIV 1984)

[31] Matt. 9:13 (NIV 1984)

[32] ibid

[33] Ps 51:17 (amp)

[34] Heb 13:15 (NIV 1984)

[35] 1 Sam 15:22-23 (NIV 1984)

[36] Lev 6:5 (NIV 1984)

[37] Num. 5:8 (NIV 1984)

[38] John 8:7 (NJKV)

[39] Rev 12:11 (NIV)

[40] Gen. 3:15 (NIV)

[41] ibid

[42] "Forgiven and Set Free" by Linda Cochrane, © 1986, 1991, 1996 Care Net, 1996 Baker Books, div. of Baker Publishing Group, p. 91

[43] ibid p. 92

[44] Ps. 103:12 (amp)

[45] Rom. 8:1-3 (amp)

[46] Lam. 3:23 (NIV 1984)

[47] Deut. 28 – 29 (NIV 1984)

[44] Deut. 30:19 (NIV 1984)

Suggested Resources:

"Freedom From Your Past" by Jimmy Evans and Ann Billington

"Forgiven and Set Free" by Linda Cochrane

You Tube: Claire Culwell http://www.youtube.com/watch?v=rk0cW6MGLas

You Tube: Gianna Jessen http://www.youtube.com/watch?v=kPF1FhCMPuQ

"unPLANNED" by Abby Johnson

"Your Scars Are Beautiful To God" by Sharon Jaynes

"Overcoming Fear With Faith" by Joyce Meyer http://www.joycemeyer.org

Rebecca Kiessling's website: http://www.rebeccakiessling.com/index.html

"A Special Mother is Born" by Leticia Velasquez

Chapter 3

Divorce or Victory: the Choice Starts with You

"He said to them, because of the hardness (stubbornness
and perversity) of your hearts Moses permitted you to
dismiss and repudiate and divorce your wives; but from
the beginning it has not been so [ordained]."
(Matthew 19:8)

There is no question in most circles that divorce is bad –
even if you believe it is necessary in some cases, most
people acknowledge that a happy marriage is the goal to
reach for. It is the expectation of what we hope to happen
when we stand before a clergyman or justice of the peace
and pledge to be united to "this man…" or "this
woman…as long as we both shall live." But what about
after the honeymoon, when the pressure of kids and bills
and the realization that you and your spouse are not on
the same wave-length on a great many issues. Most of
them are probably minor, but some of them have become
increasingly more irritating - and some days seem
monumental. What then? What is plan B? Is there
supposed to be a plan B? Let's find out.

If you start reading this and see things you disagree with,
that's fine, keep reading. I, as you, have my perspective
because of what I have been through and seen personally.
Life is not a cookie cutter production and some
circumstances will not fit into this sharing. Sometimes the
most desirable options are not open to us because of
things we have no control over. But maybe in the sharing

of one heart to another, we will be able to see a point of view we hadn't considered before, one that could change us completely. That said, let's move on...

In my own experience, I have come to believe very strongly that divorce is not the way to go. I acknowledge that some things are out of our control. There are situations when there is no willingness on the part of one or both of the people involved to "fight the good fight" together (against a common enemy, not your spouse) to get through difficulties. There are two people in a marriage and both have a part in deciding what happens between them. Others may think that too much has happened for reconciliation to be possible. But there is a difference between unwillingness and impossibility.

The wonderful news is, if at least one of those people is committed to God and cooperates with Him to heal the relationship, miracles can happen – even if it *begins* with only one of the people in the union. It takes effort and a willingness to act on what is right even when you don't feel that right things are happening to you. Instead of reacting emotionally (like we have in the past) to things that promote division in our marriages, we can choose to act in a way that builds togetherness. Without that commitment and willingness to do something differently, disillusion leads to defeat and a progression of heartaches and unfulfilled longings for the "happily ever after" that the world teases us with and then decries as an impossible fantasy. But it doesn't have to be that way – or stay that way, if that's where it starts.

When two people first join in marriage, it is full of dreams and hopes for the future. Some of those initial expectations start out being completely unrealistic. They are based on fantasy, cultural norms and media which feed our desire for the perfect spouse, but give us no ability to get there. Part of the problem is we are deceived into believing that we must "find our perfect soul mate" to be happy – and there is no such thing. Soul mates are not found. They are created - developed over time in the unfolding situations that draw us together against common difficulty.

That interdependent and mutually beneficial kind of relationship is nurtured over years of two people committing to loving one another through good *and* bad times - and coming out stronger, more capable and united on the other end. Our culture's microwave mentality of ready-made partners who embody prince-charming-on-a-white-horse husbands and physically passionate, but emotionless Stepford wives who can turn on the "love switch" at a moment's notice, leave no room for daily inter-personal challenges that are inherent in the rubber-meets-the-road experiences we have in life. The car breaks down, the taxes are due, the baby doesn't sleep through the night, and you have a cold - all at the same time - and you can't stop to feel sorry for yourself or quit in the middle. Certain things still need to be done, regardless of how much you'd like to curl up under the covers like a teenager on a snow day! Start with reality and with what *is*, not with what you *wish it was*, or what you always thought *it should be* – and go from there.

Once you acknowledge that as your starting point, accepting another pivotal bit of information can save you much misunderstanding and heartache; men and women think differently. It seems obvious, but we really don't stop and realize all that little statement entails in our day-to-day interaction. While generalizations don't always accurately describe every person, the reason they are generalizations is *most of the time* they ring true.

Most men are competitive; most women are cooperative. Most men are analytical; most women are emotional. Most men see things separately as different events; most women see connections between things, weaving it all together. Each of these perspectives has inherent strengths in different circumstances, but they can also be problematic in others. There is the paradox. Each one of these traits can be exactly what is required for a successful outcome to the situation. But sometimes the traits we feel most comfortable with are the exact opposite of what is needed at the moment. That is why we need each other – to balance the relationship and keep from extremes in either direction.

We are so completely different in how we deal with conflict, money matters, children – everything. We can also have different goals in any given situation. The success of our relationships, especially in marriage, is dependent on our ability to bring the strengths of both perspectives to the table, listen to the other person's concerns and decide together what is needed in each situation. Sometimes that requires leaving what you thought beforehand off to the side, and going on with the other person's suggestions. Sometimes the correct answer will be a combination of both. It is a question of balance on a bicycle built for two. It is a learning process that takes time and practice.

The **inter**dependence needed to build this kind of communication in marriage is usually begun long after we already have our own preferences and ways of looking at life, and there is inherently much room for disappointment and misunderstanding. But it also has the potential for great success. It is built into us for a reason; to foster teamwork. Two working together, pulling in the same direction at the same time, can get a LOT of things done! It may seem strange to make this comparison, but have you ever read the *Little House on the Prairie* series?

In the book titled, "Farmer Boy," Laura Ingalls Wilder wrote about her husband's early life. One of the things she goes into great detail about is how Almanzo got his very own yoke of oxen when he was a young child and the oxen were just calves themselves. Bright and Star, we were told, needed to learn as a team. In addition to getting used to one another, they needed to adjust to being yoked together, and learn to understand and yield to their master's commands[1]. In the story, she explained that the calves needed to start training in a yoke very early so they would learn to pull together instead of fighting one another or pulling in opposing directions. Older animals had a much harder time learning team work, submitting to the yoke and to the farmer's call. It was an eye-opening revelation for me!

I have a friend who has oxen. One member of the team that they do most of their logging with was having trouble with one of his knees. He wasn't able to pull his own weight evenly anymore. So they needed to pair the healthy ox up with another one of **similar size and temperament**, training them to work together. My friend said it is more difficult to train an older pair that has not been teamed before, but it is doable. After several months of working them together, they are doing remarkably well learning to pull loads together and listening to the direction of their owners during the work.

The application of this adjustment to marriage is startling. In my marriage I am a strong personality. The dating and honeymoon stage where we were first trying to accommodate one another and learn about each other's likes and dislikes, very soon gave way to disappointed expectations for both of us. After being hurt relationally in the past, I had discovered what I liked, what I didn't want repeated and had become unwilling to yield my ideas, interests and priorities to someone else's. When my ideas are challenged I tended to take it as a personal rejection instead of an attempt on Steve's part to understand where I was coming from. Although I am progressing in an on-going process of learning godly ways of conflict resolution and pro-active communication, there are responses, past and present, that have undermined the unity we've wanted to build.

I realize now that I began stuffing stressful emotions to keep the peace, but I harbored the hurt as ammunition for later use – not knowing that was what I was doing. That hindered honest communication.

When the big changes in priorities came with the demands of new parenthood, it required us to provide for our children's needs, seemingly to the exclusion of our time with one another. This lack of time alone made it much more difficult to "build the team."

Adding in the fundamental differences in how we viewed basic things in life – many of which rarely came up in conversation before children and child-rearing were considered – increased the difficulty. We were like two older animals pulling in opposing directions and we unintentionally hurt one another in the process.

This isn't exclusive to me, I know. I have discovered this is a universal experience. But having difficulties in your marriage doesn't mean that it can't work; it just shows where the opportunities to grow together are. Dozens of couples we know who have celebrated decades of marriage together are still happily married! How do we get from the struggle stage to the comfort of working together as a team and complementing one another? By determining to take the time and committing to practice until it happens. Just like training the oxen, it doesn't happen without effort.

Proceeding with this analogy, we can illustrate the principles of marital unity-building very well! In the initial struggle stage, it is awkward as each of us is trying to see where we fit together. Hurts build up from the tugging and pulling in different directions at differing rates of speed. Without outside input, the stronger personality in the relationship ends up being the directing force – and that can be dangerous when that person can't see the other side of the road! Bruises and raw spots wear away at us under the yoke. We pull against one another, trying to avoid the pitfalls on our side of the road, not knowing that the other person sees the ditch on their side and is trying just as desperately to avoid that.

Left untended and open to more irritation, these injuries begin to get infected with toxic thinking, self-protection and resentment. Once you reach this point in marriage, silent avoidance and blame-shifting can build padding between both spouses, as each one uses jobs, hobbies, friends or even their own children to insulate themselves from re-wounding. Although this may help minimize new friction burns, this kind of insulation does nothing to heal the previous injuries and it causes additional erosion of good will, discouraging cooperation toward mutual goals.

When spouses reach this point in their marriage, people may say, "There's just no way, things have gone too far..." The perspective many times at this junction is there are only two choices: learn to live with things the way they are or get a divorce. But that is an incomplete list of options. There is another alternative. What if instead of just trying to "suck it up and live with it" or figure out how to go it alone, you entertained a third option? What if you and your spouse started listening to a bigger voice? What if instead of letting the one who has the strongest personality in the marriage determine the direction of "the row you hoe", you started listening to the farmer, as a team, and totally changed how you respond to each other?

Both sides submitting to someone who sees the bigger horizon ahead can be the very thing we need to remove the blinders of pride and self-protection. God can help us adapt to one another, prodding us to "Gee" or "Haw" (turn "right" and "left", respectively) at the same time. Heeding His calls of where to turn, when to go and when to whoa, enables us to work together and use each of our individual strengths in cooperative effort toward the same goals.

Submitting our previous pain to Jesus' tender care balms our wounds, cleans the infections that previously kept us at a "fever pitch" and promotes healing for past hurts. Empowered by the Holy Spirit, encouraging one another every day gets us where we need to go without more chafing and discord. That is the victory of a happy marriage that thousands before us have seen as a reality. It is absolutely *not* an unreachable dream.

God can make the happily-ever-after not just a possibility, but a certainty, working with Him and listening as He advocates between and for us. Following His path for marriage is guaranteed to work with both hearts committed to God and to each other! He actively mediates between us and offers us the opportunity to submit to one another in love for the prize we so deeply desire in our lives – someone with whom to share a satisfying and purposeful LIFE. We truly can enjoy one another and look forward in hope to bigger and better things to come. But that is not the only goal – the stakes are much higher than we tend to realize.

As the foundational unit that our lives are shaped and built through, the family is designed as both a place of safety and exploration for the man and woman joined together. If it is healthy, the relationship continues to grow into a place of security and protection for both of them and, if they are so blessed, for their children to learn and develop their own abilities to navigate life. But it is critical for us to understand this does not happen without opposition. The hope, help and advocacy of God for and in us is not happening in a pristine bubble of goodwill.

Just as we have a very active advocate in Jesus Christ and the daily empowerment of the Holy Spirit, we also have a very active enemy who is working to break the family apart.

The Snake in the Garden

The devil knows that if he can separate the marriage bond, destroying the hope and unity of the parents, he gets to tear apart not only the two people in the marriage, but to also affect the children in the struggle. If he can inject fear, insecurity and blame into the mix, he can wreak his destructive intent on everyone involved. The parents have less patience and confidence as they turn painfully inward in self-doubt and suspicion of their partner. With the parents distracted by their own pain, he uses the same fear, insecurity and blame to pistol-whip our children. The resulting timidity and anger works like a two-headed monster, pulling and tearing at our little ones' hearts, forcing them to have divided loyalties between their parents, both of whom they love.

In their limited understanding of what is happening, this heartless enemy stealthily uses twisted accusations to get the children to assume responsibility and blame for their parent's pain-prompted reactions. He gets to undermine the children's sense of stability and self-worth as they seek to "fix" what's wrong and "be good for Mommy and Daddy" so that they can bring their shattered world back to wholeness. They assume blame for something they were never responsible for and therefore can never do enough to reunite. This enemy gets even more than two casualties, as the children and other family members additionally make decisions and are expected to take sides based on the injuries and side effects of the pain that result from the tearing apart of this living entity.

Marriage is a living organism - it is designed to grow and develop into far more than it started out as. The oasis of safety and growth it can become is something the "accuser" cannot stand to see unblemished, so he works overtime at every chink in the fence, every opening for discord, to bring down the boundaries of unity.

Offenses and opportunities for hurt are helped along by this enemy to inflict damage and cause withdrawal instead of cooperation toward healing. When the family unit is damaged, the reflexive withdrawal from the pain stops the progress and support each member lends to the others and the stability of each member is in danger. When people in that union feel the loss from their unmet needs (and the damage from the various ways we seek to alternately meet those needs) it is a recipe for disaster that leaves this truly evil enemy of our souls gloating over another target of his attentions.

You must understand something pivotal: he **hates** you and me and he stops at nothing, pities no one young or old, and keeps on the attack until he sees his twisted plan through. He may be invisible, but his effects can be clearly seen. The problem is, most of the time we blame his pokes, prods and antagonism on the other *person*, instead of the real source of strife. Like having someone else wind you up like a top, watching gleefully as you spin out of control hitting and bumping into the people you love the most, our enemy revels in the misplaced blame and carnage he instigates. Not realizing the discord is being introduced by a third party, the people we bump into then react to the pain we inflict on them, by retaliating on us and the battle is on.

I am not in any way saying that "the devil made me do it" or that we are not individually completely and solely responsible for our own actions and attitudes. We need to take responsibility for the junk we engage in and inflict on others. But we have the opportunity to change what we do, make amends for the past, learn a new way of doing things to build up one another, and forgive the other people in our lives.

When we resist retaliation and choose to forgive, we not only give others the chance to start with a clean slate, but we set ourselves free from the hurt, pain and guilt that weighs us down. We can leave the debilitating results of the past in the dirt with the accuser and instigator who used every trick he could think of to start the friction in the first place!

I got a mind-blowing picture in my head a few years ago that truly illustrated how oblivious we are to what happens in the unseen atmosphere in our homes. Did you ever read Greek mythology? Strife and discord are not merely attitudes, they are personalized. They are depicted as demons sent by Hades to stir up trouble between people so they can all gloat over the dissention that resulted from their prodding.

Like invisible but very irritating pokes in our souls, they keep at us until we look around to see who it is that is so aggravating, disturbing our peace of mind and serenity. Enter our spouse. Since "no one else is in the room", all the irritation and uneasiness that started without a focal point is now transferred onto them. To every off-handed comment, every slight they ever inflicted on you – whether they meant it or not - and you retaliate toward them for your uneasiness. They are totally blindsided by your foul attitude, as they walk unsuspectingly into the room. All they know is that you are getting on their case "for no reason." The focal point that had been missing now has a visible target – but it was not what started the tension!

All the while, the unseen instigators of this invisible drama are rolling on the floor laughing at their continuing success rate of mayhem and division. This scene is not something new in human history. From Shakespeare's "Mid-Summer Night's Dream" to fairy tales, Greek and Roman mythologies to modern-day "fiction" like Frank Piretti's "This Present Darkness", this concept of invisible interference in the affairs of man is a common theme. There is inherent credence to something that is shared so widely in so many different cultures and time-frames. It *is* real, they *are* there, and they are intent in their twisted purpose.

Strategic Weaponry and Powerful Allies

But we are not without effective weaponry for these battles and we do not have to let them succeed. Our enemy is sneaky and he is invisible, but he is not invincible or unbeatable. He **can** be stopped. Once aware of their treachery, we can fight *for* one another instead of against one another! Like spraying a can of spray paint on the invisible man, making him visible and targetable, once you see and accept the reality of this interference, you *can* stop it. Take responsibility for your own actions, allow other people to take responsibility for theirs, and then defend *one another* against these formerly invisible attacks. You can stand back-to-back and use specially designed armor and offensive weapons against the *real enemy* instead of battling your mate. You can prevent additional pain from happening and work together to heal the injuries that occurred earlier.

Even when there are things you need to change in your own heart and between you and the other person, it's not something we have to try to figure out all by ourselves or muster up the strength to do (or stop doing) all on our own. No matter how tired or hopeless you may feel right now; it doesn't have to stay that way. You don't have to lie down defeated and let the destruction continue. You can fight FOR one another and your children, instead of succumbing to the lie of the inevitability of divorce and the evil deception that whispers promises of freedom and a fresh start but only delivers more pain and disappointment. The darkness does not have to continue to pull you and your family down! You CAN truly be happy! Not just "happy again" like you were when you first got married, but MORE excited and experiencing a depth and richness in love that you've NEVER had before because of the added triumph of success against this common enemy!

And we do not do it alone! We don't have to just act like all the junk that happened earlier doesn't matter. The pain is real and the wounds are there and are still tender to exposure and re-wounding. (check out the fence analogy in the next chapter on anger) But it doesn't have to stay that way. The "holes in the fence" can be filled. True healing is not only possible; it is an attainable prize unmatched by any other! You have options open to you that can work dynamically in your life, in your marriage and in your family for generations to come to be really whole! It's yours for the asking. There is power available for you to win. You just have to cooperate with it.

Just as certainly as there are things we can do to expose and minimize the destructive interference in our lives, we can also connect with the constructive and healing assistance of our tender and capable God – He is not known as the Captain of the Hosts for nothing! He has been battling these instigators on our behalf for centuries. He knows what we need and can give us help beyond any level of "expertise" we can muster up in our individual lifetimes of trying.

We are each created with a room, an empty place inside our soul, just for Him to live. From there, He fills us with love and heals us from the inside out, where no one else could possibly reach. Expecting another person or anything else to fill that emptiness by human effort is a frustrating endeavor guaranteeing disappointment. But pursuing relationships from a position of already being filled with God's love enables us to give and receive love out of that abundance instead of from desperate longing and need.

If you are a believer in Jesus Christ, you have a connection with the most powerful love ever known, a power living inside you that can derail the destruction that is trying to break apart your family. If you have not asked for the love of God to help you, there is no better time than right now. Life is way too hard to go it alone. Having a relationship with anyone – even our own children – is difficult at best unless we accept direction and guidance from the One who *designed* us. We can get the customized help we require to restore us completely, while simultaneously taking the prescribed actions that heal the damage better than any human restoration system imaginable! It's an inside job! But it doesn't come *from inside* ourselves – it *comes to dwell inside* us. There is a distinct difference.

I recently heard a perfect explanation of this by Jimmy Evans. Two people are sitting, each with a glass of water. They are only able to give water to the other person if they get some *from* them. It's a "closed system" so to speak, and they never have more to give than what someone else gives them. If the other person stops giving them water, while they keep giving it out, it is not long before they have nothing left to give. It breeds discontentment and unhealthy dependency – us depending on that water from the other person, and they not being able to continue giving it consistently. The enemy induces fear, so that we all get possessive of what little we have left and each drink up our own supply, trying to satisfy our own needs, until we all run dry.

We feel rejected because the other person is no longer supplying us with what we need, and we feel used because we gave some of ours to them earlier. The mutual need drives more fear between us for where to get more water. And instead of being supportive of one another, we become suspicious, self-protective and resentful.

BUT if we're getting our water from a never-ending source, from the well that never runs dry, we have our needs met *and* have a constant supply to meet the needs of others who are still stuck with a single cup.[2] The inference is, when others see you with a consistent supply of joy and peace, they will want to know where you're getting your water and you can point the way to the eternal source.[3]

When I heard this I felt like someone finally understood how I felt! He described perfectly what I had been unable to communicate in ten years of trying! As I thought more about this analogy, other points came up.

- The more we just keep swapping water back and forth from one to the other, the warmer it gets. It stops being refreshing and energizing. The lukewarm water that results reminded me of drinking through a garden hose on a hot day.

You're expecting a cool drink and get tepid or warm instead and spit it out. It's not satisfying to anyone. How often have we been swapping water back and forth with our spouse, expecting them to understand what we're going through, how we're feeling, what we need. Then when their reaction is nothing like we anticipated, we recoil back in unexpected pain from the misunderstanding. Enter that accuser and instigator again. He will use this time to interject thoughts of more happiness in the arms of someone else. The thoughts arise that if my spouse doesn't understand, after all this time, what I meant or what I am going through, then maybe someone else would. Maybe this was all a mistake. Maybe I should have…. Stop! Realize you are being PLAYED - but not by your spouse! Adjust your perspective and see what is really happening in that unseen realm.

- When we realize we aren't getting what we need, we start getting more protective of "our own water", and hold back our affection, attention, and help. It is the reaction to that holding back that each of us is responding to. "If you're not going to meet my needs, then why should I respect you?" "If you're not going to respect me, why should I meet your needs?" It does no good to stand there arguing which came first the chicken or the egg. We need to break the cycle. Self-protectionism and stinginess never helped anyone – it builds walls, not intimacy. We were *created* for mutual aid! Water that doesn't flow like a spring-fed aquifer gets putrid like a kiddie pool left out in the sun – after a while the green builds up, and it's not useful

155

for anything but breeding mosquitoes! Water needs movement to stay fresh and useful.

- There's a well that never stops flowing that we can access! If we are getting refilled and renewed by what Jesus called the Spring of Living Water, we're not giving from a limited source like the "human" cup or pitcher, but from a limitless supply that not only fulfills our own needs, but supplies refreshment and life to others around us. If more than one of us is drinking and sharing from that same eternal spring, there's no telling how many others could be healed and live a truly wonderful life, splashing around in it like a well-tended pool in August! No matter how "hot" life can get, we can be one of the people who gets continually refreshed and shows the way to the pool to others! There are millions of people who don't know the way to the pool! They don't know there is any other way than being in a desert of lack and want, each one swapping cups of water with one another. But they don't have to stay out there and neither do we.

Spring Cleaning

When we are discouraged and beaten down by life, with circumstances we can't seem to get out from under, we feel hopeless. When we can't see any way out of the downward spiral, when there is no end in sight, just one cry from our dark place to God can stop the descent! That's all it takes! God *promises*; "For everyone who calls upon the name of the Lord will be saved."[4] Period. Saved from what? Grammatically speaking, the phrase "saved from…" requires an object. Saved from Hell – of course! Saved from destruction – undoubtedly! Saved from the emptiness that drags you down and threatens to overwhelm you in your longing for connection – yes! Saved by *Someone* who will understand what you are going through without degrading you – absolutely! And that's only the beginning! The applications for this promise of God are as limitless as the stars in the universe. Let it soak into your heart. "WILL BE SAVED"…not might be, not could be, not if you jump through enough hoops, but "everyone who calls on the name of the Lord will be saved." The priceless opportunity for life beyond anything you ever imagined is "in your heart and in your mouth."[5] Call out for it!

We begin at the "spring" - the well-spring of living water we just talked about. First we submit ourselves just as we are and cooperate with God to get the junk out of our own "pitchers!" There are "leaves" and "sticks" (attitudes and past behaviors) that have been decomposing in there and contaminating our water; they block up the refreshment coming from our pitchers. But we don't have to leave them in there – the same refreshment that fills us from the inside can rinse out the junky stuff that leaves a bad taste in our own mouths! It can be the "spring cleaning" we all need!

When you're on a plane about to take off, the stewardess explains that "if the cabin pressure decreases and the oxygen masks drop in front of you and you have a small child near you, put the mask *over your own face first*, so you are able to help them with theirs!" In a similar way, you need to make the effort to seek God's wisdom yourself, before you can share it with others. Quiet time with Jesus enables you to "feed" on the good stuff. In doing so, you will be equipped to also pass that blessing and the tools required for victory to the next generation for stable and gratifying relationships.

This chain reaction of supportive cooperation is much more powerful and constructive than the destructive cycle that division tried to set up. You *will* win out over discouragement and accusation, if you make the choice to stick with it. It is never too late to turn around and walk together toward the goal you agreed to when you first said "I do", or reset the goal together to a place beyond anything you once thought possible – you *can* make it!

But what is the process from here to there? We're not talking about a walk in the park. It's true. The steps can be hard work at times – especially when we've done marriage the "wrong way" for many years. How do we start doing it right? What is the motivation to do the hard work of rebuilding a marriage when improvement and happiness seems so illusive? Especially if the feelings we've felt in the past for our spouse are a distant memory and the hurt built up between the two of us looks so insurmountable. Wouldn't it just be easier to start again with someone else or even just be on your own for a while, away from the upset, turmoil and restlessness?

Understand this: giving up on the battle FOR your marriage is not a one shot deal. If we give up on developing the skills and abilities that can save this one and move onto the next relationship, when the glitter wears off the next one, we'll still be in a place of having to learn those same lessons with that one! The lessons are much better learned the first time around with the person we've already invested so much time and life in! We *can* begin to turn this around here and now.

More Than Determination

If you've lost the desire to try again for your marriage's sake, then let's look at an alternate motivation: the little ones who you DO still have feelings of love for. Let's consider the impact on them. This is not a guilt trip or stating that we do what we do "for someone else." Any 12 step program will tell you doing something for someone else without a heart-attitude adjustment won't bring lasting change. Outward motivation doesn't last very long – it's got to be an "inside job." I'm also not saying to just stay together for the kids, without addressing your issues that continue to be a source of unresolved conflict and contention. Of course that kind of battlefield in the home is not good for anyone involved. But let's look at the situation from a child-based perspective, simply to dispel some misinformation.

They already know there's a problem. The tension and stress between you is something you can't hide for long – they know something is wrong. If the language and communication between the two of you has been harsh in front of them, they are already being torn between their love and loyalty for both of you. They want to defend each of you to the other one at different times. You may have had the same confusion and pain when your own parents had difficult times in front of you. Many times it turns out to be a learned behavior that carries over to the next generation.

In the same way that you used to be oblivious to the accusations and irritations from our unseen enemy (that you thought were coming from your spouse), your children are dealing with the same challenges. The added problem for them is, due to their tender years they don't have the ability to filter through lies and deceptions that are so obviously untrue. The enemy is filling their heads with the same false garbage he successfully tried on you, but his focus is slightly different.

The enemy uses the same tactics on our kids that are clearly seen in child abuse situations. Just like any other form of abuse, the enemy tells our children that everything they are going through is their own fault. If they hadn't done X, Y, Z this wouldn't be happening. There must be something wrong with them if they are going through all this pain. If they tell anyone what they are feeling or going through, they will hurt the people they love the most... one of them will disappear... everyone will know it's their fault... or no one will believe them. The lies are endless and cruel.

Step back and listen to what your kids are being exposed too and think about how it affects them. (Listen to the excuses they are already making to explain away what they feel! "It's okay Mommy, I know you're tired.", "Daddy's just working a lot and he doesn't have time to do that with me." "I'm ok, I don't really need to....") And the enemy pulls them down one notch at a time while we escape from our own pain by retreating to the club, or the links, or the gym, or in video games and social media – ouch! I know! Self-medication comes in many forms - I said it was personal experience! We have to see what is REALLY happening. We have to stop abdicating our responsibility and losing out on our enjoyment of one another and our kids!

As parents it is our job to protect our children from the enemy! They are so innocent and so loving; they never suspect the attack they are under. And when our marriage has sunk to this level, we are so caught up in our own pain, in our own unmet needs that we are too busy to see what the enemy is doing to them. We are far too focused in the wrong direction to protect them, to be united against this common enemy. We are preoccupied with listing each other's infractions and licking our own wounds. Please see this! If you are a child of divorce, or grew up with this kind of strife in your home – the name calling, the angry voices, the cold silences begging to be filled with *anything* positive - you only have to look back a few years to see the truth of this scenario!

And the decision to divorce could make things much worse. In addition to the hurt you feel and the memories of all your spouse's infractions you are carrying around, you are now going to be put in a situation to use those memories to defend your own position in legal proceedings. You are about to say all kinds of horrible and destructive things about your spouse to fight for custody over your children in front of strangers. I'm not saying those things aren't true. I'm not saying those things never happened. I am simply saying that the most difficult times you've had will become the main focus of your thoughts, while the good times and the attributes you each liked about one another, even if they seem distant right now, are about to be negated and minimized as something counterproductive to the legal case. This is not just a hypothetical "what if." This is reality. It has proven itself over multiple generations now – one divorced and disintegrated family at a time.

I am not saying that a time of separation is not in order to work through the unresolved conflict or personal issues that remain troublesome for the two of you. If there are issues that need to be addressed, you both need to have the opportunity to be away from the battlefield. Dreading coming home from work isn't good for anyone. But divorce is not the answer.

I recently heard Mark Gungor, the man behind "Laugh Your Way to a Better Marriage" say he is against divorce but a strong proponent of separations. It seemed counter-intuitive. How is it possible to have both views? For exactly the reasons cited above. In a (temporary) separation, the "break in hostilities" should be used to assess what is of pivotal importance in the marriage. What is just a pet peeve can be irritating and in the big picture is merely an annoyance that requires minor adjustment. There are things that are significantly more hurtful that need to be dealt with using stronger measures. In some cases personal safety is a big factor. Deal with it head on, but with the ultimate goal in mind. If a separation happens, the separation needs to be done from a perspective of repositioning the two of you for reconciliation and regaining what was lost due to hurtful actions, misplaced priorities and battle-fatigue.

Before succumbing to the fear of "how am I going to do this all alone" and having people come out of the woodwork to suggest a dozen authors who can give the 6 steps, 9 ways or 4 methods of successful single-parenting – there is SO MUCH opportunity to make those resources irrelevant by resolving the issue.

162

Of course it is *possible* for one parent to raise children if that becomes necessary and these books have value in the case of a parent's death or in circumstances when mediation and resolution has not worked. But it should be a last resort after a **serious** effort toward reconciliation. The optimal situation is a team of two parents, each with their own strengths contributing to the effort. God's plan is that they work together to raise children assuring stability, loving discipline, training of life-skills and development of character. The family is designed to be a safety zone for children, a haven from harm, bad company and negative influences. It is a place to get your children ready for their own contributions to life and to the *next* generation.

Divorce derails the very foundation of the safety zone, pitting one parent against another to fight over which one loves the kids more and who will be a better provider of the financial and emotional needs of the kids. Each parent strives to project that they are the more competent caretaker – and damages the other in the process. Each one comes up with as much dirt as possible on the other, to come out the winner in a verbal bloodbath! How is that good for the children? How is that good for anybody? Why does it continue?

Cultural Motivation Behind Divorce

Divorce is big business! It makes money for attorneys! It makes money for the housing industry. It makes money for toy stores. Think about this, this is not a cynical conspiracy theory without any foundation. There are billions, probably even trillions of dollars spent annually including attorney's fees, child support payments, court costs, rent for multiple apartments, babysitters and daycare fees. Then add the bribes and apology gifts given to make up for missed school functions and postponed visitation. Many are missed because you're working extra hours to earn enough money to spend on *your* weekend with the kids and many doubled bills! If you thought your financial situation stunk before you separated, how do you think the same amount of money is going to be enough to pay for twice the housing, twice the electricity, twice the phone, twice the cable bills and so on? It is an industry that has grown to skyscraper proportions following the demise of the Ozzie and Harriet and Cleaver generations. Unfortunately, many of us know far too much on the subject from personal experience.

Understand that no matter how callous and stingy you think they are being by not *wanting* to come up with the child support or not being able to be satisfied with what they have, it comes down to basic math. There are certain things you do have to have. There are times when you need to have a break and get unstressed for a little while to be able to fulfill your responsibilities. There are some things you don't need and there are things you can cut. But you can only spend the money you have once.

That's true no matter what your living situation is. If you are suddenly paying for a second rent and the associated costs for a second dwelling, there is simply less money left over to spend on clothes, school supplies, trips to the aquarium, museums, parks, apple picking, pumpkin patches, beach trips, whatever – all the stuff you used to enjoy together as a family. Priorities need to be carefully weighed, and little luxuries you've been used to getting may need to be abandoned in the new reality. This said, purchases made during a time of separation, maybe with a tinge of "I deserve this", "why shouldn't I..." may not be the wisest choices of how you spend what limited resources you have.

You have good *reasons* why you do the things you *have* to do, your spouse always has *excuses* why they *can't* do theirs. Don't go there. The accusatory tone these conflictive thoughts set up in our minds - that these attitudes and purchases made by the other person *prove* that they *obviously* don't care about the kids - is false. These decisions should not be used as proof of their insensitivity – or of yours. Re-focus. You're fighting the wrong battle.

It is not true that you can't work things out beyond this point; this is another lying sneak-attack from that accuser. The question to ask is not "Why do they keep pushing my buttons?" The question to ask is "Why do I HAVE a button?" What is it about that one situation that sends you up the wall and always results in a blow up? You're being played by a bigger adversary than your spouse! Don't let him succeed! He is trying to perpetuate the cycle of divorce. That's what he does. See it for what it really is.

Many of us have dealt personally with this as *children* of divorce. Statistics say we are much more susceptible to getting divorced in our own marriages. They also state that once you get divorced, the chances of getting another doubles with each one. If you had a 10% chance of divorce before your first marriage, it increases to 20% with your second and 40% with your third! The baggage you bring with you as a child of divorce (or child of a dysfunctional family that stayed together and didn't learn how to work things out) sets you up for the demise of your own marriage incrementally more than those who grew up in a stable home. You are still affected by the unresolved pain and misconceptions you learned growing up. It's all doom and gloom with little hope for escape from the defeatism that comes from tearing a child's secure family life apart.

But there IS hope! Please understand it doesn't have to be that way! This is not inevitable! Statistics and averages are just an opportunity for God's Light to shine the way to a miracle recovery. There is a hope that lifts your heart to see infinite possibilities of something better! I have lived it – am still living it! And I want to assure you it's not a pipe dream! *Your own choices can guarantee it!* [3]

I was a child in a divorced family. Those statistics set against my own marriage were daunting, especially with the strong personality I have. The battles I saw growing up, the power struggles and disappointments on many different levels between my parents and the resultant consequences for us as kids, set me up for attitudes and perspectives on marriage that handicapped my ability to build a strong foundation. The model that was ingrained in my own responses to conflict was the one that resulted in my parents' divorce. I meant well, and I did do some things right. But when the honeymoon wore off and I got closer and closer to conflict and disagreement issues, my own attitudes directly opposed the goal I had determined in my heart and mind to reach. Proverbs 14:1 says it very clearly, "Every wise woman builds her house, but the foolish one tears it down with her own hands."

In my case, my hands had lots of help from my mouth! Sarcasm and demeaning comments (mostly snuck in on the sly or in a group conversation) created holes that weakened the integrity and stability of my marriage. My

166

passive-aggressive responses to conflict degraded our emotional bond. My own dream started to crumble right in front of my eyes! I wanted to change how I was reacting; I wanted to have the happy ending that eluded my parents and so many other couples around me! I wanted to make the necessary adjustments and cooperative effort to stay married, but I didn't like the odds. I made an inner vow that I would not get a divorce, but when push came to shove and disappointed expectations early in our marriage hit both of us with daily realities, I came closer to that decision than I ever wanted to! I am so grateful for the outside Help and the "inside job" that was done on my behalf to overcome the handicap of my early years!

* * *

My pre-teen years were a struggle. I had the responsibility of being the chief cook and bottle-washer while my Mom went back to school and back to work to try to augment my Dad's income.

Although my father had worked in a non-union shop with no vacation or sick leave benefits (if he didn't work, he didn't get paid) all his adult life, he did work hard and took as much opportunity for extra hours as he could. He had been born again when I was 9 and had a good work ethic from long before that with his upbringing, but that didn't necessarily carry over into his view of family accountability. We went to church and he actively pursued understanding the Bible, but seemed uninterested in using that knowledge to address some of *his* less desirable character traits.

He had an anger problem and struggled with the differences in financial standing between what he experienced as a kid and where he found himself as a married adult with children. He had a hard time with financial priorities and realistic money management. He took the attitude of, "I worked for this money, and I should be able to get the things I want with it." He then gave my Mom what was left to run the house. I'm not talking about extravagance or addiction, but little self-gratification things like eating breakfast and lunch at a local diner instead of eating at home or packing a lunch. He'd spend money on a few games of pool at a club after work to "wind down". It doesn't seem like much, but when we were so close to just paying the bills, the impact was more detrimental than anticipated.

My Mom couldn't make ends meet with the money he gave her, even after she got a job to help with the bills. This was a constant source of contention and financial frustration. His feeling of primary entitlement with the reality of the limited finances and his responsibility to his family signaled his lack of priority to my mother. This had her scrambling to increase the family income to satisfy her own financial security and left her feeling rejected in the process. Her disappointment over his lack of tenderness and encouragement made her withdraw further. My mom's inability to keep up with the housework and spend fun companionship time with my dad increased the distance. Her withdrawal was an indication of her disregard and growing disrespect for him. It was a vicious cycle.

In the application of any given circumstance, it is often not the situation that is the problem, but the attitude and the perceived reasons for the need. The financial conditions in and of themselves did not have to produce that emotional tone in our home. I have known other families that have multiple jobs and difficult living conditions, but are doing so in the spirit of mutual cooperation and a realization that this is a temporary situation. They are united in purpose and make the most of the limited time they do have together.

Physical intimacy should never be the sole expression of emotional connection in marriage. Showing respect, spending quality time, sharing kind words, and doing nice things with and for one another, are all ways that we communicate love. If these other avenues of communication are diminished or missing, physical touch and sex become merely self-gratifying exercise routines. Without the emotional connection, resentment and distance replace affection.

My parents' jobs were a separate scramble to increase household income, but it was not a mutual partnership toward a common, agreed-upon financial goal. It was a resentment-ridden struggle to keep up with family necessities. In doing so, things that needed doing around the house were left undone and resentment on both their parts made our house (the place that should have been a haven from outside pressures of the world) a mess to be avoided until the need for meals and sleep brought us all together. It was not pleasant. And it got worse.

My dad lost his job when I was 12. This added more pressure and tension. He was out of work for over a year before finding a new job 30 miles south of where we lived. When I was 13 we moved to reduce the commute. Moving from our home (and school) to a new town closer to the new job, reset some of the baselines for a temporary improvement in some areas, but made other things harder to deal with. My parents "tried" for two more years to make it work. Each of them worked long hours in physically demanding jobs trying to provide for 5 children from age 1 - 14 in a rented apartment.

Financial frustrations and conflict were not addressed correctly. But there were also social changes in the family dynamic. As the oldest girl a lot of the "mothering" duties fell to me. I didn't want to be responsible for mountains of laundry, making dinner for seven on a budget for four or trying to balance homework and housework while still trying to figure out how to "be a kid". I didn't want the responsibility of being the first-born daughter.

I had no idea what a great training ground these things were in my pre-teen and teen years. I learned skills that would serve me very well when I had a family of my own. But the seeds of discontent and accusation were being sown in my heart by that same accuser, with the help of some well-meaning people who saw my struggle but didn't understand the equipping process it was building in me.

I had multiple people around me telling me that I "shouldn't have to miss being a kid because of someone else's needs." And "it's such a shame you don't get to have any fun!" These comments ate me up inside, depriving me of the counsel of reason and reality, and of seeing the positive aspects of my situation. I was gaining skills, experience and strengths... acquiring knowledge and confidence by managing a family much earlier than my peers. I looked at it all as a burden instead of an opportunity.

My younger brothers and sisters each dealt with things in their own way, each situation impacting them differently depending on their age, personalities and perspective. Anger issues, seeking attention and acceptance from others, finding hobbies that distracted us from the conflict...

After many years of emotional struggle my parents hit a breaking point. Unresolved offenses combined with compassionate but misguided acquaintances fed the developing animosity. These "friends" were not encouraging a Godly resolution and cooperation toward reconciliation, nor were they encouraging each of my parents to take personal responsibility for their part in the problem. They were encouraging the culturally approved cut-and-run option of divorce. And some of them were quite vocal about it.

My parents, too overwhelmed by their own unmet needs, beaten down by disappointment and legitimate hurts and fears, didn't seek other alternatives. My father did not want to divorce, stating quite clearly it was wrong. However, he staunchly held to an unwillingness to learn different ways of communicating and resolving conflict between the two of them. He felt counseling was a waste of time and was unwilling to "air their dirty laundry in front of an outsider." On the other hand he wouldn't take the time to try to discuss and work through specific points of frustration on his own with my mother either.

After years of trying to adapt and make due, my mother tried to convey her frustrations and desires for their relationship to my dad. She had made many accommodations along the way that she hadn't wanted to make and the resentment over the one-sidedness of the

171

effort had come to a head. My dad still refused to see what was happening and how his actions were impacting all of us. He was holding onto the status quo (never did any of that stuff before, why start now?) and his "rights" in lieu of what the Bible clearly shows in Ephesians 5:24 and 6:4 about being a loving leader and teacher in the home: protecting his wife and gently raising the children in the "counsel and admonition of the Lord". Instead, his heavy-handed authoritarianism demanded compliance with no accountability for his part of family relationships. He seemed to have no intention of changing what he was doing or seeking out help for becoming a better husband and father. In the face of confrontation from my mom about his behavior, he would laugh or make jokes, somehow shrugging off responsibility, putting the ball back in her court to deal with the consequences, like she had done for years.

As a result, my mom's heart became hardened. Frustrations solidified into a seething resentment, and she began to *anticipate* offenses. This set her up for reading sinister motives into some situations that weren't meant that way at all. Her angry responses during these times confused my dad and prompted retaliation or withdrawal.

When the hurt was intentional on either side it cut deeply with feelings of betrayal. The expectations they had for marriage were far from what they were experiencing. A husband is supposed to be a protective provider. A wife is supposed to be a supportive partner. She wanted to feel loved and cared for. He wanted respect and companionship. But their responses to one another didn't communicate these feelings very often.

Their actions and attitudes often fulfilled one another's fears, prompting them to add another layer of self-protection thus continuing the merry-go-round. It was not a fun ride. (When I went to my first 12 step meeting in my twenties, I was given a pamphlet called "The Merry-Go-Round of Denial." I didn't take much convincing – I'd lived it personally! Although my dad didn't drink often, the "isms" that accompany alcoholism were glaringly apparent to me when I read that tract.)

Without accountability and outside help, my Mom decided she couldn't fight "the inevitable". My parents split when I was 15 and my youngest sister was 2. During this time our family was even more financially depressed.

Things had been tough for us for all the previously mentioned reasons, but it got much worse after the split. Now we faced two rents, two utility bills and other multiplied financial obligations added to court-mandated child support. The welfare system gave my Mom more than my Dad could financially, but not enough to meet our growing needs. We were still struggling and trying to make it to the 1st and the 15th every month as our financial dependence just shifted to a blue-lettered envelope twice every month.

The on-going division of loyalty and search for stability tearing at all of us was gut-wrenching. No one could see a way out of the frustration and need, except for the reconciliation we older kids wanted so badly. We remembered what it had been like previously, long before the layoff and the move. We longed for and, in our own ways tried to obtain the reunion, mediating disagreements and "trying to be good" to decrease the tension. But at times we acted out of our own feelings for what we felt entitled to as well. We remembered our younger days when we had fun times at picnics and swimming and family get-togethers. We wanted that back.

Let me be completely clear in my appraisal of both of my parents. My dad wasn't acting this way out of thin air. He had his own fears and disappointments in life and his insecurities and doubts added to his legitimate need to be respected and honored. He felt insecure with physical limitations as he dealt with threatened blindness from a vision condition that began when he was much younger. That boulder of fear over the threat of possible blindness and other issues was constantly hanging over his head. He needed encouragement and emotional support. When he did not act honorably, he was deprived of the respect and appreciation he needed and the cycle perpetuated itself, adding to his fears. He was pushing away the respect and honor he needed from my mom with his own actions and words.

My mother needed the safety and security that she knew in her heart comes from a loving and self-sacrificial husband. She had seen how devoted and hard-working my Pepiere (her dad) had been. He was gentle and kind even when he got upset about something. This was what my mom was expecting but not experiencing in her marriage. When she was required to take on a greater degree of responsibility for financial security without receiving the tenderness and emotional support from my dad, it added to her fears, and frustration solidified into bitterness.

Communication was not a strength they shared. When one of them would make an effort to improve the relationship, the other one would still be stewing over that last infraction and vice-versa. Both of them were absolutely justified in their longings and heart-felt desire for things to be different than it was! But in their pain and disappointments, they were reacting in ways that actively tore down the very foundation they each wanted so desperately to build and it escaped their grasp.

They hadn't done everything wrong by any means! There were good times and they overcame some of the handicaps they had been dealt earlier in their lives. But other things they did - like all of us - were not conducive to the changes they wanted to make and created more roadblocks for themselves. I've seen this same dynamic repeated many times over the past decades with many other relationships, including my own. But divorce does not offer the answer!

Society lies and tells us that the tension will decrease and everything will "be so much better" if you split up and "not subject your kids to all this turmoil." That couldn't be more wrong. Kids are more resilient than we give them credit for! With proper direction our children can learn that these are *opportunities* to learn how to manage conflict and resolve differences *if they are given the chance to see their parents model pro-active problem resolution up close and personal where they live*! Divorce doesn't fix the situation; it postpones the lessons we need in healthy relationship-building skills from the people who are responsible to teach us just that. Without learning these skills, the pain delays growth and adds more tension.

My parents' divorce created divergent outlets of additional emotional strain. This frustration and resentment trickled down to us kids. Who am I kidding, it wasn't a "trickle"; some days it was a deluge! It dramatically changed our ways of interpreting others' actions and words and in many ways still influences how we handle conflict.

At the time it affected how we related to our parents and to each other. Dad was the one who made a joke of everything or made hurtful comments to get out of a situation he was uncomfortable with. Mom was the strong but frustrated one, forcing solutions to get the best outcome she could manage. They were both successful in their own way to some extent, but it wasn't enough. They were both in pain and wanted so much more in and from their life together, but didn't know how to reach it. Our parents are long-since gone, and the legacy they left us in this area is a battle some days.

We are still all struggling with different aspects of how this break down affected each one of us. Sometimes we address our issues in healthy ways like forgiving others, engaging in physical exercise and talking things through. Sometimes we resort to avoidance, blame shifting, denial, excessive sleep or working too many hours. When we rely on the unhealthy coping mechanisms, it perpetuates our inability to resolve legitimate differences!

As an adult now, I can see my mother's perspective much clearer than before. While her marriage and our family were disintegrating, she was hurting because she could see the goal and felt she had no way of attaining it. In my young eyes, not understanding the scope of the struggle she was undertaking just to make it through the day, I often took my father's side – the quintessential Daddy's girl. That added more pain to my mom's loaded heart. Later, when I saw what my Dad contributed to the mix, I hated him for years for not being the husband he should have been. I have to admit that I held his infractions and unreasonableness against him (even after his death). It took a long time for me to see things with a more balanced perspective. Our home wasn't healthy for anyone, but it was what it was. "If only I/he/she had tried something else…" Regret is a bottomless, exhausting lie – and not a good substitute for life!

I am very happy to interject here that my mom found salvation and God's gift of eternal life before she was taken from us in a car accident. My strained relationship with her was a heart-break for both of us. I wish so much we had repaired our relationship before she died. I *was* able to resolve some of the accountability issues I had with my dad before he died just two years later with some amazing resources and mutual effort that have had a lasting impact on my heart, my life and my own marriage.

I have tools today that they knew nothing about. With everything in me I will seek God for the opportunity to use and communicate every single resource to prevent the same deception and hopelessness from infecting other hearts and homes! My family is still surmounting obstacles and winning many victories that our parents were not able to enjoy in their shortened lives. I want very much to overcome all these hurdles and share the way to that victory – to let everyone know that the goal is most assuredly reachable!

We don't have to go into the fray blind, trying to pioneer a new territory through the hazards and pitfalls on our own without the experience and guidance of others! We have a tremendous and helpful loving God whose strength we can rely on and take full advantage of every day. He can make our goal a reality instead of regret!

The first step in realizing this goal is basic determination: stick your stake in the ground and anchor your tent on this spot – Divorce is **not** an option. See it for what it really is: the suggestions of the enemy of Marriage – the accusations of a liar - specifically interjected to divide and destroy your family one thought and action at a time. Don't fall for it!

Instead of succumbing to the lie of inevitability ("it's no use, it's gone too far to stop it now") and placing hope in whispered false promises of freedom and a fresh start with someone else, reject that path. Refuse to give into the slander that passing the dysfunction onto another generation propagates. See it all for what it really is: going from the frying pan into the fire! Make your "fresh start" with your own spouse! Know that others have been where you are, fought their way back and are experiencing the process of the happily-ever-after you're longing for! You CAN truly be happy!

Do not fall for the lies that somehow dissolving the marriage will make all the problems disappear – it doesn't. It creates new ones and magnifies the current issues by an order of magnitude. Though it may be a simplification in some situations, it basically comes down to a pride problem. "I am hurt by what you did, are doing, are refusing to do anything about and I can't take it anymore! I am right, you are wrong and I can't keep going like this!" Don't allow this line of thought any space in your head!

Very Big Provision: If abuse is involved, whether you are the husband or the wife, your first priority is the safety of you and your children. Insure that safety - with physical distance if necessary. Then, from a position of safety, address the issues. Prioritize regular time together to work it through. Resist blame.

Instead of defending your hurt feelings (however justified you are in those hurts) seek resolutions that heal both of you, restore your family and protect your children. Outside intervention can be very helpful. If counsel is sought, Godly counsel is mandatory. People, however well-intentioned, are limited by their own experiences and hurt and can give truly horrible advice based on those hurts. We undoubtedly fail if we are leaning on other people's understanding of the situation. Even "trained professionals" have days when they don't bring their A-game for any number of reasons. We're human. We're limited.

Pray. Pray before you get together. Pray together. Pray after you meet. Pray for Wisdom, discernment and direction. Pray not to take offense. Prayer is not an after-thought. It is essential for everything. If we follow the direction we get in prayer and seek and listen to *God's insight* in the situation, miracles happen. God's grace, when accepted, is never-failing. It strengthens us to persevere when we get tired from trying to force our own solutions.

Remember, you're looking for conflict resolution. Identifying issues is important to solving them, but if a counselor is promoting blame and division in your relationship, it's time to look for another counselor. If the counselor is pointing you to God as an active participant in the healing and growing process, you're probably on the right track. Healing your marriage is about doing what you know is right, regardless of what your emotions are screaming in your head about it not being "fair", or "it's his/her turn to..." (you fill in the blank).

You can do the right thing to and for others when the wrong things are happening to you. God promises us that all things work together for good to those who love Him. You can be the one to pull your marriage off the death-list, with determination, prayer and powerful marriage life-support from the organizations I refer to at the end of this chapter. You don't need to rely on your own feelings, human wisdom or culturally-accepted cut-and-run tactics to satisfy your search for a happy marriage. You can be the one who seeks transformation and renewal for the one you're in now! It can save you tons of regret in the future.

I saw an online video by Lysa TerKeurst where she spoke about a dear friend of hers. The friend felt she couldn't take it anymore, decided to leave her husband and be happy with someone else. She had not been willing to listen to her friend offer Biblical encouragement for staying in her marriage and working things through. Just two and a half years later, when Lysa suggested they get together and have lunch to get caught up, she asked her friend to tell her about her new husband. She hesitated and said, "He's hairy." Lysa said the answer took her off-guard. Her friend, who had refused to work things out with her ex-husband, who had been so totally enthralled with the expectations of a new start with someone else, who was so excited to spend time with her new spouse, now unexcitedly describes him two short years later simply as "hairy." Her friend then burst into tears and told of her regret and the difficulties her children were going through. She hadn't listened and now wished that she had resolved to repair her original marriage in the first place.[6] This painful hindsight happens far more than anyone thinks.

The rise in post-divorce and blended family resources is proof positive of that!

Let me make a statement in the most adamant terms I can. It is a truth I learned from the chapters of my life, from my personal experiences and those of close family and dear friends. **Divorce is not an end of anything except the unity and security of a family created to be a stable haven for all who are part of it.** Although our culture tells us that divorce promises a better life, it delivers something much different. It delivers prolonged family decomposition worse than any natural death. Death, although painful and sometimes mixed with regret over what might have been, brings closure. Death has a real and recognizable time frame with a beginning and an end.

Divorce on the other hand is a prolonged, continual reopening of painful wounds inflicted on many levels between all the parties involved. It can damage each person in the family and extended family for generations. Custody issues, child support, schedules for who gets to spend time with whom and when, broken hearts as children are passed back and forth, loneliness and regret all promote division instead of closeness. The intimacy, mutual aid and support between family members are lost. Divorce does not just create an awkward situation at weddings and holidays, but perpetuates a continuing erosion and distrust that eats away at family members and can affect every aspect of their lives forever if left unaddressed.

Divorce is also contagious. The recent statistics of people who divorce one another show at least two other couples in their circle of friends and close acquaintances that support, condone and contribute to their downfall and are or end up divorced as well. Divorce is a cancer that erodes and invades parental abilities and trust. It affects the children's formation of moral and ethical standards, their feelings of security, sense of stability and their future abilities as spouses, lovers and parents. Conflict resolution is compromised as avoidance of uncomfortable relationships becomes the primary tool in family interaction. This avoidance spreads between generations, as parents' model this abdication of instruction vital to the building of relationships. It robs their children of learning that in real life situations some things are worth fighting for even when it is difficult.

The chain reaction of ill-chosen words and actions by multiple people in the relationship compromises the strength and stability of the family. Bad decisions made in haste and pain without seeking God's wisdom can open the door for attitudes and behaviors that attack and damage the family's weakest members. Bad choices can create a downward spiral of consequences not possible when unity and proper decision making is preserved. After a divorce, the absence of key family members exposes weaknesses that are exploited by our enemy.

Similar to a pack of predators who, through multiple attacks, will chase a herd to separate and reach the weak and defenseless, our enemy will attack the family with divorce to fracture and separate it. Without God's guidance we cannot predict the onset of problems created by divorce. Increased pain and pressure may lead to other bad decisions that may include the need to trust untrustworthy people with child care, detrimental choices made due to increased financial stress, loneliness, fatigue and all the negative side effects that come with these choices. The results are increased guilt, shame and regret that further compromises honest, encouraging marriage and family communication.

This cancerous condition can only be healed and redeemed by intensive, continuing support and counsel by Jesus Himself. He often uses people who have "been there, done that" who, with His help, have broken free of those painful snares. Nothing short of God's answers and guidance will ever be able to reach, identify, repair and heal the shards of a fragmented family. No matter how our culture "puts lipstick on this pig and sells it," divorce destroys families! I believe with all my heart that this perspective on divorce is not over-stated. The ripple effects, the pain and the damage are far reaching. Many times they are beyond a hurting person's comprehension. The generational and personal degradation of divorce makes things worse, not better. The price is much higher than commonly anticipated. But we are not without warning.

"God hates divorce."[7] It's right there in black and white. If God hates it, then it's something that will harm us – generally in ways we can't see at first. Jesus explained to the crowds that it was due to the hardness of our hearts that Moses allowed divorce. But God never intended it to be that way. Historically, divorce was seen as the last resort for women who found themselves in abusive situations with men who were not willing to stop using their wives and children as outlets for their frustrations and rage. In more recent times, men no longer have the perceived corner on spousal abuse. Some women are turning on their husbands, physically enforcing their will and emotional upheaval on their families. It should also be noted that not all abuse is physical – verbal and emotional abuse is on the rise from both sexes. We need to stop it all now!

Divorce dissolves commitments that are supposed to last a lifetime, when two adults are not willing to work at the give-and-take that marriage requires to be successful. We didn't always see divorce as the automatic solution to marital conflict. But in our present society of drive-through everything and instant gratification; patience, moderation and anticipation for long-term objectives have taken a back seat to "me, mine, now." A spouse has become just another thing to trade in for a different model when the paint gets scratched and the newness wears off. I am sorry if that sounds too simplistic or callous. I understand the hurt and disappointment of dear people who find themselves trying to make it through each day wondering how they can take it if things don't change. I am not making light of the pain involved in this, but we need to CHOOSE a different way.

Fix the Problem - not the Blame!

Marriage is not designed to be an ensemble of individuals living in the same house where one person is receiving the benefits of others' hard work and enterprise. All must contribute; all must give and take responsibly and fairly, for the family as a whole to function. Family is a team. Each one in the family needs to take personal responsibility for its success and contribute to the work involved in making it so, or the damage to all its members increase over time. The answer to the broken factors contributing to its degradation is not dwelling forever on who did what, but resolving them! Another 12-Step principle in action: Fix the Problem, not the Blame! Instead of pointing fingers, sit down and work together to overcome the obstacles.

Marriage and the family unit need to be something that is protected, tenderly nurtured and defended. It must be fought for on a daily basis through love, education, and compassion. It takes humor, understanding and adherence to godly principles to make two people realize that what they have together, even when it gets damaged, is precious and worth fighting for. Certain compromises and concessions in personal preferences may be called for in different situations, but it should be a shared decision and something that happens with all parties involved. It should not be a one-sided ongoing acquiescence by one person time and time again for the sake of a peace-less cease-fire.

None of this comes naturally! We need to *learn* things we've never known before because we've never been in this situation before! No one is born happily married, but it is absolutely a worthy goal that needs to be actively pursued. A successful marriage is something we must build each day in love for each other and patience with one another's foibles. We are all defective humans, ourselves included.

Start at the beginning to see the end goal: the happy and productive union of two people. Anything you are thinking, saying or doing should be checked against that goal. If what you are about to say is in opposition to that goal, then throw it out. If what you are about to do compromises what is good for the two of you as a couple or the safety and security of your children, then run away from it. Don't even entertain it as a thought. Get rid of it. The division won't survive if you don't feed it; "The beginning of strife is when water first trickles [from a crack in a dam]; therefore stop contention before it becomes worse and quarreling breaks out."[8] They don't call Proverbs *The Book of Wisdom* for nothing! Anticipate the presence of conflict and put a plan in place for what you will do when it comes up. Don't let it catch you off guard. It's not a blame thing, it's to be expected.

One thought-provoking analogy equates the journey of marriage to two rivers coming together and becoming one. As they come together, there is a lot of turbulence. The water is roiled and splashes a lot where it intersects and begins to settle into its new boundaries of banks, rocks and sandy shoals. But as the traveler continues down the river, they find the water isn't so turbulent, the shores are not so prone to erosion and the water becomes more peaceful. That is the way it works in marriage as well! After the initial honeymoon, the next several weeks and months begin discoveries of things as silly as which way you prefer to feed the toilet paper off the holder and remembering to put the cap on the toothpaste. It builds to things more substantial like keeping track of checkbook deposits and withdrawals or the necessities of keeping up with the laundry and dishes.

Merging the two strong currents in the beginning is not always easy, especially when you started out so excited and with such high hopes, happily going over the Beach Boys song in your head... "Oh Wouldn't It Be Nice!" The tragedy for many marriages in our country is that young couples don't wait long enough for the early turbulent currents to merge and settle down into the peaceful, winding, shared journey to the sea.

People we know who are happily married can share knowledge with us if we open ourselves to hear them! Thankfully, some of us have parents and grandparents who have "merged turbulent currents" successfully, are still together after decades of marriage. I had role models that have been married for more than 50 years! They are such an encouragement to me!

For those who do not have these kinds of mentors in their immediate families, there are lots of great marriage resources out there to help young couples begin (and older couples reclaim) their relationships. We can renew our mindsets and help our marriages grow strong and be fulfilling, the way they were meant to be.

"Marriage Today" is an excellent source of valuable marriage training. Its founder, Jimmy Evans, has developed invaluable resources such as "Every Great Marriage", "Our Secret Paradise" and "Marriage on the Rock." They can help us begin to strengthen marriage by realistically revealing the starting point and recognizing how unrealistic our initial expectations were. They can then assist us in moving along toward smoother waters.

Jimmy's tongue-in-cheek observations bring humor to the sometimes rude awakenings that can occur following the wedding ceremony: "Prince Charming has bad breath and his feet stink!" and "I knew she was my 'Mrs. Right' – I just didn't know her first name was 'Always'!"[9]

He poses several realizations to consider: Marriage is the only institution that we expect to do well in without pursuing training and education! We go for driving classes, nursing courses, cooking school and job training. We learn manners, rules and laws. We practice sports, spend hours learning to play musical instruments or speak another language, but we expect that two of the most important things we do in life – marriage and parenting – are just supposed to happen naturally!

Invest in Your Marriage

Our perspective is skewed. Another point Jimmy made is this: instead of looking at marriage as a vending machine (what can we get from it) we need to look at it as an investment. When we begin to look at life in terms of investment and reward, we have a better understanding and a surer foundation to build our marriages on. This is not a cold calculation; it's a mind-set that changes how you react to every situation. The terms are the same, but the meaning of some of the words change.

You get a return on what you invest in. If you don't put money in the bank you don't get interest. The more money you invest the greater the return. That is the way it works on your job, in developing friendships, in hobbies and in sports. Anything you want to do well needs an investment in time and practice. The more you practice, the more proficient you get.

If you don't invest time and effort into marriage, you don't get interest and confidence in the security of the relationship. Without pre-marriage counseling or time studying God's word on the topic, there is no "starting capital." Without both partners working on it together after the ceremony, there is no "working capital" to insure growth.

Once the investment has had time to mature a little, another consideration of smart investing is timing. Jumping in and out of the market can be disastrous; let your investment grow. You've invested a lot of time and effort into learning about each other and navigating those waters together. Selling off an investment because of a lull in the market, or walking away from the capital you've put in so far, is like "buying high and selling low." A stock investment has highs and lows, so does a marriage. This does not mean the quality of the investment is diminished! Don't sell during a temporary dip... don't divorce during a rocky stretch! This is fiscal and relational disaster.

Equating this ill-advised strategy to marriage, taking the little energy and confidence you're left with after a crash and investing it in an untested new relationship, results in a risky position on the new and the loss of everything you earned in the old.

As Jimmy Evans also points out in his teachings, you get results in the area that you put the effort in. If you are spending all your energy, time and effort at work, in your hobbies or somewhere else, don't expect a huge payoff in your marriage. If you find that you have spent the quality time, effort and passion of your ideas in another area of your life and your marriage has become dry and unfulfilling, it's not too late. He points out that if you put the same energy into studying your spouse again, trying to rediscover his/her likes and dislikes again, as when you were first dating, that spark can come back in a week!

Reinvesting time, sharing fun, communicating, building memories and acknowledging victories with your current relationship can result in the marriage of your dreams with a real soul connection, not magically granted, but fought for hard and well-earned – with all that history behind you to appreciate the journey!

I heard a story of a woman who went to a lawyer and wanted to initiate divorce proceedings against her husband. The attorney advised her to go home and be attentive, cook meals he liked, greet him nicely dressed and groomed when he came home, expressing interest in and doing things for him she knew he liked. Then, he reasoned, when she divorced him, it would hurt him all the more and he would see just how much he was losing. She went home and started right away. Several months had passed and the lawyer had not heard back from the woman about when to begin the divorce papers. When he called and asked when she was coming in she exclaimed, "Oh, no! I'm not divorcing him now! We're happier now than we've ever been! He's doing everything I've ever wanted, why would I get rid of him now?" The investment she put in, not expecting it to make any positive difference, was all that was needed to turn everything around.

Taking the time to learn the easy way, through the experiences of others who have gone before us, and doing what is needed to come out on the other side with a happy and stable marriages is time well-invested in the second most important relationship of your life. Happiness and fulfillment follows when we align our priorities correctly... God first, family second, job third.

You can do it! There is so much help in the Bible, in divinely inspired books and from teachers who can help us along the way! As we briefly mentioned earlier, in the book of Matthew 19:3-9 (and reiterated in Mark 10:2-12) Jesus clearly addresses the topic of divorce as a failure due to hardness of our hearts. He does not say it is a solution to our marital disappointments. "So they are no longer two, but one flesh. What therefore God has joined together, let not man put asunder (separate)...He said to them, Because of the hardness (stubbornness and perversity) of your hearts, Moses permitted you to dismiss and repudiate and divorce your wives; but from the beginning it has not been so [ordained]..."[10]

Guard Your Heart

So if God says, "I hate divorce" and He knows we have issues with one another, what is His solution to the problem? He tells us how to avoid it: "For the Lord, the God of Israel says; I hate divorce and marital separation and him who covers his garment [his wife] with violence. Therefore keep a watch upon your spirit [that it may be controlled by My Spirit], that you deal not treacherously and faithlessly [with your marriage mate]."[11]

To keep us from this hardness of heart, God tells us to turn our hearts toward Him, and says this perspective will result in faithfulness toward our mates. He gives us examples by using His relationship with the church as a model in Ephesians chapter 5. The funny thing is He doesn't tell us to make our mates change, He tells **us** to change! He points out that we have been unsuccessfully trying alternatives to fix things, and then narrows the vision a little more, directing us to change *our own* attitude and actions.

He doesn't tell wives to train their husbands or husbands to dominate their wives. Instead, He warns women not to succumb to fear, and tells them to respect and adapt themselves to their own husband.[12] He then tells men to love and tenderly nurture their wives the way they care for their own bodies and implies if they choose not to their prayers will be hindered.[13] The only "training" that is supposed to be going on is "training up their children in the nurture and admonition of the Lord."[14]

Both spouses are directed to "be subject to one another out of reverence for Christ."[15] We need to return to the original intention of marriage: doing for our mates – in love and tenderness of heart – the things we used to do before we got into the day-to-day grind of bills and housework - when the other person was the thrill of our lives: "I know you are enduring patiently and are bearing up for My name's sake, and you have not fainted or become exhausted or grown weary. But I have this [one charge to make] against you: that you have left (abandoned) the love that you had at first [you have deserted Me, your first love]. Remember then from what heights you have fallen. Repent (change the inner man to meet God's will) and do the works you did previously [when first you knew the Lord], or else I will visit you and remove your lamp stand from its place, unless you change your mind and repent."[16]

You are not called to be responsible or accountable for the others person's attitude, but for your own. However, it is also not a directive made without promise! God includes a sneak peek at the reward of the hard work this self-discipline will bring. It sounds very much like the instructions to the children of Israel facing their enemies in Chronicles: "If My people, who are called by My name, shall humble themselves, pray, seek, crave and require of necessity My face and turn from their wicked ways, then will I hear from heaven, forgive their sin and heal their land."[17] Make no mistake – a happy, mutually fulfilling marriage IS a promised land!

The solution to our faltering marriage is *not* that we try to get God to "fix" what's wrong with the other person, but that we work on our own short-comings. We are to determinedly change (in His empowerment) the things we ourselves do that add damage in our marriage, relationships and workplaces and cooperate with the Holy Spirit to heal both of us. We need to look at things differently to make that change.

Grow Your Garden in Love

Once again, it takes a change of perspective – from a consumer mentality to a gardener mentality. Jimmy Evans explains that a *consumer* purchases what he wants and if he is dissatisfied with what he gets, he brings it back to the store for a replacement. But a *gardener* mentality goes deeper and looks for the underlying problem with that lack of anticipated growth. Instead of starting from the supposition that something is irrevocably wrong with the other person, a gardener explores options for nurturance and a change of behavior. He asks, "What nutrients am I not providing for the growth and fruit I want to see?" More tender care, water, pulling weeds that sap the strength from the plant, sunshine and...*poof!*, miracles result!

Heads up: Those three little dots before the *poof!* signify a waiting period between the effort and the results. Instead of being discouraged by the wait, accepting the reality that the *poof!* REQUIRES TIME to manifest itself brings the thrill of anticipation and hope: "For a dream comes with much business and painful effort..."[18] It takes work, but it is SO WORTH IT! And we are not doing this alone.

We are not *designed* to meet our own most basic needs. Jesus told us so Himself: God is the master gardener and Jesus is the vine we stay united to[19]. With these pre-requisites in place, we are free at all times to go to God's tool shed to avail ourselves of the fertilizer, Son-shine, and "water of the Word"[20]. We can renew our minds to pull out the weeds of worry, darts of discontent, arrows of arrogance, pins of pride and all our unhealthy self-reliance. We can't succeed in a partnership project on individual effort, but we can work together with God and our spouses to grow our own healthy garden. If both people in the relationship trade in their consumer mentality for one of nurturance and meeting each other's needs, we can succeed beyond our highest hope.

You CAN have the marriage of your dreams – it takes forgiveness of the past and a commitment to help one another with whatever obstacles we are facing or will face. Learn new things, new ways of approaching life situations alongside your life-partner. The longer couples wait to learn key principles, the more damage we will inflict and receive as each one blindly winds their own way over and around these obstacles.

If we return to the analogy of the two rivers coming together from earlier, we can foresee some of the problems (or rocks) we need to watch out for.

Navigating the Rapids

We've seen that rough waters, rocks and waterfalls also form rapids. They are not isolated to just the area that is merging together in the beginning. So too in a marriage there are times along the way - even long after a couple unite - that situations and circumstances come up to create issues. Some of them are so common that they can be predicted well in advance.

The seven-year mark is a much talked about dangerous time. For some reason, whether dating or married, when seven years passes in your relationship together, things start to fall apart. Frustrations, disagreements, disappointments and other everyday occurrences build to a head and before you're really aware, they become larger issues and you start thinking, "What did we even start this marriage for!?" This was something I experienced personally.

Steve and I were together two years before our wedding. On our fifth anniversary, Steve and I threw a huge party where we invited all the people we had at our wedding and the people we'd become friends with since. It had been planned for months. The problem was, by the time the party started, we weren't speaking to one another! We didn't want to cancel and miss seeing everyone, but we generally avoided one another most of the day. It's something we laugh about now, but it was anything but funny back then.

Hollywood made a movie called, "The Seven Year Itch". It was a comedy that re-enforced the label for the difficulties that many encounter at that particular point on the marriage timeline. If you are nearing this important milestone in your marriage, plan ahead. Talk. Make up your minds ahead of time how you will handle the stress of issues happening together. It will make a big difference in the outcome!

The first two or three years of your children's lives are another set of rapids. During this period the round-the-clock care of children necessitates that so much of your time be focused on your new arrival. And if you have a succession of children close to one another in age, it extends the period of turbulence. It leaves your energy much depleted and you are both challenged to make time for one another. Meet that challenge head-on with help from family and friends. It won't happen accidently. It takes purposeful effort to navigate those years successfully. Mutual babysitting swap-nights with friends are a great help for this one!

The first year that all your children are in full-time school is another tricky current to navigate. It's another time that mutual aid helps with the feelings of "forced disconnection" for everyone – parents and children alike – commonly known as "separation anxiety". Finding healthy and productive ways to enjoy the new "away" time will make the together time enjoyable instead of a "make up for lost time" scramble.

The empty nest time is a longer version of this earlier lesson, with the addition of its own unique challenges that add age, health issues, work status and financial considerations to the mix. Only you can determine whether this will be a time of rekindling romance and enjoying more time together or times of awkward silence or distracting yourself with outside activity.

Of course there are other obstacles that are unique to your own family that fewer people are required to deal with: unique medical issues, untimely family deaths, job changes and so on. Although not everyone deals with these particular challenges, there are "seasoned guides" who can help you navigate these places too. One woman told me (after we started building our own house!) that her husband specifically promised her that he would NEVER build his own house — that being one of the things he had seen in someone else as a marriage crusher. Thankfully, my husband and I navigated that one successfully with prayer, forgiveness and acceptance of those things that didn't go the way we thought they would...but now it's done. We learned a LOT during our house building adventure and now know things about each other and house construction that we didn't know before! However, the likelihood of us actually trying to build a house together again (to put those lessons learned into practice) is pretty slim!

Each patch of rough water requires a slightly different navigation technique. Knowing that these trouble spots are out there ahead of time can help you. So can knowing that it is likely each of you will initially have a different solution to address these challenges. You have the perspective you have because of what you've been through in the past — so does your spouse. Putting your heads together in an attitude of mutual cooperation and openness to differing options is essential to your healthy marriage. Listen to what they suggest without taking it as a bash on *your* ideas on the subject. Just because his or her approach is different, we should not conclude their ideas are a personal assault on ours. (There are days I still need to work on this one!) Differing viewpoints can be valuable and eventually a source of mutual amusement as a marriage matures.

We have choices. We can go down this river of life trying to keep our heads above water in the rapids, getting battered by the rocks as the waves try to determine our course, or we can choose a better way by learning God's navigation skills.

Have you ever seen those documentaries on National Geographic or outdoor channels of the white-water rafting trips? We can learn a lot sitting on the edge of our chairs, holding our breath as we watch them almost come out of the water at times! The rapids can be scary at first, but they are best navigated by a team working, leaning, and paddling together.

There are also times of adjusting your positions and, if needed, being wise enough to get out of the water and portage around the roughest spots on land. Sometimes the wisest thing we can do is avoid the areas that could break up the boat if you "went there." Learning how and when to face things directly or avoiding the situation completely, takes skill and help from more experienced rafters! These are the "seasoned guides" I referred to. There are great marriage mentors out there, take advantage of their experience! They are a great source of help that when sought out, are more than willing to give aid and direction when the going gets rough.

Check your equipment, navigate as a team over the rapids and feel the exhilaration of the ride! It seems like a no-brainer to me after years of not doing it right! Get in the raft and get your gear on! Learn to lean at the right times, use the paddles to steer and push off the rocks! Listen to those who have been down this river before! It's not always smooth sailing, there are days of rain and stretches of rapids ahead, but the clear waters of a strong and steady life-long marriage are yours for the making!

White-Water Marriage Guides

I've already referred to Marriage Today. Jimmy Evans reveals tips and practical solutions to everyday misunderstandings that he has experienced with his wife Karen in a nearly-failed marriage which is now over 35 years strong. His extensive experience with marriage counseling and related resources through other relationship-building groups are powerful resources. HIs web site (www.marriagetoday.com) and others, who, like him, have a passion for restoring the strength of marriage, are a well of refreshment in a barren land of broken hopes and relinquished dreams. For a taste of what I am talking about go to http://www.marriagetoday.com/the-lie-of-easy-divorce/ and view links on their web page. This is the title article as of the day I am typing this is, "The Lie of Easy Divorce" includes the research that proves what I was sharing with you. Their website spotlights other marriage mentors' resources as well as video clips from Jimmy and Karen's marriage-building library.

They are not alone in their passion to champion today's disintegrating state of marriage.

Gary Smalley (http://smalley.cc/,)
Joe McGee (www.joemcgeeministries.org),
Mark Gungor (www.laughyourway.com)

Les and Leslie Parrot, (www.realrelationships.com) Emerson and Sarah Eggerichs (www.loveandrespect.com) and many other excellent resources teach us, through laughter and a common sense application of sound marriage principles, how to navigate the joining of two lives with remarkable success.

But they all have one "catch" – they are only as effective as the time *you are willing to invest* in your future and that of your family. If you allow their passion for strengthening your family to become contagious and put *your* effort and *your* time into the restoration process, you will be able to watch the return to romance and reap the harvest of the promises you made to each other – seeing your marriage blossom before your eyes!

The key ingredient that makes any of this work at all is your personal reliance on God for the direction to navigate. We can make all the plans in the world, but if we are relying on our own ability to anticipate what's ahead, we are going to hit rougher water. As the old saying goes, "Man proposes and God disposes." If we seek God while loving others along the journey in practical ways, He can make solutions visible that we don't see in our limited perspective. If we try to force solutions when others are not ready, we delay the true resolution. We may distract their focus from the task at hand and push them to view our advice as interference. I am still learning this too; I hope I am learning it well!

In the meantime, quality time of laughter, sharing family stories, practical help, not getting bogged down in offense and hurt feelings, all help calm the waters. Remember the guidance from 1 Corinthians, chapter 13, which is read at many weddings? Be patient, be kind, don't take offense at things, don't look down your nose at others in pride, don't hold prior infractions against someone, love one another in the moment and leave the things you can't change in the past. Faith, hope and love go a long way in smoothing over those rough places in the river! And the family stories you share along the way (which after divorce are often few and far between) not only pass on the legacy of the family, but can inadvertently answer a lot of questions and give the opportunity for sharing great conflict resolution tips!

I should also interject here that the love that is needed to build this kind of relationship is not a gooey feeling or the pounding of your heart when someone walks in the room. That is a temporary and fickle thing – not strong enough to base a life together on. The love that is required for a high quality marriage is a determined commitment to make decisions based on the well-being of the other person. It is a self-sacrificial choice to do and say the things that help the other person reach the heights in life they were created to reach. When both people in the marriage are working toward that goal, it is unstoppable! And laughter is the oil that smoothes out the rough spots when the gears don't always meet the way they should! Facing conflict with humor (not sarcasm and bitterness, or passive-aggressive comments said with or without a smile) can diffuse the damage that everyday stress can throw at people. Learning to laugh at yourself and to enjoy the good things around you at that moment may seem trite compared to what you're dealing with – but it is pivotally powerful!

Dealing with Mole Hills before they become Mountains

When friends of ours were going through a pretty tough time in their marriage, they realized one day that little things were getting to them and were sparking some of the real frustration with the bigger things they hadn't been able to resolve yet. So they made up a song! They started coming up with a bunch of little things that irked them about one another and put them to a simple tune and sang it to one another – and then shared the song with us during one of our campfire-in-the-backyard times: "You didn't put the cap on the toothpaste baby, I don't wanna be with you! No, No, No, No, No, No! I don't wanna be with you!" They'd just change out the toothpaste thing with something else and sing it again, making fun of themselves and how silly it was to get so upset about such little things. It was a fun way to remind one another that whatever they were getting heated about didn't really matter as much as it was escalating to and they diffused the situation that way. So when the bigger things came up, they didn't have all the little stuff clogging up the works, it worked great!

The ability to laugh off the little things, to let things go quickly and to work toward mutual cooperation is counter-cultural. "Keeping short accounts" lets people be what they are and who we are and move on to the next day without a bunch of baggage getting in the way. That's what it means when the Bible says not to let your anger "last until the sun goes down"[21] or not to "let the sun go down on our anger."[22] Deal with things while they are fresh, respectfully and with a goal of seeking clarification. Maybe the other person just didn't know that what they said or did was taken the wrong way. Sometimes in giving one another the benefit of the doubt, we avoid the heart-ache of unintentional pain that can lead us toward retaliation and the feeding of more bad feelings. Cooperation and using your gifts, talents and energy to make things better keeps us united. It takes determination to let go of the past and to use all the tools we can to put our marriage back together! In addition to the human "guides" on the river, we have a Healer bigger than any damage, a peace-speaker who can reach deeper than any pain can hide, and a unifier who can overcome and reunite two hearts. He can repair relationships that *people* think have gone beyond the point of no return. That's not just wishful thinking. "Nothing is impossible with God."[23]

We don't need to face our lives in regret, thinking "if only." The spirit of defeat is a liar – we can ΛLWAYS begin with a clean slate and rededicate ourselves to deal with life in practical acknowledgement of our inherent differences. Instead of being divided by those differences, we can use them to help one other. Like two hands working together to clap - it's impossible to do it alone.

Dear friends of ours had problems early on and separated a couple times in the beginning of their marriage. They had some pretty serious problems that happened mostly because of the immaturity of youth and the lack of knowledge of how to deal with conflict resolution and anger. (Sounds like all of us just starting out.)

Because we were close, I knew details that unfairly biased my attitude against the husband even though we liked each other and I had known him before I met his wife. When she decided to go back to him, I was doubtful it would work and with all good intentions at the time, I advised her not to. I was projecting past occurrences into the future and told her all the reasons it was a bad idea. I was being protective of her at the time, not allowing for some pretty powerful prayer warriors in the equation, because I wasn't following God at that point in my life. God had other plans and was definitely at work in both of them. I am so glad now that she was strong enough to tell me flat out: "Don't rain on my parade!" (exact words) She wanted the dream, she wanted to make it work and so did he. She wanted me to celebrate with her instead of being a wet blanket on the rekindling embers of their relationship. I cautiously told her that I would support her in her decision. I *was* happy for her. In a very short time we were all having barbeques, celebrating our kids' birthdays and sharing *life* together! It was a huge victory! We need to remember past victories and let them be an encouragement to us in the present toward a great future.

When I look back at the transformation they went through in their lives together, I can see the 30+ years they have been in relationship with one another. Time has passed and they are definitely not the same people they were back then. I am grateful she didn't listen to my good-intentioned all-be-it horrible advice! What the heck did I know anyway? I was the same age as she was. Now in my fifties, I still remember that time of our lives and hope re-kindles in my heart as prayers build for their future.

I see so many couples going through difficulty. They think they made a mistake or that their relationships are not repairable. I can say confidently that no relationship is beyond the healing reach of God! When someone says they can't take it, that the other person is beyond hope and thinks that this is the way he or she will always be, I have demonstrable proof it doesn't work that way!

None of us are the same people we were when we were younger! The question is: do we have counselors and mentors that point our way to Jesus for the ability to work things out and stay together until we can enjoy the outcome? Are we letting God work inside *both of us* until we grow into the maturing, caring, responsible, reasonable people He sees in us? Or are we still acting like spoiled children in big bodies? Do we give up and take what we think is "the easy way out?" Please hear me: Divorce is not an easy way out! The pain you're feeling when you want to cut and run because you can't take it any more can be INVESTED into your future instead of being a dead weight you are forced to carry into the next part of your life! Learn from it, find the treasure in it! It all happened for a reason — take the good things you can from these situations and use the rest as buoys and markers of where *not* to go later on in the trip!

Again, just like in the chapter on abortion, if this choice has already been made and your first marriage is already dissolved, start with today. Seek the instruction, communication skills and conflict resolution opportunities you can for today. I've heard many testimonies of renewed vows, re-married divorcees, and successful second marriages. Don't let self-condemnation (or other people's judgement) rob you of a successful marriage!

We can't control other people or fix them, but we can seek God for the wisdom, insight and ability to change *us*. Ask God to show us what **we** are doing wrong in the situation (He *will* show us!) and repent – not just by apologizing, but turning a heart-felt regret over our part in the mess into a daily cooperation with God to stop doing the things we are doing that add pain and delay to the joy we can be living in! Then, while we are busy with that *full time job,* He is free to work on our current and/or ex-spouses and change all our hearts! It works! I'm living it! I am currently 32 years into my own marriage; I'm not perfect by any means and we still have struggles to be sure. But the problems we are working through are normal challenges in life! We have victories under our belts that we can look back on and smile about and use them as springboards to launch over the top of the issues that are ahead of us!

You can do it! You can have the marriage of your dreams instead of the apathy, difficulties or outright nightmare you are living in now! Roll up your sleeves, take hold of it with both hands and refuse to let go – the victory is yours for the making!

Footnotes

[1] <u>Farmer Boy</u>, from the "Little House" series by Laura Ingalls Wilder, Pub. Date: October 1953, HarperCollins Publishers

[2] Jimmy Evans Marriage Today from the teachings "Our Secret Paradise" and "Marriage on the Rock"

[3] John 4:29 – 30 (amp)

[4] Rom. 10:13 (NIV 1984)

[5] Deut. 30:14 (amp)

[6] Lysa TerKeurst from an online devotional on You Tube: http://www.youtube.com/watch?v=gcA2IXXlPcg&feature=related

[7] Mal. 2:16 (NIV 1984)

[8] Prov. 17:14 (amp)

[9] "Our Secret Paradise" Jimmy Evans © April 2006 Regal Books

[10] Matt. 19:6, 8 (amp)

[11] Mal 2:16 (amp)

[12] Eph 5:22- 24, 33 (NIV 1984)

[13] Eph. 5:25 – 33 (NIV 1984)

[14] Eph. 6:4 (NIV 1984)

[15] Eph 5:21 (NIV 1984)

[16] Rev 2:3 – 5 (NIV 1984)

[17] 2 Chron. 7:14 (NIV 1984)

[18] Eccl. 5:3a (amp)

[19] John 15:5 (amp)

[20] Eph. 5:26 (amp)

[21] Eph. 4:26 (amp)

[22] Eph. 4:26 (NIV 1984)

[23] Luke 1:37 (NIV 1984)

Suggested Resources

www.Marriagetoday.com

"Marriage on the Rock" Jimmy Evans

"Our Secret Paradise" Jimmy Evans

"Every Great Marriage" Jimmy Evans

"The Mountaintop of Marriage" Jimmy Evans

www.laughyourway.com and "Laugh Your Way To A Better

Marriage" by Mark Gungor

www.joemcgeeministries.org   Joe McGee Ministries

http://www.smalley.cc/ Smalley Insitute

"Love and Respect" series by Dr. Emerson and Sarah

Eggerichs

"The Five Love Languages" by Gary Chapman

http://proverbs31.org/ "Proverbs 31 Ministries"

"Love and War" by John and Stasi Eldredge

"Your Time-Starved Marriage" by Drs. Les and Leslie Parrot

"Your Heart's Desire" by Sheri Rose Shepherd

"The Grand Demythologizer" by Tim

Keller www.thegospelcoalition.com

Chapter 4

Anger and Fear

"But now put away and rid yourselves [completely] of all these things: anger, rage, bad feeling toward others, curses and slander, and foulmouthed abuse and shameful utterances from your lips! " (Colossians 3: 8)

"Let all bitterness and indignation and wrath (passion, rage, bad temper) and resentment (anger, animosity) and quarreling (brawling, clamor, contention) and slander (evil-speaking, abusive or blasphemous language) be banished from you, with all malice (spite, ill will, or baseness of any kind)." (Ephesians 4:31)

I heard stories a long time ago about how some elephants are trained. When they are small, the trainer tethers one of the elephant's hind legs with a heavy rope or chain. The small animal pulls and pulls against the tie that binds it to a very small area or boundary. No amount of trumpeting, pulling or tugging extends its boundaries. After a long time of trying, the animal finally gives up, accepting its confinement within the length of that rope. The trainer can then reduce the size of the rope, as it is no longer necessary. Long after the animal has grown stronger and can easily break the tether, the elephant remains defeated "knowing" it cannot escape.

Reading in Ephesians chapter 4 this morning, God revealed my similarities to this regal, but captive behemoth. I have been tethered. The tether is not one of rope or chain, but it is just as restrictive - and more difficult to recognize. Although it is not a physical object, it is far from invisible. It is anger. At times it has kept me from logical thought, deeper relationships, intimacy with those I love and many personal goals. The destruction it has instigated in my life has fostered fear, helplessness, distance and caution where I wanted to have self-confidence, closeness, and freedom. I have been limited by this tether for years, while trumpeting loudly that I wanted to escape its hold on me. I began to believe that there was nothing more I could do to overcome its grip.

But even while succumbing to its deceptive restrictions, I have been growing. God has been helping, directing and teaching me. My faith is stronger. This year I have marching orders. This is the year that rope is broken and I go free. When I began reading in Ephesians 4 this morning, it was very clear that this was not a resolution of my own making – it is a divine assignment. Habitual anger is not easily set aside. But it is NOT inescapable. It will be far more difficult than sticking to a diet or fitting into a certain dress size by Easter. But it is imperative that its hold is broken. There is a lot more at stake than I ever realized before. When I got to verse 29 and read to the end of verse 32, I knew this was to be the victory I strive for each day. As I read these verses, I saw the elephant in the room that no one wants to talk about. And I now know what I need to do...

I refuse to be restrained by anger, confined to this tiny space any longer. I have been angry about something for as long as I can remember. "I come by it honestly" as the saying goes; both my parents were angry people. My dad was explosive in his anger and my mom was on a continual "simmer" after years of frustrating circumstances she saw little control over. My anger expresses itself in a blend of both. It is not a happy combination. Our home was tainted by its poison for years. And unfortunately, like all emotional states, it is contagious.

Sure, there were happy times, undoubtedly. It wasn't a 24/7 thing in either my birth family or in the family I was blessed with as an adult, but looking back over my life I see now how anger in different forms has damaged a lot of the relationships I hold dearest to me.

It poisons the atmosphere, choking out positive communication. It begins as self-protection, with someone trying to get their needs met in an uncertain situation. Fear threatens that this will not happen. Anger pushes back and demands compliance. The internal battle turns outward and bleeds over to others, who respond with either flinching withdrawal, egg-shell walking hesitation or their own resentment and retaliation. As it reproduces itself, it breeds defiance and division between its participants. It ends up being a prison for everyone involved – a cycle that does not willingly allow deviation or escape. I know. I've lived it.

I now have the ability to end the tyranny of habitual anger in my life. I am no longer willing to surrender my health, my family and my peace of mind to its many relatives: fear, depression, frustration, rage, crying, guilt trips, manipulation and imposing my self-centered demands on others for one more day. I will not remain in the whirlpool of emotional turmoil where I have been both a victim and a perpetrator for years. I will be free and I will release the people I have tied up with me to this post. Jesus is my liberator.

"Facing" Anger

I also refuse to surrender my face to anger anymore. It sounds strange to put it that way, I know. Let me explain. It is common knowledge that emotions change how we look. When the Bible refers to this fact, it doesn't talk about just temporary expressions, but our "countenance" – how our face reflects what is in our hearts. If we maintain emotions long enough, those feelings not only become how people characterize us, but they are ingrained on our faces. "A glad heart makes a cheerful countenance, but by sorrow of heart the spirit is broken."[1] Daniel and Nehemiah both experienced "sadness of heart" – they were questioned by kings as to why their "countenances" were sad when they were grieving over the state of their nation.[2] Hannah was characterized as having a "sad countenance" before Eli told her she would indeed have a son.[3]

Moses' countenance was so radiant after his time on the mountain with God that the Israelites asked him to wear a veil over his face! [4] I can't imagine that. To be so happy and joyful that people don't want to see your face? Evidently being that close to God created more than laugh lines!

Sometimes emotional states morph into something else over long periods of time – this is clearly seen in Naomi's life. After suffering much personal loss, Naomi's sadness and disappointment turned into bitterness – she even told people to *call her* "Mara" (bitter) [5]. This clearly showed on her face.

But joy and sadness are not the only emotions to affect our faces. Anger too changes our appearance. Saul's countenance toward David was changed - and not for the better.[6] His jealousy over David's sudden popularity with the people morphed into anger and twisted his face to reflect the hardness of his heart toward David. This is evidently not an isolated occurrence; it can affect anyone. Proverbs, the book of Wisdom, warns against slander by telling us "a backbiting tongue brings forth an angry countenance."[7] Speaking ill of others, even when they can't hear you, hardens you inside and out – first toward them and then spreading inward, becoming a filter that everyone is seen through. Suspicion and accusation make you question others' motives, souring your expression as you look for hidden intent behind misinterpreted actions.

That's not just theory. I have seen what long-term anger can do to people's faces. We all have. You can tell a bitter old man or woman long before they open their mouths to complain by the thinness of their lips and the lines creasing their faces! I *do not* want to surrender my face to those kinds of lines!

Thankfully, I have a choice in this. Unlike many a mom's admonition that "your face will stay that way", unflattering facial distortions don't have to be permanent! We find out later in Naomi's story that God provided comfort and provision for her in her distress. After years of grief and loneliness following the loss of her husband and both her sons, God worked through Naomi and her daughter-in-law to redeem their futures in joy. Naomi's wise advice to Ruth had been offered in tragic circumstances from a prison of accumulated pain, but it resulted in healing for them both in God's provision. And it was evident on her face. When she was able to cradle her grandson in her arms, her hope was restored and her countenance was changed - to the point where even her neighbors were talking about it! [8] Her new joy erased years of bitterness that had been etched into her appearance.

"A man's wisdom makes his face shine, and the hardness of his **countenance** is **changed**"[9] (emphasis mine). Like hundreds of other tips for successful living in the Bible, this promise is not just for Naomi. If we refuse to allow toxic emotions to gain a permanent anchor in our hearts, they will not adversely impact our appearance. And if we are already seeing these effects, then a change in focus can rescind the damage. I want to exercise that kind of Wisdom. I am determined to not allow anger any more time to work its destruction in my life, my face and my relationships!

I am done with it and am going to follow the Great Physician's prescription to treat this malady at its source until I am well and whole. At 49 years old, I made up my mind and heart to renounce the primary cause of it all. It is an on-going mission. I want to turn away from fear that morphs into frustration over unmet needs, resulting in anger when I feel powerless. I want to proactively communicate with others with positive and reasonable expectations. I want to respond to difficult situations in faith, knowing that all things can work out for my good. I love God and I am determined to trust that somehow each difficulty I face is actually an ingredient in His ultimate plan and purpose for me. Any other perspective is self-destructive, at best. The emotional habits I have been defaulting to are hurting me and the people I love, and I don't want to cooperate with that oppression anymore!

There IS a cure for these side-effects. I have become determined to renew my mind daily and as often as needed to break free of this bondage to anger and to holding other people hostage to my moods. Today is a new day and His mercies are new every morning! I am a branch, attached to The Vine, and I will grow and thrive and be healed. I know I can't do this alone and I have no illusions of perfection, but in Christ I can do all things! [10]

The Gift of Instruction

Meeting these goals will take a fundamental change in how I deal with frustration and stress. Simply knowing what I should do is not enough. I need to feed my spirit daily on God's instruction if I am going to see these promises fulfilled in my life. I am *finally* learning that instruction is not something to be avoided or dreaded, but something to run eagerly toward! Proverbs has a lot to say about this.

A comparison found in Proverbs 9:7-9 says wicked men respond to correction with hatred and resentment; wise men appreciate the correction, knowing it makes them wiser. God can use any time and any situation to teach us anything He wants to, of course, but I am finding that the best way to be fully open to His leading is to set a specific time each day to be alone with Him. For me this "Quiet Time" is first thing in the morning. Before anyone else is awake, before any scheduling or preparation gets my mind cluttered with my to-do list, I have my time alone with God. It is primarily a time of instruction. It's a time of Bible reading, prayer, watching Christian programming and teachers online, and writing down what I am learning. This is a precious time of communion with my Savior - for me to build up my spiritual reserves for a day of challenges and to increase my ability to encourage others who are going through their own difficulties.

The observations and instruction I receive in my quiet time each morning are about obtaining personal liberty. The funny thing is, liberty is most effectively found in God's *correction*. He points out things I am not doing the right way, He helps me let go of ill-advised choices in my past, and He encourages me to make better decisions today. He gives me assurance of His tender care and helps me release resentment and anger I sometimes hold against other people's painful contributions to my journey. I have learned that nothing – good or bad, past or present – has to be wasted, but can fulfill a specific purpose in God's design for me. Everything He allows to happen is a brush stroke from God's artistry, as He completes the mural of my life.

Understanding this helps me forgive myself and others more freely and shortens the times of difficulty I go through as a result of poor choices – mine or others. Whether situations were pleasant or unpleasant, cheerful or painful, it can all be beneficial if I allow Him to use it as a teaching tool to correct the way I do things in the future. It all makes up a part of the stronger, more capable and confident person I am becoming.

It's funny that as I first started learning about this, Beth Moore was doing a series called "How to Thrive in a Season of Chastisement."
(http://lifetoday.org/video/thriving-in-a-season-of-chastising-part-1-2/) It fit right in (of course) with the revelations that God was leading me through. Accepting chastisement, correction for what we do outside of God's will for us, is a challenge. We seem to have a much easier

time spotting someone else's flaws; but we're told we need to get the plank out of our own eyes first!

When God drew my attention to yet another fault I needed to correct recently, I started to feel defeated. But something stopped me in mid-thought. I had a choice. I can always look for someone else to point at who I feel is acting "worse than I am", and deflect the attention to them. But I know if I accept God's conviction and confess my own fault, I will see good things happen at a result.

Each victory I have experienced in the past has fueled my determination to tackle another self-defeating habit in the present. When I feel unsure, and begin to get into blame shifting to deflect attention from my own junk, and respond instead with faith and self-examination, it leads to more victory. So, with this in mind, I decided to cooperate with Him.

My reactions to many situations are changing, which changes the unpleasant situations I'd rather not have to be going through. This seems backward to me! When I try my hardest to change *things*, I bang my head against a wall of obstacles; but when I determine to let God change *my reactions* to things, the situations I want to adjust often become resolved. Without constantly having to force my own solutions, I can enjoy my relationships more instead of constantly "working on them"! All of us win.

This morning's realizations were the culmination of so much prayer and Biblical input over such a long time. Now I am *running* to the cross, submitting myself to God and allowing Him to remove this deep-seated anger plank out of my eye!

Change Begins With Me

Ever since I was a little girl, then growing older, getting married and having children of my own, I have continuously allowed myself to be both a victim and perpetuator of fear and anger. Which role I stepped into depended on the situation and the people present. I never saw it before, or maybe I ignored it and just went with the status quo because it was easier than facing it and changing. My self-righteousness over all of it gave me the excuse that I was acting better than *other people* - and I denied my responsibility for things that I didn't want to address.

It hasn't been hard to avoid dealing with this behavior pattern because I am not this way in public and with people I don't have repetitive, personal contact with. I am like this most often with the people I feel safe with: my husband, my children and a few very close friends. In situations with outsiders I am much more likely to take on the peace-maker role and adopt principles like "looking for the best in others" or "not taking offense" or "giving someone the benefit of the doubt" and "cutting them some slack." I try to take into consideration that maybe what they said or did had little to do with me and was just "the straw that broke the camel's back" and I should just "let it go."

But I am realizing how little I give the benefit of these same principles and courtesies to my own immediate family members. I tend to be much quicker to assume that the motives behind their behaviors and words were intentionally harmful, therefore justifying my own reactions. I claimed my right to be offended and often made them pay with angry words, cold shoulders, dirty looks, rolled eyes, belittling attitudes and a host of other self-righteous mannerisms and reactions.

God is showing me that these responses to conflicts do little to resolve the underlying issues. They block constructive communication, tear down goodwill and damage the safe sanctuary of the home that I have always wanted to foster. I was "tearing down my house with my own hands" as mentioned in Proverbs 14:1. Sometimes I erupted if I wasn't getting what I wanted and then bemoaned the fact that there was an undercurrent of tension in the house. In the past when I did take responsibility for something I did wrong, I used to swing way over to the other side and determine "never to do that again", compounding the harm done by doing the opposite extreme.

God has been showing me this is not a recent event or even a bad habit. This has been a sin issue for me both as a child and as an adult. (Sin may seem like a harsh word to use, but by definition, "anything that is not done of faith is sin" according to Romans 14:23 and I can't fix something if I deny it). It began when I was very young and has been creeping deeper into my attitudes and behaviors for a long time. I had become comfortable with it, not just to the point of acknowledging "that's just the way I am" or defending it, but not even recognizing it as part of my character. I can readily point this tendency out in others who suffer from it– the seething undercurrent of anger that colors any given situation and manipulates changes in the people around me – but I was clueless that it was firmly imbedded in the armor I created for myself.

It was harder to see from inside because I am also pretty adept at the principle of "minimum effort for maximum results." My anger *can* involve blow ups and other effusive demonstrations of my "displeasure", but I usually got the desired results from sulking, sarcasm, dirty looks and surreptitiously slamming things. Why expend more energy than necessary to get what you want done? I wasn't really aware of the individual thought processes that went into my reactions, but it was true none the less.

It's not pretty or comfortable to talk about, but it has become too real in my life and I want to be free from it. A verse in James says the only way to rid myself of this junk is to face it honestly and confess it as a "fault" or "sin"! If that is part of the solution I'm ready. Maybe you can see yourself in some of these same struggles. Maybe you can benefit from what I am learning too. We can begin by confessing our angry behaviors today, and seeking alternatives to our usual responses.

Iniquities and Inner Vows

It wasn't until recently, when those behaviors weren't accomplishing what they used to, that I realized how big a part of me they had become! Jimmy Evans illustrates these destructive tendencies – what the Bible calls iniquities – with a word picture that got through to me very well: if you go to the seashore or on a high mountain where the wind blows in a prevailing direction most of the time, the trees that grow there develop a bend in them. They grow sideways in the direction that the wind blows on them. So when the bark and roots and trunks develop, they stay that way. Even if you were able to transplant those trees into an environment that no longer had winds blowing, they would still be bent after growing like that for so long.

It's the same thing with iniquities. People get "bent" living in the emotional "currents" they develop in when they are young. This is true regardless of the emotional tone. If it's an atmosphere dominated by a positive outlook, then their perspective on situations tend to remain positive even in negative situations. But if they began life in an anger- or fear-based situation, their perspective usually tends to be dominated by negative responses. Even when they are older and the people they used to have this negative contact with are no longer a daily reinforcement of the behavior, they're still bent - habitually responding in similar ways – even to innocent or harmless occurrences. This then initiates a new breeding ground for these undesirable "currents".

Jimmy warns us that two of the ways people usually respond to these influences in their own lives perpetuate the "bend" into the next generation. They are 1) inner vows or 2) continuing the iniquity ourselves.[11] What's the difference?

With an inner vow, we make a decision that we will not do something as an adult that someone else did in the past to hurt us (usually as a child): "I'll never let anyone hurt me like that again" or "I'll never hit *my* kids" or "When I grow up, I'm going to do with my kids all the things I didn't get to do!" or "I'll never be this poor when I grow up!" These kinds of vows end up being a funnel that your decisions flow through to get you where you've determined to go – or keep you from going.

But just saying it doesn't necessarily determine your actual responses in the moment. Someone who felt unloved due to harsh "discipline" as a child may themselves be harsh (continuing the iniquity themselves) despite their abhorrence for what was done to them. But they may go the opposite extreme, enacting an inner vow. In the case of child abuse, someone may be so fearful or determined NOT to repeat what was done to them that they become too permissive or indulgent with their own children, avoiding conflict at all costs. The problem with this is that without sensible limits and reasonable expectations for behavior, another extreme is fostered. As a result, children can become boundary-less and resistant to instruction. In trying to make sure our kids don't experience the same kind of deprivation *we* felt, we create a different problem in *the next generation*.

In this example, we substitute seething anger for complacent allowances and fail to fulfill our responsibility to teach our kids restraint. This can lead to them learning to control us by asserting their own angry outbursts to get *their* way when we try to set boundaries for them. This perpetuates the previous generations' anger response to control the next and the cycle continues unabated. The pendulum swings from one generation to the other from controlling and angry to indulgent and permissive unless we seek healing.

There are other substitutions as well that this principle applies equally to, but what it all comes down to is fear. Fear of rejection, fear of being unloved, fear of not being valued and the list goes on. Fear is a cruel taskmaster. We are left wondering why we can't escape the pits we keep falling into in our dogged resolve to avoid them! Unless we learn to respond differently, learning healthy conflict resolution skills, beginning pro-actively to *practice them* in our own lives and passing them on to others, we will be unable to stop the pattern.

Sometimes our behavior choices are based on noble aspirations, but differences in personalities and individual situations mandate differences in application. By making set determinations as absolutes to direct our own behavior based solely on human insight, we make ourselves god in those situations. Without the grace and love of God guiding us through these emotional mine fields, we are insufficient to the task of freeing ourselves from the offending characteristics. We need to let God direct us. Remember, He sees everything a lot more clearly than we do! If we submit to His teaching and develop increased sensitivity to His lead, He can prevent our short-sightedness from carrying destructive patterns forward into another generation.

This is not a weak-kneed, fatalist position of helplessness. This is an unvarnished awareness of our true, unsanctified human nature! When we come to God in humility, requiring our faith to reach out for the help to achieve the healing we need in His strength, we overcome obstacles in God's powerful Grace. Without God's intervention, we easily perpetuate our pain and sinful behavior toward the ones we love most.

We need Jesus and the Grace of God ourselves and through us toward others to escape these pendulum swings that keep whipping our family trees from one extreme to another. If we are going to grow and be able to nurture the coming generations to be confident in love and acceptance, while still pursuing His moral standard – which includes rightful and necessary discipline - we need a Guide Who already knows the Way.

God is the only One capable of maintaining the ability to balance these ingredients without falling over into one side of the ditch or the other! And as I spend more time seeking His will and guidance in my life, I find I more readily recognize the right path for these balances instead of reverting back to my own self-powered reactions.

It is exhilarating to be able to experience these victories and changes when they happen! It doesn't happen overnight – but neither did the "bend!" However, with Jesus' help, it doesn't have to take as long to get rid of the undesired reactions that it did to acquire them!

I remember as a young child, in response to my mother's comment one day that I couldn't "go 5 minutes without talking", I determined not to say a word to anyone for 1 hour. (The fact that the comment was "5 minutes", and I turned the rebuttal into "1 hour" is a sure sign of pendulum/ditch thinking right there!) I did it in anger to prove her wrong and hid the hurt I felt about her comment. I buried it, not wanting to look at the pain of it and went very quickly to anger and self-defense, another behavior that God warns us is bad for us. "Do not repay evil for evil"[12] for "God is my shield and the lifter of my head."[13] Any other way takes too much energy and leaves us defeated by keeping us side-tracked from what we were supposed to be doing with those minutes and hours.
I didn't realize what I started doing that day. In taking my mother's comment as a challenge not to speak for an hour, I built a wall between us. I lost those silent minutes

in a bad attitude and forfeited whatever positive interaction I could have had with her that afternoon. I can tell you now as an adult, it wasn't worth the self-satisfaction I got by proving her *unintentionally* hurtful comment wrong.

Visiting the iniquities...

Many people misinterpret a critical warning in the Bible given by God to the children of Israel. As a result most completely miss the promise that follows it! In fact, this point is so pivotal in its importance that God repeated it 4 times (Exodus 20:5-6; Exodus 34:6-7; Numbers 14:18; Deut 5:9-10) in slightly different ways. The common thread of His instruction is this: "Thou shalt not bow down thyself to them (false idols), nor serve them: for I the LORD thy God am a jealous God, *visiting the iniquity of the fathers upon the children unto the third and fourth generation of them that hate me*; ..." (emphasis mine). This last part most people see, but misunderstand. We think that God is going to punish our children, our grandchildren and our great grandchildren for sins we've committed.

In the terminology used, "iniquity" is not the same thing as sin, and "visiting" is neither retribution nor blind punishment. Iniquity is a tendency in our own personality toward doing something evil as a result of our fallen nature, things we saw growing up or experienced from the people we most associate with – the "bend" we discussed earlier. The deeper meaning is accepted in both Biblical circles and secular psychological professions, even if the wording used is different.

Alcoholic behaviors in children generally have roots in alcoholic parents and grandparents, abusers were generally abused by their own caretakers or parents when they were children. The same goes with bigotry, addictions of any kind and other personality traits, like anger and fear. The terminology for the "carry over" of these things is known as "generational sin"; the "iniquity", or "bend in character" that results from those behaviors are "visited" on the following generations.

This is certainly not to say that we have no choice in the matter! God is a God of Redemption and everyone everywhere has the opportunity (and the promise!) of deliverance and freedom from these tendencies simply by seeing and grabbing hold of the second part of this passage. Look at the very next line: "And showing mercy unto thousands of them that love me, and keep my commandments." Anyone who is willing to make God the priority in their lives, who truly wants to live a godly life, is *guaranteed* the enablement of the Holy Spirit to walk in victory over these things that have tripped up us and our ancestors for generations!

Once you begin to understand the heart of God, you realize this verse is not a curse or retribution coming on innocent children for someone else's sin! In fact, God addressed this false perception when He spoke in Deut 24:16: "The fathers shall not be put to death for the children, neither shall the children be put to death for the fathers: every man shall be put to death for his own sin." We each bear responsibility for what we choose to do.

But for us, in post-resurrection promise, we need not retain that guilt, habitual sin and consequence of death.

We each can claim Jesus' death as the penalty paid for our sin simply by believing in Him and choosing to follow His leading. The enablement for victory over everything that we face is proclaimed time and time again in the Bible. In the book of Deuteronomy, chapter 4, verse 7, it says, "For what great nation is there who has a god so near to them as the Lord our God is to us in **all things** for which we call upon Him?"(again, emphasis mine) not some things, not sometimes, but **all things** for which we call upon Him!

We can overcome any obstacle, no matter how long it has been a problem! Matthew 19:26 says, "But Jesus looked at them and said, 'With men this is impossible, but **all things** are possible with God.'" Romans 8:28, 2 Corinthians 4:15, 2 Corinthians 5:18, and Philippians 4:13 also use the term "**all things.**" The apostle Paul tells us there is nothing outside the power of God in our lives. I can do everything I need to, to break free of the mire that threatens to suck me down into another pit – I **can** break free! And I can share with others that same grace and power I have found so that they may use it to deal with their own challenges.

I am quite incapable of managing other people's lives and choices. My own emotions are challenge enough, thank you! Like trying to hold an inflated beach ball under the surface of the water in a pool – trying to subdue my emotions in one area just forces it to pop up higher in another one. I am not able to see where it's trying to pop up next until it's too late.

I have a history of running into walls of other people's emotions (and my own behavior patterns) with very little success. I have a lot of "aha!" moments as a result to show for it. I am so tired of 20/20 hind sight! I am learning that I don't have to dwell on them and stay there. The pain from areas I haven't been able to let go of yet can be the impetus for me to do something about them. I am learning to see a bigger picture. And I am learning to submit one day at a time to where God wants to take me. I need to believe Him when He promises: "I know the thoughts and plans that I have for you, says the LORD, thoughts and plans for your welfare and peace and not for evil, to give you hope in your final outcome." [14] When I take that to heart in faith, then the real peace can flow.

God is teaching me deep lessons as the years go by about believing that acceptance and trust are tools to help me enjoy the journey. The things I previously stumbled over can actually make the journey easier as I learn to avoid repeating them! We can get irritated about all the stones we keep falling over, or we can ask God for help in leaving behind the painful memories of past debris AND help in learning to navigate over the new ones that come up along the way. Stones and debris ARE in the way – that's life. But God's direction of "...forgetting what lies behind and straining forward to what lies ahead," is a matter of focus and is a choice over which we have *complete* control. We can "press on toward the goal to win the prize to which God in Christ Jesus is calling us upward."[15] We can choose to use the debris as stepping stones to get a clearer perspective.

And we don't have to *feel like it* to **do** it. Just like looking at a sink-full of dirty dishes, we rarely *feel like* doing them. We make ourselves **do** it for the end result. We need to realize that the same principles apply in the heart. If we do the things that need to be done, even if we don't feel like doing them at first, the reward is worth the effort. When we choose to do the right thing, even when the right thing doesn't feel good at the time, God works in our hearts and in the situation and our emotions get us in line with His desired behavior for us. "For the time being, no discipline brings joy, but is grievous and painful; but afterwards it yields a peaceable fruit of righteousness to those who have been trained by it."[16]

I now know many ways not to let my fears and frustrations build into anger – the choice is mine to use that knowledge to avoid the destruction previous iniquities led to and gain additional insight to be wary of distractions...

Destruction and Distraction

Beth Moore said in a *Wednesdays with Beth* teaching (now called Wednesdays in the Word) on Life Today that the devil uses various techniques to keep us from our destiny. (Destiny doesn't have to be the grand scheme of things, or the big finale at the end – it can also be what you are supposed to be doing at any given moment.) As believers in Jesus, we are protected in Christ from a myriad of destructive things. (Psalm 91:4-10) With this protection in place, it is impossible for the devil to destroy us. (2 Cor. 1:10 and Phil 1:28) But he doesn't give up easily.

Beth declared: "if satan can't get us with all-out destruction, he will try to get us with distraction." [17] He uses every trick in his book to keep us from our purpose. It can be an aggravation, focusing on little annoyances (attitudes, offenses, and misunderstandings) or it can come in the disguise of pleasant things (like social media, games, or TV). Either way, these distractions keep us off-balance or off-task. If an off-handed comment or incidental event can keep you running in circles of hurt and distract you from what you are supposed to be doing, don't think for one second the enemy won't use that against you!

Unfortunately, I can personally attest to that truth from more instances in my life than I can possibly count. I've lost out on positive *personal* interaction and time accomplishing things I truly wanted to do because of hurt feelings and taking offense when things didn't go the way I thought they should. I avoided honest communication about my own expectations, not wanting to make waves. But "not making waves" did nothing to address the problem. The disappointment over unmet expectations or desires, bred frustration I didn't know how to handle. I missed out on a successful resolution to the problem by blame shifting, not initiating positive action or direct communication. Often I distracted myself from the resulting distress by watching mindless TV programs or online videos or scrolling social media, only to realize hours had gone by and the issues still went unaddressed.

When we give in to these "fret fests", we perpetuate frustration and apathetic distance we want to avoid and we set ourselves up to *keep* it going when we give in to petty distractions. We need to recognize this at the beginning and strive to keep focused on real goals. Succumbing to it time and time again steals our life a little at a time; and the destruction of our purpose comes just as surely when it creeps as when it crashes.

Like a classic bait and switch, distraction contaminates our past, present and future and extends its tentacles into each area of our life. It's not that we are unaffected by others actions, or that we are never supposed to be "off-task" or take a break. Staying in a perpetual state of having to accomplish something productive all the time is harmful. (Hence the instruction to work 6 days and then take a day of rest!) But we need to realize how important it is for us to pro-actively address interpersonal issues when they are small. We *will* feel hurt by certain things; we *do* need relaxation time. But we can't let unresolved emotional issues overshadow life. These smaller issues based in fear of unmet needs, frustrations over others actions, hurt feelings and harboring offenses are the foundation that anger builds on.

If we allow them to go unchecked, *we* become weakened; getting side-lined by our own emotions if we meet these challenges by defaulting to anger. We lose our *enjoyment and our purpose*, compounding current ineffectiveness with the unhealed memories of a sometimes painful past. This distracts us from pressing forward in hope to our future. But we can stop this process dead in its tracks! We can dismantle it before it has a chance to go any further.

When recognized for what it is - and who is helping perpetuate it – we can use this awareness to our own advantage. Instead of being a frustrating cycle we cannot escape, the realization that destruction and distraction are both hindrances to us can prove to be the motivation we need to turn to the One Who sets us free and gives us repeated victory!

Dismantling the Foundation of Anger

Two of the resources that have recently helped me dismantle the chemistry of hurtful memories and the results of these "bends" in my own character are "Who Switched Off My Brain" by Dr. Caroline Leaf and "The Hurt

Pocket" by Jimmy Evans. Understanding the foundation that anger is built on gives us the knowledge and power to dismantle it and rebuild our foundation on stable footing thereby changing the structure of our lives. They have been instrumental in my journey to freedom from this destructive trait.

According to Dr. Leaf and other neuroscientists, thoughts are not just emotional, fluid, random happenings that we can't do anything about. There is a visually detectable anatomy of thought and cognition that builds continuously in the construction of our brains. Extreme magnification of these areas shows trunks and branches with differing densities very clearly. Dr Leaf calls them the "magic trees"[18] of the brain. They are made up of nerve cells, axons and dendrites, that all have minute spaces between them that require chemicals to bridge those gaps, conducting the thoughts - electrical impulses - across them. Chemical enzymes, hormones and physical nerve cell groupings or knots form in the web of tissue in our brain with each memory. These knots, or "trees", can either house good memories or bad memories. The more often these connections are visited by our conscious thought, the bigger and denser these trees become. This can be a good progression which elevates our outlook on life, strengthening and building us up or a detrimental reinforcement of despondency that perpetuates the problems we so want to be released from.

The knots for good memories release endorphins and other "feel good" chemicals into our bodies when we think of them. Bad or painful memories are dark spots in our brains that look like a bare and twisted tree. They release toxic chemicals that poison our bodies with depressive hormones and enzymes and increase the toxic effect of those memories with each remembrance of that thought. That is the reason God told us in Philippians 4:4 and again in verse 8 to "rejoice in the LORD" and to "think on things that are lovely, wholesome, excellent, praiseworthy, pure..." etc. It makes us stronger and creates a chemical flow of regenerating strength in us. "A cheerful heart is good medicine, but a crushed spirit dries up the bones."[19] Science is now proving truth told thousands of years ago! The "meditations of our heart", the things we keep running and re-running over and over in our heads, can either build us up or tear us down – quite literally!

In "The Hurt Pocket", author Jimmy Evans picks up where Dr Leaf leaves off and tells us that these toxic memories collect in a kind of "pocket" where they hang out together and act as a weapons locker. This locker becomes the arsenal from where satan (whom Jimmy calls "the hurt whisperer"[20]) retrieves those memories and adds emotional messages that piggy-back along with them, etching the memory deeper in our thoughts and compounding the pain.[21] The memories serve as the delivery system to bring accusations and lies forward into our present to damage our now. These added messages can go undetected for years, molding and shaping the way we process information and acting as a filter through which good information and encouraging messages have a harder time getting through.

Our general outlook on life itself depends on what we think about... and what we think about what we're thinking about! If we keep remembering the good memories we have about particular people or places, it acts like an anti-depressant, a mood elevator, a feel good training session for our brain. We get physically and mentally stronger and then we are more able to handle the things in life that are less than what we hoped for. We are better able to have victory over life's challenges.

But when we keep repeating (in our own heads or to an all-too-willing audience) all the things that hurt us, made us angry, discouraged or depressed us, it actually weakens us inside and makes us less able to face the challenges and situations that threaten to derail us and drag us off the desired course for our lives – lives of purpose, fulfillment, and joy. By building walls in an attempt to protect ourselves we actually wall ourselves into a self-made prison, perpetuating our own pain. If we repeatedly meditate on hurtful episodes we've had in the past, things that continue to frustrate us in the present and things we fear will happen in the future, we become self-defeated by our own dark preoccupation! [22]

I am finding that the chemicals associated with this pain additionally act as a quick retrieval link for those dark memories later on. When I feel that same emotion again, in reference to something else that is happening now, the emotional link associated with it brings up other memories from the past with that same pain signature and snowballs itself with even more layers of those feelings.

This is most evident when having a conversation with others. One person starts talking about something hurtful or aggravating and the other one chimes in with something similar. Pretty soon it becomes a competition to see who can come up with the worst example of what you're talking about – whether it's a general irritation on a certain topic or an increasing list of someone else's offenses. One memory or infraction leads to revealing another until you're all so wound up about it you can't stand it.

The same thing happens in our own heads when we dwell on distressing thoughts. A black hole of sorts is initiated and sucks us down into a deeper level of that emotion, making it more difficult to "shake it off". They pull harder on our focus and form a mental quicksand of depression, doubt and disappointment over the past and initiate fear and dread over the future. These emotions are draining on spiritual and emotional strength. They weaken our resolve and our ability to overcome daily challenges. When I become aware that this kind of thought-spiral is happening, I get anxious to get out of its pull.

In my attempts to deal with this in the past, the strategy I used most often for escape was anger, resentment or rage. These emotions carry surprising power with them, which, although it provides the energy I need to break free of the draining emotions in my heart, the anger does more damage on the way out. Like a hollow-point bullet, it punches its way through the draining, weakening emotions and gives me "strength". But this kind of strength is destructive in its application and hurts everyone more in the process, leaving a bigger hole in the end than I started with.

We need to realize we are doing damage when we "indulge ourselves" in the "right" to have these outbursts. Once we acknowledge this, then we can advance toward a change in our own responses. Rage, sarcasm, blame, belittling others, addiction, transference, denial, repression and avoidance are all destructive ways of handling these uncomfortable situations. We need to see them for what they are to be free of them.

Coping Skills

The psychiatric community calls many such attitudes and behaviors "coping skills." I have some difficulty with this term because using the word "skills" makes it sound like a positive way of successfully handling difficulty. While they can act as safety valves or quick *temporary* ways of dealing with unmanageable situations in the moment, perceiving these learned responses as an achievement can be very deceptive. While the "coping" part of the term may arguably be accurate, "skill" not only implies something is learned, but also beneficial. This could not be more misleading. But that's the way deception works: wrap a lie in a partial truth and, once the truth part can be verified, repeat the lie part more and more until it is simply accepted as fact.

"Coping" is not meant to be a permanent way to deal with life, and "coping skills" are a human way of dealing with difficulty that already has a divine prescription. The Bible tells us we are "more than conquerors and gain a surpassing victory..."[23]! In accepting society's ways of coping as our default mode, we are selling ourselves and our loved-ones far shorter than we are intended to live.

Continued reliance on them as a response to conflict adds to the damage it perpetuates. One offense or hurt wraps around another until it all snowballs, and the pain becomes more and more unmanageable. Not accepting the benefits of godly conflict resolution skills doesn't just lengthen my pain, but hurts the ones I love standing near me at the time. The ones that I want so much to love, protect, teach and lead by good example are left hurt and in need of additional healing because of my reliance on psychological diversions instead of God's truth. There are superlative alternatives to ineffective psycho-babble.

The same verse that told us "we are more than conquerors" goes on to tell us the condition for that victory: "...through Him who loved us." We don't do it on our own; we attain this "surpassing victory" by abiding in Christ and following God's instructions on the matter - which absolutely includes *conquering* difficulty. And the Bible is *full* of instruction on successful living in many, many arenas!

As a comparative example, let's look at dealing with anger with cultural justification and psychologically suggested "coping skills" and then through Biblical conflict resolution.

We can repress it, ignore it, deflect it, blame it on others, or vent it. Justifying our outbursts with phrases like "he/she just made me so mad", "that's the way I am (Irish/Italian/Latin temper, etc.)" or even "I'm PMS-ing!" This implies there's nothing you can do about curbing it; that's simply not true.

God says, "A [self-confident] fool *utters all his anger*, but a wise man holds it back and stills it."[24] (emphasis mine, amplified version) Other versions refer to the fool "giving full vent" to his anger. Did you catch that? Wisely handling anger involves "stilling" it and "holding it back", not finding better ways to "vent it". Imagining the other person on a dart board, a pillow you're punching, or some other kind of substitute "targeting" while you're rehearsing and retelling their offenses over and over again in your head and to other people, perpetuates the turmoil; it doesn't resolve it. Being wise involves self-control and conflict resolution of a higher level, regardless of the other person's actions or what modern culture says.

Of course it's easier to view *other's* angry outbursts and see "the fool" in them. But in order to break free from our own destructive cycles, we need to stop focusing on other people's stuff and look at our own contribution to the problem. Acknowledgement is the first step to freedom. We need to accept the fact that *we* often are the fool.

When we address the situation God's way, we can appropriate the resolution, the healing and the assurance that strengthens and equips us for the next challenge. God's solution to adversity avoids additional damage, strengthens our confidence in Him, and allows us to use lessons learned to help others. Repeated success encourages our continued implementation of these principles for the next challenge as we build *positive* snowballs!

Deflecting or redirecting anger doesn't work. Punching a pillow or a workout bag, may be better than a face-to-fist confrontation, but it does nothing about curbing the emotions welling up inside you or about resolving the conflict behind those feelings. Verbally slamming someone to their face or behind their back does lots of damage to relationships. Later on, when you've cooled down, you have regret and other repercussions to deal with that you could have avoided - and verbal assault damage can last far longer than a bloody nose or a black eye. "Stuffing it" or "going to your happy place" is outwardly better than outright aggression or retaliation, but it does nothing about the source of frustration and how you deal with personal boundaries being violated. If we're not supposed to lash out, and we can't just ignore it, what are we supposed to do with it? We need a more comprehensive battle plan.

God acknowledges that anger is something that comes up - and that there are times that getting angry *is* the proper response! But He doesn't leave us hanging there; He tells us what to do about it. "Be angry… and sin not." [25] "Don't let the sun go down while you are still angry." [26] In fact, God addresses anger over 260 times in the Bible. Check it out: go to Biblegateway.com and type in "anger" and "angry" – it's pretty impressive what insights come through on the pages in so short a space.

If we let God show us a different perspective, take responsibility for our own responses, and allow the reason behind it to motivate us to change how WE respond, we can then forgive others and release the offense before it has a chance to simmer in us and work its poison.

This illustration helped me see this process: A man was talking to his son about his son's temper. He instructed his son to go out to the corral, choose one board in the fence and every time he got mad and lost his temper to hammer a nail into it. That sounded like a good way to relieve some of his anger so he got to it with enthusiasm – each time he got angry, he hammered another nail into the board with everything he had. In a few weeks, the son had hundreds of nails in the fence. This surprised him. The son went to the father and reported that now he could see how many times he had gotten angry in such a short period. He didn't want to continue to react in anger and decided to calm down instead of just blowing his top.

In seeing a physical "record" of his outbursts, he was more aware of his lack of self-control. It motivated him to change – it became a personal challenge to keep from adding more nails to the fence. His father said it was good that he recognized that and added another instruction: instead of just putting a nail in the fence when you lose your temper, now each time you respond to situations with patience instead of blowing up, take one of the nails *out* of the fence.

In a couple months, after both adding and taking out nails from the fence, the board was clear of nails. He was pretty proud of himself for his accomplishment, but now the son realized something else. What was left behind was a board riddled with holes and dents. The board had been weakened by all the hammering and no longer had the structural strength to do what it was supposed to. It needed to be replaced.

This story taught me a big lesson. In the real world, you can't replace people. Your anger, snide comments, sarcastic words and cold shoulders may give you a temporary satisfaction in the beginning as you pound nails into the board of their hearts, justifying your actions with the pain you are in because of what they did. But if you were able to see them as these boards, you would be able to see those "nails" accumulating and building up inside them. Even after you act with kindness and patience, gaining control over some of your habitual responses, the holes left from previous nails still leaves damage and hurt. But there is a solution.

Thankfully, we are not boards in a fence. We don't need to be thrown away and replaced. We can be repaired. The holes can be filled and we can become stronger than we were before. God's love and walking in a personal relationship with Him is more effective than any wood putty. He fills in our weakened areas with Himself. Jesus can be the healing that rebuilds a once-damaged board into a solid plank of emotional maturity, including patience, slowness to anger and thoughtful responses instead of angry outbursts.

The question is: are we willing to let Him change our reactions to things? It's not comfortable to change how we act and it takes time and effort to learn a new way of doing things. But it is much harder to fix the broken and damaged people around us, than to stop ourselves from reacting that way in the first place. Make no mistake – it's worth it to learn! The feeling of victory when we keep ourselves from going down that tired old road is very exhilarating! I know – from personal experience! I'm in the process of taking those nails out – and God is filling those holes.

Interrupting the process of anger begins best before it has a chance to become a word or an action; the time to dismantle that foundation is while it is still merely a thought.

Taking Every Thought Captive

Resolution isn't simply "sucking it up and moving on". In order to break free of a thought stronghold of anger we need to understand the difference between sheer human determination and following God's lead. Previous attempts to handle things just by trying to be "nice" - and multiple failures – showed me I was merely being silent when I was upset about something. But not "speaking angry words", didn't stop my mind from racing forward and going over and over the offending thought, what I wanted to say and how much I wanted it to change.

I found out first hand that this is why God warns us to "take every thought captive"[27] and resist the devil at "his onset."[28] Instead of letting those thoughts get engrained in our hearts producing depression or lashing out at someone else in anger, we can make better choices. We can use our own thoughts to improve situations by changing our responses. It is a decision we make in the moment; it doesn't just "happen naturally." It takes work – and LOTS of practice! This is the beginning of emotional healing.

I was in someone else's car one day and a song came on the radio. It's a beautiful song, don't get me wrong, but when I hear the words singing about how this father is going to keep dancing with his little girl while he still can because he knows she will be gone someday, living her own life, it gets me.

I got a lump in my throat and started inwardly bewailing that my daughter and her family lived so far away. This time, however, my reaction was different than it had been in the past. I couldn't turn the song off, like I had done before. I didn't want to have to explain to the other person why a song they were enjoying (in their car!) was "making me" sad. So I stopped myself. Instead of allowing my usually despondent reaction to have free reign in my emotions, I fought that negative thought from the beginning – taking the accusatory thoughts captive and countering them with truth.

I knew why my daughter was not living nearby, there wasn't anything I could do about it at the time and allowing this emotional tide to rise was going to do nothing positive for anyone. So I fought back. I answered my emotions with practical facts. I did not succumb to the temptation to start talking, yet again, about how much I missed her and her family and I allowed myself to enjoy the memories of her and her dad dancing the Father-Daughter dance at her wedding a couple years before and... it felt great!

I countered the depressing thoughts with faith and truth. I thought... "No, I am not going there again. Jenn is where she is for a *reason* and a *season*. There are lessons being learned by everyone in this situation (the *reason*) and it will not be a permanent situation (it's only for a *season*). God is in complete control of all of it. Either I believe that or I don't. If I don't, then I am in much sadder shape than just a song making me cry. And if I do believe it, (which I do!) then I have no need to cry. I can enjoy the music, the company, the sentiment and not let my emotions push me around and instigate more of those depressive chemicals!"

I stopped the lump in my throat before it had a chance to get a hold of me and after sneaking in a few deep breaths, I felt great – I won! I expanded and strengthened a positive connection of cells in my brain and decreased some negative ones. It started with a decision - and *doing it* gave me victory.

Natural vs. Intentional

As we've seen earlier, we need to guard against deception that the line "time heals all wounds" plays in our thinking. Emotional healing doesn't just happen "naturally"; we need to be intentional in how we respond to conflict to see the victory we've discussed. Our natural tendency toward conflict is to avoid addressing issues directly with the people we have unresolved problems with. We need to actively guard against two very specific "coping skills" in this area: gossip and avoidance.

Two ways most people handle interpersonal conflict include talking about it to people who are not part of the conflict itself (gossip) or ignoring the situation and hoping it goes away (avoidance). Both help us deflect our responsibility for our own anger by assigning it elsewhere. When we try to make ourselves feel better by spreading a sour view of someone else, we medicate our hurt by gaining someone else's validation ("misery loves company"). Talking with others, who will be supportive of our meditation on the injury in the form of complaining or back-biting, perpetuates the problem and it often back-fires in the future. If we taint others' view of the person we're upset with, and later have an opportunity to resolve the conflict with the original person, the damage to their reputation by our gossiping with others is difficult, if not impossible, to wipe away.

In the opposing direction, by using avoidance or procrastination to sidestep our contact with the ones we are taking offense against, we allow the infection to fester until it invades our perspective in other areas. If we have been hurt by one type of person – whether the grouping in our mind is gender, race, age (or other category)-based - we begin to guard ourselves against people with similar attributes. For example if a woman was abused by a man, she could become wary and suspicious of all men, not just the one who hurt her. If someone had a bad incident with a dog, they could become fearful around all dogs. In so doing we may be separating ourselves from the very people who could help us resolve the issue (and the puppies we could be having fun with!). Either way the damage has no way of experiencing the healing we're looking for.

When we view it this way, we can see that gossiping, back-biting, avoidance and procrastination are <u>deadly</u> to our healing. But what is the alternative? Without making a determined effort to resolve the conflict, address the issue, and rectify the situation, the hurts we carry continue to fester. They build and begin to crowd out other things in our lives that are good and enjoyable. We become obsessed and overwhelmed with the pain, trying harder to make sense of it and gain control over what was done to us. This inward battle poisons other relationships and builds walls we sometimes don't even know are there. These walls can solidify into self-protection and envelop us in a cloak of darkness of unforgiveness, resentment, fear and anger. Using either method allows the pain to be perpetuated - and this poisoning is again gleefully observed by the enemy of our souls.

But just as surely as we have an enemy, we have a Friend of the Broken-hearted! We don't have to do this alone! He knows what to do! It is as simple as reaching out from the prison doors that we have locked ourselves behind and becoming willing to try a different way – our Creator's way. To heal the painful wounds we've been carrying, we acknowledge them, allow our Great Physician to clean them out and heal them – and resist picking at the wound repeatedly while the damage is repaired.

We need to work and live cooperatively with one another to grow and be healthy. Division fosters heart sickness and a heavy heart drags down the body. The words Abraham Lincoln spoke hundreds of years ago as our country was going through heartache and division in the Civil War apply just as surely to us and our families today: "A house divided against itself cannot stand." He was quoting Jesus (Matt 12:25 and Mark 3:25). Division wounds. Unity Heals.

The Family Stronghold of Anger

Godly conflict resolution involves constructively and cooperatively communicating disappointments or desires, asking for the other person's input and mutually arriving at a solution that both people can live with. Many a marriage counselor and comedian have repeated: "if you want someone to know what you're feeling, you have to tell them, they are not mind-readers!" That tired old line accompanied by tears of... "If they cared, they would know what I am going through!" or "If they loved me enough, they would stop doing X, Y and Z!" is not true. This perspective is counter-productive to any goal but martyrdom.

But this was my response to frustration and disappointment. Many times throughout my life, I got resentful about another person's lack of understanding of how conflict was affecting me. I felt tired all the time, and fatigue doesn't make for a bright outlook on life! I felt like a twin-sized sheet trying to cover a king-sized bed. No matter where I turned and how carefully I tucked one corner, there simply wasn't enough of me to cover everything. I thought if only I had more help, I could be happy. To make matters worse it wasn't just one situation with one person. It was a bunch of things going on with several people all at the same time: different applications of unmet needs, denial, frustration, and disappointment- each one keeping me off-balance and away from the peace I wanted so badly. One conflict morphed into another, each one building more lines of personal defense inside my heart. It became a habitual state of mind that I wanted to escape – I didn't want to keep feeling like this, but I saw no way out. I thought I had to make other people do what I needed them to and had no way of enjoying time with them if they didn't. It was maddening! It never occurred to me that the common denominator in all of these issues was me! I discovered that if "it" was going to change, *I* needed to change. God's freedom from inner turmoil was completely within my grasp the whole time.

It seems so strange to look back and recognize the futility of my own self-defeating attitudes. Like the commercial, "Wow! I coulda had a V-8!" It's a matter of perspective and priority.

If you have a broken arm, you don't take an aspirin and hope it gets better – well, not if you want a healed, functional arm, you don't! You go to someone who knows about broken arms and have it set properly, give it time and protection to mend up, maybe some exercise or physical therapy in that area and then you'll be able to use it like it was designed to. Comparing other people's arms to yours and getting frustrated that yours can't do what theirs can do does nothing about making your arm better. Neither does brushing your hair or putting on a different pair of shoes – your arm is still going to be broken. Do what you need to do for your broken arm!

It's the same thing with emotional damage. Distracting myself with enjoyable diversions like baking, shopping, video games or TV did nothing for the cause of my frustration. I still had the same issues when the cookies were gone, the bills came in and the program was over. Cleaning got something positive done, but then gave me something else to complain about, that I was doing everything all myself and didn't have time to enjoy anything or anyone. I have the same time available each day that everyone else has. Where was it all going? And what did I need to do differently to get the results I wanted?

I needed to address the "broken arm"! I needed to identify the "break", target the area with healing, and get some positive emotional "therapy". I had to be honest about myself to myself. I had anger issues stemming from frustration over unmet needs and problems communicating those needs constructively. I couldn't stand the turmoil anymore. John chapter 14 says "Let not your heart be troubled...trust in Me" Matthew 6:33 says "Seek Me first and all these things will be added to you". I seriously started praying that God would somehow help me be the person I wanted to be on the inside. I started reading my Bible more, started going to adult Sunday school and women's conferences. I heard lots of things that helped me see things differently.

It sounds so basic, but I started reading Christian books about conflict resolution! Following a Women of Faith conference, I got ahold of a book called "Big Girls Don't Whine" by Jan Silvious and laughed till my sides split. It was a fun way to gain perspective on my own contribution to the problem. I learned a lot about taking personal responsibility for my own emotions. Then, following an "Iron Sharpens Iron" women's conference, I read Deborah Pegues' book "Confronting Without Offending". It concisely shared practical ways of dealing with conflict by intentionally and calmly working cooperatively with others instead of avoiding conflict or bullying my way through.

"Boundaries" by Dr. John Townsend and Dr. Henry Cloud gave tips to determine healthy expectations (inside me and toward others), how to avoid resentment from misplaced boundaries – and how to set and enforce reasonable ones. Dr. Gary Smalley's book, "The DNA of Relationships" was a huge eye-opener how fear plays into all this.

Dr. Charles Stanley's 5 part series on Anger was amazing with helpful tips and practical application of proven solutions. All of these resources combined together to teach me how to create a win-win situation so everyone's needs can be communicated and addressed. Intentionality makes all the difference! When I decided to take advantage of reliable resources and prayer to change me, instead of avoidance or blame, I unhooked the talons that had been dug in for so long and walked away from it, one step at a time!

Now that I am experiencing the difference, I want more! I understand how merely "coping" destructively perpetuated the problem. I no longer want to settle for isolating within the pain or addressing it out of those dark emotions. Instead I want to keep challenging the hold they had on me by seeking out God's help to break free of it all in the light! Consistently bringing each situation before God in prayer sets me free from the turmoil. This process works wonderfully no matter how long it has been an issue - in both preventing new problems and addressing things still stuck in the past.

The previous scene I shared about my mother's comment, "can't you go 5 minutes without talking?" is a perfect example. The false message I brought forward with the comment from my mother was... "You're always talking, but what you have to say isn't important and has no value." I know my mother's heart today, not only did she not say that, she never *meant* that. She was making an observation (and chuckled about it at the time) that I rarely stopped talking when I was little. I was not mindful of the right time and place to talk – or that there were times not to speak at all. I had lots of observations and lots to say about everything. (My elementary school report cards all have "talks too much" or "needs improvement" in this area). It wasn't a bad thing, just a part of my natural, out-going personality, and age-appropriate socializing.

But the "accuser" was right there, waiting for his opportunity to drive a wedge between me and my mother, which then added to other misunderstandings and created more distance and division. Instead of laughing along with her, I took offense and interpreted it to be derision instead of amused truth.

Today, I try to look at painful memories in light of the new things I am learning. I can search out the lie in messages that come with memories from my past. Then I hold it up to God and ask Him to grow His Truth over it. In this way, although I still remember what happened, the pain of false messages that come with the memories is healed in my heart and the lies are discarded from my mind. Dr. Leaf details this process in her book, "Who Switched Off My Brain?"

I can cooperate with God's healing and live in joy if I develop the practice of doing this with hurtful situations. It diffuses the power of the pain and keeps me from reacting with dramatic emotional pendulum swings. I can choose to respond appropriately if necessary with smaller "course corrections". Like driving a car, it takes time and practice to develop this skill.

Before you learn to drive a car, you think you just point the car in the right direction and it goes. Once you get behind the wheel you begin to realize that it is necessary to continually move the wheel ever so slightly, constantly readjusting your direction to stay between the center lines and the gutter. Frequent adjustment in little doses makes for a much smoother ride than stiffly sticking to one direction until you come near a tree or a gully and jerking the wheel in another direction. This is the case even when road conditions are good. If there are adverse weather factors added to the mix, it requires even more adjustment to keep on the right track. It takes a little more finesse, but it is still do-able.

Slight corrections at lower speeds keep your car headed in the right direction. When you start to slide and fishtail, if you point your wheels in the direction of the drift and continually re-compensate for the slide, turning it first one way and then the other in small adjustments, you become centered and in control again. Over-compensating and jerking the car in the opposite direction results in certain off-road collision and more damage and cost than we want to deal with. It's the same in life.

If you're dealing with someone else who is highly stressed, or your day is already not going the way you expected it to, you're feeling ill, you're going through a big life-change or other adverse "road conditions", slow down, make your thoughts more deliberate, be cautious about the likelihood

252

of over-reacting. If you give people the benefit of the doubt, cut yourself a little slack, give yourself more time to "get there", you can navigate these tougher emotional roads with more success and without needing to call a tow truck to get you out of the ditch. I claim no perfection in this area whatsoever! But I defer to Will Rodgers who humbly observed: "Good judgment comes from experience, and experience comes from bad judgment!" I have good reason for humility in this area.

Fear To Rage in 2 Seconds

One of the most dramatic experiences I had with navigating these roads the wrong way occurred when my children were young. I was trying to be a good mom, playing with and taking my kids to neat places, teaching them how to bake and cook, learning about nature and enjoying lots of different activities. I brought them to church, got them involved in junior choir, Sunday school and youth group. I knew from my own upbringing that teaching my children about God and instilling a set of morals was something good parents were supposed to do for their children. The truth of that statement is not in question. However, this fact did very little to build up my reliance on God for everyday living. Sunday school was something that children did to learn Bible stories. Adults listened to sermons once a week, and that was sufficient. Wasn't it? What more could I learn from a collection of historical stories and commandments that I didn't already know?

I already shared I had problems with communicating my disappointments, misplaced expectations and frustrations.

But I wasn't seeking instruction for my ignorance in this area. I figured that "I was doing the best I could" and left it at that. I was acting better than lots of people I knew and that was good enough for me. I thought, "I'm a strong, competent woman, I can do this on my own." I didn't have time to read much or even breathe some days with everything that was going on. My quiet time back then involved quick prayers with my kids at their bedside and 1 minute devotionals as I was drifting off to sleep. I was not relying on God's strength or direction for my parenting or my marriage.

When I would have times of frustration, insecurity or disappointment, I would white-knuckle my way through, taking deep breaths, counting to ten, and try to reason out the situation in my own understanding. That only goes so far. When I reached the end of my own limits, it would inevitably morph into anger. Some days, it took much less provocation than others.

The problem was it rarely stayed where it started. My anger would spill over in other areas of daily activity that had little to do with why I was simmering inside. Raising kids and trying to succeed in marriage doesn't really go the way you think it should before you start doing it. Navigating these roads without godly instruction and a good support system of people who've been there before you to encourage you gets hard fast. Compounding one thing after another, causes a lot of stress when you realize you've made BIG miscalculations through just not knowing key information.

When the unexpected happened, I would stuff it, trying to "suck it up" or "be good" about it, and then transfer the frustration to some other situation, usually with my children. Most of the time they weren't doing anything earth-shatteringly wrong, they were just being kids But I would scream at them, sometimes hitting them in anger over their behavior, disobedience or defiance, instead of a measured response that was offense- and age-appropriate. I could have been using these opportunities to teach them things like appropriate conduct, listening skills, and conflict resolution.

In my ignorance, I ended up teaching them by repetitive example something far different than I intended: passive-aggressive anger response, emotion repression or explosion to get what you want, and blame transference for the guilt experienced afterwards. The "iniquity of my father" (and mother) was being passed on to the next generation by me. The emotional simmer would give way to the angry explosion. Then I would beat myself up for losing control. This cycle repeated often, but never with more intensity than this one afternoon.

With my kids in the minivan and a pie on the floor between the two front seats, we were on our way to a campground to visit friends. It was something were all were excited about: swimming and a picnic smorgasbord awaited. On the way, I pulled over to the side of the road to talk to another friend who was driving her kids somewhere else, momentarily leaving my kids in the car with instructions to "stay in the back seat, I'll be back in a minute." A few minutes later, from just 10 feet away, I realized the minivan was rolling backwards toward a fence that was blocking a now-unused canal that dropped about 20 feet down to a dry creek bed. Apparently, getting impatient about reaching our destination, one of my kids had climbed into the front seat to call me back, and had inadvertently moved the gear selector into reverse.

I screamed as I ran to the van, slammed the gear selector back up and proceeded to unleash my terror-turned- rage onto my kids. At this point they were 6 and 4 years old, no longer in car seats, but in seatbelts. As I screamed about the car almost going over the cliff, I noticed how it was stopped by the fence, since it wasn't going more than a slow roll backwards. Thank you, God! What would have happened if they had stepped on the gas to push themselves up higher to see better or get my attention? The terror of what *could have* happened spurred on my anger instead of diffusing it. I never once hit them during this tirade, but the damage I was doing with my mouth was clear to see in their faces and body language.

As I considered with heart-stopping realization that I could have lost both my children by my stupid act, I deflected the blame to them for not staying in the back seat. Then I realized in addition to everything else that there was now a footprint in the middle of my pie. I screamed even more, making a quick mental calculation about the size of the footprint. I directed my fury for the spoiled pie toward my son, the youngest, while the two of them held onto each other for dear life. They were petrified at my reaction and crying while repeating they were sorry. I finally sat back in the driver's seat, calling out to my friend something about seeing her later, still yelling while rushing home to trade the spoiled pie for one I had left on the counter for our family for later. On the way to the campground, I began to calm down. I started doing deep breathing, measuring out my words, and I explained to them that if they had done what I told them to, then I would not have gotten so upset.

This was absolutely a behavior I learned from my father. I deflected the blame for my angry outburst to them for disobeying my direction to stay in the back seat. I blamed them for the danger they were in instead of taking responsibility for leaving the car running. I took more than the minute I said I was going to take talking to my friend. Her children were also in her car and my kids wanted to say hi to their friends too. My conversation was delaying our trip to a fun event I had hyped up to them all morning, and they were age-appropriately trying to get me to hurry up so we could have the fun I had promised.

Instead of accepting responsibility for my negligence, I unleashed my rage on them. My apologies to them on the way to the picnic were watered down by "if you wouldn't have done… then I wouldn't have *had to* do that". It was not fair any way you looked at it. They were getting the punishment and blame for my stupidity. I was repeating the same outbursts as an adult I objected to so strongly when I was young.

Accountability and Change

Upon arriving at the campground I was still trying to wind down and my mind was racing. I told the two families we were visiting with what had happened to make us late. They thanked God with me for His protection that my children were still alive and gave me hugs of understanding about the fear and relief. But they also helped me see my over-reaction. Now that the danger was over, they gently pointed out my own responsibility and gave me the Grace I needed to safely own up to my own actions. Once that was out of the way, we were soon were laughing about the pie, effectively putting out the fire of any residual anger. (about half-an-hour too late!) Their support and non-condemning accountability for my actions was exactly what I needed right then!

I was overwhelmed with relief that the worst hadn't happened. Then came the guilt; I started crying. I was so upset with myself for terrorizing my children with my reaction and actions that had put them in such grave danger. The memory of them holding onto each other for dear life during my tirade awakened memories of my own childhood and my father's heavy-handed, verbally magnified "discipline". I called my kids over to me and cradled them in my arms, tearfully apologizing for my horrible outburst and swearing to them that I would never do that again. After repenting to them, we stayed for the fun we originally intended to have, enjoying swimming, hiking and picnicking. (How forgiving little children are, especially toward their parents!)

At the end of the day I brought my kids home and tucked them into their own beds. My daughter came downstairs wanting to talk about what happened. I assured her that everything was okay and she could go back to bed, that I wasn't angry any more. But she still needed to talk about it. She haltingly told me, "Remember when you were yelling at Tom about the footprint in the pie?" I said yes. She tearfully continued, "Well, it wasn't Tom's foot in the pie, it was mine." I wrapped my arms around her, laughing through my tears. I told her how brave it was of her to tell me after my reaction was so horrible earlier and I told her that it was okay, that I wasn't upset about the pie anymore and she could go up to bed again. I carried her up the stairs and tucked her in, assuring her I loved her and everything was fine. I went downstairs but heard her footsteps again a few minutes later. She still had something she needed to get off her chest and that something brought her back down to me.

She again brought up the pie: "Mommy, do you remember how when you were yelling at us there was no pie on my shoe?" I couldn't help it, I grinned and said, no, I hadn't noticed. "Well, the reason there was no pie on my shoe was because I used your scarf in the van to wipe it off...." Her tears began to fall anew as she wailed. "...and it's still out there!" I took her in my arms and laughed and cried and told her it was okay, that I could wash the scarf and I was so proud of her for coming downstairs to tell me this after I had been so angry that day. I gently carried her upstairs again, overwhelmingly grateful that my children were safe. I repeated that everything was fine and I promised I would never go off on them in anger like that again. And I have kept that promise.

What I realize now is that the power struggle to keep my anger controlled instead of dealing with it God's way, (by confessing my inability to manage it and asking for Him to heal me from the lingering after-effects of my own childhood) *increased* my *inability* to resolve the issues that were manifesting this way against my children. I made an inner vow never to be angry with them, never inflicting on them the same distress I felt when I was a child dealing with my parents' anger. What I didn't realize at the time was that anger wasn't the root problem, it was a symptom. Anger was the result of not knowing how to handle conflict and not knowing what to do with the frustration, fear, hurt or disappointment that begins the chain reaction that *turned* into anger.

Instead of seeking the One Who has the answers; I tried to "do it myself." I tried to handle it the way I had been shown as a child, modeled in two different ways by my parents. My Dad's heavy-handedness in situations tended to create more conflict than there was in the beginning. His method was to force your way. The more you force it, the louder you get, the quicker the problem goes your way. That was ineffective at best. No matter how much you hit something or someone, it doesn't fix anything. It just puts more nail holes in the fence. Since his anger resulted in pain for us as kids, as an adult I didn't want to hurt my kids. I resolved to just not get angry, not taking the time to sort that one out fully. I was oblivious to the fact that this is humanly impossible, but I tried it anyway.

As the pendulum swung to the opposite side, I began to be more permissive with my children and avoided conflict. I missed situations that I should have used as opportunities for "teachable moments." I missed opportunities to teach about consequences and instructions about restitution and repentance – which ultimately brings freedom from condemnation, instead of dealing with guilt and repressed anger.

I realize now that the time immediately following my explosion in the minivan was the time-frame my anger began to go "underground". (Not that I was really dealing with my anger that openly before.) I remember when a friend was staying with my husband and me for a while, she commented one day. "Oh for cryin' out loud, will you guys just fight and get it over with? You just snipe and pick at one another and never just say what's bothering you!" That observation was like a glass of cold water, snapping us out of a clueless state, unaware of that particular dynamic in our relationship! Her outside perspective helped us to see things clearer. Old habits die hard and it's sometimes easier to avoid addressing issues. We repress and ignore them in our busy lives rather than say the uncomfortable, "Let's Talk". The seed was planted by her comment that helped us recognize our avoidance patterns.

Looking back I can see that each time a traumatic incident happened that was not sufficiently dealt with, I stuffed it, trying to act like it didn't matter or that with enough self-control I could go on and just do better next time. I began to measure and meter out my words carefully, pausing between words and phrases to insure I didn't lose control of my voice volume and content. I did this partly to make sure I explained my objections rationally and to insure the person I was talking to would accept what I was saying and secondly to sensor myself from profanity. (a godly goal that, when achieved, gave me the opportunity for instruction.)

One way I found to stop myself from swearing was to substitute nonsensical syllables strung together. That allowed me to let something short out in that moment, without teaching my kids words I didn't want them to hear from me – and have to punish them for saying later! The trouble was I ended up sounding a little like Yosemite Sam. Which as alternatives go, ended up being pretty funny. ☺

My anger was diffused and the kids understood they had crossed a behavior line, or that I had stubbed my toe or something, without me being a source of egg-shell walking fear. Soon we were all laughing. It was a more preferable outcome to previous reactions! I substituted "Gosh" for "God" in anything closely resembling those swears and took the opportunity to explain to my children we can't use God's name in vain when we get surprised or angry, because His name is so special. It was a great teaching opportunity and made it much easier to break harmful speech habits when I found substitutes for things I didn't want to *say* anymore.

So I also began looking for alternatives to *behavior* patterns that I wanted to break. I needed help. I knew I needed to change how I responded, but thought I had nowhere to turn that wouldn't cost me lots of money a struggling young family didn't have. I went to several counseling sessions to get me through some really trying periods here and there, but even with medical insurance, counseling fees add up quick! I found additional help in friends, referrals from books they were reading on the same thing, other families I knew in church, and in my Bible. Parenting and marriage Bible studies – especially studies that focused on personal accountability – were very helpful. The study that helped me the most was Beth Moore's "Breaking Free, Making Liberty in Christ a Reality in Life". Her chapter on generational sin hit this nail right on the head and the way the whole study addressed key points in my life started my pursuit of right living and faith in earnest.

James Dobson (www.focusonthefamily.com/parenting) and Kevin Leman (www.drleman.com) have wonderful parenting resources that teach the difference between punishment and discipline – an emphasis on training and instruction instead of retaliation. Two of their books "The Strong Willed Child" (Dobson) and "How to Make Your Child Mind Without Losing Yours" (Leman) are great starting points to give parents guidance on how to raise children according to their own personalities. Cynthia Tobias also has great material on "Surviving the Strong Willed Child", "You Can't Make Me! (But I Can Be Persuaded)" and "Every Child Can Succeed" about learning how to teach our children with different learning styles in mind, without breaking their spirits and doing damage to their perceptions of God in the process! I did not have these books when my children were small but value them now.

There is a difference between agreed upon consequences for disobedient behavior while training and communicating appropriate behavior... and a swift, punitive reaction toward our children when they do things that irritate us or embarrass us. Unfortunately, most of us have been guilty of the latter, myself included. Because of my dad's heavy-handedness in demanding obedience, my impression of God was impacted negatively and it took many years for me to understand I could trust Him as strong protector, abundant provider, powerful defender, and tender comforter, instead of just a punitive law-giver. Early negative examples are hard to overcome sometimes. But we don't have to simply continue the path that has been modeled to us earlier in life; we have choices. Now I know better and run to Him when I need help. I have learned new ways of dealing with the unexpected – and to anticipate or prepare for things I've never dealt with before by relying on others who have.

In re-training myself to respond differently, I incorporated what I was learning about not using "never" and "always" statements (like "you never listen!" or "you're always making a mess!"), taking responsibility for my own behavior and being clear in my expectations. I was being very careful to make sure my family understood what else was going through my mind, that helped me arrive at the request I was making or boundary I was enforcing. But it took so long to get there that usually the other person (adult and child alike) "tuned me out."

I took too much time for the "set up" before saying what I needed or wanted at the moment. My husband calls it "taking the long way around the barn." When the situation would not change and I didn't get to the goal I was looking for, the frustration I felt would build because I had no idea how else to get the results I wanted. (I am still working on trying to be more concise, coming up with a "Readers' Digest version" of what I want to say!)

I heard I should redirect the anger I was feeling constructively, so that my "accomplishment drive" could be satisfied in this somehow. When I would get frustrated about something, I would begin to clean. Sometimes I would do one room. By the time that was done, I was back in control. But if it was a bigger issue or if it was something I couldn't resolve on my own, the whole house was my target. I was trying to work off the negative energy that needed a volcanic eruption as all that emotional lava was building in me.

I reasoned that by cleaning or doing yard work, at least I was putting my time and the energy to good use. But I have learned that no matter how clean my house got, without using principles of "taking every thought captive" in my mind while I was cleaning, I did nothing to diffuse the generation of more junk and harmful emotions. Now I understand that I first need to work the frustrations out with God to let Him "create a Way (in Him) where there is no way (in me)." Psalm 51:10 says, "Create in me a clean heart, O God and renew a right, persevering and steadfast spirit within me."

One day recently we were all sitting around the living room laughing about family stories, when one of my kids said something about the house needing cleaning before a party we were going to have and one of them said, "No problem! Just get Mom mad, the house will be spotless in a few hours!" I had mistakenly thought that it was some kind of secret! They knew. It stung a little when they said it, but it made me realize my past behavior is still having an impact on them. I'm praying for healing – for all of us.

The Importance of Healing

While watching Beth Moore on Life Today one morning, she shared a story she read in Gilda Radner's book, "It's Always Something". When Gilda was a young girl, her pregnant dog had an accident with the family's lawn mower and her back legs were mutilated beyond repair. When they brought her to the vet to try to have her fixed up, the vet told them that he could stitch up the wounds, but her legs were not fixable. He assured the family that she could still have the puppies, that they were uninjured and that the momma dog would learn to get along without her legs. Sure enough, as the wounded area healed up, the momma dog would walk forward with her two front legs and them skooch up and hop her back end forward everywhere she went, not bothered at all by the new way she had to get around. She said that to their amazement, the puppies were born perfectly healthy and physically unaffected by their momma's injuries. But when they were learning to walk, even though they had four perfectly developed legs, *"they learned to walk just like her!"* At this point I got a huge lump in my throat as Beth Moore recounted what went through her mind when *her* daughter was born.

She told how, after everyone had left and visiting hours were over, she was alone with her new-born daughter. Beth started un-wrapping her to see her little toes and fingers. With hushed tones and a sense of overwhelming urgency, she recalled how she asked God how something so beautiful and so perfect could have come from her, as broken and damaged as she felt. Remembering the things that had happened to her when she was younger and the resulting self-destructive choices she made as a young woman, she was overtaken by a feeling of intense fear and a desperate heart-cry: "Please! God! Don't let my past affect this perfect little one!" She told how she became desperate to do anything she could to make sure the effects of her past would not be passed down to her children! She called out to God to do whatever He needed to do to her and in her to keep that from happening. I am sure there was not a dry eye within hearing distance of this story, either in the studio audience where they were filming, or in countless Bible studies and living rooms across the country when it was later broadcast. Many of us have cried out with that same heartfelt appeal for our own personal situations.

I began to wish I had "determined" long ago to have my own personal quiet times with God, letting Him wash all this junk out of my heart His Way as I finally do today. The 'accuser of the brethren' kicked in at that moment, working overtime to follow through with his initial temptations and schemes, with the 1-2 punch of condemnation. The devil uses every opportunity to drive a wedge of self-recrimination and guilt, blame and resentment between us and other people – he thrives on it! But God simply wants to help us to stand up and let Him dust us off while He tells us how dearly He loves us and reminds us that His mercies "are new every morning".[29]

I can't do anything now about the choices and decisions I made when my marriage was new, my children were young nor about things that happened last year or even last week. They are all in the past and cannot be taken back. But I can confess those things as God instructs us to. He says that "if we confess our sins, He is faithful and just to forgive us our sins and to cleanse us from all unrighteousness".[30] I can confess my errors, lack of obedience to God's promptings, avoidance, fear, willful ignorance and other things falling into the category of "everything that does not come from faith."[31]

I can lean heavily on God's Grace to teach me not to deflect my focus to others' infractions and missteps. I can release it to the past as a bad memory that I will learn from, but will not hold me back. I can give the grace I want to receive to others when I feel slighted by their words or actions, and then I can move on with a peaceful heart. I want to enjoy the freedom, peace and rest promised in God's word and to give those same benefits to others in my life!

My heart-cry now is to leave the legacy of the latter years of my life as a beacon of hope and freedom to my children who are unintended recipients of my pre-healed walk with God. Like Gilda Radner's puppies, my children have witnessed a drag-and-hop faith – knowing there is faith and believing in God, but not taking the opportunities available in His power for change and victory.[32]

I want so much for them to learn to walk with Jesus without my spiritual "disabilities!" Fear tries to step in and show me a picture of the future without the hope of God's work in them. But I see the deception of that now. I can celebrate progress. And when I find the slightest change, I can allow that to reinforce my hope. I need to remember the opportunity that comes with past failures – my own and others'. When we turn the responsibility for redemption of these failures over to God, we are set free from trying to initiate changes that are not ours to make. It is far better to cooperate with His direction to make progress. Not getting it all right now does not mean we won't get it right ever. It's all about attitude.

It is very interesting to me that when confronted with multiple failures in his attempts at inventing, Thomas Edison was undeterred by his critics. When jeered at for the numerous failures he experienced and their assertions that developing an incandescent light bulb was all a waste of time, he replied, "I have not failed 700 times. I have not failed once. I have succeeded in proving that those 700 ways will not work. When I have eliminated the ways that will not work, I will find the way that will work." [33] No one remembers who his critics were now – but Thomas Alva Edison will always be known as the father of the incandescent light bulb. He literally lit up the room! With that kind of optimistic perspective on any situation, we too can move on from our own failures and missteps and allow others that same Grace for theirs. We can each advance hopefully and expectantly into our future, in freedom, and with God's help we can light up our own corner of the world.

Little Victories

Last year my husband and I were preparing to get some wood ready for heating our house. It was January and we had less than a cord split and ready to burn. We used the tractor to drag out some trees we felled earlier in the year and got ready to use the chain saw to cut them up. The saw flooded. So while waiting for the flood to dissipate we dragged a couple more logs out. It flooded again. A third drag, this time from the big, seasoned log pile. No "go" on starting the saw, it needed tuning before we could use it.

Going back to the house and seeing how little we had left with so much more winter weather still ahead of us, I started getting edgy. Not an overt panic, just an undercurrent of uneasiness I wanted to avoid. With each attempt to distract myself from what I was feeling, the uneasiness grew. I didn't face it, identify it and deal with it. I substituted something else to do. I reasoned that I still needed to clean the house (my original plan for the morning), so I got out the vacuum cleaner and mop and cleaned the downstairs. It took effort to stay on-task with this as yet undefined emotion eating away at the edges of my consciousness, but I kept going.

The usual lift I get from the accomplishment of a job well done was totally lost in the moment. When I went upstairs, I was just more disagreeable and felt overwhelmed by how much was still left undone and how little time I had to do it all. Instead of empowering me, I felt drained and paralyzed. What should I do next? The Christmas tree still needed to be taken down, but the last thing I wanted to do at that moment was taking on the wrapping and storage of each of those little ornaments!

Steve looked over at me and asked me why I looked sad — or was it fearful? He couldn't tell which, but he could see something was wrong. I said no, I wasn't sad and told him about too much to do and not enough time to do it all. He understood that predicament well. But it went deeper than that. I started to do a self-diagnostic and got honest — to a point. I told him I felt frustrated that there was so little wood and that we couldn't do anything about it that morning with the saw acting up. He assured me that he would take care of it on Monday when I was at work and we would be good to go. He suggested since I had already cleaned the downstairs and worked with the tractor with him in the morning, that I could just sit and enjoy a movie with him. I left it at that, curling up next to him on the couch, and within a half-an-hour, I was taking a much needed nap while he watched TV and read. The New Years' activities had left both of us sleep-deprived from the previous couple days and it was a much needed refresher.

It wasn't until the next morning, two seconds after hitting my knees for my "Thank you for this day..." prayer to God that I realized I had missed the critical point and the prescription for what I had semi-diagnosed as "uneasiness" the day before. The verse that popped into my mind once I began my morning prayers was "Be anxious for nothing, but in everything by prayer and supplication, with thanksgiving, let your requests be made known to God, and the peace of God, which surpasses all understanding, will guard your hearts and minds through Christ Jesus."[34] I *was* scared. Steve saw it in my eyes that afternoon, but I missed the symptoms. If I had faced the truth of it the day before, I would have seen it. All I needed to do was go to God myself right when it started and ask Him!

I was afraid of running out of wood for the woodstove for the rest of the winter, worried about our depleted supply. Instead of facing that fact and turning to God for the confident reminder that He would, of course, provide what we needed when we needed it, I distracted myself with "busy work". Yes, it was good to change what I was doing when the first option didn't pan out. Yes, it was good to take a break and a nap and enjoy the time with Steve afterwards. But leaving the fear behind the frustration untreated tainted the afternoon. In that moment on my knees, I realized I had skipped a couple necessary steps: turning my fears over to God, asking Him for the provision of wood we needed and resting in the peace that He would make it happen in time for our need. THEN, moving on to cleaning the downstairs and the nap and time with Steve would have been more enjoyable instead of the aforementioned "fret-fest".

But even in this arm-chair quarterback review of the day before, there was victory. I acknowledged that in the past, feeling this same frustration and fear would have mushroom-clouded into accusations and blame-shifting. I could have let my frustrations explode into anger about other things and directed the fallout toward Steve or one of the kids about the causes for not being able to do what we were "supposed to be doing." I could have transferred it through the similar emotional signatures of other events stored in my memory, to some completely different situation entirely, leaving us all confused as to "where the heck did THAT come from?" I was so happy to be able to see the progress in that moment instead of beating myself up in self-condemnation again!

I am learning to go by God's direction instead of my own feelings in many things. It definitely works out better that way instead of being led around by the nose after being offended. I am beginning each day with a new resolve to start with a clean slate – and give other people that same gift - watching what happens when I don't have all the past baggage tripping me up. Wow! I get a lot more done without that knot in my stomach from unreasonable expectations! Apprehension and past offenses aren't clogging up the pipeline of appreciation or the sense of adventure that each day can hold!

I am setting the goal for myself to help at least one other person - <u>without an expectation of pay-back or feeling of indebtedness!</u> Each day I can feel the chains of, "you-owe-me" falling off as I lean in close to God to keep those old attitudes from climbing back into and onto me again! I've done it the wrong way for so long, I couldn't see that was part of the mix. It feels natural to keep the impatience and fear and it's hard to shrug it off at first.   But when I allow Love to burn off that junk - *recognizing it as* junk and throwing it as far away from me as I can in prayer and faith in God's protection and provision - it is a wonderful freedom! I want to feel that way more each day until the old, stressed, habits die of neglect! I want to forgive others and prayerfully they will forgive me for the harm I did to them when they were close enough to get fall-out from my "getting out of the pit" process!

I am gaining an increasing appreciation for the Apostle James' instruction to "confess your sins to each other and pray for each other so that you may be healed."[35] As my many teachers have shared their personal struggles with me, it helps pave a way of resolution through the jungle of my life. As I share my struggles and victories with you, we are all beneficiaries of a lighter load. Cares and difficulties shared, "one to another", fall away in the light of God's unconditional Love. Experience the healing this verse promises! Trust that the same Healer Who is working in me to get rid of my unnecessary burdens will also repair the damage done (willfully or in ignorance) to and in you as you allow Him entry into your heart.

The anticipation of the adventure can begin anew each day as we each learn how to build up one another, encourage one another and protect one another! The words of a beautiful song cheer us on... There is now no condemnation, there is now no separation, if the Son has set me free, then I am free, forever FREE!

I am making progress – that tether of anger, holding me to the ground is being uprooted. I can hardly wait to see what else God has in store as I cooperate with Him to get that thing off me once and for all! This little elephant is ready to fly!

Footnotes

[1] Prov. 15:13 (amp)

[2] Dan. chap. 7, Neh. chap. 5

[3] 1 Sam. chap. 1

[4] Exo. chap. 35

[5] Ruth chap. 1

[6] 1 Sam. chap. 18

[7] Prov. 25:23b (amp)

[8] Ruth 4:14-17

[9] Eccl. 8:1b (amp)

[10] Phil. 4:13

[11] "Building an Emotionally Healthy Marriage" by Jimmy Evans, www.Marriagetoday.org

[12] Rom. 12:17a (NIV 1984)

[13] Psalm 3:3 (amp)

[14]Jeremiah 29:11 (NIV 1984)

[15] Philippians 3:13-14 (NIV 1984)

[16]Hebrews 12:11 (amp)

[17] Beth Moore, teaching on Distraction and Destruction on Life
Today http://lifetoday.org/video//?search=Beth%20Moore

[18] "Who Switched Off My Brain" by Dr. Caroline Leaf

[19] Prov. 17:22 (NIV)

[20] "The Hurt Pocket" by Jimmy Evans

[21] Ibid

[22]Ibid

[23] Rom. 8:37 (amp)

[24] Prov. 29:11 (amp)

[25] Ps. 4:4 (amp)

[26] Eph. 4:26 (NIV 1984)

[27] 2 Cor. 10:5 (NIV)

[28] 1 Pet. 5:9 (amp)

[29] Lam. 3:23 (NIV)

[30] 1 John 1:9 (NKJV)

[31] Rom. 14:23 (NIV)

[32] 1 Cor. 15:58, Eph. 3:16-19 (amp)

[33] http://www.fadedgiant.net/html/edison_thomas_alva_quotes.htm

[34] Phil. 4:6-7 (NKJV)

[35] Jas. 5:16 (NIV)

Suggested Resources

"The DNA of Relationships" by Dr Gary Smalley

"The Bait of Satan" by John Bevere

"Me and My Big Mouth" by Joyce Meyer

"Big Girls Don't Whine" by Jan Silvious

"Confronting Without Offending" by Deborah Pegues

"Boundaries" by Dr Henry Cloud and Dr John Townsend

"Battlefield of the Mind" by Joyce Meyer

"Fight Like a Girl" by Lisa Bevere

"Wild at Heart" by John Eldgredge

"Get Out of That Pit!" by Beth Moore

Chapter 5

Encourage Yourself in the Lord

"David was greatly distressed...but David encouraged and strengthened himself in the Lord his God."

1 Samuel 30:6

While we all need training in discovering there is "a time to be silent and a time to speak" [1], there is nothing inherently wrong with the speaking. God **gave** us the gift of speech and one of the joys (and challenges!) in life is learning to put it to good use. As we've just seen, the key to using your *words* beneficially is monitoring and adjusting your *thoughts*. Instead of being pushed around by your emotions, you have the more productive option of training yourself to follow Paul's instruction to the Corinthians to "take every thought captive" [2] and become a sentinel of your own thought life.

Life can be hard and there is much room for disappointment. When you are tired or disappointed, you are much more susceptible to thoughts that whip you up into a frenzy or drag you down further into a pit of despair. You don't have to allow every thought that pops into your head free reign in there!

Let's be blunt. Some thoughts are worth considering, and some need to be taken out like the trash they are. Think about it: when you first put garbage in a container, it's not too bad. I mean, it IS garbage, but it's manageable. If you take it out right away, there's no smell, no problem. But if you leave it in there a while, it starts to decompose. As more time goes by, it starts to liquefy and run into other things. The smells blend together in a stomach-turning odor that attracts flies. Leave it there a while more and a few flies become dozens. If you leave it there still longer, the flies reproduce and soon you've got maggots crawling around in there. And the longer you wait, the stinkier and more putrid it gets and the harder it is to get rid of. It's the same with trashy thoughts. It doesn't stay in the can very long without festering into a bigger mess.

Trashy thinking yields trashy talk. The tendency to repeat these thoughts, leads to giving them an outlet in your words. As the words reinforce your negative thoughts and produce more words, they soon turn into actions. The actions build up as they are repeated and become habits. These habits become the evidence of your character. A trashy character yields a trashy reputation and a trashy life. A trashy life is not good for you, or anyone you care about. Trashy thoughts are a LOT easier to get rid of than the progression to words, actions, habits, character and life that follows it. If you discover specific thoughts aren't leading you in a positive direction, get rid of them as soon as possible!

If you've already accumulated some trashy thoughts, words and actions and you want to get rid of the garbage, don't despair – you can rescue your habits, character and life beginning today. Don't cover it up. Start by taking out the trash and cleaning the can!

James 1:21 says, "... get rid of all uncleanness and the rampant outgrowth of wickedness, and in a humble (gentle, modest) spirit receive *and* welcome the Word which implanted *and* rooted [in your hearts] contains the power to save your souls." How do you decide what is "unclean" and "wicked"?

Paul is a great help! In Ephesians chapter 4, verses 29-32, he shows us both what to get rid of AND how to "clean out the can" – replacing it with good stuff: "Let no foul *or* polluting language, *nor* evil word *nor* unwholesome *or* worthless talk [ever] come out of your mouth, but only such [speech] as is good *and* beneficial to the spiritual progress of others, as is fitting to the need *and* the occasion, that it may be a blessing *and* give grace (God's favor) to those who hear it... Let all bitterness and indignation *and* wrath (passion, rage, bad temper) and resentment (anger, animosity) and quarreling (brawling, clamor, contention) and slander (evil-speaking, abusive or blasphemous language) be banished from you, with all malice (spite, ill will, or baseness of any kind). And become useful *and* helpful *and* kind to one another, tenderhearted (compassionate, understanding, loving-hearted), forgiving one another [readily and freely], as God in Christ forgave you." Sounds like a tall order!

But we have more help from Paul. As we've seen before, Philippians 4 tells us we can choose to think in ways that replaces the trash with good things that encourages us and others. 1 Corinthians 13, the "love chapter", is another place we can pick up great advice on what thoughts can stay and what thoughts should go. For example, is what you're thinking kind? Is it gentle? Is it based on believing the best about the other person? If not, it's probably time to take it captive and replace it with something constructive in an attitude of godly resolution instead of acting on accusation. Accusation is satan's territory – and he doesn't need any help from us!

It's not rocket science; it's practical common sense - something we can even teach our children to do with age-appropriate instruction. Like Thumper in the classic Disney movie "Bambi" put it so very eloquently long ago: "If you can't say somethin' nice, don't say nothin' at all!"[3] The difficulty in putting this into action is if you're depending on your own self-control to keep from speaking nasty when you are habitually thinking nasty, your success rate will not be very high. Jesus taught: "For out of the fullness (the overflow, the superabundance) of the heart the mouth speaks."[4] If you aren't thinkin' something nice, you'll soon be saying something that's not nice. That's what's in your heart if you're dwelling on all those past offenses. Look for something positive to think about. Keep at it until your attention is refocused in a more positive direction - and your words will follow!

It is not easy to do when you're in the middle of an emotional mess, but it is a simple tactic that anyone can employ to lift their view beyond the immediate difficulty. You can't stay depressed, angry, fearful or discouraged for long if you start flooding your mind and heart with positive, honorable, pure, lovely, kind, excellent and praise-worthy thoughts. Using this strategy will empower us with "the joy of the LORD" that we are told very plainly "is [our] strength".[5]

Trust in the Lord

Part of the problem lies in not wanting to think well of someone you are currently upset with! We often feel so justified in our hard feelings. Getting to the point that you default to "believing the best" and "enduring all things"[6] takes work. Try ignoring the current situation just long enough to seek a peek at the end goal. How do you want to feel in the next hour? Stomach still knotted and a headache building, or enjoying the day? What about next week or next month? Frustrated or joyful? You have the power to get to either destination by what you choose to think about next. If you eventually want to have a constructive working relationship, a better rapport, a deeper level of trust, or a loving relationship with that person, ditch the justification and give them the level of respect, consideration, courtesy, etc. you eventually want to receive from them.

Contrariwise, if you want to hold onto your justification and frustration, continue to approach each interaction with suspicion, accusation and antagonism. Then any conversation can be a source of additional conflict and distrust by repeatedly anticipating an adversarial attitude. Either approach – toward the negative or the positive – becomes a habit that reinforces itself. You choose which one you foster by determining which way you process each interaction. The one you choose most often becomes your "default" setting.

You can choose to believe the action you are tempted to take offense to is either intentionally destructive or just a simple misunderstanding. Based on that step, you can withdraw and/or retaliate - or make allowances and respond in kind ways. Even if the other person verifies their intent and you can see a harmful pattern of interaction between the two of you, you can still choose the high road.

You determine the tone of your relationships with everyone around you by your choices. Like Paul directed us in Romans 12:17-18: Repay no one evil for evil, but take thought for what is honest *and* proper *and* noble [aiming to be above reproach] in the sight of everyone. If possible, as far as it depends on you, live at peace with everyone."

Everyone? Really? Even the people who seem to enjoy the conflict? That seems like a pretty lofty goal to accomplish alone. It is – but we aren't. ☺ The previous verses we looked at in Ephesians 4 – specifically verse 32 - shows us our motivation for such a big undertaking: "And become useful *and* helpful *and* kind to one another, tenderhearted (compassionate, understanding, loving-hearted), forgiving one another [readily and freely], as God in Christ forgave you." Not as they forgave us the last time we did something against them, not as we forgave them the last 6 times, but "as God in Christ forgave you".

That's a much higher standard to meet. But God's point is clear: He has forgiven more from us than we can recall – and it cost Him more than we can imagine. God, Who created us, Who loves us, Who gave His all to save us from hell, in His own unfathomably sacrificial love for us, traded our sin and degradation for His perfectness and righteousness. By giving up His own Son for us in a particularly gruesome fashion, He adopted us. In the middle of all this pain, purposely inflicted by jealous, insecure men with political and religious authority, He chose to speak words of Grace instead of retaliation from the cross in Luke 24:34: "Father, forgive them for they know not what they are doing."

That's how we are supposed to forgive other people. Like I said, it's a lofty goal. Impossible to reach on our own, with our emotions screaming inside us how "unfair" it all is. But we are not alone in reaching that goal. God Himself walks us through every difficulty to help us truly reach forgiveness of others. All we have to do in the beginning of the journey is pray to be *willing* to forgive. He takes it from there.

This principle works not only in our horizontal relationships with people, but also in our vertical relationship with God. How is that possible? Forgiveness is a choice to let go of the offenses and hurts we've held against others for what they've "done to us", right? What if the one we need to forgive is God? What if the offense we're taking is against Him for the difficulties we're in and the things God is "allowing to happen" to us or to the people we love? Let's be real here. We accept accusations against God all the time – like we saw in the previous chapters, the enemy accuses in every direction, including God to us. The same steps work no matter who you need to forgive.

We can't succeed in this task without His help. We need to "encourage ourselves in the Lord". Let's see how this works in action.

Something happens that we don't understand: a tragedy, a loss, or some other difficulty. We may have a basic understanding that God is in control, even though we might not be able to point to chapter or verse for proof. We have a choice to believe the best, that the reasons God has for allowing a painful or difficult situation is for our ultimate good, like He said, or we can believe that He's just being mean or careless concerning us. Based on whichever assumption or accusation we choose to believe, we either lean into Him for the strength to get through it, trusting His good intentions, that He has "a good plan for us"[7] and will provide us with the necessary tools to navigate the opportunity successfully, or we could pull back and scream and swear and distance ourselves from Him, to prove we don't need Him or His guidance to live through it. We "wing it" and hope for better times soon.

When and if we choose the former way of dealing with life's challenges, and lean into Him for help, we find He is eagerly waiting to dispense the ways and means for victory and the know-how to use them with amazing results, even in the worst possible situations. That's Grace in action. The victories on the other side of each challenge increase the likelihood that when faced with the next, we will "believe the best" about Him and "endure all things" reasonably certain that He is the answer to the challenge, not the cause of harm and destruction in our lives. This affinity to positive thoughts in His direction builds trust and our anticipation of His response for good in the next opportunity we have for belief - or doubt – even in familiar situations.

But what if we don't have the advantage of familiar territory? What if we're facing something we've never faced before? We can still choose to trust His good intentions toward us. This is by no means something I claim to be an expert in – I am still definitely growing in this area. But we can choose to walk through even unfamiliar circumstances holding tightly to God's hand, believing He is for us, not against us, and make amazing progress in places and situations we've never been before.

He has big shoulders, He can handle your raw, unvarnished questions and emotions – and He can help you shed the weight of the turmoil you're in. First, ask Him for the *willingness* to process your understanding of this situation with Him. He will. Then ask Him for the ability. He does that too – with a love deeper than anyone can measure! Hebrews 4:16 tells us we can "come boldly to the throne of grace, that we may obtain mercy and find grace to help in time of need." He WILL meet that need!

If we recognize the sacrifice of His Son on the cross as the pinnacle of His selflessness towards us, then we can re-interpret any accusation that comes about the alleged negligence or retribution of God through that filter. That alone should give us reason enough to trust His beneficent intentions toward us, even if we can't see the whys behind some of the difficult things we are dealing with. He's already proven His heart and good intentions toward us. He will bring us to a place of acceptance and healing as we get to know Him, seek understanding and find Him faithful in all of it!

With Him by our side, acknowledging all He is doing for us, walking us through forgiveness in our relationship with Him, then we can readily apply those principles in our horizontal relationships! How can we not give other people the same consideration and deference He continually offers us? Forgiving others sets us free from the pain and sets us up for amazing things – even if there are struggles along the way. I'm not belittling the struggle – far from it! I'm saying God is bigger and better than the difficulty and WILL show you a higher, nobler way of responding to down-right horrible circumstances!

Check out the story of Joseph some time. His older brothers couldn't stand him because he was daddy's favorite and they decided to get rid of him. In Genesis 37, instead of killing him, they decide to sell him into slavery and make a few bucks in the process. This poor kid pleads with them while he's being dragged down the road by slave traders, never to see his home again. Years and chapters go by. The only thing we know about this time in his life is that he is promoted from slave to overseer in an Egyptian official's home because he fulfills his duties with excellence, which gets the appreciation of his new master.

Someone can surmise that the religious training and moral character of this boy began at a very early age for him to take on an attitude of excellence even in this horrible situation. He had options on how to act, and he chose to roll up his sleeves and do everything well, regardless of his circumstances. Well, this gets the attention and gains the trust of his new master, who puts him in charge of everything in his house. Unfortunately, his good looks (and arguably great body from all that manual labor) attract the attention of his master's wife, too. Not willing to commit this sin against his master or his God, he resists her repeated suggestions and finally flees when she manipulates the situation and intensifies her advances. Insulted by his refusal, the wife retaliates. Joseph is accused of attempted rape, thrown in prison and left for dead.

I'm pretty certain this would make me bitter...and vocal. I probably would not have maintained the amazing attitude of trust in God and commitment to excellence that Joseph displays here. He decides to become the model prisoner – helping others and his jailer – and ends up being put in charge of the people there! The story follows him through Genesis 40 with more betrayal, more prison time, and a continued display of service and excellence without complaint from Joseph. Even from his jail cell, he is noticed for his integrity. By Genesis 41, he's in charge of all Egypt and all the people in surrounding nations are surviving a multi-nation famine because of his prudent management of the crops in one country. Wow!

But wait – he must have been harboring some kind of blame or hard feelings, right? He just didn't *have the chance* to pay any of his brothers back for their betrayal and accusation, right? In classic, God-style, what-goes-around-comes-around fashion, guess who shows up to buy food from their "little brother"? Does Joseph turn them away? Does he sell them as slaves and return their lack of compassion?

No. In fact, he gives them the food for nothing, sending them back home with not only the grain, but the purchase price still in their sacks (unbeknownst to them)! When they return to Egypt with double the money for the second load of food, they get arrested for stealing (which they didn't) and begin to reason between themselves that the trouble they're in now *must be* God's pay-back for what they did to Joseph. Joseph, overhears their regretful speculation and he begins to cry. He yells at all the Egyptians to leave the room and reveals his true identity to his brothers. He then brings all the family to Goshen to feed them throughout the famine, and is finally reunited with his father and little brother. It looks like a happy ending - but it gets even better.

His brothers evidently don't trust his graciousness and forgiveness – guilt is still condemning their hearts years later when their father dies and they are gripped once again with fear. Will he retaliate now that their father isn't around to see his vengeance? Joseph shows his true colors when they come to him begging for their lives and the lives of their children after their father's funeral.

Joseph knows full well what their original intent was, but that does not determine his response to them. He utters some of the most gracious words in the Old Testament and throughout history: "But Joseph said to them, 'Don't be afraid. Am I in the place of God? You intended to harm me, but God intended it for good to accomplish what is now being done, the saving of many lives. So then, don't be afraid. I will provide for you and your children' and he reassured them and spoke kindly to them."[8]

Talk about keeping a good attitude! I can guarantee he couldn't have been so gracious if his heart was clogged up with all kinds of bitterness and resentment stewing in his thoughts all those years over what they'd done to him. At some point early on in his life, Joseph made a decision not to harbor ill-feelings and trusted that even though he didn't understand why he'd gone through so much garbage, God had a plan to make everything he was going through worth the effort. He still does.

So what will our response be when we know others meant to harm us? Will we choose to trust God with the outcome? If He allowed these painful things to happen instead of intervening, can we choose to accept both the promotions and the tragedies and allow God to use them for "the saving of many". Trusting God enables us to do amazing things – even in painful circumstances!

Take Peter for example. The man *walked on water!* People usually focus on the dip he took in the ocean by taking his focus off Jesus when he noticed how boisterous and threatening waves were. But don't lose sight of the fact *he got out of the boat*. He followed the invitation to join Jesus on the waves, and he walked on the water! He TRUSTED Jesus. We are capable of walking on the waves of some pretty intense storms too – as long as we keep our focus on the One Who *controls* the wind and waves. It's a matter of trust. Again, I can share I am no expert in this either. Knowing something deep in your soul and doing it in the moment of trial are two totally different things! But when we do, it's AMAZING!

Trusting that God knows what He's doing even when we KNOW we don't have a clue can be so hard sometimes! No matter how far I get in my walk with God, there are situations when times of uncertainty happen, when the intensity of the fear (or other strong emotions) that attacks me from left field still surprises me. I don't know why. I seem to fall apart momentarily, panicking over things that later seem so inconsequential when I compare them to the greatness of my God and His love for me!

In Proverbs 3:25 we are commanded, "Do not be afraid of sudden fear, nor of the onslaught of the wicked when it comes; For the LORD will be your confidence and will keep your foot from being caught." I am grateful that I am much quicker to recognize opportunities to apply this thought and to reject the rising panic (or anger) sooner than at previous times in my life. Running straight to God, knowing He is faithful to His Word and will reveal the next steps on the path shortly, is the best antidote to the poison of fear! Let me explain using a situation that happened earlier.

Unexpected Situations

One day I got a call from one of my best friends - who happened to work as my "relief" at the local Post Office for my first five years as Postmaster. She worked every Saturday morning and on days during the week that I needed to be out of the office. When I decided to apply for this job 5 years before, others warned me against it and said I would never be able to find someone who would be willing to work such crazy and unpredictable hours (4 hours one week and 44 hours the next) all for $9.00 per hour. At the time I laughed and said that I already had someone in mind. Deb is a home-schooling mom who lives about ¾ of a mile from the Post Office and didn't care about only getting 4 hours work once a week. If she didn't get more hours, she was plenty occupied with her children's home-schooling, a nursing home ministry one day a month, various music lessons and tutoring. But if I needed to call her in, she appreciated the extra funds that more hours provided.

It was a perfect fit for both of us. The fact we were friends to start with and shared our faith and priorities in life was a bonus. It helped to smooth over the times that expectations for what needed to happen in the office conflicted with both of our family plans. God provided for those situations by giving me two other people I could borrow from other offices for coverage when Deb and I both had plans of the same day. It was a temporary fix, but it worked for a while.

In the ensuing months, as our families changed and grew, my absences increased in frequency and I had begun to question my ability to take more than 1 or 2 days off at a time. My daughter's family was living in Oregon and my son's family was growing. Grandchild number 3 was expected in a few short months. I had jury duty scheduled and a postal-related convention in a month and a half. I was increasingly finding myself in situations that I needed to be away – sometimes unexpectedly - and due to similar happenings in her family, so did Deb.

Around the same time, I had a bad dream one morning. In the dream, I was to host a dinner at my house. It was already dark outside and the guests were beginning to arrive. I hadn't done the cleaning, gotten the extra table and chairs out of the garage or even purchased the food! I asked my son to please run to the store to get the food while I attempted to get into the garage and enlist our guests' help to retrieve the extra table which still needed to be wiped down.

As I woke up, the word ringing through my head was, "Prepare! You need to do what you can *now* to prepare for what is coming!" This is not a new admonition for me, but the urgency of it this morning contained a new intensity that I had not previously felt. This urgency added to prior lessons I was learning from the parable of the ten virgins during my quiet times.

In Matthew, chapter 25, five virgins were wise and prepared and were welcomed into the wedding feast and five were foolish and unprepared and lost out on being wed to the King! The intensity of the emotion that lingered after that dream drew me to my loft with certain anticipation that God was going to tell me something really important this morning.

I went upstairs like I usually do for my morning reading and computer time, listening to Life Today, Joyce Meyer and others. The teaching and references I "just happened to be getting" (like my son would note: LOL!) were all about preparation and not just winging it, but making a *specific* effort to do what is necessary to get the things we need ahead of time. Reminders that once properly equipped, God can use the Holy Spirit living in us to "bring to your remembrance everything [He has] told you"[9] and that we will "[...never be at a loss] to know how you ought to answer anyone [who puts a question to you]"[10] along with admonitions to – "do it courteously and respectfully"[11] were impressed on me in a way I can't accurately describe. These thoughts seemed to be aimed somehow toward new circumstances about work scheduling, but I was unsure of what one thing had to do with the other.

Trust or Fear?

I went to work that day and received a phone call from Deb requesting four Saturdays in May off so she and her family could do foster care classes to prepare for the next ministry God had led them to – taking in little ones who needed a stable home life as foster children. She excitedly explained how there was a room in her house that needed cleaning for a while and out of the blue, she just decided to start it the day before. She had only intended to begin it, work on it for a couple hours and then move onto something else. But once she got started she couldn't let it go. She kept at it until everything was sorted, containerized and the room ready to use. Then her voice got even more excited as she told me that just a little while after she had finished the room, she received a phone call from the foster care program, wanting to schedule a home inspection and begin the process of certification. She said she was so grateful that she had already tackled the room and that, if she had not done so, she probably would have put the woman off for later and missed the beginning of this class. She realized she had been motivated by an unseen Hand to keep at it. Now she was prepared; having already taken care of one of the requirements, she scheduled the visit.

Normally it is an 8 week course, but the agency had recently made arrangements to offer these classes on Saturdays in a 4-week format. Her husband would also be able to attend the classes in this format as he worked during the week! She was calling me to let me know of these recent developments and asking for this time off for the classes. My initial feelings on the subject were selfish – not wanting to give up my Saturdays off for a month. But because she had already told me about events leading up to it and that this was something she was *clearly* meant to do (so many pieces fell into place to make this possible), that her excitement and enthusiasm for what was happening right before her eyes was contagious. I said I would notify my boss about my needed authorization to work non-scheduled overtime for the next month. I truly was excited for her and said, "Go for it!"

What I got back from my boss stunned me. After sending her a three paragraph email explaining the situation, I got back a 6-word sentence: "You need to get another PMR" (Postmaster Relief). WHAT?! I couldn't believe what I read. Seriously? Over 4 days off? Was this an over-reaction or what? I let Deb know that was our boss's answer to the situation and what she emailed back to me was basically her resignation. But it wasn't an "oh well, too bad for you" thing. Deb's response was a very touching "thank you" for the last 5 years, along with her belief that her responsibilities in my office had been a "sacred duty" – a fact which I was very aware. Her dedication to the office and to each customer was something I cherished and made me completely confident when I left things in her care.

This sudden development from someone who clearly didn't understand the situation and the resultant loss (to the office, my customers, the Postal Service and me) made me want to cry. My initial thoughts on the subject were not very godly. I had one of my own over-reactions – the thoughts of retaliation I referred to earlier. I wanted to lash out… to forward Deb's letter to our boss with a nasty declaration attached from me in admonishment for discarding such a dedicated employee who was so well trained and passionate about the job. I could add arguments about the time and costs associated with hiring a new trainee in the current economic environment, the overtime that would be incurred in the process far outweighing just 4 Saturdays' worth of training time and so on.

I didn't. I took a deep breath. Who am I kidding? I took *lots* of deep breaths! I shouted out loud, "Are you kidding me?" and then whispered "God help me." (Yes, I am aware that is backwards from what I could have done in proper priority, but there it is). With the realization that I had no control over this situation right then, I knew an angry response toward my boss was not the right thing to do. "For man's anger does not promote the righteousness God [wishes and requires]."[12] There was that "bringing to your remembrance"[13] thing again...

The strange thing is that after the initial thought of that nasty return email went through my head, my refusal to write it and following prayers of "God, what am I going to do now?", some most unexpected thoughts came through my mind. I almost immediately felt a sense of seemingly misplaced peace, thinking, "Maybe this is a good thing". Maybe this was the answer to my on-the-back-burner concerns about office coverage for longer periods of time. Maybe this was a friendship-retaining way of God allowing for both Deb and I to be able to move onto the next chapter of our lives without setting aside our loyalty and support of one another. Maybe this was God's doing...

Then I started reasoning things in my own thoughts, (not recognizing them as that at the time)...maybe this flip decision from the district management was all smoke and mirrors and would come to nothing due to a lack of applicants for the job anyway. The email I sent next was not to my boss, but to Deb, thanking her for her touching response, and her dedicated service. I added in my own hopes that this probably wouldn't come to anything with the inconsistent hours and level of responsibility related to the job for prospective applicants. I hit the "send" button on the email and went home for the day.

The next day I got another email from Deb. She told me how the situation was progressing. She told me she and her family had discussed the whole situation the night before and that this seemed to them to be the green light they needed to proceed as foster parents. They felt a new season had arrived and the previous one was over. She said she would cover for me for the month as needed during the week, since she could not work Saturdays, and then she would be done.

Another brief panic as those words sunk in... But then God's peace returned again. I had people telling me five years before that I would never get someone for so little money, with all the responsibility required for the position and that proved to be wrong. The fact that the responsibility has increased dramatically since I hired Deb did not change the Truth that I still had the same God, the same provision and the same opportunity for someone else to step into five years later! My mind raced back and forth between confidence that if it happened once, it could absolutely happen again, and panic over the ever-increasing list of what if's. Fear or Faith? Which would I choose? I went back and forth longer than I'd like to admit.

But there was still a peace that would not let go inside me. It reassured me that things were supposed to happen this way. Psalms and other verses of assurance were just rising in my memory, affirming that everything was going exactly according to Plan. It wasn't *my* plan, obviously, but all the elements of what was happening were too "coincidental" to be accidental.

Realizing this gave me the assurance of God's purpose in the process that was unfolding, even if I didn't know what that was. It's not the first time I've gotten panicked over some situation where I couldn't see the good that was going to come next. I was ready to try a different tack from the beginning of this trip!

The next few hours were a race of thoughts, a blur of emails and multiple phone calls to two fellow postmasters and the Human Resources office. I needed to know how to begin the job posting process. All the while, the doubt and fear of not finding someone and visions of working 6 days a week and "never getting out of the office" bombarded me. But the God I am getting to know more and more each day reminded me of another time of another time of doubt 5 years before. He reminded me He was still able to make a way where, to human eyes, there is no way of getting from here to there. "Behold, I am doing a new thing! Now it springs forth; do you not perceive and know it and will you not give heed to it? I will even make a way in the wilderness and rivers in the desert." [14]

I sat there and started thinking about something I had recently written entitled *Faith and Trust*; how God continues to bring deeper levels of commitment and trust from my heart each time I am called to meet increasing needs. I know I cannot meet them myself and that raises the bar up another notch each time I meet challenges in His strength, not my own understanding. No pole vaulter can ever take me over the bars of difficulty that God has lifted me over! Would I be willing to trust Him with this one?

I thought of 1 Samuel 30 (though I didn't know at the time where it was). The Amalekites had come to Ziklag when King David and his men were gone and carried off the women and children, and everything they owned, and burned the city. The men, who had been fighting side-by-side with him hours before, returned to see their wives and children taken captive, their smoking town pillaged, and all their belongings stolen. Thinking all was lost, they needed a fall guy to aim their overwhelming grief at; they turned to stone David. Their fear for their family members' plight brought on a panic-turned-rage. "...But David encouraged and strengthened himself in the Lord his God."[15]

Just like he had done when facing Goliath, David reminded himself about previous victories and refused to let his concern for his family and the families of the men who were his constant companions deter him from seeing the truth of God's presence in all situations. He turned away from the threat of stones and turned to the priest, asking for the ephod to inquire of God what the next step was: "Shall I pursue...? Shall I overtake them?"[16] This was not easy, but David had had lots of practice with other people's fears, doubts and anger.

Same strategy, Different day

When David was a young boy, he was rejected, overlooked and misunderstood by his older brothers and his father. 1 Samuel chapter 16 recounts that when the prophet came to anoint one of Jesse's sons as the next king, David's father paraded all his other sons before the prophet for consideration. Samuel was told by God that none of them were the one He had chosen. Puzzled, Samuel asked Jesse, "Is this it? Do you have any other sons?" Jesse's response was a weak one: oh yeah, well "there is yet the youngest; he is tending the sheep"[17], but he's just a kid...

Really? A prophet comes and specifically tells you to bring all your sons to a feast so he can anoint one of them the next KING and you leave one of them out in the field!? Far from Jacob's favoritism toward Joseph, Jesse seemed to completely forget David qualified as his son. Even if he wasn't the one chosen, wouldn't that be something you would want the whole family there to experience? His own father hadn't thought to include him. But *he* was the one – the one God had chosen as the next leader of Israel. His brothers belittled him and his own father discounted him, but God hadn't. Samuel corrected their oversight and declared, "We will not sit down to eat until he is here."[18] and he anointed David as the next king, leaving them all stunned.

But he was still young and the time had not come yet for David to rule. He went back to caring for his father's flocks. Nothing had changed in his circumstances, but he had God's anointing. Even with all this rejection from his own family in the background, he was still faithful in herding and protecting the sheep in his charge (sounds a lot like Joseph!). David was developing and maturing in his experiences; he was trusting God in the moment and believing God is who He says He is and can do everything He says He can do! The current king wasn't gone yet – and there were many years of training still ahead for the young teen. He had fought lions and bears to protect his father's sheep and grew in his relationship with God.

All this talk of royalty and succession must have seemed so far away as life had returned to "normal". Then King Saul, hearing from someone nearby that David was a skillful player and a warrior, requested David's father to send him to the palace to play the harp for the king when he was troubled by an evil spirit. Not long after, he became the king's armor bearer.

Set and match. God made a way for David to be in the company of the king instead of his father's sheep fields.

But then what? From common shepherd to royal musician is a big enough step. How could he possibly make it from harpist to king? God wasn't done yet – not by a long shot.

We don't know how much time went by between chapter 16 and 17, but evidently David was back at home with his father in Bethlehem by verse 15, feeding his father's sheep again. Jesse, concerned for his older three boys who were soldiers in the royal army, sends David to bring food to his brothers and their commander, and tells him to bring back word from the battlefield. When he reached the battle front on his father's errand, he found the army of Israel was cowering in fear from a challenge that had been issued by the biggest bully they'd ever seen.

Goliath, a giant from Gath who was fighting on the side of their enemies, had called out for a substitution match. Instead of the whole army fighting from both sides, he suggested a literal winner-take-all death match between himself and one champion from the Israelite army. If the champion from Israel killed the giant, he said, all the Philistines would serve Israel; but if Goliath was able to kill the Israelite champion, then all Israel would become servants to the Philistines. Then the trash-talk started. For 40 days, morning and evening, He challenged Israel to send someone out, calling them cowards and defying their God, pointing out that none of the other nations had been able to stand against the army of Philistines, so why would the Israelites be any different? The men were terrified and fled from him. The king had resorted to offering a three-prong bribe, oh, sorry - *reward* - for anyone who would fight Goliath: great wealth, the king's daughter's hand in marriage and their family's freedom from any future taxes. But still no one would come forward. Not until David showed up.

This is the scene David came upon when arriving on his father's errand. Faced with what looked like insurmountable obstacles, he chose to ignore the belittling insults his brother hurled at him, accusing him of pride when David asked what was going on. He focused on the task at hand and gathered the information he needed. David asked again, "what shall be done for the man who kills this Philistine and takes away the reproach from Israel?"[19]

David volunteered to represent Israel and fight the giant. The nay-saying king told him he'd never succeed – even tried to get him to wear armor several sizes too big for him for protection. No doubt the very armor he had carried for King Saul in the previous chapter. He respectfully addressed the king and reminded him who he was fighting for: the Living God of Israel! He told the king about the challenges God had given him victory over in the past and declared with confidence God's sure deliverance. He ran quickly to the battle line, calling out to a falsely confident Goliath, not in his own strength, but "in the name of the Lord Almighty... whom you have defied!" He shouted, "...I'll strike you down and cut off your head. This very day I will give the carcasses of the Philistine army to the birds and the wild animals, and the whole world will know that there is a God in Israel."[20] David knew and said out loud that the same God Who delivered him from the lion and the bear would deliver this unbelieving, God-taunting enemy "into [his] hand".[21] And He did. With the death of the giant, the army of Israel found their confidence again, routed the Philistines and won the battle.

The victory God provided for both Saul (the current king) and David (his future successor) resulted in a mentoring situation where the young shepherd again moved into the castle. God created a way, where there was no previous way to human eyes, for David to get from where he was to where he needed to be. Here he could learn from the older king, who was now his father-in-law, eating at his table, living in the palace, experiencing the day-to-day decisions up close and personal that he would one day be faced with.

He had opportunity for learning things he would never been able to learn any other way. He not only learned what to do, but also what NOT to do from Saul. As a result, David was called a man after God's own heart, not perfect, but intent on pleasing Him and repenting when he messed up. In this way, he overcame both the hard things thrown at him from others and the results of his own sins, in the strength God provided him.

We can also overcome "through Him who loved us"! [22] God sees us in our youth too – in our inexperience and our spiritual immaturity, but anoints us as His chosen ones. He understands that He has much to teach us and makes known "the end from the beginning."[23] God knows all the while what He will bring out of us in His time and for His glory.

Application in Action

With all this in mind, I changed my discouragement-tempted heart's focus to one of relying on the finished victory that God had already given me. I reminded myself of "previous victories" and repeated it when necessary over the next few days! I confirmed it by telling Deb what God showed me in David's encouraging example.

"I know now that God is doing something amazing in these changes. Just as God provided you as my substitute 5 years ago when everyone else was saying I wouldn't be able to get coverage, just like when I got this position, going from letter carrier to postmaster, as probably the least qualified at the time (as my "big sister" Lynn was praying in the car during my interview), just like when I took a demotion from being a full-time to a part-time letter carrier instead of allowing myself to be reassigned to another office when my mail route was cut...enabling me to have more time with my family and then compete for this vacancy, just like so many other times when God already had a resting place in mind, a landing strip. He has always prepared places for me that surpass where I've been and I know He is doing something amazing in this!"

I realized an additional bonus: God was now using this situation, not only to give both Deb and me what we needed now, but also to share that benefit with someone else! For both of us, the road was still shrouded in unknowns; what foster child would be assigned to her, how long would it be, etc. Who was going to replace Deb at the office? How long would it take? But then the next thought hit me – who was supposed to be the incoming employee? I didn't know who would be my next PMR, but I knew now God had already prepared the situation for who would be filling the job. All I had to do was pray for the wisdom to realize who He wanted here when they came in to interview!

With that relief in my heart, I went to sleep. I had been sleeping pretty well during this time – with working 6 days in the office and then doing the usual housekeeping when I got home, solid sleep was not a problem! But this night something weird happened.

I woke up the next morning from a nightmare that seemed to go on for a *long* time. In the dream I was searching for someone (I had no idea who, just that it was a girl) who had been kidnapped by evil. Yeah, I know. My dreams can be off the wall sometimes and disjointed with lots of things that don't really make sense until later, if ever. Chinese pagodas, exploding fireworks, chases, betrayal, escapes, rescues, danger, and hand-to-hand combat, had me in knots when I woke up - not the stuff of my usual dreamscape. Faces and names were changing and not clear through most of it, but it felt so real. Even after my eyes were opened the images were so vivid and my emotions still so intense, it was disturbing! And it wasn't dissipating with waking.

I got up from bed and went to the living room. I needed to change my focus. I needed to start my day in a peaceful attitude. In my experience, out-of-the-ordinary disturbances take out-of-the-ordinary measures to dissolve them. I prayed Jesus' names, titles and promises; everything that came to mind came out of my mouth. Glorious Savior, Mighty God, Prince of Peace, Everlasting Father, Lamb of God Who takes away the sins of the world. Then I started singing songs I love with soothing tones and reminders of the closeness of God. "Jesus Name Above All Names", and "Thy Word is a lamp unto my feet and a light unto my path..., when I feel afraid, fear I've lost my way, still You're there right beside me, and nothing will I fear as long as You are near, please be with me to the end! ... I will not forget Your love for me and yet, still my heart forever is wandering, Jesus be my guide always at my side and I will love you to the end! Thy Word is a Lamp unto my feet and Light unto my Path." (Based on Psalm 119:105)[24] All this was running into Phil 1:6 "He Who has begun a good work in you will continue till the day of Jesus Christ right up to the day of His return developing that good work and bringing it to full completion in you." These and other verses were giving me peace and confidence again. This went on for a while.

I had begun this quiet time, trying to shake a disturbing nightmare, but somewhere along the line it turned into something much more! I felt the truth of something else beginning to emerge: "He who believes in Me [who cleaves to and trusts in and relies on Me] as the Scripture has said, From his innermost being shall flow [continuously] springs and rivers of living water."[25]

As I started praying every verse that was coming into my head and singing parts of hymns and praise songs, several people who also were all going through various kinds of difficulties in their lives right then all came to mind and all this stuff started coming up and out to encourage *them,* too. I started writing notes and sending emails and included the references that were coming up in my heart: Jeremiah 29:11-12, Hebrews 13:5, Hebrews 4:1-2 and other verses interspersed with my own words. "He loves you dearly and will never leave you nor forsake you - even when it looks too hard... God is doing a *new* thing and He wants you to come along for the ride and enjoy the new things and the new you He has around the corner, instead of wishing the past would come back - can you see it yet? Are you excited?"

I was doing a new Bible study at the time by Beth Moore called "Living Beyond Yourself - Exploring the Fruit of the Spirit." The things I was learning were suddenly reaching a deeper impact on my heart. Each chapter was perfectly timed in the situations I kept finding myself in during this

10 week period. It is amazing how excited I can get in a house so quiet while everyone is still sleeping, when it's just me and God and a book and some questions leading me through promises and getting to know God's character and heart towards me!

The day before I had been in a chapter called "A Painful Deliverance" based on Acts 27 through Acts 28:10. Beth had observed that not all the places God takes us are comfortable, but His plan in all of it is to deliver us from where we are to the place He has already prepared for us in advance. He's not winging it, He knows what we need to jettison overboard so we can be sure to reach the shores of Malta – "a place of miracles, a place of healing and a place of supplication."[26]

God had evidently been showing me these particular verses because I kept looking back and wishing I hadn't made some of the choices I made. Satan had been using the fatigue from the extra work hours and other trying circumstances I was going through at the time to wear me down and beat me up with regret and second guessing: If I had only done some things differently my daughter would not have moved 3000 miles away to Oregon and everything would be better,... restoration, salvation, grandkids, family happiness and so on in my perfect little plan. But I kept being brought back to the realization that God's ways are higher than my ways and He has reasons for why things happened the way they did and all of it *is* combining together, working out His perfect plan and helping all of us grow and reach (sometimes desperately) toward Him for the answers when our world is disturbingly rocked.

Making these realizations for myself, I was praying for my friends and family members and I felt so tender-hearted toward the many different situations they were going through. I am very grateful for the internet and email! Physical distance, differences in time zones and work schedules didn't have to mean that communicating was impossible or inconvenient. I was using it all to share what God was showing me for mutual encouragement and concentration on Him instead of the stormy times we each were seeing as a disaster.

I shared what had come as a rush of encouragement to me and offered it to them. I shared assurances that everything that was happening in their lives was part of God's Plan A, in His sovereign and abundant love for us all, not a mish-mosh of junk that was coming to overwhelm them. None of this was a surprise to God and He was well able to get us all through to the other side of these difficulties. The words were a message to look hopefully forward to the future. And as I was assuring them, these truths anchored themselves firmly in my heart as well.

I was being given the amazing opportunity to see a different perspective – and getting it in a way I'd never experienced before. Like Beth Moore has said many, many times: "When God is all you have, you realize God is all you need – and everything else is a bonus!" God sees all the things we go through as the refining pot and furnace that He uses to melt off the chains we never knew were there. As we turn to Him, He ends up burning off the ropes that are holding us, but leaves us fresh and faithful and exuberant and not even smelling like smoke, just like the men in the fiery furnace in Daniel! I was reveling in the beauty, the provisions and the Grace of Jesus and Daddy Abba God. As each verse came up, it fit together perfectly with others like a continuous conversation directly from Him. Hebrews 4 led to Psalms 37 which led to Philippians 3 and so on.

So instead of being afraid and expressing it to everyone who would listen…instead of feeding everyone negative words like, "I am going to be stuck working 6 days a week, my house is going to be dirty all the time, I am never going to have time with Steve, nothing ever changes…" I realized that I needed to be more concerned about losing my confidence in the Promises of God. Promises that continually assured me that He was providing glad tidings and was in the good news business and I would **not** be chained to the office, the things that needed doing **would** be done and none of the difficulties would last forever. The lies we listen to about "this (horrible thing) will never stop" but "this (wonderful thing) can't possibly last" is meant to discourage us. *Everything* changes, good and bad. None of it lasts forever! So encourage yourself in the bad times that this too shall pass – and enjoy the wonderful times completely while they are here because this too shall pass! That's a GOOD thing! Believe in the good report! Correct your heart of pessimism! His reminders in all of these things seemed pretty straight-forward to me. Instead of panic, I could commit every step to God and let Him direct me where the next turn would be. I could let my faith be exercised -and stretched! - and believe Him, and watch what He would do with it!

I heard a wonderful story the other day that totally captures this truth: The king in a faraway country decides to plan a banquet and invites everyone in the kingdom to come. But, he says, everyone MUST wear royal clothes. No one will be allowed into the palace with common attire. A slave, hearing this invitation, decides to be bold enough to ask for help. He goes to the gate of the palace and asks a guard if he can speak with the king. The king sends for him and asks what his question is. The slave haltingly explains that he really wants to attend the banquet, but he only has rags to wear. Would the king be willing to provide the clothing required for him to attend the feast? The king smiles broadly, commending the slave for his wisdom and asks the prince to clothe the slave with royal robes. The prince leads the slave into his own room, giving him an entirely new outfit, from turban to shoes. Nothing is forgotten. He is royally dressed from head to toe. The prince then explains these clothes will never wear out or need replacement; he will never need his rags again. The slave is excited and gratefully attends the feast, enjoying it immensely. But he's not sure he can trust the prince's assurances that he will never need his old clothes again. Never? Really? Surely something will come up. Surely there's a catch somewhere. The slave is plagued with his doubts and carries his old clothes in a bundle, sometimes in his lap, sometimes under his arm, but never really letting go of the smelly rags. It hampers his ability to do some things because he won't let go of the bundle. A long while later, the slave realizes the prince is good on his promises and he never did need the rags after all. He finally lets go of the doubts - and the bundle - and is free to fully enjoy his new clothes.

God does the same for us: He offers us Christ's robes of righteousness, His salvation, His Grace, and everything we need to attend the banquet of Life lived in His presence - forever. But often we hold onto doubts. Is it really going to last? Is this really all we need? I have to admit that I still haven't released all my doubts. It's not that I don't want to; old habits are hard to break sometimes - but I am learning to let go of the old self, and become a more consistent version of the new. The wonderful thing about God (well, one of many) is, He's not mad at us when we fall short of what He desires for us. He's not disappointed in us at our frailty. He doesn't yell at us for our humanity and our difficulty. He tells us He understands! "Inasmuch then as we have a great High Priest Who has [already] ascended *and* passed through the heavens, Jesus the Son of God, let us hold fast our confession [of faith in Him]. For we do not have a High Priest Who is unable to understand *and* sympathize *and* have a shared feeling with our weaknesses *and* infirmities *and* liability to the assaults of temptation, but One Who has been tempted in every respect as we are, yet without sinning... (which brings us to the text at the start of this chapter) ... Let us then fearlessly *and* confidently *and* boldly draw near to the throne of grace (the throne of God's unmerited favor to us sinners), that we may receive mercy [for our failures] and find grace to help in good time for every need [appropriate help and well-timed help, coming just when we need it]."[27]

He keeps reassuring us and helping us shed the smelly old rags of our past, our doubt, our fear...and continually gives us the grace to live each day in His robes of righteousness, without shame, living in faith, and in forgiving relationships with other people.

God had been trying to make His point earlier that week and I was having trouble accepting it without adding in my "yeah, buts...." He was telling me, "I am God, I have said it, I will do it, you can rely on it. Just trust me!" I hadn't quite shaken the doubts off, and I hadn't realized that was the cause of my uneasiness. God knew all this was lingering under the surface and gave me impressive help to remind me – the apostle Paul. It seems that even the man who wrote 2/3 of the New Testament by divine revelation had times when he was tempted to look at new situations with fear and doubt, rather than trust and excited anticipation of the good things God has planned. But he didn't stay there – he "encouraged himself in the Lord".

He told me to redirect my focus from the past, to something better: "...forgetting what lies behind and straining forward to what lies ahead, I press on toward the goal to win the [supreme and heavenly] prize to which God in Christ Jesus is calling us upward."[28]

"Straining" and "pressing forward" sounded like effort to me! If Paul, the 14th apostle who had directly heard and spoken to Jesus, needed to "press" and "strain" then maybe my own difficulties weren't something I had to feel guilty about! How could I get over these feelings that wanted to hold me back? 2 Timothy 1:7 is a valuable promise; it was the first verse I ever had my kids memorize when they were little and having nightmares. It reminds us that fear does not come from God. It told me not to give in to the fear that was telling me, "It's too hard, back off!" We have the power of God's love, self-control and self-discipline to make it! You can do it!

Encouraging answers to my questions just kept coming, one after another – it REALLY WAS a conversation with God! He was answering each thought, each question as it was coming up!

God is not a man. He doesn't lie. He doesn't go back on His promises. If He says it, He will do it. Period.

One after another the words were flowing out. It was like the Holy Spirit just held up a mirror and asked me plainly if I was going to "be a doer of the Word"[29] or just a forgetful hearer. Yes, the Word I was getting that God placed on my heart that day could absolutely encourage other people, but then He asked me if I would apply this wisdom to my own life, to my own heart? Would I walk away from my loft and forget that "appeal *and* encouragement in which [I am] reasoned with *and* addressed as sons"[30]? Would I simply trust Him that each of these situations were specifically designed by God Himself to help *me* grow? These verses were a conversation from Daddy to Daughter! And that realization thrilled me!

When I walked away from my loft and headed out to work, it didn't take long for the battle to re-engage. The doubt and fear kept coming, through the mouths of different people around me and in my own head. "Who in their right mind is going to take on this much responsibility, with so few hours, for so little pay?"

But with such strong messages of encouragement during my quiet time, so many verses as armor and ammunition that I had gotten that morning, I now had a new outlook. That time in my loft with God had a direct impact on my state of mind and built a faith shield that God tells us so clearly will "extinguish all the flaming arrows of the evil one."[31] It was so reassuring to read, "Trust in the Lord with all your heart, lean not on your own understanding. In all your ways acknowledge Him and He shall direct your path."[32]

Okay God, you've got the reins on this one and I am <u>not</u> going to grab them back this time! I have no idea where we're going, but You do! Thank you for taking me along for the ride!

I didn't know what was going to happen. I liked working with Debbie. Part of me wanted it to be like it had been because I was comfortable with that; I knew what that felt like. But Joyce Meyer and others repeatedly tell us that stepping out of our comfort zone is where growth happens. *Working* with Deb is now the past, but our friendship - and opportunity for future collaborations - are still unfolding. The past was good in its own time and season. What is ahead for each of us is better, if we let God steer us down the roads, over the bridges and through the next seasons of our journey.

Although I had been *really* tempted to fight my boss's "solution" and use legal and labor relations options to hold onto Deb, God showed me all these affirmations of His care through the whole thing. I decided to let go, in faith, of what was back there and stretch beyond myself to the good things that God already prepared for the future. Okay God, pry my fingers loose, I want to let go of what is and reach forward, it's just my hands are stuck from holding on so tightly! More words popped into my head "...I know whom I have believed and am persuaded that He is able to keep that which I've committed unto Him against that day!"[33]

I embarked on the new experience of being the interviewer. I took the training, made my lists of questions to ask, set the dates and only two of the four applicants showed up for their interviews. Even so, the choice was hard to make. Both were qualified, both enthusiastically passed the process with flying colors. Which one? I had to make a decision. Both of them would work fine from what I could see. Which one was the person God had placed in my path? Which one did I have "peace beyond understanding" about? It had to be about more than what was on paper. I had to apply discernment and purpose. How could I be sure which one to choose?

I am now on the other side of that decision after encouraging myself in the Lord as He taught me to do. I was now ready to give an answer to those who asked the same questions that were running through my own head, "Who in their right mind would possibly take this job …?"

Her name is Rachel. She was a perfect fit. We complemented each other and helped one another and she completed her training very quickly. There are too many details that just emphasize how great this situation was for both of us, but her details are not mine to tell.

Suffice it to say that there is no doubt in my mind that the right choice was made. And in the perfect provision, sense of humor and rightness of everything God does, the adage of "what goes around comes around" in life is on full display here. Rachel's grandmother, and before that her great-grandmother, were previous Postmasters in this very same Post Office!

When I was a young girl, dealing with all kinds of pain during my parent's divorce, Rachel's grandmother, Betty, was a rock of support, encouragement and advice during hours of conversation over this very same counter! Two generations ago, I was encouraged and given the gift of family wisdom and sound counsel. At that time I had no idea I would be on her side of the counter someday. And now I am in the position that enabled me to give her granddaughter that opportunity to share the joy, sense of contribution and responsibility in our community. God knew that everyone's needs would be met; my own, Deb's, Rachel's and the foster child(ren) assigned to Deb. Our little rural Post Office is not overlooked by a loving, giving heavenly Father. He won't overlook your needs either.

More time has passed. Things have changed in so many ways since then. I was able to plan another trip to see two of my grandkids in Oregon – before they moved back home. I was also able to take some time off when my third grandchild was born. We took a trip to see her once in Florida a couple of years ago. Steve and I went sailing for a week for our anniversary – and we're planning other trips, confident that the people I work with can handle whatever comes up while I'm gone.

The ripples go on through all our lives: Deb's "foster" situation turned into an adoption – and she is a blessing, no "disguise" needed. It was a perfect fit for everyone involved. But the panic it began with hadn't felt like it at the time. Like I've heard lately: when it feels like things are falling apart, you can choose to trust God that things are actually falling into place!

Nothing stays the same for long – and amazing things can result from change! Rachel's "local job, flexible hours, and room for advancement" led to better things. She has moved on to a bigger Post Office, promoted and sharing her abilities and personal touch with a new community. And three other people have been interviewed and placed in my little rural post office since then – and moved on to other things themselves. The person in there now will likely be moving on to have a shorter commute in the next year or so. I have had the opportunity to hire others – for three different offices. The best choices were made not relying on my own understanding, but on God's. He has never failed me. I simply can't ask for more than that. He "who is able to do immeasurably more than all we ask or imagine"[34] has everything under complete control.

I am grateful for the assurances, the guidance, the gentle hand and the direction I am privileged to experience in God's care. The things He leads me through are not always comfortable, but He is always gentle and never leaves me to face anything alone! I can trust Him implicitly – even when there is pain involved. Like a parent tearing off a band-aid when the purpose for it is over, it hurts more than you want it to, but it's over quickly and then you move on.

The challenge is translating this trust from past victories to present struggles where I am not as calm. The solution is found in following David, and Joseph, and all the "great cloud of witnesses" who "look to Jesus, the Leader and Source of our faith..."[35] Encourage yourself in the Lord, in the past victories, in the past deliverances, in the past guidance – and trust Him to safely guide you through each new challenge.

God has repeatedly proven to me that the battles we face in life are won or lost in our minds before we even begin. We must prepare our attitudes to face situations in His peace, provision and protection. I repeat: I am still a work in progress – I know there are certainly more circumstances that will give me opportunities to test these principles again in my life. But I believe with all my heart that getting to know who God is and what He is trying to tell me in His Word, sharing others' teachings and struggles and victories - and letting them share mine – we will all be victorious! Getting there is half the battle! The great news is, as Keith Green so wonderfully put it, the battle is already won! It was won on the cross; believe it and become a child of a loving generous God, Who ALWAYS takes care of His own.

The Battle is Already Won

Well, the battle is already won,
And the race has already been run,
It's all been done, you just have to claim the victory.
And the future is already made,
The foundation was totally laid,
When He paid the bloody price for you and me.

Oh my friend, have you heard the story,
What my Jesus has done?
We will share his triumphant glory,
For the battle is already won.

Then the sign of the end shall appear,
Fill the sky with a message so clear,
All will hear the beloved calling of our Lord.
Every tongue will confess to His name,
All His children and angels proclaim,
He's the same for now, for now, for now and every more,
He don't change.

Oh my friend won't you join the chorus,
Singing praise to the Son.

From the day that He laid His life down for us,
The battle was already won.

Raise your banners high,
Praises fill the sky,
Mountains tremble and fall,
Hallelujah sing, glory to the King,
Lord Creator of all.

Well, the battle is already won,
And the race has already been run,
It's all been done, you just gotta claim the victory.
And the future is already made,
The foundation was totally laid,
When He paid the ugly, bloody price for you and me.
Oh my friend, have you heard the story,
What my Jesus has done,
We'll return in triumphant glory,
For the battle, it's already won! [36]

Have your own conversations with Jesus. He already won the battle for you, let Him show you how it applies directly to the situations you are in today. He *does* speak, you *can* hear Him! Instead of being fearful of the unknown and shrinking back in fear and defeat before you even begin, "run quickly to the battle line" and "encourage yourself in the Lord." "...Has He spoken and will He not bring it to pass?"[37] Of course not! Ready, set, go! See you at the finish line!

Footnotes

[1] Eccl. 3:7 (NIV)

[2] 2 Cor. 10:5 (NIV)

[3] "Bambi" Walt Disney Films 1942

[4] Matt. 12:34b (amp)

[5] Neh. 8:10 (NIV)

[6] 1 Cor. 13:7 (amp)

[7] Jer. 29:11 (NIV)

[8] Gen. 50:19-21 (NIV)

[9] John 14:26 (amp)

[10] Col. 4:6 (amp)

[11] 1 Pet. 3:15 (amp)

[12] Jas. 1:20 (amp)

[13] John 14:26 (amp)

[14] Isa. 43:19 (amp)

[15] 1 Sam. 30:6 (amp)

[16] 1 Sam. 30:8 (amp)

[17] 1 Sam. 16:11 (amp)

[18] ibid

[19] 1 Sam. 17:26 (amp)

[20] 1 Sam. 17:46 (NIV)

[21] ibid

[22] Rom. 8:37 (NIV)

[23] Isa. 46:10 (NIV)

[24] "Thy Word" copyright © 1984 Meadowgreen Music Company (ASCAP) (admin at CapitolCMGPublishing.com)/ Word Music (ASCAP) All rights reserved. Used by Permission.

[25] John 7:38 (amp)

[26] "Living Beyond Yourself – Exploring the Fruit of the Spirit" By Beth Moore, p. 158 Life Way Press 1998

[27] Heb. 4:14-16 (amp)

[28] Phil. 3:13-14 (amp)

[29] Jas. 1:22-23 (amp)

[30] Heb 12:5 (amp)

[31] Eph. 6:16 (NIV)

[32] Prov. 3:5-6 (NKJV)

[33] 2 Tim. 1:12 (NKJV)

[34] Eph. 3:20 (NIV)

[35] Heb. 12:1-3 (amp)

[36] "The Battle is Already Won", written by Keith Green and

Wendell Burton copyright © 1987 For The Shepherd Music

[37] Numbers 23:19 (amp)

Suggested Resources

"How To Think When Life Stinks" by Jimmy Evans

"Living Beyond Yourself – Exploring the Fruit of the Spirit" by Beth Moore Life Way Press 1998

 "Your Scars Are Beautiful to God: Finding Peace and Purpose in the Hurts of Your Past" by Sharon Jaynes

"Living Free – Breaking the Cycle of Defeat" by Robert Morris and James Robison

Chapter 6

Growing Your Faith and Trust in God

"Trust in the Lord with all your heart and lean not on your own understanding; in all your ways acknowledge Him and He will direct your path." Proverbs 3:5-6

I woke up this morning with part of a song by Darius Rucker running through my head: "It won't be like this for long..."[1] It is not just a coincidence that God happens to be using these words to rouse me from sleep this morning. I am thinking of some things that are happening in my life that aren't very comfortable right now and after just writing the previous chapter, to "encourage myself in the Lord", I am looking back on what God has already gotten me through and realizing that the state I am in right now "won't last for long". This is a good thing...

In a recent teaching by Jimmy Evans called "How to Think When Life Stinks" (funny how that title just jumps off the page at you!), he talks about two different ways of thinking that can either help you in times of trouble, or leave you feeling hopeless. You can succumb to the pain and pressure from the devil, who is called "the father of lies", to leave you defeated, or you can choose an attitude that insures you cooperate with God to use the difficulty you're going through to make you better, stronger and more capable than you were before. Jimmy calls these two perspectives photographic and prophetic thinking.[2]

Photographic or Prophetic?

Photographic thinking is when you focus on a situation and project that the pain, illness, poverty or difficulty you are going through right now is the way it is always going to be. The "accuser" holds up a picture of what you are experiencing like a photograph, and tells you "it will never change", "things (or people) will always be just like this", "you'll always be broke", "you're stuck with a loser", "It'll never get better", and so on, as a means of cutting the hope and promise of a better plan out from under you - especially during times of high stress.[3]

If you take the time to think it through, you realize that's a lie, but most times we are so distracted by the overwhelming tide that kind of thinking projects, that we can easily get pulled down into it. This negative perspective is an emotional drain. It limits your ability to resolve the issues and move on positively to the next step.

The alternative is called prophetic thinking. To exercise prophetic thinking means that we reach outside of the three dimensions we usually live in: the physical (what I can see, touch, smell, taste, and hear), time (things happening in a linear progression from start to finish), and emotional (what I think, want and feel), and become increasingly aware of the fourth dimension – the unseen world of faith.[4] That is when we realize that everything in the first three dimensions changes.

God is the God of new beginnings and new mercies every day. Armed with this perspective we become mindful of the impact of things that we cannot see, and allow our perspective of what is seen to be changed. By anticipating and claiming peace in our possibly uncomfortable present we can "be still and know" it will not stay like this for long.

By exercising prophetic thinking, inner joy is obtainable even in difficulty because of the certainty of the influence of God's Grace in our circumstances and into our future. Things WILL change, they always do. Whether they change for the better is greatly dependent on the attitudes we choose.

I say "*exercise* prophetic thinking" because it usually doesn't happen naturally – in the positive. We don't need to train our minds to be negative in our mental projections – we do it all the time: "Oh, I know I am going to be late!", "I just know they aren't going to like my presentation!", "I'll never get this done in time!" We get stuck in a mode of projecting temporary difficulty in the present as a permanent condition of misery or disappointment into the future.

It's easy to see the deception in this view, because we all know *everything changes*! Nothing stays the same but God. We go through seasons in life just as we go through seasons in weather. Children grow, we get older, life offers new opportunities and things change. Prophetic thinking looks forward in hope and acknowledgement that nothing stays the same – and that the future is something to look forward to.

God says in Jeremiah 29:11, "I know the thoughts and plans I have for you declares the Lord, plans to prosper you and not to harm you, plans to give you hope and a future." And to the extent that we look forward to that good future, we have hope, peace and joy, even in the middle of a difficult time. This is much more than just relying on the power of positive thinking. It is a pro-active cooperation of thought, preparation and determination. As we believe in the good promises of God, we do the things we need to prepare for the future, rely on God's provision and opportunities, and keep our eyes focused on the satisfaction that we will get on the other end – if we persevere in doing the things that need to be accomplished for that goal.

My brother sent me a text the other day: "This difficulty did not come to stay, it came to pass". Knowing the hard time we are going through now is temporary, gives us the ability to break it down into smaller more manageable bites. When I deal with it one day at a time instead of taking on the whole thing at once, I can get through it victoriously. It is only when we stop, discouraged and weary, part-way through the journey that the enemy wins over us. We CAN do this – and like everything else in life, we are not without examples to show us the way.

Goal Orientation

Although most of us will never face the kind of opposition Jesus faced, check out how the Bible tells us He got through His trial and execution as an example of how to deal with hard times: "Who, for the joy set before him, endured the cross, despising its shame, and is now seated at the right hand of the throne of God".[5] He felt the pressure of the torture that He knew was coming – even while they were still shouting "Hosanna"![6] A few days later in Gethsemane His "sweat was like drops of blood falling to the ground".[7] He knew what was happening, He told His disciples even before the Passover meal they shared about some of the specifics. But the Bible tells us that instead of staying overwhelmed by the tremendous weight of taking on all our sin and the rejection He endured on the way to the cross, He kept His focus on the joy of being reunited with His Father in Heaven after His purpose (our salvation) was fulfilled. He told Peter this was *why* He came, and asked him, "Should I not drink the cup that was prepared for me by My Father?"[8]

If He had not kept His imminent return to the glory He shared with God since before the foundation of the world in mind, what else could have prevented Him from saying "I quit! This is too hard! The heck with this! They're just not worth it!" But He looked continually at the goal, not the things that were happening at the time.

We have a secret weapon in any battle we face that we certainly do not use as often as we should. We are told we "have the mind of Christ"[9]! We can endure hardships with that same purpose always in front of us, relying completely on God for the ability to do it all![10] Prophetic thinking establishes the attitude that even situations as difficult as Crucifixion Day may seem unbearable from where I am right now, but I know Easter morning's comin'! The resurrection promised is always the resurrection fulfilled in Him – even if it looks bad for now. "He will never leave you nor forsake you"[11]

God is faithful and is The Redeemer, The Savior, The Healer of the Broken-hearted, and He promises His Grace is All-Sufficient.[12] His Amazing Grace **will** lead us home – not just to a sweet-by-and-by Promised Land in heaven, but in a faith-resting, Spirit-filled, abundant life here while we await His coming retrieval of those "who are being made holy"[13] (sanctified). Grace and Mercy are what Jesus said He desires.[14] He wants us to live by the Law of Freedom, not bondage again to fear[15] He wants us to be confident in the power of His work in us so that we can echo the apostle Paul's statement: "I know that in all things, we are more than conquerors and gain a surpassing victory"[16] and fully believe our Savior when He says, "nothing is impossible with God"[17] Instead of old habits of fear and self-recrimination, I choose to have faith that God is healing all of us, just like He promised, and that all of us will be stronger and better people due to the process!

We can train ourselves to exercise these internal attitudes that acknowledge the Power of God we have in Christ. The ability to make this choice is a wonderful gift and it's **ours**!

Perspective

In the last chapter we saw the story of young David before he became king, going to the battle lines and seeing and hearing what is happening – battle-trained soldiers shaking in their boots, looking at a nine-foot-tall bully who was cursing them, cursing God, and challenging the nation to send one champion to decide which group would serve the other from then on. It was all a question of perspective.

The King and the other soldiers acted on what they saw and the fear of the risk before them. David saw the situation in the light of years of being out in the wilderness with God and some sheep. He saw the giant in front of his face in relation to the enormity of his all-powerful God, the One he had been comforted and protected by all his life and Whom he loved with all his heart. In comparison to the loving and omnipotent God, this giant didn't look very big at all! David readily saw the other dimension that his compatriots had not exercised - yet. When David won they had a "vision correction" and, where moments before they had been avoiding the battle, they rushed forward and routed the entire Philistine army! [18]

The Bible tells us we are supposed to "walk by faith and not by sight".[19] how do we develop this ability to rely on the unseen realm when the physical, temporal and emotional senses are so obvious and so overwhelming sometimes? Practice! David had plenty of practice out in the fields by himself.

David used cooperation, preparation and determination all the time! When he was a young boy shepherding his father's sheep, he found himself in pastures alone with wild animals trying to pick off stray lambs. He was keenly aware of the presence of God and relied on His enablement to get the job done – and done well. Having personal experience with the unseen power and protection of God, combined with the religious instruction he was given as a Jewish boy, David was well acquainted with the comfort and tangible presence of God. His past deliverances gave David confidence in his future; he knew and trusted God with his present.

Sleeping outdoors, tasked with the safety of his helpless charges, he had to prepare the way for them: a safe pasture to eat, eliminating the prickly and poisonous plants that would harm his sheep, a safe place to lie down, careful of holes that could be harboring snakes or serve as leg-breaking fissures in the ground, anointing them with oil against small but deadly parasites, and keeping them all together, in the safety of the flock. Joyce Meyer and Max

Lucado have done intensive studies of Psalm 23 and explain line by line the meanings and details of this most famous Psalm. (I encourage you to get their studies, learn from them, and share them — the insights and the understanding of how faithfully and tenderly God cares for you will absolutely change your perspective on His sovereign leadership forever!)

David also needed to exercise dedication. There was no way for him to be half-hearted in his vigil. He couldn't decide to give up or take a break from his duty to his flock. No matter how tired, or sick, or out-of-sorts he became, they were fully dependent on him to provide for them. Their lives depended on his faithfulness to his assigned task. He knew it was imperative for him to bring his "A" game. He used music and praise and practiced the presence of God to stave off the discouragement and loneliness that he encountered in this solitary life — the psalms are full of examples of these battles.

But you don't have to be a shepherd out in the wilderness to develop these traits. You can begin just by looking at your own life. If you look at the things you've survived, the situations you made it through, when others looked at you and said "Wow! You should be dead!", "Boy, are you lucky! No one should have survived that!", "How did you do that?" then, work your way through the surprises and unexpected thrills you've experienced — from sunsets, to seeing an ultra-sound, to the birth of your children, to a call from a long-lost friend at "just the right moment", you will see the evidences of that same care in your life. There is ample proof of a Power working for our benefit, Who is sadly under-appreciated for His loving attention toward us.

But we can change that. We can overcome the obstacles and purposefully cultivate awareness of the Invisible and Devine. We can change our perspective of everyday situations to reject the photographic perspective that uses "always" and "never" lies ("It's *always* the same, work, work, work, and what do I have to show for it?"..."No matter what I do, I *never* win!") Defeat is *guaranteed* by a negative attitude! Why create your own self-fulfilling prophesies of doom and gloom when you have repeated opportunity to change it?

Once we understand what the obstacles are, we can soar above the emotional bog of what we are going through at the moment and have trust in the unseen – the "prophetic" – good that is waiting on the other side of this current valley.

Overcoming Obstacles

Now back to "prophetic" and "photographic" as related to David's encounter in the valley. Jimmy Evans illustrates three obstacles to prophetic thinking from 1 Samuel chapter 17 in the person of Eliab, David's older brother, King Saul, the leader of the nation of Israel at that time, and Goliath, the enemy whose physical strength was much superior to David's. When David was told he couldn't overcome this present situation by all three of these men, he relied on his faith in God in previous experiences to combat their negative declarations. Their comments toward him came with different motives and intentions – from an elder sibling's distain and invalidation, to a king's prideful self-righteousness and dependence on physical armor, to an enemy's pre-battle trash-talk. Their negativity and counsel could have ended David's victory before he even got started! Instead of getting sucked in by the discouragement and offense that could have deterred him, he shifted his focus away from the visible. He didn't accept what they said. He met each obstacle with its counter-match in faith.

- **Invalidation v. Godly Value** - It doesn't make sense sometimes that the people we love would not be our biggest cheerleaders. But sometimes the people we have known for a long time don't allow for the possibility that we've changed, out-grown childish or self-destructive behaviors, and still view us with the same immaturity we may have demonstrated years earlier. Eliab was such a person in David's life. He knew him "way back when" and would not accept David as anything more than a foolish, adventure-hungry, kid-brother. As a result, instead of encouraging him and recommending him to the king, he tried to assign evil motives to David's questions and discounted his ability to contribute positively to the solution.

Notice that in rejecting his older brother's accusations, David did not instigate a screaming match trying to defend himself. The Bible says David asked, "What have I done now?"[20] but when Eliab starts railing on him about leaving "his few sheep"[21] unprotected, he doesn't debate with him, he simply turns away from Eliab and asks someone else the question.[22] He respectfully but firmly disarms his older brother's disparaging remarks and seeks information from someone who will answer him on an equal level.

He chose to slip free of the constraint of invalidation and rejection by family who "knew him", and extinguished those accusations on his shield of faith. He knew he was well-beloved and protected by God. Knowing his value in God's sight made it possible for him to turn away from the distraction of his brother's verbal barbs and execute the most famous victory in history.

Do you have an Eliab in your life? You don't have to let their condescending attitudes stop you from reaching success and defeating the giants in your life. Look how it all turned out – everyone knows about King David, not many people recognize the name Eliab. I am sure that after the battle, seeing Goliath's head in his little brother's hand, Eliab changed his opinion of David and was cheering with the rest of the soldiers - albeit somewhat sheepishly! Sometimes we need to walk away from others' opinions of us, and let it ride for a little while – time proves our worth to them soon enough.

- **Appealing to Authority** - Next David respectfully *asked permission* of the authority in place to fight the battle in his own way. When King Saul tried to make David fight the battle wearing the king's armor, he asked the king to understand that he couldn't succeed by methods that he was not well-practiced in. He gave the king his verbal resume' of previous successes and won his consent for initiating an alternative battle plan. He pointed to previous situations guarding his father's sheep and said, "When a lion threatened my father's sheep, God delivered them into my hand and I killed a lion and I killed a bear, and I will kill this uncircumcised Philistine who has defied the God of Israel!"[23]

332

He didn't negate what the king told him. He tried on the armor, and demonstrated that his unfamiliarity with it would be a hindrance instead of a help in the current situation. He submitted to the authority at hand and made an appeal for change in the day's standard operating procedures with respect and honor for the king's position. He pointed to God Who had saved him many times before and applied that implicit faith to Israel's covenant with God for the victory that he knew was surely coming!

David knew that God's favor rested in being set apart (sanctified and consecrated) to God. The symbol of this consecration for the Israelites, by God's arrangement with Abraham, was physical circumcision. (For us as post-resurrection believers, it is circumcision of the heart. – see Romans 2:29). David reasoned that if they (God's army) were circumcised and consecrated to God, then they *certainly* had the favor of God with them. His confidence that this "uncircumcised Philistine" was bereft of that divine protection superseded any dependence on physical armor. Based on God's enablement, he kept repeating: "this uncircumcised Philistine" was not in covenant with God, and David would surely win the victory.

He trusted God Who says "Behold! I do a new thing"; he rejected the weapons of sword and spear that required him to get too close to a VERY long-armed enemy or wearing armor that restricted his movement. David appealed for consent to face the giant with a familiar weapon more advantageous for the current situation (his slingshot) unencumbered by extra weight and a learning curve he could not afford to indulge just then.

- **Trash-talk v. Trust** - When faced with a bully, who decried the powerlessness of the Lord of Hosts and blasphemed the name of his God, David ran quickly to the battle line, grabbing a few stones (he only *used* one!) and spoke loudly <u>to</u> this mountain of a man that he would be the victor. He was not being *self*-confident or cocky - he was facing this braggart as the representative of and in complete dependence on The Defender of Israel - "I will cut off your head. And I will give the corpses of the army of the Philistines this day to the birds of the air...the Lord saves not with sword and spear; for the battle is the LORD's and He will give you into our hands"![24]

Instead of absorbing the threats and jeers of Goliath's trash-talk, he answered back with his own confident declaration of victory and won the battle with a weapon that enabled him to strike the fatal blow well out of range of those arms, and then used the enemy's own sword to cut off his head, render him powerless, and mightily encouraged the rest of Israel's best warriors (who had been shaking in their shoes) to pursue and defeat their enemies.

Over and over in the Psalms, David builds up his faith in God by using his words to reinforce his faith in times of unrest, uncertainty, and even the consequences for his own disobedience. He knows that God is merciful and faithful. He knows that God has never abandoned him and "will not suffer His servant to see corruption"[25]; confident that "no evil will befall" those who trust in the LORD.[26] Check out a concordance and look up the word Trust sometime. Just in Psalms alone, there are more than enough references to revive your confidence in Your Mighty Shepherd! It is a study well-applied to life's difficulties.

I am now free to apply these same concepts to my own behavior and experiences...my own lions, bears and Goliaths in life. When I look back at the times in the past when God has brought me through situations that I thought I could never make it through, I can access the multitude of "stones" of faith of previous victories with which to run quickly to the battle-line. I don't need to look far to see when things around me and my own challenging thoughts could have crumpled me into a pile in the dirt! But as I reach into the bag of stones I picked up earlier, I gain confidence in the track record of my Redeemer. He is NOT distant! He is an "ever-present help in times of trouble"[27]!

Learning a New Battle-Plan

A recent study in Beth Moore's "Living Beyond Yourself – Exploring the Fruit of the Spirit" encourages you to draw on your experiences with the Father of Faith to "strengthen your feeble knees"[28] and shows us the pattern of belief to follow, exemplified through "believing Abraham."[29] As I was reading these passages, the Holy Spirit, in the dark and quiet of my loft, applied the Truth of it to my own experiences and my heart started to soar! God WANTS to apply His Word to our hearts individually. He WANTS to lift us out of the pits of despair and discouragement – and we don't have to go too far to let Him! Do you have battles with bad habits you are desperate to escape? Health issues you struggle with? Pride driving wedges between you and the ones you love?

Do you have children or grandchildren you have worries about? Do you have family members or dear friends who don't personally acknowledge God in their lives? God spells out promises all over the Bible for you to claim and see manifested in your life! Just like in David's life, the battle is not yours – once you put your faith in Jesus to be your Lord, Savior and Teacher, all the results in your life become His deal and He is ALWAYS faithful to complete His responsibilities!

Read Romans 4: 17 – 21 and insert your own areas of doubt and fear: "[17]...God...Who gives life to the dead and speaks of the non-existent things that [He has foretold and promised] as if they [already] existed... [18][For Abraham, human reason for] hope being gone, hoped in faith that he should become the father of many nations, as he had been promised, So [numberless] shall your descendants be. [19]He did not weaken in faith...[20] No unbelief or distrust made him waiver (doubtingly question) concerning the promise of God, but he grew strong and was **empowered by faith as he gave praise and glory to God, [21]Fully satisfied and assured that God was able and mighty to keep His Word and to do what He had promised**." (emphasis mine)

What situation did you insert here as a replacement for Abraham and Sarah's childlessness? For Tracy, human reason for hope being gone, hoped on in faith that she would....as she had been promised,...She did not weaken in her faith when she considered the (current situation)...No unbelief or distrust made her waiver (doubtingly question) concerning the promise of God, but she grew strong and was empowered by faith as she gave praise and glory to God, fully satisfied and assured that God was able and mighty to keep His Word and to do what He had promised"! Did that just get to you the way it thrilled me!?

God plainly tells us He "is not a man that He should lie, neither the son of man, that he should feel repentance or compunction [for what He has promised]. Has he said and shall He not do it? Or has He spoken and shall He not make it good?"[30] Of course the answer is a resounding "NO!" He is faithful! Don't get distracted and discouraged by what things look like in the physical realm right now. The Bible very clearly says when you "delight yourself in the Lord", He gives you "the desires of your heart."[31]

This verse can be understood in two very distinct ways: When you make God the delight of your life (not a chore or a time clock you have to punch in to get your brownie points), God gives you what you most desire. In some cases this is a request granted directly. In other cases, the meaning of the promise changes slightly. Sometimes the things we think we want most (the desires of *our* heart) would absolutely not be good for us. However the same promise still applies: when we make God our delight, instead of elevating those earthly desires over our time with Him and His plans for us, He gives - or *places* - new desires and wants into our hearts that we appropriate as our own. He fulfills His promise in a different way by replacing self-destructive or less valuable desires with higher aspirations - "giving us the desires of our hearts".

God may not (Very Big Smile and Laugh Out Loud!) do things the way *you think* He should, or in the timing you think it should happen, but you can absolutely be assured He does things the way they should be and must be to get the results in us He is looking for! Either way, He is "giving us the desires of our hearts", and we can trust Him implicitly.

Look back over your life and take stock of the times when God winked at you and did something (big or small) that let you know He was caring specifically for you. Recognize the times that God was delighting in surprising you or providing something you needed or protecting you from something horrible you later found out about. Think of them as individual stones of faith that you keep in a pouch or bag at your side that you always have access to, to load your slingshot against the Goliaths in your life. Let those victories help you build your shield of faith "so that you can extinguish all the flaming arrows of the evil one!"[32]

Use those times to apply that faith and trust to your God Who promised "never to leave you or forsake you"[33] and to be Himself "your abundant compensation and reward"[34]. Don't let fear (**F**alse **E**vidence **A**ppearing **R**eal) make you back down from what you hold dear in your heart! You and I both have had times like that in our lives – see your current situations in light of past victories. It will absolutely change your attitude!

Attitude Determines Altitude

Our family suddenly needed to get a new vehicle. My husband went ahead of me while I was at work and picked out the one he felt best suited our needs, in a low enough price range for us to afford. When we went back together after I got out of work, my attitude was off-the-scale irritated. The battle I was engaged in in my head showed all over my body. I was sour-faced, lips pressed together and thinned, arms folded and not speaking two civil words together at a time. My facial expressions and body language were screaming louder than any objection I hadn't verbalized anyway, so it was no secret how I felt.

As the salesman and my husband pointed out the little pickup truck and all its benefits, I was torn between two very different considerations. On one hand, I was resistant to incurring a car payment again. Having a long-term financial obligation on top of the other bills we were already committed to was instigating financial fears. But then considering our family's transportation requirements pulled the deliberations in the opposite direction. I began telling them that with two teens still at home, a second vehicle should be able to fit all four of us in it. We should get one with a king cab. Two opposing factors – expense and size – were warring against each other in my head. There was **no way** for them to satisfy both. And I was taking my frustrations with the situation out on them.

God was admonishing me the whole time to straighten out my attitude. There are many things I am supposed to be as a believing wife, and most of them are clearly spelled out in the book of Proverbs. Let me just say, I was not a "jewel" to my husband that day[35]! I was the *other woman* in Proverbs, the contentious woman who was compared to a "continual dripping" on a leaking roof, the one the husband goes outside to get away from[36]!

I kept hearing God's instruction to calm down and cheer up and that my attitude toward my husband was dishonoring and embarrassing him. My husband needed to be able to "trust in" me "confidently" and "rely on" me, getting "comfort" and "encouragement"[37] from me. I should have been able to give calm and rational input, but I kept justifying my lousy attitude with the costs of this purchase. "We can't afford this! I don't want another car payment for the next two to four years! I can't work this into the budget, it's too much!" and so on.

In that show room God allowed me to battle this out with His Unseen Presence for just long enough to get my full attention, no matter how many people were around me. It became very clear to me I was not going to dictate the outcome of this engagement. God was not accepting anything from me but complete surrender.

I knew I needed to change my attitude – but I was so worked up at this point that it was going to take a lot of help! Do you know that God will help you follow Him once you make up your mind to do it? I started thinking "God! Please help me! I know my attitude stinks. I don't even want to know what this salesman thinks of me right now! I have been such a shrew! (yes, sometimes I call myself names...) But I am so wired about what this is going to cost – we can't afford this AND we need another car!"

I promise you I heard God "think" to me – "your attitude is *your* responsibility, provision is *My* responsibility. I will take care of the money. Stop letting your fear ruin this day – **just trust Me**." He flat out told me that my main objection – years of car payments - was not going to be an issue. I didn't know how, I didn't know what inside scoop He had that I didn't know about, but I just knew it was going to be okay.

During the test drive (we had to go separately because the three of us couldn't fit in the truck at the same time!), the salesman was trying to pacify my frustration and sell me on my husband's purchase of the truck. I apologized to him for my lousy attitude, trying not to make excuses, but explaining my reservations. It was a lame attempt, but he accepted it and told me he understood.

I apologized to my husband when we got back to the dealership. He graciously accepted my apology and put his arm around me, assuring me everything would work out fine. I got less stressed and we went in to fill out the paperwork for the financing of the truck. Then God threw in another condition - proof of His own special brand of "humor".

Since my husband had co-signed a loan several years back for someone who had trouble making the payments, his diminished credit rating was going to make it more expensive to finance this purchase. In order to get the lower percentage rate on the loan, I was going to have to be the primary owner. Not only was I supposed to straighten out my attitude, I had to take an integral role in the purchase! I would not be allowed to sulk on the sidelines and be able to hold this against my husband as ammunition in future arguments – I had to be the one signing on the dotted line! (You are too funny for words, God!)

The frustration and fear cloud that had taken over my attitude previously was now replaced with guilt. The realization that I had done damage to my husband and my marriage during that time filled me with regret. (Have you had the opportunity to find out yet that the very things the devil tempts you to do or say are the exact same things he then rubs in your face when you fall for it?) Financial fears had dropped my emotional altitude into a crash landing. My behavior at my husband's side was "as rottenness in his bones" instead of being "a crowning joy"[38]. Now I had emotional wreckage to sort through.

341

I apologized again to my husband and determined to remember God's promise and direction that afternoon. It didn't take long for Him to follow through with what He promised.

A History of Provision

Can I state any more clearly God is good, God is faithful, and God knows what we need? Each time I was tempted to get worried and fume about the bill for this, God reminded me of His promise. I also reminded myself of earlier times when God had come through for us. In thinking back, I remembered these situations.

When we moved into our first house, we were finally going to be able to have pets for our kids, but hadn't gotten around to doing anything about it yet. We were still getting financially adjusted to our mortgage payment. One March afternoon when our daughter was 4 ½ and our son was 2 ½, the dog warden showed up at our doorstep and told me he had an unclaimed dog who he didn't have the heart to bring to the vet to put down, and wondered if we were still interested in getting a dog. (We were well acquainted with our local dog warden, both of our daughters - the dog warden's youngest and our oldest - went to preschool together and we had need of his services earlier with neighbor issues).

As my husband came up the stairs and heard the last part of the question, I turned to him and said "Honest, honey, I didn't call him!" We went out to Tim's van to see what we were in for – a beautiful, but very thin tri-color coon hound hopped out of the sliding door of the van and stopped short in perfect hunting point, motionless as he sniffed the air coming from our back yard! My husband commented, "Oh yeah! There's lots of stuff for you to hunt out there!" Really? My husband doesn't hunt. Why a coon hound? It wasn't a breed of dog I had considered before, preferring something more "fluffy" like a spaniel or retriever.

Just then, the front door opened and our two-year-old stepped out to see where Mommy and Daddy went. Running full tilt at this dog he had never seen, and more importantly had never seen him, our son wrapped his arms around the dog's neck and squeezed, claiming "My Dalmatian!" 101 Dalmatians had come out as a Christmas re-release that year and the kids had practically worn out the tape! It was only then that the adults of the family noticed that each white patch on this dog was flecked with little black spots – my little boy's prayers for his own "Dalmatian" had been answered.

The dog never flinched, never growled, never tried to get away. He just let this enthusiastic little boy smother him with hugs and the excitement of the fulfillment of his deepest desire at the time. In spite of our new mortgage being double what our previous rent had been, we knew this was now our dog and we made the necessary arrangements to keep him. I didn't know where the money was going to come from but I chose not to think about it right then. We just knew this was one of those things that was "supposed to be" – we never thought to give God credit for it or question why – until later:

The following winter when the kids and I were gone somewhere, my husband had taken his usual place in our not-too-often-quiet house near the woodstove in the basement to read. As darkness fell outside, with him engrossed in his book, the house darkened inside as well. Suddenly, Steve startled from the story-line, heard the dog's claws on the hardwood as he jumped to the floor, barked and roared around the corner from his resting place on our bed, down the hallway through the kitchen and toward the front door. Steve heard the door bang shut - followed quickly by a car door slamming out front! My husband ran upstairs in time to see a pickup truck, with all its lights off, driving very quickly away from its previous position – backed up to the front door with the obvious intent of emptying everything they could. They hadn't known that someone was home with no car in the driveway and all the lights off! God only knows (and we suspect) what might have happened if the dog had not been there. Steve could have come upstairs completely unprepared, thinking that it was his family returning home...we all shuddered to think beyond that point.

That dog was suddenly worth a lot more to us than a reason to buy dog food and pay vet bills! It was then that God got the credit for us acquiring our dog. God provided for and protected us before we knew it was an issue.

A couple years later, we had financed brand new replacement windows for our house to keep the cold out- the 45 year-old wooden-framed windows that came with the house were very leaky. We upgraded in the selection process to get tilt-in style windows so we could wash them more easily. They were $495.00 each, installed. It was going to take a big chunk out of our budget for a couple years, but we knew we needed them. We looked at it as an investment in heat savings, not an empty expense. Four months after the windows were installed (after paying extra money at the last minute for disability insurance for the term of the loan) my husband was hurt at work and the insurance we didn't think we would need (but got anyway "just in case") paid the balance of the loan. We got the windows for very little out-of-pocket expense. Yes, the situation that made this provision possible was not what we would have wished for by any means! But the silver lining was clear to see: God provided for those windows before we knew it was going to be an issue.

I was reminded of these things, in addition to other situations in the lives of our whole family where good things came out of uncomfortable circumstances. In light of this new car payment, I not only noticed that God had previously provided each one of these times, but also that with each incident, the amount that we needed to believe Him for was increasing! First a few hundred dollars for a higher mortgage and dog related expenses, then the tally increasing to nearly $500 dollars each for windows. God took care of it all. Now it was a test of faith for even more. Would I believe Him for thousands in car payments based on His previous faithfulness or was I gonna "wig out" and worry.

We needed the vehicle. We couldn't afford a bigger truck with a king cab or more horsepower. Would I just relax and believe Him? Would I encourage my husband and be a true "helper" for him, or a shame? Faced with these as my options, I asked God for the grace to be the wife He wanted me to be. He delivered on both accounts – just as He promised "Far above all that we [dare] ask or think [infinitely beyond our highest prayers, desires, thoughts, hopes, or dreams]"[39].

We only made two payments on that truck. I got a check in the mail I was not expecting from an inheritance that covered the cost of the truck and more. God provided before we could know it was going to be an issue, and all He wanted from me was a good attitude.

After these situations and many others I have experienced in the meantime, I have learned to trust that God knows what He is doing. I should probably state that "I am continually learning", because this is not past tense, it is a daily process – things that I know in my head still need help getting from head knowledge to heart attitudes on a regular basis.

I know this is what Paul was saying when he told us all he had not "already attained"[40]! But he determined to "press on toward the goal to win the prize"[41]. In our weakness, God's strength and "grace is sufficient"[42] – if we only take the time to depend on Him for it! Even when I can't see with my human eyes how any good can come out of a situation, I can choose to let Him remind me of His past provision.

Long after the truck incident, when we built our house and had the potential for even more financial stress, I was reminded again that worry solves nothing, creates physical distress and emotional distance for no good reason. When God admonishes us not to fear, He is not just "blowing air up your shorts" (sorry, I don't know where that phrase comes from, but it fits). When He says "Seek ye first the kingdom of God, and His righteousness, and ALL these things will be added to you as well"[43] (emphasis mine), He comes through. God has always provided beyond our vision at the time and He always will. Even when we have our hissy-fit moments of floundering, yelling for help in something we feel is too much for us, it's never too much for Him. He calls to us to trust Him and then lets us re-discover why He says we are His children.

Sometimes in hind sight, after a situation "resolves itself", I can see I've once again made a fuss over something that turns out not to be anything much at all in God's provision. I can picture myself laying in the bottom of a kiddie pool calling out to God that I can't handle one more thing: "I'm drowning!", and He gently but insistently calls me to "Just stand up". You can too. He knows what you need. He has already provided for it before you knew it was going to be an issue. If I stop insisting on my own way, in my limited perspective and how I prefer the situation to go, He shows me I am capable of much more with Him than I previously thought. The same goes for you. He sees farther than you can – and He loves you deeply – you can absolutely trust Him!

Providing Miracles

Oh, by the way - the follow up on that truck incident: in 2006, a few years after we bought the truck and two months after getting his license, our son was driving that little pickup truck on an icy road. As he went from a sunny and sanded part of the road to a shaded and icy stretch following a snow storm, he lost control of it and became air-born. Without any ability for him to steer it, that truck went up, wedging "itself" perfectly between two large trees and a telephone pole, landing on top of and sliding along a now-shortened 4-ft tall stone wall built up on a 2-foot- tall berm on the side of the road.

My son walked away from that truck without a scratch on him, walking a ¼ mile down the road to have a friend of his "help him get the truck down before Mom and Dad could see it". We saw it. We took pictures of it. It took two tow trucks and 45 minutes with three grown men from the local garage to get that thing off the stone wall – and then we drove it home! A bigger truck would not have become air-born, rising over 4 feet in the air to land *on* the wall. A bigger truck would not have fit between those trees, leaving just enough room for my son to get out simply by opening the driver's side door. A bigger truck would not have been light enough for the telephone pole's guy wire to act as a guide cable to straighten it out and keep it upright instead of rolling over on the hood, crushing it flat on the rocks. There is no doubt in any of our minds who saw the aftermath that day – that truck was placed by Divine Hands between those trees with only 6 inches to spare on one side of the nose of that truck, leaving the driver's side door free to open. The "king-cab" truck I was trying to insist on a few years before in that showroom would not have fit between those trees leaving my son walking around and vehemently promising to pay us back for the damage. God did.

He fulfilled His promise to "give me the desires of my heart" in a way I never anticipated: He provided for this situation, substituting a second-rate "desire" from my heart with a far-superior one from His. By preventing the purchase I thought we needed, He again provided for our needs before we knew it was going to be an issue. He gave me my son alive and in one piece instead of a truck I thought I wanted! He is truly faithful and He is worthy of my trust – and yours.

Dozens of other incidents happened in our lives (most of which are undocumented and fail us for our waning memories as time goes by), like our 11-year-old daughter walking with a friend as a car slowed down to ask directions - just as another car came around the corner, making the first car drive away leaving the girls with a weird feeling, not knowing why. Later that day we heard that a stalker was in the neighborhood and had already abducted some kids in neighboring towns. God provided again.

The birth of my two children, after multiple miscarriages - weathering spotting during the first trimester for both of them, delivering them safe and sound through different challenges during each pregnancy - and now they have children of their own. God prevented more heart-ache and blessed us with ever-increasing miracles.

My marriage, health issues, job changes... life in general takes its toll, but we celebrated our 32nd anniversary this year! We need to remember these things. These memories are weapons in our arsenal to defeat fear and dread over the future for which God promises He has "good plans"[44].

Be a David. "Encourage yourself in the Lord". Take the time to look back at your own life and remember the situations when you just "happened" to get what you needed. Take time to notice the people and resources that mysteriously showed up in the nick of time. Allow those times to help you build your faith and trust in the God Who numbers every hair on your head, knows every tear you've cried, understands every desire of your heart, and has a glorious plan for you – far above anything you can possibly hope for yourself!

Make up your own "book of remembrance" – record previous deliverances. Apply the faith and trust developed in the past to the situations you encounter today. When faced with present challenges, look to the past successes that you never saw coming and declare God's provision and protection into your future.

Worry isn't helping you get what you think you need. It just shortens your vision and tenses up your gut. Take it one step further: Change your focus - let go of what is giving your own heart the flutters and make up your mind to prayerfully *be* the solution to someone else's difficulties. While you're sharing God's love for them, know that He has your issues firmly in hand and is working through His pre-determined solution for you! I may not be able to see how I get from where I am now to the favorable outcomes that I've experienced over and over again. But I know God will get me there. He always has. He always will.

Footnotes

[1] "It Won't Be Like This For Long" Darius Rucker

[2] "How To Think When Life Stinks" Jimmy Evans

[3] Ibid

[4] John 18:11 (NIV)

[5] Heb. 12:1-2 (NIV)

[6] Matt. 21:9, Mark 11:9-10, John 12:13 (NIV)

[7] Luke 22:44 (NIV)

[8] John 18:11 (NIV)

[9] 1 Cor. 2:16 (NIV)

[10] Phil. 2:5-13 (NIV)

[11] Heb. 13:5b (NIV)

[12] Heb 12:9 (NIV)

[13] Heb. 10:14 (NIV)

[14] Hosea 6:6, Matt 9:13 (NIV)

[15] Rom. 8:15 (amp)

[16] Rom. 8:37 (amp)

[17] Luke 1:37 (amp)

[18] 1 Sam. 17:52 (NIV)

[19] 2 Cor. 5:7 (amp)

[20] 1 Sam. 17:29 (NIV)

[21] 1 Sam. 717:28 (NIV)

[22] 1 Sam. 17:30 (NIV)

[23] 1 Sam. 17:35-37 (NIV)

[24] 1 Sam. 17:46-47 (NIV)

[25] Ps. 16:10 (NIV)

[26] Ps. 91:10 (amp)

[27] Ps. 46:1 (NIV)

[28] Heb 12:12 (NIV)

[29] Rom. 4, Gal. 3:8-9 (amp)

[30] Num. 23:19 (amp)

[31] Ps. 37:4 (NIV)

[32] Eph. 6:15 (amp)

[33] Heb 13:5 (NIV)

[34] Gen. 15:1 (amp)

[35] Prov. 31:10 (NIV)

[36] Prov. 19:13, 27: 15 (NIV)

[37] Prov. 31:11-12 (amp)

[38] Prov. 12:4 (amp)

[39] Eph. 3:20 (amp)

[40] Phil. 3:12 (NKJV)

[41] Phil 3:13 (NIV)

[42] 2 Cor. 12:9 (NIV)

[43] Matt. 6:33 (NIV)

[44] Jer. 29:11 (NIV)

Suggested Resources:

"How to Think When Life Stinks" by Jimmy Evans

"Living Beyond Yourself - Exploring the Fruit of the Spirit" by Beth Moore

"The Lord is My Shepherd" by Joyce Meyer

"Safe in the Shepherd's Arms: Hope and Encouragement from Psalm 23" by Max Lucado

Chapter 7
Misunderstandings and Motives

"For what person perceives (knows and understands) what passes through a man's thoughts except the man's own spirit within him? Just so, no one discerns (comes to know, comprehend) the thoughts of God except the Spirit of God."
1 Cor. 2:11

The ways my days start are just mind-blowing sometimes – and I love it! This morning, I was just becoming aware of being slightly awake. You know, that time when the dreams and thoughts of the subconscious give way to the feel of the room, needing to get up, and the first thoughts of the day begin forming. What am I going to do today? What day is it? It's mostly a solitary time, but there are times it becomes a conversation – as it did today.

My granddaughter Natalee's favorite song, "Hallelujah" is running through my head as I begin to be aware of waking up. Not the Hallelujah Chorus of Handel's Messiah, but the song by Leonard Cohen. It was a joy for me to hear my son and (then) 2-year-old granddaughter sing this together! (But I digress...) I thought, "What is our Quiet Time together today? *Girls With Swords*? (the book I've been reading by Lisa Bevere) Sure, I'm game." With thoughts of maybe snuggling down a little longer under the covers, I got back an answer to a question I hadn't asked: "I know." "Wait ....What?"

A long pause passed while the double meaning of *that* sunk in through the fog of the morning. He wasn't done. God issued a clear challenge: "Do you want to come upstairs and stop being 'game'?" There was no room left for the fog as the inference took hold: I can be prey or I can stand victoriously against the predator of our souls and kick some enemy butt. But I can't do that without the armor God gives me to put on, or the training I need to wield the sword of the Word against him effectively. No time like the present! Another Quiet Time begins...

"Be sober and vigilant for your adversary the devil roams about like a roaring lion seeking whom he may devour." [1] Another verse right behind it reminds me - "Put on the full armor of God so that you may be able to stand against all the wiles of the devil ...belt of truth,...breastplate of righteousness, ...your feet shod with...the gospel of peace...helmet of salvation...sword of the Spirit"[2]

I've unknowingly fallen into edit mode when this passage comes up, condensing what is actually said with a shorter version to make it fit the analogy more simply, but the re-read brings out precise detail. It doesn't say feet shod with the shoes of the Gospel or the shoes of peace, as I so often seem to condense it. It says, "...feet shod with *the preparation* of the Gospel of Peace". The amplified version says: "And having shod your feet in preparation [to face the enemy with the firm-footed stability, the promptness, and the readiness produced by the good news] of the Gospel of peace."[3] Preparation. Stability. Readiness. Gospel.

Gospel literally means Good News. What good news? The Good News of Peace. Not just small "p" peace, but "the peace of God, which transcends all understanding."⁴ Even when it doesn't make sense, even when the storm seems loud and boisterous around us, even if we don't understand why something is happening, we can remain supernaturally peaceful. Stable. Ready. Peace beyond our circumstances. Peace that transcends human understanding in the midst of the storm.

This Peace is only found in one place. Jesus said, "Peace I leave with you; My [own] peace I now give *and* bequeath to you. Not as the world gives do I give to you. Do not let your hearts be troubled, neither let them be afraid. [Stop allowing yourselves to be agitated and disturbed; and do not permit yourselves to be fearful and intimidated and cowardly and unsettled.]"⁵

The Good News of the Gospel of Peace is ours because Jesus is "Immanuel (which means 'God with us')"⁶ and told us we need not be afraid. Jesus said, "I have told you these things, so that in Me you may have [perfect] peace *and* confidence. In the world you have tribulation *and* trials *and* distress *and* frustration; but be of good cheer [take courage; be confident, certain, undaunted]! For I have overcome the world. [I have deprived it of power to harm you and have conquered it for you.]"⁷

There is a peace of mind that comes when you've trained with the Master. When you've prepared for the lesson, gotten the proper gear together, and learned how to use it. There is a confidence when you stand ready for the bout and know that you're not standing there alone.

But why is this preparation so important? What does this Gospel of Peace prepare us for? "...that you may be able to stand against the wiles of the devil."[8] Various synonyms for "wiles" include trickery, deceit, slight of hand, and distraction. We've already looked at several ways he uses these tactics to wreak havoc in our hearts and lives. Knowing the character of the enemy and the weapons he uses helps us defeat him. But our ability to defeat him is not an off-the-cuff, "winging it" as we go kind of thing – well, not if you want to be victorious in it. Preparation is critical because it gives us familiarity with the weapons we wield in each battle and this gives us God's peace in the storm.

The Bible tells us that satan, the great deceiver, uses weapons not made of flesh and blood. The weapons he uses against us are invisible and aimed at our affections. Visible weapons like swords and spears would be easier to see, but he uses weapons like fear, deception, and accusation. He wants to steal our joy. To weigh us down, wear us down and tire us out to make us more vulnerable to his attacks. Make no mistake he's not satisfied with stopping at the hunt. He wants to tear us apart and take us out of the picture entirely.

Jesus warned us Himself: "The thief ", satan, "comes only in order to steal, kill and destroy"[9]. But Jesus didn't leave us with just that declaration, He added: "I came that they may have *and* enjoy life, and have it in abundance [to the full, till it overflows]"[10] Panic feeds the enemy's attack. Peace dismantles the weapons he uses against us. Preparation before the battle and prayer in the face of the enemy gives us peace. Together, we have opportunity to fight against our enemy as a team, encouraging one another, praying for one another. But we can't do it without the *preparation* of the Gospel. Preparation is key.

Going back to the announcement Paul makes that satan's weapons are not visible, he also tells us the weapons God gives us to fight him are also not visible weapons of flesh and blood – and that's a good thing! God not only gives us armor – the aforementioned shield, helmet, sword and breastplate from Ephesians chapter 6 – to defend ourselves against the enemy's weapons, He gives us instructions on how to prevail in these battles - battles that take place on a very different kind of battle field.

Conditioning the body strengthens and builds stamina and endurance. When you feel better, you have a stronger immune system. And while a healthy body is a good starting place for any combat, spiritual battles require more than physical endurance. Strengthening your mind and soul is critical for victory. Because victory (or defeat) for emotional and spiritual warfare doesn't begin on a physical battlefield, it begins in the mind. Although we've already introduced the concept of "taking every thought captive" in a previous chapter, this barely scratches the surface. There is much more in the context of the passage.

2 Corinthians 10:4-5 says: "For the weapons of our warfare are not physical [weapons of flesh and blood], but they are mighty before God for the overthrow *and* destruction of strongholds, [Inasmuch as we] refute arguments *and* theories *and* reasonings and every proud *and* lofty thing that sets itself up against the [true] knowledge of God; and we lead every thought *and* purpose away captive into the obedience of Christ (the Messiah, the Anointed One)".

The arsenal we use to fight is more powerful than the attacks we are faced with. But we need to be on our guard. We need to be aware of incoming attacks and meet them head on as soon as they begin in order to be victorious. These engagements happen as we take captive the thoughts that begin the enemy's attack. Being wary of common pitfalls (depression, discouragement, and worry, to name a few), we can train ourselves to think differently. Think to win.

A now-common definition of insanity, sometimes attributed to Albert Einstein, is doing the same thing over and over and expecting different results. To get the results you want to see instead of being stuck in a pit of failure and discouragement you've been in, change how you're thinking. Thinking in ways counter to our previous natural tendencies, gives us the stamina and endurance to overcome the enemy's attacks. Just as in physical combat, different attacks require different defenses and counter attacks. Knowing which ones to use when is a skill - and a gift. It gets easier with practice.

We've already seen how "encouraging ourselves in the Lord" and looking back over previous successes can bring victory in your attitude over new challenges in life. And we've gotten deeper into how to specifically build your faith and trust in God as the result of this encouragement in the past. Now let's look forward and apply them in battle against four specific "wiles" satan uses against us and how we can defeat them: Fear, Accusation, Comparison, and Guilt.

"Fear Dancing"

Fear is one of the most-used weapons in satan's arsenal. It comes in many forms and from many directions. Fear is so prevalent, they've created lists of different fears and given them each their own names: Achluophobia (fear of the dark), acrophobia (fear of heights), agoraphobia (fear of open spaces or crowds), arachnophobia (fear of spiders), and that's just some of the A's. Fear paralyzes us and keeps us distracted from our true purpose – and victory over the enemy.

Fear in relationships is a weapon satan can use almost imperceptibly. Fear of what people think or say – some call it "peer pressure" - is a huge influence on our words and actions, not only for kids and teens, to whom it is most commonly used in reference to, but for adults too. Many times we don't recognize it for what it is. That's how it sneaks under the radar.

Dr. Gary Smalley's book "The DNA of Relationships" brings a new awareness of how this works on a daily basis in a way I never expected. When I first picked up the book, it was to get some tips on how to correctly deal with my relational frustrations and enable me to show respect to those I have conflict with. I wanted help combating my default attitudes of withdrawing or getting passive aggressive when I felt upset.

Instead of a rehash of old information, I found Dr. Smalley's book to be fresh and inspiring in uncovering what happens in my heart and head every time I am preparing for an interaction with anyone! The concept of interpersonal communication being based on core fears, and our frantic attempts to get our needs met to allay those fears being the foundation for every interaction we have, was like a paradigm shift in my thinking. The conversion from fear or disappointment to anger can happen so quickly in my mind and heart that I never stopped mid-trail to see the steps I took to get there!

Dr. Smalley's description of the "Fear Dance" and the examples he gave of his family members' interactions to illustrate how it progresses was eye-opening. He poses the question: "What are you *really* mad about?"[11] He challenges us to realize that the real problem is not the argument that is currently happening, but the *fear* over what we think is going to be the *outcome* – our needs not being met. He poses the theory that our reactions (especially anger) to another's behavior, is our way of trying to make the other person meet our needs so we can return to a feeling of safety or security – at least until the next time. The picture I got in my head as a result of this explanation surprised me.

Like the mild-mannered mayor in the familiar story by L. Frank Baum, stranded in the strange land far beyond his ordinary Kansas, we struggle to regain a sense of stability. Our insecurities morph into intimidation of others to keep us from feeling weak and off-balance. Sometimes our attitudes are barely noticeable, and sometimes they reach detrimental degrees easily seen by others in threats, rages and fury. We expend so much energy, distracting and redirecting attention from the reality of what is, to obtain from others what we think we cannot attain without all the misdirected effort. We become manipulators, unwittingly pulling strings and levers to bolster our own confidence - the Wizard in a bigger-than-life Land of Oz where nothing is at first familiar. We hide behind curtains of deception, to make our own way, sometimes without even knowing we're doing it! After a while, we may find out that we don't need to do this to get what we want, but then we fear *discovery* which instigates more fear – and temps us to keep the deception going.

But discovery of the deception is inevitable and the betrayal and disappointment of those once fooled into completing our assigned tasks can become ugly and cruel. Without the Grace of Forgiveness to smooth the way forward, they can retaliate with demands and expectations of their own.

Even when others try to help us, unhealthy relational habits can hinder our progress. We try to do the right thing, but not all the variables are under our control. The balloon escapes the confines of Oz and we need to find a different way back home. This parallel struck a chord in me.

I don't want to bully anyone into jumping through my self-imposed hoops to allay my fears! Given the choice in Christ, I would much rather allow Him to cleanse me of the fear and give me the power and Grace to trust Him – freed from striving for *self*-protection and resting in His! (His protection is a LOT stronger and far reaching than anything I could possibly come up with on my own anyway!) This also opens doors for willing cooperation and blooming opportunities - each person being able to use their own gifts and talents toward the good of all. That is a much-preferred option instead of coercion – whether obvious or passive-aggressive (refer back to the anger chapter)!

Having been shown the "man behind the curtain" in my own mind, God is helping me to look at myself and my reactions more clearly, without condemnation and shame.

This enables me to look back on lots of previous interactions – even with family members long gone and situations whose painful wounds still can distort my current perceptions. I need to allow Jesus to re-frame my thinking and heal the past so the future is built on Truth and Light instead of pain and fears.

Referring back to the timid mayor-turned-wizard, we can see behind the scenes; clearly, he wasn't evil. His bravado concealed his true motivation. His demands and actions were easily observable, but the motivation for what he did was based in fear. No one saw that; they saw the mask he projected. The same is true of us.

Actions are viewable. Attitudes can be felt. But assuming other peoples' motives can be a tricky business and leaves SO much room for error! As we noted at the beginning of the chapter, 1 Corinthians 2:11 clearly states no one can know what is in a man's thoughts, except the man's spirit within him. Trying to discern *why* someone else does or says something can lead us *way* off base – and open wide the door for conflict. We can't correctly assume *why* someone else does anything. They think differently than we do because they have different experiences and personalities than we do. Even siblings growing up in the same house have different perceptions on identical situations based on their birth order, body chemistry, age at the time, and so many other factors! (check out Dr. Kevin Leman's books on Birth Order) We seriously need to give one another a break, cut them some slack and try to understand – or ask them directly! – what they are going through and thinking about. It would save a lot of time, miscommunication and division.

The good news is we don't have to let previous misunderstandings about others' motives continue to hurt us. Someone said, "Where there is Life there is Hope"; today can be a new start. It may be embarrassing or painful in the beginning, but the effort is worth the investment of time, energy and honesty. This is freedom in progress. Looking back on things I cannot change in my past is not an empty regret-grasping agony, but a treasure hunt to find the jewels God had hidden in the trials I missed the first time around. Sometimes I missed the point was because I was too young to see it; sometimes it was too painful at the time to try. I realize so many times, I believed a lie – and proclaimed quite loudly that I could not "take it anymore" and fled the scene, before claiming the jewel in the victory!

Just like Moses fleeing in fear from Egypt and God using his time in the wilderness to prepare him to return for his truest destiny, we can let God redeem our past experiences and build us into the mighty men and women He created us to be through faith. Leaving the mud and weeds in the past, we can appropriate the confidence in God's provision developed in earlier situations and apply them to the circumstances we find ourselves in today. It's not a trip to the wood shed; it's a journey to the ultimate safe deposit box. It's not a matter of punishment, but of becoming equipped with our inheritance in Christ. We can let Jesus sanctify our hearts, bring out His Light through our eyes, and lead us home - excited about the journey, not dreading the ride.

Instead of allowing the devil to convince us that the only way to get our needs met is to deceive and manipulate one another, we can follow Jesus' model of faith and prayer to combat fear. Very often our fears turn out to be empty threats of the enemy and not much of what we think "might happen" actually does. If we face each fearful situation with honesty, faith and trust in our Heavenly Father's sovereign will, we gain the courage to deprive fear of its power over us.

This discovery is an amazing relief which is perfectly portrayed in the movie "Labyrinth" by the genius of Jim Henson. Sarah is going through adjustments in various family dynamics with a step-mom and a new baby brother, and finds her new responsibilities are more than she wants to handle. As a result of some rash words, she finds she must battle the Goblin King to get her kidnapped little brother back. As she journeys through the maze and all its traps, she discovers the labyrinth keeps changing and she cries out, "It's not fair!"[12] The Goblin King isn't interested in fair, he wants to win! His unfair advantage of making up his own rules and throwing one curve-ball after another intensifies. He uses various deceptions and fears to try to turn her from her determined rescue mission. But she's not battling him alone. She gets help from some very unlikely friends she meets along the way that help her meet each new challenge. With their help, even temporary forgetfulness of who she is and what her purpose is doesn't deter her for long.

Facing one fear after another, she gains confidence. Her final stand in the battle finds The Goblin King pleading with her to "love me, fear me, and I will be your slave!" in essence: you can have everything you want – if you submit to me! She had already unveiled that everything she previously "wanted" was junk compared to what she was truly seeking, and now she makes the final discovery.

Everything he has used on her throughout the journey has been a lie. It's all smoke and mirrors, a sometimes terrifying temptation for her to veer off her course, but he never had the ability to choose for her. The look on her face is priceless as the thought transfers from her favorite book to her own life. With that declaration, all his deceptions fall away and his influence over her is broken: "You have no power over me!"[13]

The same realization can be ours. Paul tells us clearly that "No temptation has overtaken you except what is common to mankind. And God is faithful; he will not let you be tempted beyond what you can bear. But when you are tempted, he will also provide a way out so that you can endure it."[14] This awareness of how fears and temptations have influenced many of our decisions can break the hold they have on us. We can look for and appropriate those "ways out" that God promises to provide and be victorious over our fears.

Acknowledging the influence of fear can have another benefit too. If we are willing to accept the possibility that other people have these same "fear curtains" that conceal their true motivations and drive their actions, we can dismantle the next weapon in satan's arsenal: accusation. We deprive accusation of its power by acknowledging the possibility that instead of intentionally attacking, annoying or tormenting us, the motivations of others could be based in *their* fear. We can revisit times when we assumed ill in others' motives and allow that maybe, just maybe, the things we were hurt by were not true, but merely the smoke and mirrors of someone else's self-protection.

Other possibilities include lack of knowledge, misunderstandings and miscommunication. Being open to considering alternate motives is a great equalizer against accusation. Accusation divides; extending grace, believing the best of others in difficult situations, and applying compassion to their struggle brings unity.

This frame of reference is not just a good way to build a foundation for future events and handle current interactions more peacefully, but it is also a good way to deal with hurts in the past. Just because the injury is old, doesn't mean it can't be mended. We can heal.

Healing the Accusation Breach

When I first heard Kathy Troccoli sing "Goodbye for Now" about her losing her mom to cancer, I thought about how thoroughly our past experiences affect our now. The hope she embraces and the comfort it gives her to know that she will see her Mom again someday is something I want to convey when I write sympathy cards. I want to share that wonderful hope in gratitude to God that I will be able to see my own mom again and to say all the tender things I want to be able to say to her.

But this is a fairly new attitude for me in my relationship with my mother. Some would even say it's too late for that now. You see, my mom is no longer in this world. And the relationship we had during my teen and young adult years was more unpleasant than enjoyable – for both of us. Unlike Kathy Troccoli's tribute, my relationship with my mom toward the end of her life was not something I would write a song about. Describing my relationship with my mom as "rocky" is like the understatement of the year. Others may have unhealthier recollections to avoid; some are better, some are worse, but they are mine. They color my motivations and my actions to more of a degree than I realize sometimes. This directly impacts my accusation quotient in the present and I cannot afford to leave that kind of damage unhealed.

Things between us were mostly adversarial – for several reasons. With the onset of (my) puberty, our interactions took a nose-dive. Mostly it was centered in my being clueless about the pressures she was under. Expectations and dreams almost attained and then, through circumstances – some of which were out of her control – taken away or denied her, left her feeling disillusioned with the differences between what was and what she thought should have been. That carried over into her relationship with my Dad, with us kids, and with other people she came in contact with - as it does for all of us. She was an amazing woman, stronger and more determined than she gave herself credit for sometimes. But her God-given resilience to meet these challenges and her inner strength developed an edge to it in the forge of frustration and fear that turned on her and others.

Even though I have great appreciation for her determination, I see many of the same obstacles setting up in me, and I want to change the course I am on. Her progress in this area was interrupted by a fatal car accident, and we haven't gotten to see the fulfillment of the changes God made in her journey to that freedom. I saw it starting before she left, I just didn't recognize it at the time. I was 27. She was 46. She had begun talking about expectations, boundaries and open communication – some of the same things God has been bringing me through in the past several years. I had no intention of listening to her. I didn't get the benefit of her knowledge because of my attitude – and the accusations against her that I harbored in my heart.

As I grew up a little and began to understand some of the things that were a mutual struggle for us, I had a new appreciation for some of the things she went through, and the things she tried to do for me. But by then, I really couldn't tell her anymore (or yet, depending on your perspective).

Misunderstandings and my immaturity were a big cause of our problems. I can see now that my assuming evil or mean motives for her and my father's actions is probably the biggest contributor to the conflicts between us.

As a 53-year-old mom and grandmother, some of my preparation and refining process have included forgiveness - both given and requested. Sometimes I need to extend it; sometimes I need to ask for it. It's been humbling, but it's been worth it. Viewing my parents' decisions and actions in the light of my own experience with spousal and parental frustration makes forgiveness easier. Financial pressures, medical issues, job conflicts, differing goals and methods of parenting and discipline preferences, exacerbated the stress between them based on their personality differences. This division contributed greatly to emotional barriers between them. Ironically, these are the same challenges I face on a daily basis.

That kind of constant emotional instability magnified the impact of events that would otherwise be merely annoyances easily confronted, had not other issues already eroded out the foundation beneath us. Realizing that this background discord all plays a part in how dramatically a glass of spilled milk, or broken dish plays

into my current responses and delivery of retribution for the surface offense, is a real eye opener.

If I am having a good day, the dishes are done, the air conditioner is working and the car isn't in for repairs, I deal with the happenings around me with a lot more finesse, than I do and did when my kids were smaller. When these other things are still hanging over me and it's day one of the cramps and the headache is on day three and the bills are coming in and the checkbook is sadly lacking, and...you get the picture...it's a completely different story!

So I started on a journey to apply this more adult understanding to my own past, to revisit the stressors that trigger undesirable reactions in me and develop more healthy responses now. Looking back at situations that happened when I was the child in the equation, I can see some things way more clearly – even if I don't recall or never knew what the other aggravating factors in the situation were for my parents. Some things are not so easily understood. How can you find out why something happened when the person you shared painful experiences with is no longer alive? I still wanted resolution, but was unsure about how to get there. I knew I needed a special grace to get through those memories.

370

Asking for Clarity Works!

While talking to a Christian counselor about generalities, I became increasingly aware of something from my past that I was still holding against my mother - and she had already been "deceased" for 23 years. I was stuck in unforgiveness over an event that happened when I was a child. As I was talking about it, I verbalized the thought that I would never really know what her motivation was for that particular decision that had affected me so deeply. She was dead and there was no way I could ask her now. I didn't know at first why it still hurt so badly, but my counselor posed an option that I had never considered before.

I have had times in the past when, in answer to a thought or a prayer for understanding, I have been directed to a passage in the Bible or I ended up watching a program on TV or sometimes just got a sudden "knowing" – a realization that I know I never had on my own – that explained the whole thing and brought clarity. At the suggestion of my counselor, I decided to see if God would help me understand the root of this particular long-held bitterness.

I prayed, "God show me what I need to know here! I really want to let this go! I don't want to still be angry with my mom over something that happened years ago – long after her death!" I sat with my eyes closed, expecting an answer, determined to take the time to listen for it. I didn't have to wait. What happened next was truly strange. Instead of going directly to an explanation, in one moment in time, several things happened all at once.

First I *felt* "I Love you" repeated several times quietly, "off to the side", knowing it wasn't coming from God this time, but not knowing who it was. Then the verses in 1 Corinthians 13 about "love always believes the best" popped into my thoughts. Simultaneously, a very vivid memory came up of my Mom holding me while I sobbed heart-wrenching sobs about a boy breaking up with me over the phone in 6th grade. She sat there on the couch and held me, crying with me and saying all those Mother things about him "not being worth it" and "if he only knew what kind of treasure he was losing", and so on for what felt like all afternoon.

I know I cried until there were no more tears left, my body shuddering with every breath. She stayed with me the whole time, smoothing my hair back and holding me in her arms, rocking me back and forth. I was 11 years old and it was the most overtly painful thing that had happened to me up to that point. I was completely helpless to change it – and so was she. She would have done anything to make me feel better at that moment. And I knew it. It's a good thing she didn't know this little 6th grade boy's phone number. I can just imagine...

Anyway – the realization that she wanted to take the pain away, if she could have, made me feel better. This certain knowledge is much more easily understood by me now as a mom who went through some of those things with my own children. I was tempted to make some of those phone calls myself!

Now with that as a backdrop, God reminded me of the original situation: my Mom told me that she couldn't let me go to my grandfather's funeral because she needed my help at home with two of my younger siblings (my youngest sister had not been born yet), while my Dad and brother (both named after this grandfather) went to the funeral over an hour away. I was so upset! I cried and screamed and can't imagine that I was much help to her that day with the attitude I took up for this.

It got even worse afterwards. When my dad and brother came home, they recounted all the family members in attendance that we rarely, if ever, saw and how they'd laughed and talked about family memories and ate and talked some more. I was so angry about missing it! Years later, when I was an "adult", I talked with my mom about it, but it wasn't much of a discussion. I was still angry and she was defending herself. She told me she remembered the reason I didn't go was I was sick at the time. I growled back "I was *not* sick, you TOLD me you needed my help and THAT was why you didn't let me go!" Maybe she was the one who was sick; maybe it was my younger brother or sister, maybe that was why she "needed my help". I don't know. She said that wasn't it and she honestly remembered *me* being sick. (there is a very real possibility I was sick...and didn't remember that part) Between the two of us, we never really resolved what had happened.

Somehow in the context of the two memories being brought to my attention so close together, God let me in on a secret no one else could have told me, something not even my mom remembered later on: my mother's true motive for keeping me home that day.

The boyfriend thing happened several months before my grandfather died. The thought that came to me in that moment was that my mom had speculated, if the pain I felt when some boy in school broke up with me was that intense, what degree of pain was I going to be in if I was at a funeral for the grandfather who loved me deeply, who I loved so dearly and had spent so much time with in my very young life? Whatever the reason at the time, she was not going to be able to go herself, with two young children under the age of 3. She would not be there to hold me while I cried worse than any boyfriend could have hurt me.

My Dad would not have been able to help and comfort me, going through the loss of his own Dad at the same time. (Not that my Dad would have reacted that way anyway. Even if it was someone else's loss we were dealing with, he wasn't the type to "be there" for me like that. Consolation was my mom's purview).

She was not trying to deprive me of my own grandfather's memorial. She was trying to save me and protect me from that pain as best she knew how – and all she got for it was yelled at and insulted by a grieving 11-year-old. I realized again, that someone's motive can be honestly sincere, and still enable you to make what later turns out to be the wrong decision – in someone else's eyes. Arm-chair quarterbacking seems easy after the plays are complete, but no one has the benefit of hind-sight before something happens except God.

It then became clear in that moment of revelation who was *feeling* "I love you" to me when I first began remembering the situation. It was my Mom. I had not understood her true motivation of protection and feelings of helplessness in her own inability to be there at the time. I had applied an accusation to her motives that was selfish and self-serving: that she hadn't wanted to deal with my younger siblings by herself for the day so she was keeping me from something I really wanted to do. I had repeated that accusation many times over the years in my head whenever I thought of this situation, cementing it in a dark cloud of bitter memory. I knew now I was so wrong! In an instant, I was able to let go of that bitterness and the ugly hold it had on my heart.

I saw my wrong assumption of her motive was one more brick in a wall of distance between us. It was good to be able to get rid of it. Motives are tricky things. Most times you can look at a situation and be fairly accurate as to *what* happened. But determining *why* someone did something is a gamble at best. Sometimes, if we're honest enough to admit it, we don't even know why *we* do some of the things we do. So how can we be so confident we know why someone else did something? That's the heart of accusation.

Isn't that how the devil tempted Eve to reject God's instruction in the garden? *God's holding out on you. You won't really die, you'll become like He is and He doesn't want to share that kind of knowledge with you. You can handle it. Don't listen to Him. Take it for yourself*. God's motive for withholding the tree of the Knowledge of Good and Evil was based on His love for us. Accusation said otherwise. Accusations don't need to be true to do damage. That applies to our view of God and toward others, who are created in His image.

If we truly trust that God is Love and that everything He does is out of Love, we more readily trust that even difficult situations we endure have purpose and benefit in our lives. This perspective can also help us trust in those same qualities in people: "Love bears up under anything and everything that comes, is ever ready to believe the best of every person, its hopes are fadeless under all circumstances, and it endures everything [without weakening]."[15]

The verses here in 1 Corinthians 13 can become an accusation-quencher when we are tempted to guess at other people's motives. I am now able to see another thing more clearly instead of "through a glass dimly …when I was a child, I thought like a child, I spoke like a child I reasoned like a child. Now that I am grown, I am done with childish ways…Now I know in part (imperfectly), but then I shall know and understand fully and clearly, even as I have been fully and clearly known…"[16]

The unforgiveness and anger I held for so long toward my Mom over that incident has melted into a motherly understanding of knowing she was making the best decision she could with the information she had at the time, and regretted it afterward. Second-guessing herself after they returned from the funeral was useless for both of us. She really had been acting in love; it just didn't seem that way to me at the time. Lord knows I've been there myself many times now!

Yes. There are other not very pleasant memories I have in confrontation between us that, if I dwell on them in accusation, they can still hurt and tempt me to wonder how she could possibly have treated me that way. But now I can step back and realize I don't have all the information with any of those situations. I can choose to let them go with forgiveness and Grace, just like God gave me the opportunity to do with this one, knowing that I have been dishing out not-so-pleasant memories myself. I can easily identify specific times she must have asked herself the same questions of my behavior and disrespect towards her! But when I talk to friends of hers, the things they remember were the times she told them how proud she was of me and how well I was turning out. This just added to her regret that we weren't closer. There was no condemnation or ridicule of choices I was making that she disagreed with, just a heart-break for the distance between us and a longing for something better.

That is the true heart of a mom - of my Mom. And I know with all my heart that if she could have changed the past and times that she lost it, or reacted in a way that turned out not to be the best solution at the time, she would have - she would have moved heaven and earth to do so. I feel the same way toward my own children. I want to make things right for them. But that's not always the best thing to do. It's also not possible in a lot of cases. They have choices to make and the outcome is theirs to navigate. My prayer is they will choose to seek the One Who sees them (El Roi) and knows every one of their answers. That doesn't make it any easier sitting on the sidelines. And there are plenty of opportunities for misunderstandings.

Just as Jesus as prayed, "Father, forgive them, they don't know what they're doing", when I experience situations now that could be interpreted through a lens of hurt, I can choose to hold it up to the dynamic between my mom and me all those years ago, say a silent "I'm sorry Mom, I didn't understand" about the past and move on with additional understanding. I am learning that I can accept that knowledge and adjust possibly misplaced expectations and live today well, while I wait to see her again. There is peace about that, even through occasional tears.

I am so grateful for this opportunity! God gave me a gift of being able to correct a faulty memory, and it has made an amazing difference in my perspective! There have been other times when He has interceded in my thinking and made a difference in relationships that are being built right now, and situations I have benefited from, even though they were really hard at the time. These are not isolated incidents. He does that kind of thing more often than we realize – He is the God of reconciliation, after all. And it's not only with family relationships. Sometimes it's with people you think won't make a difference if you ever bother to get closer to them – and then He gifts you with another friend out of the experience...

A Different Strategy

When I was working in a previous job, I had a supervisor that was "on the strict side". Part of it was her job and part of it was her personality. After a while, it seemed that she just got even more unreasonable in her expectations, and as my supervisor, and with my work station right next to her desk, there was no way of getting away from her. The situation just got harder for me to handle and the other people she was supervising and I often got stuck in complaining sessions about her behind her back. I knew it wasn't the right thing to do, but I found myself obsessing and thinking about negative things relating to her all the time.

One day, while I was at home I started thinking about (and dreading) the next day at work. That was the end. I just started talking out loud: "God! You've got to help me! This is ridiculous! I am standing here in the shower thinking about her! - *I don't want her in the shower with me!*" (yup, I know go ahead and laugh, but that is the point of frustration I was at.) Now I wish I had prayed about this a long time before that, because instead of joining me in my angry pity party, God "thought" me something I kind of knew, but hadn't given much attention to. And the funny thing was all this information was just there. It didn't take individual sentences for Him to download the thoughts into my heart. I just knew with a deeper understanding what was happening.

He is such a "Daddy"! Like <u>Little House of the Prairie</u>'s "Pa" explaining to his "Half-Pint" or Andy Griffith explaining it to Opie, He didn't wag His finger in my face and scold me for being critical, He gently showed me a perspective I hadn't tried to see before: "Tracy, not everything that is happening is out in the open. There is pressure you don't see and frustration that has nothing to do with you or work going on here. (what?) She was just diagnosed with diabetes recently (we all knew that at work) and that means lots of changes – remember when you were a diabetic during your pregnancies? You only had to deal with it for a few months, and controlled it by eating differently for a little while, knowing as soon as the baby was born, you could go back to sweets and fats and carbs just like before. Inconvenient and annoying, but temporary. She's insulin-dependent, with needles and blood checks and the knowledge that the consequences of not doing what she needs to can be fatal. There's a lot to get used to: having to make sure she's back home from

379

visiting or shopping to test and take her shots and all the things you never had to deal with. Do you know the fears that go along with this? What happens if she forgets to take juice with her? What happens if she starts to have a reaction – too much or too little are both bad. Instead of complaining or defending your own actions, why not offer to help her?" (What can I do about that?) "You could offer to be a 'back up' for her. Offer to learn how to administer emergency insulin if she starts to have trouble at work." (Seriously. That's Your answer?) "Try it. See what happens."

It was something I never thought of at all! But of course, I had just read an article about it recently while waiting in a doctor's office, so the seed had already been planted. God doesn't ask you something without somehow preparing you for it ahead of time! So after I became willing to get rid of the knot in my gut, I finished my shower free of the obsessive frustration. Would it really make a difference?

The next day, when no one else was around, I asked my supervisor if I could talk to her. I told her that I knew that she had been diagnosed with diabetes and asked her if she had anyone at work that would be able to help her if she went into a diabetic shock. She was wary and seemed surprised at my question, and said "No, why?" I asked if she would like me to learn how, seeing my desk was right next to hers.

You probably could have knocked her over with a feather then and there. I don't remember what the rest of the conversation was after that. I don't think I ever did learn what to do. But I had offered. And I guess that's all God needed to happen. After that day, she didn't seem to let the pressure of work get to her as much, she wasn't as rattled when stuff went wrong with the job, and we had nice (and sometimes personal) conversations after that. We even met after work a couple times sharing gardening tips and a walk near a marina one afternoon.

She moved shortly after that and I haven't seen her in a while, but who knows? Maybe all she needed to know was God "had her back" and wasn't going to let her down with her latest struggle. He let me be the person He used to tell her. It doesn't get much better than that.

God also used this as a lesson to me in applying His Word to believe the best and not assume that others are being mean or short-tempered just because they want to be. Maybe we need to allow for the possibility that they have stuff going on that we are completely clueless about and that one interaction you have with them at 8:15 in the morning really can be either that last straw that pushes them over the edge, or the life-line that brings them back from the brink.

Motives and Compari-sin

The fact of the matter is nobody's perfect. What we are able to see from our limited perspective of others often does not show us reality. There are big differences between what we see from the outside and the totality of what we each experience. Some experience more upheaval than others. Some are more peaceful than others. What one person finds to be an easy task can completely baffle someone else. Situations that some take in stride and somehow learn to overcome, in other's lives may completely devastate.

We each have strengths and weaknesses. They are built into us by Divine design. We need God and each other. Each of our differences and strengths were given to enable us to contribute to the betterment of one another. But sometimes we use them to divide us. The temptation to evaluate one another based on these differences is strong. This is where comparison comes in, and it's never a productive thing.

Andy Stanley, an internationally known pastor and son of Dr. Charles Stanley from Atlanta, Georgia, recently gave an amazing teaching on "The Sin of Comparison". He told how "There will always be someone with a bigger –er than you"[17]. And this is a problem in both directions: in the envy direction, (pretty-er, smart-er, skinny-er, rich-er, healthy-er) we feel defeated and like we'll never measure up to the ideal we are comparing to. In the condescending direction, (ugly-er, dumb-er, fat-er, poor-er, sick-er) we tend to feel "superior-er",[18] and look down our noses at others who we feel could be and do better, if only they'd be more like us – or at least listen to our advice. Either way, envy and pride steals the joy of our relationships and sets us up for defeat.

It's a sword that cuts either way. Andy pointed out that's the sin in "compari-sin" – and the admonition "Do not be wise in your own eyes…"[19] keeps us from trouble and foolishness.

To use a wonderful phrase from my years in Al-Anon: "Don't judge your insides by someone else's outsides". When we "judge our insides" (everything that we know, feel, experience, the complete package of all the internal "us" combined together) by comparing it to "someone else's outsides "(the *appearances* we are only able to see from what is visible of others from the external "them" they choose to show us), the assumptions and decisions we will make will be faulty. We are unable to completely know other people's thoughts, motivations and pain. We know our own too deeply sometimes. And the apostle Paul tells us "when they measure themselves with themselves and compare themselves with one another, they are without understanding *and* behave unwisely."[20]

The decisions we make when we are comparing what we see in others and what we know and feel on the inside of us are unwise, and often damaging. We've all done it. It's part of being human. And it perpetuates misunderstanding in others and continues between generations, between families, between individuals – each making their own erroneous judgments. Like ripples in a pond, guessing at and then comparing what we think others' motives are affects more than we realize. That is why we need the Holy Spirit and the principles laid out in the Word of God to keep us from these foolish errors.

Re-read 1 Corinthians 2:11: "For what person perceives (knows and understands) what passes through a man's thoughts except the man's own sprit within him?..." You don't know for sure unless you ask. That is why so many counselors advise "reflective listening" – while someone is speaking to you, asking them "Do you mean...?" and reflecting back to them what you think you heard them say. Sometimes it matches, but sometimes it doesn't. That way, when there is any way that you misunderstood something they are saying, you can know about it right away before damage and division sets in.

Someone can say something in a short phrase, meaning a lot more behind it, and others may interpret it (based on their own thoughts and emotions at the time) and infer something totally different out of it. They can be hurt by misunderstanding something you meant completely differently.

One such situation happened in a conversation I had with my mother-in-law several years after my father-in-law died. (Let me take a break here to interject something critically important: "mother-in-law" is exclusively a descriptive term here. Estelle was a dream, a heaven-decreed life-line in my life. She in no way fits any proverbial references to our culture's sarcastic understanding of "mother-in-law". She was a true blessing to me and there are no undertones of anything negative in our relationship. She is a true saint. Barbara Johnson, acknowledging her son's wife for her dedication in her book, "I'm So Glad You Told Me What I Didn't Want to Hear", put it perfectly by calling her "Daughter-in-Love". I thought that was so beautiful. Estelle was my "Mother-in-Love"!)

We were on the deck of Estelle's house enjoying a family barbeque with Steve's side of our family. My husband was dealing with the results of a work injury; he was unsuccessfully dealing with his new limitations and attempting to do things he had previously been able to do with ease. He was stiff and was having trouble moving around after a particularly tough day. As he waved me away from helping him with something, it reminded me of his dad. Suddenly my thoughts went into Mr. Peabody's Way-back Machine and it was déjà vu all over again:

Years before, we had been visiting Steve's parents. His dad's health issues often caused him to be short of breath but it seemed to be affecting him pretty intensely that day. As I got up to help him, the look I got from Steve's mom, with a slight shake of her head, let me know I needed to sit back down and let it go. It made no sense to me, and I am usually not aware of subtle cues like that, but the intensity of even her subtle reaction was too clear to ignore. I sat back down without saying anything. Later on, she explained.

She and Milton had an unspoken agreement that when he was going through things like this, he wanted her to just let things lie. He didn't want her making a fuss over him, saying there was nothing she could do about it anyway. It was a carry-over from his WW II Army Medic attitude, "Don't make a big deal, it'll be fine". She seemed so calm! I was in awe. "How can you do that?" She told me how hard it was for her to sit there and act like everything was fine, when what she wanted to do was jump up and *do* something – *anything* – to ease his trouble. She told me it was one of the hardest things she ever had to learn. But it was one of the things she needed to adjust to and it's just the way it was. That stayed with me for a long time.

Years had passed since that conversation, but the memory of it had come full-force into my awareness while watching my own husband that afternoon. With a little sadness in my voice because of the shared helplessness I felt, I leaned over toward her and said softly, "like father, like son". I was relating to that story like it had just happened, but she had not been thinking about that at all – go figure!

A few minutes later, seeing her shoulders slumped over and acting quieter than before, I asked her if she was okay. She tearfully told me, "Milton was a wonderful man, a great provider, a wonderful husband...why is "like father, like son" a bad thing?" She was hurt by the thought that I meant it as a derogatory comparison. I hadn't meant it like that at all – but she had no way of knowing how my thoughts had traveled so far from that moment. I thank God she told me what she was thinking!

I immediately agreed how wonderful Dad was, hugging her and telling her how much I admired him and was saddened that I hadn't gotten to know him better before he died. (I love hearing Milton stories – he really was an incredible man!) And I am so glad I had the chance to correct the misunderstanding with Estelle! When I explained what I had been thinking behind that statement, she knowingly nodded her head and said, "Yes, he didn't want me to make a big deal about that kind of thing." I had made my comment actually looking up to her and admiring her guidance on how to "stay seated" when faced with those helpless feelings and the strength to remain calm during my husband's (her son's) physical trials.

The initial hurt gave way to an alliance of shared strength during another difficult time, and it made my task easier to handle. Talking it through helped our relationship deepen. I shudder to think of the distance and division that could have shadowed us if she hadn't told me what she was thinking at the time. Estelle was without doubt one of

God's most precious gifts to me, both before and after my own mother died. I am glad she didn't keep the hurt of that misunderstanding to herself!

This particular experience cast me in the role of child. I have had multiple opportunities to play the parental role - being misunderstood and misunderstanding my own children's words. At any given time in our lives, no matter how old we are, we can step into either set of shoes - or both depending on the situation. Both happen continually in every relationship. It's just a fact of life.

We need to realize we do indeed, "see things dimly"[21] right now, and we need to extend grace to others. If we are to live in any degree of peace and joy, we need to make 1 Corinthians 13 more than just something we hear at a wedding. We need to apply it to everyone we encounter - most importantly to our relationships as parents, children, and siblings. If we are going to experience the Life Jesus died to give us, we need to develop patience, kindness, and humility, and reject resentment, jealousy, pride and a quick temper. We need to "be ever ready to believe the best of every person"[22].

If something happens or is said that hurts us, we need to use the grace and power that the cross has extended to *us* and give the other person the benefit of the doubt. It is helpful for us to apply "grace" to them, understanding that other things in their experience - whether today or in years past - have brought them to this place or situation. We need to develop the ability to overlook their current words or actions that are hurtful and release them in acceptance. This is at the heart of being quick to forgive and slow to take offense.

Believing that their recent action or words I am tempted to hold against them is just "the straw that broke the camel's back" and that a great part of the current attitude I'm seeing from them may have nothing to do with me, enables me to take a step back and not take something (as) personally.

All of us have lots of other contributing factors that others are unaware of at the moment. Just as we would like them to cut us some slack when we are not at our best, we need to cut them some slack too. It is not easy. It takes practice but fortunately we all have lots of opportunities for this! The more we practice it, the more readily we will retain our peace. If on the other hand, we dwell on these misunderstandings or the difficult situations we've been through with regret and direct accusations inward with second-guessing ourselves and others, it can morph into another one of satan's weapons: Guilt.

The Division of Guilt

In a recent teaching by Beth Moore on Life Today, she addressed the dangers of guilt and its detrimental effect on our victory over affliction. She defined affliction as anything that afflicts us. Any troubles, trials, temptations, tough situations, that have the effect of stealing our joy and peace of mind can adversely affect our ability to fulfill our purpose in life. She warned that sometimes we bring affliction on ourselves by our own choices and that can tempt us toward guilt. Teaching from Psalm 25, she makes a bold statement: "Untreated guilt is the most fertile soil on planet earth for affliction."[23]

Untreated guilt can grow lots of trouble in our lives. Guilt leads us to distance ourselves from God. Distance from God makes us more prone to temptation. Temptation submitted to gives way to more sin and more sin makes us feel guiltier. It's a horrible cycle of defeat. But, she says, it is a path we can jump off of. We are supposed to come boldly to the throne of Grace so we can find help in times of trouble, according to Hebrews 4:16. But often our guilty conscience tries to get in the way, deterring us from the very confidence we are supposed to have in the Love of our Heavenly Father. "Our afflictions are supposed to bring us into submission to Christ, not defeat us. No matter what your affliction and your trouble, ask God to forgive all your sins and mean it...instead of crying 'woe is me, my sin caused all this', here's the remedy: when you confess and repent, you're forgiven...it's done,"[24] said Beth.

"Let us draw near to God with a sincere heart and with the full assurance that faith brings, having our hearts sprinkled to cleanse us from a guilty conscience and having our bodies washed with pure water."[25] We can shed the guilty conscience with full assurance because God is true to his Word: "If we confess our sins, He is faithful and just and will forgive us our sins and purify us from all unrighteousness."[26] Instead of a continued cycle of day after day continually asking God to forgive you for sins you've already confessed, when they come up again in your memory, take a different tack. "The next time you are tempted to get into guilt over it, stop and this time thank Him [God] for doing it."[27] This dismantles all the power the enemy is trying to exert over you with guilt.

With Fear, Accusation, Comparison and Guilt out of the way, you can view the enemy's wiley attempts to defeat you with understanding and say with confidence, "You have no power over me!" We can share this confidence with others. And we can implement these changes from a different vantage point: one that rises from who we are instead of what we do.

Grace-filled Change

With all these foundation stones in place, believing I know what needs to be done, I have tried sometimes unsuccessfully to act and feel differently by sheer will-power. Will-power alone doesn't get me very far. God showed me a keystone that opens all this up in another teaching I saw on-line. The biggest misunderstanding I have been able to identify in why I can't seem to get above a certain behavior level for very long: my misunderstanding of identity.

Bob Hamp, from Freedom Ministries at Gateway Church in Southlake Texas, was teaching on Levels of Change. Among other things in the teaching, he diagramed the levels of change we experience and why we are so frustrated sometimes in trying to change our undesirable behaviors. He explained that each of the lower levels create a ceiling or cap, that restricts people to the level below it. If we try to change merely at that level, it keeps us confined and unable to make lasting progress. I was furiously taking notes and making connections to all these other things going through my head.

He showed the lowest level of change is Environment.[28] (This is commonly known as the "location-"or "geographic cure" in 12-step circles; in psychology it's a form of escapism.) We think if we just change jobs, change marriages, change living conditions, or move, then our lives will be better and we will see the results we want to see. This is a fallacy due to one inescapable fact: "No matter where you go, there you are."[29] This is not a new thought. A quote by Thomas a Kempis in Imitation of Christ ca 1440 AD states: "So, the cross is always ready and waits for you everywhere. You cannot escape it no matter where you run, for wherever you go you are burdened with yourself. Wherever you go, there you are." [30]

No matter the trouble, we take us with us wherever we go. Differences in our environment *can* shake up things – in good ways or bad, but we cannot expect lasting change inside ourselves just by changing our location. So this is the lowest level of change in Hamp's diagram.

The next level of change is Behavior.[31] He then assigned behavior two different contributing factors: thoughts and feelings. He showed how our thoughts and feelings can affect our behavior in positive and negative ways. This is a more effective level of change than just changing your environment, but the power of positive thinking alone is not enough to raise you past the level of your own experiences. If you are having a bad day, your feelings are dragging on the ground, your thoughts tend to be negative and you resort to familiar - and sometimes destructive - behaviors.

We can change our environment and get temporary, surface change. We can advance to the next level and change some thought patterns and emotional responses for short-term improvement in behavior, but without rising to a higher level of change, there's an invisible ceiling restraining your progress.

The next level up is Capabilities.[32] At the capability level, it's no longer our own determination or will-power that hinders or advances us. Our success in change at this level is based on our natural capabilities. Your capabilities are a stronger starting point than your environment, feelings and thoughts, but capability also implies limitations.

This level acts like a thermostat on what you allow yourself to do or how high you think you can attain based on your past experiences. If you have struggled with something in your past, you may tell yourself you can never get over that thing, you'll always be an alcoholic, you'll never be financially responsible, you'll never get past a certain weight limit, etc. People that are blocked from change at this level will often, even subconsciously, sabotage their own success in a particular area because of the thermostat-like cap affecting their behavior. If they think they can't, then they can't. In order to break through the boundaries of this level, we need to advance to the level of Belief.

According to Bob Hamp, Belief is different from thoughts in several ways. Generally a belief is held in your heart, not just a thought in your head. It can be faulty and is often not a conscious process, but is a "sense" of a feeling, not something easily expressed in language[33]. It is a filter that strains every bit of information before being processed in your head. For example, someone who was verbally abused can feel badly about themselves no matter how pretty or intelligent they are in fact. They believe they are stupid or ugly or useless or incorrigible, or any number of derogatory things they heard over and over, even if they may not be able to put it into words or define why.

Sometimes it's a question, "What is wrong with you?" leaving anyone with influence in their lives to fill in the blanks for them. People may believe they will never escape an addiction or a behavior because they believe they were "born that way", or "it's just too hard". External affirmation does little to dispel the lies that trap people at this level. It's has to be "an inside job".

Bob told a story of a woman who had been depressed for 11 years, stuck in a cycle of inactivity, sleeping pills, and discouragement, sleeping her days away in remorse for not being there for her family. She had sought Bob out so he could help her son with *his* problems. When Bob asked about her issues, she revealed her belief that even though she was a Christian and believed in God, "it's too late for me. This has gone on too long. Just help my son."

He didn't merely contradict her belief with shallow affirmations. Instead of arguing with her, he asked her to read aloud a list of verses that spoke of God's sovereignty, Jesus' resurrection power, and her capabilities in Christ. She would be hearing her own voice, but this was not merely self-talk.

He asked her to listen to what she was reading, receiving it as God speaking these things directly to her heart. At first she was stoic and distant while she read the first few lines, (you can almost hear the "Yeah, yeah, whatever..." of the enemy) but then, as the list proceeded, listening to her own voice reading God's truth about what was True in His Word and applying it to herself, as God intends for us all to do, she got more and more excited. "Why didn't I know these things before?" Her beliefs about what was and was not possible changed deep inside her heart because she listened to a Voice bigger than her own. "...Faith comes by hearing and hearing by the word of God"[34]. Don't ever underestimate the power of God's words spoken to a grieving heart! It truly is ALIVE! If we surround ourselves with God's truth, listen to His Word to shape our beliefs, about Him and about ourselves, we can see greater change from that level instead of constantly getting disappointed and frustrated with setbacks from the limitations of the other lower levels.

I read something that applies here very well: "My Son, be attentive to My Wisdom [Godly Wisdom learned by actual and costly experience], and incline your ear to my understanding [of what is becoming and prudent for you]. That you may exercise proper discrimination and discretion and your lips may guard and keep knowledge and the wise answer [to temptation]."[35] I read this and stopped short – I didn't want to miss this. The phrase jumped off the page to me and chipped away some more self-righteous indignation about something someone else "did to me" the other day.

When I read the phrase "wisdom learned by actual and costly experience"...I caught myself in the accusations that had been building in my thoughts toward someone and I recognized the junk that God was trying to skim off my hard heart. Wisdom is not cheap, experience and the lessons we learn by it costs us something, it hurts, it's hard, - and then it's ours! We can apply it because we got it the hard way - I needed to hear that. It helps me from being so judgmental of others who have not had the same experience "lessons" I've had. And it humbles me when I think of the things others have gone through that I've been spared.

My attitude toward this particular situation I was dealing with was overflowing with self-righteousness. I was, in effect, agreeing with the enemy's accusations about this person being foolish, followed by an assertion that "if they would only listen to me…, they would be making wiser choices". While it may have been true, my expectation that they would (should!) accept my input was driving a wedge in our relationship. My attitude was becoming an obstacle between us. So I needed to take personal responsibility for my own choices in action and attitude and renew my mind in God's truth at the belief level.

"For man's anger does not promote the righteousness God [wishes and requires]."[36] I can be *right* up, down, and sideways, but being *right* – and getting ticked off at others because they don't see it or care if I'm right – is a very poor substitute for a loving relationship with them. My expectations of them understanding what I know, without them having had the experiences or capabilities I have was a futile waste of time AND an opening the enemy was using to create dissention. I do not want to cooperate with that kind of sneaky junk anymore! I believe that just as God has been working in me and producing and allowing certain situations to help teach me the things He wants me to learn in His perfect timing, He can and does do that in others' lives as well. My attitude needed to be adjusted by that belief.

We don't have the responsibility of others' choices. We have the responsibility for our own. Instead of applying this verse to how to correct *their* misunderstanding and what we consider "error", we can choose instead to pray that God gives opportunity for us to learn godly Wisdom, and understanding so that we can "exercise proper discrimination and discretion" and guard our own lips to "give a wise answer to temptation"[37]. We can also pray these things for them – without destroying our relationship in the process - by giving them the dignity and respect to believe that they too will be able to learn their own lessons based on their own experiences. We can then take off the martyr hat, the Holy Ghost Jr. T-shirt and just be free to be ourselves. There's a LOT less pressure that way! And we will be able to enjoy the purpose we were created for instead of trying to run someone else's life.

The temptation is common. God's prescription for this malady is prayer, humility, and repentance – not for others' faults but for our own. "If my people, who are called by my name, will humble themselves and pray and seek my face and turn from their wicked ways, then I will hear from heaven, and I will forgive their sin and will heal their land."[38] I have no trouble accepting my "land" needs healing. I know where to turn. And that's a good thing because we've got one more level to go.

Environment, Behavior, Capabilities and Belief: all these previous levels of change concern what we do. If we try to change our behavior in these first four levels, we will have repeated times of failure, for which God promises us we can always receive forgiveness. But the greatest and highest level of change is not based on what we do, but on what God does for us. This is the level of Identity.

"Who are we?" and "What are we worth?" The answers depend on your criteria. If who you are is based on earthly, material standards like what you do, who you hang out with, what you drive, where you live, your financial standing, your roles in life, or even religious standards like how "good" you are, how much you give to the poor, etc., your answers will be vary greatly depending on who you ask. If your answer is based on how God created you carefully and intricately "in your mother's womb"[39], then comparison with others is eliminated entirely. No one of us is less valuable than another. We are each unique. Each of us shares that creation point: God created us with purpose, on purpose, as we are, with a yearning for us to get to know Him better.

The degree to which we successfully change is most impacted by our understanding of our identity. Are we a sinner, with a death-defined "old man" at the center of who we are? Or are we a "new creation" [40] in Christ? If we start at the lower levels of impact, we will struggle uphill. If we begin at the top and accept God's assessment of who we are in Christ, as a born-again, Holy-Spirit in-dwelt, sanctified over-comer, then the other lower levels of change will take care of themselves from the top down. Yes, there are challenges we still need to face, but they are no longer insurmountable if you truly know who - and Whose - you are. Bob Hemp's teaching goes far beyond what I've cited so far and I encourage you to listen to the teaching in its entirety. Reviewing it periodically helps me get beyond the distractions of the immediate and reset my focus toward a Bigger perspective.

I wonder what other things I have stored in my memory that are tucked away with impressions and emotions that are faulty and detrimental to my understanding. Clearly my perspective on other people and events in my life have led to misunderstandings and shaped my motives.

Situations that I took to heart didn't mean what I thought they meant and shaped how I acted in hurtful ways.

I realize now that, even if the offenses I've harbored were intentional, it is not doing me any good holding onto them, poisoning my perceptions of other things. I want to "See to it that no one (including me!) falls short of the grace of God and that no bitter root grows up to cause trouble and defile many."[41] God, I pray that the other things that I still unknowingly harbor in my heart in unforgiveness would be illuminated in Your Light. I want to repeatedly shed these dark spots inside me, to enable the freedom of Truth and Love to heal each one. I want to be open for the realizations I have no way of seeing with my own natural eyes, like I saw that day about my mom, to help me walk away from the weight of burdens I was never meant to carry!

I want to wait expectantly for Wisdom, not just to use my quiet times to talk to God, but to hear Him, apply what I am listening to, to my own life, making me more open to joy - which I seem to be sorely lacking sometimes. I want joy and peace and the emotional strength that comes from Grace. I want to daily walk with my Daddy Who tells me what paths to take in Freedom and what paths to avoid in His protection. Regret disappears as God leads me to extend His Grace to others. Acceptance of what I cannot change right now, Courage to change what I can and the Wisdom to know the difference between the two is not just a cute saying on a plaque on the wall – it is a gift beyond measure. And I am still learning...

Footnotes

[1] 1 Pet. 5:8 (NKJV)

[2] Eph. 6:11-16 (NKJV)

[3] Eph. 6:15 (amp)

[4] Phil 4:7 (NIV)

[5] John 14:7 (amp)

[6] Matt. 1:23 (NIV)

[7] John 16:33 (amp)

[8] Eph. 6:11 (NKJV)

[9] John 10:10 a (amp)

[10] John 10:10 b (amp)

[11] "The DNA of Relationships" by Dr. Gary Smalley et al, Tyndale House Publishers Inc. copyright 2004, 2007.

[12] "Labyrinth" TriStar Pictures, Jim Henson, George Lucas 1986

[13] ibid

[14] 1 Cor. 10:13 (NIV)

[15] 1 Cor. 13:7 (amp)

[16] 1 Cor. 13:11-12 (amp)

[17] Andy Stanley, "The Sin of

Comparison", www.northpoint.orghttp://yourmove.is

from "The Comparison Trap" series

[18] ibid

[19] Prov. 3:7 (NIV)

[20] 2 Cor. 10:12 (amp)

[21] 1 Cor. 13:12 (amp)

[22] 1 Cor. 13:7 (amp)

[23] Beth Moore, Life Today

"Affliction" http://lifetoday.org/video Wednesdays With

Beth Vol. 15

[24] ibid

[25] Heb. 10:22 (NIV)

[26] 1 John 1:9 (NIV)

[27] Beth Moore, Life Today

"Affliction" http://lifetoday.org/video Wednesdays With

Beth Vol. 15

[28]Bob Hamp, "Levels of Change" Gateway Church,

Southlake

TX, http://gatewaypeople.com/ministries/freedom-

kairos/media1

[29]   "The   Adventures   of   Buckaroo

Bonsai" http://www.imdb.com/title/tt0086856/

[30] Thomas á Kempis, "Imitation of

Christ" http://www.christianitytoday.com/le/2006/spring/

14.73.html

[31]Bob Hamp, "Levels of Change" Gateway Church,

Southlake

TX, http://gatewaypeople.com/ministries/freedomkairos/

media1

[32] ibid

[33] ibid

[34] Rom. 10:17 (NKJV)

[35] Prov. 5:1-2 (amp)

[36] Jas. 1:20 (amp)

[37] Prov. 5:2 (amp)

[38] 2 Chron. 7:14 (NKJV)

[39] Ps. 139:13 (NIV)

[40] 2 Cor. 5:17 (amp)

[41] Heb. 12:15 (NIV)

Suggested Resources

"Girls With Swords: How To Carry Your Cross Like A Hero"

by Lisa Bevere

"The Birth Order Book" by Dr Kevin Leman

The Sin of Comparison" by Andy

Stanley http://yourmove.is "The Comparison Trap"

"Levels of Change" by Bob
Hamp http://cdn.gatewaypeople.com/audio/Freedom/201
1/Session%202_**Levels**%20of%20Change.mp3

2013 Love Life Women's Conference by Joyce Meyer

Chapter 8

A Daughter of Royalty Renounces the Orphan Spirit

"I will not leave you as orphans [comfortless, desolate, bereaved, forlorn, helpless]; I will come [back] to you." – Jesus (John 14:18)

I am a grateful recipient of some wonderful teaching on how to take a stand against feeling rejected, second-rate, and orphaned. Yes, I said orphaned. Although my parents were both alive until I was in my late 20's, I displayed several of the emotional symptoms typically associated with orphan-hood for much of my younger life, including the insecurity, self-determination, and a strong fear of disconnectedness often associated with what some people call "separation anxiety". It is an emotional state where a person craves connection with others to obtain inner security and value. If this connection happens in a negative context, it can lead to an unhealthy dependence on other people for inner stability that can be snatched away by their departure or rejection. If the longing for belonging is not fulfilled, it can lead to a dogged determination to care for your own needs, isolating yourself to protect your heart from the hurt felt from that lack of connection. Both paths bring pain and disappointment.

I found out there are a variety of circumstances that can have similar developmental effects on you as being orphaned by the death of your parents during childhood. These can include having parents who are emotionally distant who don't have daily heart connection with their kids, who are absent due to alcoholism, addiction or other issues, or even those who work off-shifts and rarely get to spend time with their kids while both of them are awake. The effects of this lack of parental connection can be compounded by additional rejection by one's peers, not measuring up to some invisible standard of association or acceptability to those around you. In effect, it becomes a "perfect storm" – a series of detrimental conditions that make for the maximum damage to a fragile soul.

I was not aware of the dynamics of this longing earlier, so when I first heard and read verses like John 14:18, where Jesus promised not to "leave us as orphans", I skipped over it as something that really didn't apply to me, not something that was the answer to my deepest need. I had no idea this feeling was the hinge pin of so many my "issues". But a combination of events, piled one after another wore down my self-image and ostracized me from most meaningful connection. Many of those with whom I had a solid or comforting connection either moved away or died early, including 3 of my 4 grandparents, a second-grade classmate, and then a fifth-grade classmate. This left me with desperate longings for the "perfect family" and a "best friend".

In my search to attain these connections, I tottered back and forth between chameleon-like adaptation to other's needs and wishes with little consideration for the consequences, and isolation to avoid the rejection that would eventually come when I would no longer comply. It was a painful cycle to be caught in.

But there is One Who can keep us from these divergent ditches of co-dependence or willful hermit-ism and offers the rewarding state of healthy relationship with others. That One is God. He has many names and titles that show His might – El Shaddai, His provision – Jehovah Jireh, His peace – Jehovah Shalom, but one of my favorites is Jehovah Rapha, the Lord our Healer. He is the Healer of the Broken Hearted. The ways He patiently targets each one of the broken places in our hearts and brings us to wholeness amazes me. He knows how to dismantle the harmful effects of each trauma patiently and strategically with His Grace.

It is so extraordinary to me that God can even begin healing wounds we have not yet identified in ourselves! He knows us so deeply and intimately that He doesn't require us to know it's a problem before He starts to restore us. Not only that, He sometimes *hides* some of the painful details from us until He gets us to the point that the full brunt of the distress will not compound the hurt beyond what we can bear. His perfect timing of each piece of the unfolding revelation causes us to reach gratefully to Him for the rest of our healing!

So it was with me. God seemed to purposefully hide and leave unidentified in me the reason for the tears I shed at the strangest things in my life until I was in my 30's. Movie scenes and song lyrics that were supposed to be happy brought such deep sadness out of me at times that I had trouble understanding the reason for its intensity. Feelings of longing were acutely painful, and sometimes came with little provocation. I wished I could experience more sustained periods of Joy and Peace that I heard Christians were supposed to live in, but my emotions were such a roller coaster! Each high I felt was followed by a deeper, more dramatic low. It almost felt like being a windshield wiper, and it was exhausting – both to me and to my family who had to deal with the up and down and back and forth of it all.

Instead of transcendent peace, the ache and frustration of trying to get more and do more to *earn* that peace followed me as I tried to make it all happen somehow in my own effort. Like Cinderella's stepsisters trying to force their feet into a shoe much too small for them, I did whatever I could think of to make my life reflect the stability I longed for. I desperately needed to "make it fit"! 12-Step programs call it "trying to force solutions". It doesn't work.

What I didn't understand at the time was that Peace was not something I had to work to earn, or could connive to achieve. It was a gift freely given from a loving and protective Daddy. It is the result of Trust and Faith in the benevolence and provision of the Everlasting Arms of the Father and the atoning work of my Savior/Big Brother, Jesus. One of the reasons I couldn't see this is the emotional damage of being a child in a divorced family, but that certainly is not the beginning of it all.

While it is true that these feelings intensified after my parent's divorce, it was not the onset of these emotions.

I have memories earlier than 8 years old of wishing our family, and particularly my father, could be like the families I used to see on TV. In programs like Lassie, Leave It To Beaver and The Waltons, kids that did things they weren't supposed to learned lessons through natural consequences and loving instruction. Yes, it sometimes involved corporal punishment, but it was with reluctance as a promised follow-through - a predetermined consequence of disobedience done in love. It was not an out-of-control angry outburst that created more damage in its wake.

Shows like Little House on the Prairie and even the police dramas that were on at the time, showed everyday citizens and neighbors stepping in and explaining to harsh dads portrayed in some episodes that things were not supposed to be handled that way. The on-screen dads would listen, contrite and repentant, and things would be better. Some people think that is naïve or wishful thinking; I knew in my heart, even as a young child, that it was *possible* – because all things are possible with God - and longed for it to become my reality. I held onto that hope as a beacon to reach toward.

I am grateful that I had real-life models too to look up to, even in the midst of the dysfunction and sometimes harsh punishment that happened early on. At least I could see what the ideal was. Family friends and neighbors were helpful to keep that hope alive. And I could also recognize and be thankful for the times of family unity and fun we *did* have - swimming and going to the beach, walking on the breakwaters, exploring tidal pools, fishing, hunting, and so on. I had a greater appreciation for those memories and held onto them when things weren't going well.

I feel sorry for the current generations that seem to have less family time spent in cooperative activity and interaction than any other time in history. Typically more hours are spent in front of an electronic screen instead of personal dialog with the people you live with.

Today we see very different family models on TV from the Simpsons or Family Guy and shows that glorify families, real or imagined, like the Osbornes, Connors and Pritchetts. Fathers are portrayed as incompetent, bungling and incapable, or abusive. Mothers who stay home are demeaned, while the corporate-bound are portrayed as having it all together. In reality there are not enough hours in the day to both be out of the house working for 8 – 10 hours a day and have the nurturing and instructive time you want with your children, the time to do simple maintenance and upkeep on the place where you live and still have time left over for sleep. (I know this from personal experience – and so do many of you!) Something is always left "undone" – and that's how you feel in the process of trying to have and do it all.

Even on channels that air decidedly "children's programming" (now there's a double meaning for you!), kids are portrayed ruling over their parents with supposedly superior understanding. They encourage disobedience and manipulation to get what you want, while respect, personal responsibility and a healthy work ethic is marginalized or ridiculed. The identifying traits they seem to promote often focus on sarcasm, belittling one another to gain advantage, and sexual dysfunction – and they call it comedy or "reality" TV.

Video games and social media are also a drain on our time and our interaction with one another. Trying to relax after we get home from work or school can turn into a compulsion. Games are usually either mindless searches for acquiring the most points, in the form of coins, candy or other items, or a blood-bath of murder and theft in surreal worlds that do not exist, but come with increasingly realistic graphics. Things that are marketed as entertainment are so *dark*!

Yes, I know the arguments for these things include developing fine motor-skills, understanding spatial relationships, and substituting electronic aggression for the real thing on real people. But I've also seen (and exhibited!) the irritability and aggression that comes out when you are interrupted in the middle of an imaginary quest! That is proof of its obsessive influence!

Social media steals time from face-to-face interaction and draws people to a disconnected world of electronic voyeurism. I realize it has beneficial application as well, sharing encouraging and uplifting videos and emotional support even over great geographical distances. Mass communication of current events and conveying time-sensitive information is an asset in our rush of activity world, but the disconnectedness this medium fosters starves us for personal interaction and meaningful conversation. Lack of perceived accountability also plays a part in the tone of online communication. Some people disregard common courtesies and respect that would be adhered to in face-to-face exchanges.

Often the expression of ideas becomes defensive and dismissive instead of cooperative. Name-calling and outrageous character assaults on people you hardly know replace healthy debate on various topics with little to no accountability. We need to regain a willingness to engage in respectful interaction, even if we disagree in certain areas. The ability to disagree agreeably and find areas of compromise is a quickly disappearing skill. And the motivation to do so through social media seems non-existent. Things like "cyber-bullying" are on the rise and add a dark dimension to social media that diminishes us all. No wonder hope seems so dim in our culture! We have access to a LOT more information, but we have less personal communication than ever before.

"God Places the Solitary in Families"

The longings I had for the ideal family set up an emotional filter in how I saw what was happening around me and how I interpreted life in general – with a twist. I wanted happiness and I thought the opposite of happiness was conflict. I didn't understand that disagreements are unavoidable just because we're human. I believed that having a happy family meant not having disagreements, and it became my goal to avoid or diffuse all contention.

I know now that conflict is a natural part of life. Although conflict is difficult by its very nature, it can reveal opportunities to learn new things and modify your perspective by being exposed to other viewpoints. Conflict resolution is how we get from divergent mindsets to common understanding. We find out what those mindsets are by talking with one another. Reaching common understanding does not usually mean you end up agreeing on every detail. Many times it involves hashing out a compromise that combines components from differing perspectives and finding out what works for that situation and what needs to be set aside for now. There is a difference between giving in and finding mutually workable solutions.

It is important for each of us to learn healthy conflict resolution. It doesn't happen just because you get older. It is something you need to learn and develop on purpose. If we don't have parents or mentors that teach us these things while we are young, it is something we must learn for ourselves when we are older. It is one of the ultimate life-skills. Not knowing this caused many unnecessary problems in my communication with others.

I avoided conflict most of the time instead of dealing with it. I adjusted my reactions and responses based on whether or not I thought I could get my way in a particular situation. If I was facing a more intimidating personality, or someone I needed something from, I avoided confrontation and submitted to their wishes. Any sign of displeasure or resistance from another person, would quickly prompt a change in my response to stabilize the emotional tone of the moment and I would do or say what I thought they wanted. This was another example of Dr. Smalley's "fear dancing" manifested in my life. I got good at "reading people". There were times when my interpretations skills were way off base, but I would modify my responses until things got calm again.

In other situations, I would use passive aggression to change the situation toward my benefit. If I thought I could impose my own will on a situation, I went in as the dominator. But whichever tactic I used, it was from a cautious internal place of looking around and trying to "gauge the room" first, seeking a place of safety or escape for later use.

With my low self-esteem and the lack of social standing in the schools I attended growing up, I spent more and more time being solitary. Although I could see no outward reason for the ridicule I was subjected to day after day, I seemed to be singled out for derision and abuse. I had little positive peer interaction, and I didn't know why. My family was not as financially well off as some others, but we weren't wearing rags. Memories of pussy willows brought in for the teacher being stripped of their fluffy pillows on the bus before getting them to school, gum and thumb tacks left on my chair, ruining my clothes and causing physical pain, always being the last one picked for teams in gym class or recess are just highlights of my elementary school days.

I was a bully magnet. My third-grade teacher even noted on my report card that I was the class scapegoat. (How can any sane adult stigmatize the victim of such abuse by putting comments like that in their permanent educational record? I could read! The accusatory tone of that statement hurt me deeply. Recent situations with school systems and various educators/administrators since then make me question if this practice is being addressed and appropriately discouraged, even now.) I felt more and more isolated as the years went on.

I became a voracious reader. And – *in spite* of the "new" phonetic reading programs instituted in the early 70's, where "make" was spelled m-a-e-k – I was soon reading far above my grade level. While the other fourth graders were reading Hardy Boys and Nancy Drew, I was reading my dad's Alistair MacLean novels and Sir Arthur Conan Doyle's Sherlock Holmes mysteries. I got good grades, but not the best in my class. I got along far better with kids younger than me or those much older, but my own age-range seemed blocked off to me in many ways. Popularity was elusive at best. There were bright moments here and there when things looked like it would get better, but then came the crashes and disappointments when rejection would come. Fifth and sixth grade were particularly difficult. Then came junior high...

We moved when I was half-way through seventh grade, and I mistakenly thought I would have a new start in a new school, but that didn't pan out either. Now I had the added stigma of being the new kid in town. I had no support system. One shining exception was my 8th Grade history teacher, Mr. Mello. He was a mind-mannered, good looking teacher who made history interesting and fun to learn. I enjoyed his class. During a particularly trying episode between a change of classes before the teachers came in the rooms, I was the center of a verbal pig-pile. Although not every kid in the class was involved, those who were, encircled me and were intimidating enough to bring me close to tears. When he came in the room and heard what was happening, Mr. Mello slammed the door and yelled, That's enough!" He announced to everyone that this would be the "last time anything like this would be happening in his classroom" and followed it up with an even louder "Is that understood!?" No one was singled out, but the point was emphatically made that no one would be exempt from the consequences of violating his directive. He was my hero! Word got around to the other kids and to the other teachers. I felt safe from that point on if he was even in the building. The bus ride and off-school hours were a different story.

The lack of emotional and spiritual support systems was keenly felt during these years. We had attended my grandparents' church when I was younger, but by this time, we had been church-hopping from one denomination to another and had not settled anywhere for longer than a year. We were not involved in regular Sunday school class or extra-curricular activities. My parents were struggling in their marriage and that was one of the priorities that was set aside. At one point in my early teens, we attended a local church with a fairly large youth group and I went on a youth retreat weekend. My brother and I had a wonderful time! I rededicated my life to God and determined to be a different person when I got home.

413

But no one else seemed to get the memo and I still had to contend with rejection at school and conflict at home. Without positive reinforcement, I quickly reverted back to discouragement. Lighter, happier times were eclipsed by darker events. By the time I was 16, my parents were divorced and I felt isolated from everything. I started reaching out for connection in some unhealthy ways that backfired – big time! I hurt others and myself in ways that still have an impact this many years later. I became a people pleaser toward those I had no business being around and rejected those who truly cared what happened to me.

I wanted a "normal family". Even with all I'd been through, I hadn't thought that was such an unrealistic expectation. Some people say family is the foundation on which the rest of your life is built, and that the security and self-confidence we get while we are young is the spring-board from which we launch our lives. Once it became evident that the atmosphere in my family of origin was not stable enough to build on very well, I made it my goal to do things differently when I made one of my own.

Please don't misunderstand. I love my family. I have great brothers and sisters, in-laws, aunts, uncles and cousins I love dearly. As adults we are making a concerted effort to spend more time together. We have enjoyed really good times celebrating birthdays, getting together for holidays, babysitting for one another and enjoying a girls' night out here and there. The internet and Skype is also a convenient way to keep in touch with family who are too far away to drive to! But with work schedules and kids' activities keeping us all on the go so much of the time, it can get difficult to make time to visit.

As families get bigger, jobs get more time-consuming and you try not to over-schedule every minute of your life, time goes by. And everyone is different in what they need and how they connect. Some people are more reserved and others more social in their personalities, and we all have to prioritize our off-work time to be able to do what we need to get done. That's life. Expectations and priorities change. But I guess I needed more connection than what I was getting during that time in my life.

I was so grateful when I met my husband and his family. Not just his immediate family, but the whole clan. Instead of the situation we had growing up where everyone was spread out more and living in different states, seen most often during funerals and summer visits here and there, Steve's family were very close – geographically and emotionally. They ate dinner together, they worked together, and they played together. Instead of growing up in a town where multiplied thousands of families lived with little connection with their neighbors and community like mine, Steve's extended family made up roughly 1/8 of a small town of only 1500 households! There were seven to ten prominent family groups in town that made up about 2/3 of the population and the other third were "newcomers" – first or second generation residents with no blood connection to others in town. By the time you got to the third generation, the "outsiders" had either moved away or a wedding was in the works that drew another family into the "fold" and more connections were made.

Those who grew up in this little mill town couldn't walk two blocks without having an aunt, cousin or close family friend know what they were doing. If it wasn't good, they'd say something about it, or tell someone who would.

You always knew someone was watching your back to make sure you were okay – or keep you on the straight and narrow. As the saying goes: "The great thing about living in a small town is everyone knows your business; and the bad thing about living in a small town is - everyone knows your business"! Moving into a situation like that was hard, being an outsider, with no internal connection and being scrutinized by a large group of small fish in a very small pond. It was extremely intimidating.

But after I grew to adulthood and started dating Steve, I became active in the community and it became home. His family became my family too. We went through seasons of weddings and babies. Holidays were filled with much anticipated family get-togethers. Summers consisted of one picnic after another. We all helped one another when someone was moving or renovating. We mourned together when times were tough and we lost someone dear to us. This was my idea of family. I knew the truth of Psalm 68:6 long before I heard the verse: "God places the solitary in families and gives the desolate a home in which to dwell..." I now had the connection, interaction and belonging that I wanted so much. I was home.

But just like 12-Step programs and Bob Hamp's Levels of Change teaching will tell you, it is a mistake to place heavy expectations solely on "location cures". No matter how idyllic the current setting was, I was still bringing *me* into it.

It would be much later before I realized how my past affected my behavior when things would get shaky. The very coping skills that I developed to adapt to uncertain situations when I was younger turned into how I "managed" my life and the people around me as an adult.

It wasn't intentional – it wasn't even something I recognized as "my way of dealing with people". I was living my life and interacting with everyone around me the only way I knew how at the time. Most interactions went well as I learned new things and matured in my understanding of life. But when things got intense or conflictive I reverted back to old personal dynamics. I hadn't "discovered" my anger issues yet and I had no idea the depth of fear and insecurity I was dealing with.

God "placed me in a family", gave me role models and real people to give me the safety and the outward stability I needed. He was setting the stage for the inner metamorphosis He was going to bring about. Then very gently, He began to peel back layers of emotional bandages to heal my old wounds. I was clueless about how manipulative I had become in some areas! But day after day, after years of directing my steps through Al-Anon, adult Sunday school classes, and various Bible studies, it became disturbingly clear. God gradually showed me my own *modus operandi* and the behavioral habits He wanted me to exchange for a new way of doing things. I was embarrassed and mortified at some of the things He showed me, but He gently and carefully shielded me through each transition. I never felt exposed or ridiculed when He showed me the next step, so I went eagerly to Him for the fix! The changes were not immediate; it is, as they say, a process.

Ingrained personality traits and a lifetime of destructive communication "skills" don't disappear overnight. But I was not alone in His process. I now had an active support system of friends and family in my neighborhood and at church that encouraged me and graciously held me accountable for my actions. As each difficulty came to

Light and was identified and assigned for transformation, the embarrassment of the former realizations were tempered with God's Love and Grace that lead me to cooperate with Him as He made those changes without condemnation. He is "the lifter of my head"[1] while He shows me what He needs to replace in me next!

The Transformation Begins

It's funny! Sitting here right now, I am thinking of Eliza Doolittle in My Fair Lady. It's one of my favorite films – I was even in the play in high school. The first time I saw this movie, I was really little - earlier than 9 years old. My brother and I had been sent to bed, but my parents were watching the movie downstairs.

The way the stairway came down, someone sitting on the couch against the back wall of the living room could not see anyone sitting on the stairs, because of a partial wall shielding the stairway. But those sitting on the stairs could easily see the TV in the forward corner of the room. So my brother and I had snuck part of the way down the stairs and were sitting there watching the movie with my parents completely unaware that we were up long past our bedtime.

As the scenes progress, Henry Higgins and Colonel Pickering have begun an amazing transformation on Eliza, a cockney-accented, dirty-faced young woman trying to eke out a living selling individual bundles of flowers to wealthy passers-by in the streets of London. She has turned herself over to this arrogant language professor (and a kinder, gentler colleague) to teach her proper

English so she can one day open her own flower shop, a dream she believes is the pinnacle of what she could possibly reach. The transformation is well underway at this point in the story.

She is dressed to the nines and trying very hard to speak genteelly to all the high-falutin' attendees at the Ascot (horse race). The seemingly emotionless attendees barely acknowledge the happenings around them. As a specific horse is pulling ahead in the race, Eliza begins to shed her new-found gentility and starts to get into the emotion of the moment. Suddenly, after having her focus completely commandeered by one particular horse's advance toward the finish line, she slips back into her Cockney accent and screams, "C'mon Dover! Move your bloomin' arse!"[2]

In the stairway, my brother and I lost it, laughing hysterically, almost falling down the stairs. This alerted our parents to our unpermissioned presence and we were quickly herded up the stairs and tucked back into bed, with stern warnings to stay there, or else.

In the movie, Eliza realizes what she has done, not just losing control of her own demeanor, but embarrassing herself and her instructors/benefactors in front of some surprisingly familiar characters – the ultimate Pharisees. They are emotionally stiff and obsessed with decorum and "properness", condemning others' impropriety, while being so proud of their own self-control – hello! They were all at the same horse race! The biting realization for me is I have been part of that scene many times - and I have *so often* played *both parts* in my life….! (but I digress)

After I thought sufficient time had gone by, I was certain my brother was asleep and my parents were again engrossed in the movie; I carefully snuck back down the stairs. The transformation had continued for Eliza while I was banished to my room and she was now much more comfortable with her new way of speaking and behaving. They had gone through even more instruction on deportment and speech lessons. It was the proverbial good cop, bad cop situation where one (Colonel Pickering) treats her tenderly with respect and admiration for her efforts and the other (Professor Higgins) is verbally confrontative and gives her no credit for her many hours of practice. Higgins even enlists the cooperation of his mother to help Eliza develop proper etiquette in a variety of social situations.

In so doing, he inadvertently avails her of the opportunity to learn from his own mother how to simply dismiss the Professor's sometimes boorish behavior. Along the way, Eliza begins to realize his impatience is not a reflection on her, but one of *his* short-comings. She not only learns how to "speak more genteelly"[3], she is also gaining self-confidence and a sense of her own worth.

By the time I made it back to my hiding place in the stairway, they had just gotten back from the most hoity-toity society affair. She had carried herself off beautifully, even charming some of the people she met with some unexpected revelations about her perspective on a variety of topics. She spoke well, danced well, and won their hearts. She was a huge success at the ball. She and her instructors delay their celebration until they are in the seclusion of their own flat; nonetheless, they are ecstatic in their victory over some self-important know-it-all at the party saying that Eliza is indeed a princess. They congratulate themselves and dance and whoop it up in the living room, enjoying the thrill of the moment.

Eliza is basking in the emotional triumph as she is beginning to fall in love with her sometimes-crass benefactor and teacher. As she turns in for the night, she is floating around the room dancing, as the music swells, singing "I could have danced all night!"[3] She is more than just thrilled at the pomp and excitement of her own personal victory in her transformation; she is elated that she has won the approval and praise of the Professor after so much criticism and correction. She is floating on air as the maid helps her with her nightgown – what girl doesn't have secret longings for the feeling of royalty!? It just carried me away; my heart was light and soaring! I watched the rest of the movie, but most of the remaining plot was just lost on me at that point. When the movie was ended, I snuck back up the stairs before the credits got too far so I wouldn't be caught. But the words of that song wafted through my heart as I drifted happily off to sleep.

It wasn't just Eliza who had made the transformation with that victory dance - *I* was a princess. I was the one who had won over the crowd. I was the one who won over the heart of her instructor. At that point, I wasn't aware of the transference I was engaged in, but I felt good at that moment, and that's what mattered then. I am sure that I danced and sang the song the next day waltzing through the living room.

I am just as certain now that my mom would have picked up on the fact that that song happened well after the horse race but I don't remember her scolding me for it or even bringing it to my attention. It was probably one of those "mom" moments – things you realize as an adult that you enjoy with your kids "not knowing that you know". It was a wonderful high. I was experiencing how

God saw me – I *was* a princess – even if it was only for a day or two. I felt it and appropriated it for myself in that moment, knowing the truth of it. Then life happened again and the everyday took over the emotions of the "someday".

But God stored that little piece of epiphany in the back pack of my experiences, for use later on when He would begin to peel back the layers of rejection to heal my heart. I still treasure that memory.

Music Soothes the Savage Breast

"My Fair Lady" was a wonderful introduction to musicals and continues to be one of my favorites. I guess it was one of the first times that I really felt the impact of how music can lift my soul above and beyond the circumstances I am going through and impart joy in otherwise difficult situations. Another one that gave me that kind of lift was the Rodgers and Hammerstein version of "Cinderella" with Leslie Ann Warren. While being set upon by her step-mother and step-sisters, Cinderella sings a song about her own way of dealing with her lot in life. She tells those listening that she can, in her imagination, be whatever she wants to be. She goes through being a princess, a huntress, and a prima donna, to name a few, to escape the confines of her real life situation, even if it's only for a little while.[5]

It was no wonder I identified so much with that song! Obviously the step mother part did not apply, but using imagination and music as a buffer against the constant rejection I was going through were surely the same!

422

I can personally attest to the famous William Congreve line that is often misquoted, but much referenced: "Music hath charms to soothe a savage breast, to soften rocks, or bend a knotted oak."[6] Music absolutely can make difficult situations easier to bear and soften hardened minds and hearts. It can change attitudes of one person or a stadium full of people – it is a gift (when used wisely). A musical score can carry emotions on so deep a level that words are not needed to convey the writer's intention.

It was no surprise to me a few years ago, when taking a personality test from "The Gift in You" by Dr. Caroline Leaf, that I scored high in music being a determining influence in the way I process information. Music can still carry me away and lift my spirits; all its benefits are so clearly depicted in the Psalms! There are some wonderful hymns and contemporary praise music that do my heart good and pull me out of the doldrums faster than anything else if my mood takes a dip. It truly is amazing sometimes! I know you can't live on the mountaintop all the time. But if you can pick up secrets like this along the way, you can regain a good attitude when you're down in a valley!

But it works in the opposite direction too. My heart can swell with hope, or it can become anxious with fear or be dropped into the deepest depths of despair in just a few moments. (Harry Chapin pointed this out too, in his song "I Let Time Go Lightly with You", so I know I'm not the only one to notice or experience this!)

A movie, a song, or a thought about something that starts out so beautiful, instead of being an inspiration or something to reach for, can just as easily be turned around and accuse me of what I am missing. I could be enjoying myself with no cares in the world and then hear a song on the radio that ripped it all away, magnifying remorse or loss. Because of the difficulties in my relationships with my parents, "If I Could Turn Back Time" by Cher and "The Living Years" by Mike and the Mechanics still can, if I let it. I need to choose not to get on those negative roller coasters – and today, for the most part, I do. I can appreciate the tune without allowing the enemy to use regret-filled lyrics to steal my joy and rub my nose in things long since forgiven.

Identifying the Longing

Fast forward to my mid-thirty's. Both of my parents had died by this time. I and my children were attending church regularly and my husband was attending with us on occasion. I had been taking part in women's Bible studies from Beth Moore, attending Women of Faith conferences and had been seeking out lots of different teaching on being a godly woman, wife and mother. Books like Hannah Hurnard's "Hind's Feet in High Places" and Nicole Johnson's book "Keeping a Princess Heart in a Not-So-Fairytale World" had given me some wonderful perspectives on seeing my life through a different pair of eyes.

Joyce Meyer was a daily staple for me as she and others took me through the necessary transition from the cycle of defeat and that "gotta do more" feeling to acceptance that this life is a journey. I had previously internalized the thought that I had to work to *earn* my value and self-worth through what I was able to accomplish. Now I was beginning to understand the Truth that God gave me my value before I was born. In Joyce's words, I was learning the difference between my "who" and my "do".

It was a long journey; there were lots of distractions along the way and I spent many years just longing for peace and victory. I felt hollow at times grieving for what could have been my childhood, if only...and then grieving the loss of my parents all over again when they died. I was deeply concerned that I couldn't pull out of the emotional pit I was in. There were days that I seriously "willed" myself out of bed with no desire, no anticipation, only dread and monotony as I went through the motions until it was time to get back under the covers.

In a way, I wanted to keep being "the responsible one", because so much of my self-worth and personal identity were still wrapped up in what I did. But I also just wanted to curl up *somewhere* and have someone else tell me that everything was going to be okay and that *they* would take care of everything.

Teaching I heard several years ago by Jimmy Evans identified this painful longing as an "orphaned spirit". I didn't understand that was the core reason I made so many bad decisions. Some of the people I tried to connect with were not interested in belonging, just what they could get out of the situation, and honestly, there were times that was how I felt too. Some others truly wanted to help, but were wounded themselves and were not able to provide what I thought I needed. This inability translated to me as rejection, added to the pain and increased the longing for more connection. It was a vicious cycle.

Life was not all bad, by any means – I have wonderful memories of lots of things. But with the other stuff pressing in on my thoughts so much of the time then, it was harder to focus on the good parts.

I remember times of sitting in a circle around boxes of photos, lots of memories and family stories, hanging out, reminiscing. Those times have gotten fewer and farther between but they bring back the connectedness and laughter of the things that unite us. I love to be reminded of so many great experiences we've shared. You can't stay there; there's so much to do in the here and now, but once in a while, it is a nice way to reconnect, remember and laugh together. Stopping to realize how truly blessed we are in other areas can help keep a balanced perspective when things aren't looking as bright as you hoped they'd be in the moment. And as hard as some times are, there are others who have it much worse.

One day at work, things were not going well; the retail terminal I used for my postal transactions was giving me trouble. I replaced one component on Monday, the next day another component broke down. The replacement they sent the day after that was already broken and I was back to square one. I was getting so wired up about it; accusations of some unknown I.T. guy's "incompetence" had my guts in a knot. The fact that I was inconvenienced was the only thing on my mind. I made the calls I needed to make, and did what I could to fix the situation, but was still ticked off.

A colleague from another office came in and mentioned a horrible natural disaster that I was completely unaware of, not having access to the news at work. The incident left death and destruction in its wake and drastically changed hundreds of lives in just minutes. Suddenly the stuff that had me so knotted up was put back in its proper place as completely insignificant in comparison. Again, it's a matter of perspective.

God's Prescription

The strategy of enjoying your life right now, even though everything is not the way you want it to be is not denial of the past or your present difficulties. It is in fact a prescription specifically tailored for each one of us by our Divine Physician. You can acknowledge the past, or a present difficulty and then move on with great anticipation toward your future without letting the painfulness of the junky parts come forward with you! This prescription cures regret, embarrassment, shame, guilt, depression, blame-shifting, and resentment. It's a one-two punch that empowers us to rise above our circumstances and soar above any challenges we face: forgiveness and renewing your mind.

Philippians 3:13 says "forgetting what lies behind and pressing forward…" Forgive yourself. Accept God's forgiveness for anything that you regret. You did what you did (good or bad) and it's done. Maybe you did the best you could with what you had known at the time. Maybe you were being mean to get back some kind of satisfaction from pain that was inflicted on you. Whatever it was that is causing you so much angst, give it to God - and let go of the other end of it! When we bring things to Him, He thanks us for giving (forgiving) it to Him and then throws it "into the depths of the sea"[7] never to be brought up again.

When we feel the freedom that it brings to us to be released from weights we have carried for so long, we can then turn around and do the same for others. Use the same checklist for them you used on yourself: Maybe *they* did the best they could with what *they* had known at the time. We need to forgive people – release them from the grudges we've been holding over *their* heads! Forgiveness makes life a lot lighter and easier to enjoy for everyone!

The next step is what to fill that empty place with. Those unforgiving and anxious thoughts we were carrying took up a lot of room in our heads. They impressed themselves on each step we took and filled each crevice in our hearts. With the open areas that are left behind when those things are discarded, we have opportunity to redecorate. But there is some urgency in the timing!

These empty places are something Jesus Himself warned us about in the Gospels. Matthew 12:45 and Luke 11:26 both record Him telling us that "seven spirits, more wicked than the first" have the opportunity to move in if we leave those spaces vacant. We need to fill our cleaned out hearts with godly contents to keep the junk from taking over again.

Paul prescribes thought changes that are necessary to move ahead: "For the rest brethren, whatever is true, whatever is worthy of reverence, and is honorable and seemly, whatever is just, whatever is pure, whatever is lovely and lovable, whatever is kind, if there is any virtue and excellence, if there is anything worthy of praise, think on and weigh and take account of these things [fix your minds on them]...and the God of peace (of untroubled, undisturbed well-being) will be with you."[8] This *is* the prescription God personally created for what ails us!

There is *way more* good than bad in my life – and yours! It is unfortunately just a tendency in people that we take the good for granted and focus on and complain about the bad or painful things. (Just look at the Israelites' escape from Egypt. No longer slaves and miraculously delivered through the Red Sea, wearing and carrying the gold given to them by their neighbors making up for hundreds of years of forced labor – and yet they were constantly being chastened by God for their complaining and mistrust.) It's human nature's default setting. But we can select alternative preferences and come up higher than that. We need to remember how blessed we are.

By making a concerted effort to focus on and remind ourselves of the good, we become more peaceful, hopeful and stable – actually better able to handle it when life *doesn't* work the way we'd like it to and throws a curveball. God did not bring us out all this way to leave us stranded. He wants us to appreciate what is "good and excellent and praiseworthy"[9]. Focusing on what's good makes it easier to observe the undesirable things, and then determine whether it is something we can do something constructive about or realize it is out of our realm of influence to change. If it is something that we have little control over, we can pray for those who can to affect the change that is needed and then "forgetting what lies behind and straining forward to what lies ahead"[10] enjoy the now.

Mentoring v. Idolatry

One of the challenges I have faced in doing this is comparing myself to other people. I've learned it is problematic at best to base my *perceptions* of other people merely on observations. Reality is most people aren't sharing their deepest struggles with you. And to a certain degree that is the way it is supposed to be – not everyone who asks you how you are doing actually wants to hear the real answer! Some are just making polite conversation. In most cases such forthright discussions are best engaged in between people whom you share a certain level of personal intimacy. As we've already seen, basing personal comparisons on incomplete information breeds misunderstanding. It is good to remember that everyone is dealing with something. You can't see what happens behind closed doors. You don't know the challenges they are facing.

Further, if the people you compare yourself to are not even real, you are determining your self-worth or decisions on what someone wrote in a script somewhere! Real people are multi-dimensional and deal with all kinds of everyday considerations that fictional characters never need to address. (You never see a soap star at the end of a long day of vomiting kids, short on grocery money, and wondering if her husband will wash the dishes when he gets home from work, when he just had a co-worker bustin' his chops all day about the mini-van they just financed!) Comparison with real people poses enough challenges without adding in the fictional.

Similar to Andy Stanley's "Sin of Comparison", Jimmy Evans points out in one of his teachings that comparison with those weaker than us in certain areas unduly lifts our estimation of ourselves and sets us up for prideful condescension of others. Don't fall for that kind of deception. Feelings of inadequacy and condescension both make us miss out on appreciation of the gifts and strengths we each are blessed with.[11] There is a better option.

Mentoring others and emulating positive role models is a more productive goal. We can share our talents and abilities with one another to mutually benefit everyone. The Bible has lots of examples of mentoring or discipleship: Moses and Joshua, Elijah and Elisha, Eli and Samuel, Naomi and Ruth. Even though there is a certain amount of comparison inherent in choosing a mentor, mutual accountability and prayer can be important safeguards.

They can serve as checks and balances to keep you from pitfalls of putting too much dependence on the other person or taking on too much responsibility yourself, while still reaching for excellence. Older adults can offer much wisdom, encouragement and direction through difficult times, and younger "students" can just as effectively "school" their elders with fresh perspectives, respectfully and in good will. But whichever side of the relationship we are on, we need to remember they are not God.

While emulating what you see starts off positive, we need to stay alert for the slide. Those who mentor us are human beings with human failings. We need to follow them as they are following God, without following their examples when they stray. Moses was a great help to Joshua – and Joshua to Moses. The same can be said of Elijah and Elisha, and Naomi and Ruth. These mentors shared great wisdom and God's Spirit with those they mentored. They passed on their devotion and obedience to God with power, even though they each had emotional challenges to overcome. From self-doubt and anger, to depression, to overwhelming grief and co-dependency, each of these mentors struggled with the same things we deal with. Check out their stories sometime – they are fascinating to see.

But each mentoree was able to keep following God around those obstacles and each one rose higher than their predecessor following God. Take a look at Eli and Samuel. Eli mentored Samuel and instructed him in the ways of the temple, but Samuel also learned what *not* to do from observing Eli. When Eli was not faithful to do what should have been done, the nation suffered for his disobedience, his sons defamed the name of God and lost their lives and the Arc of the Covenant fell into enemy hands. Eli died with great regret and remorse. But Samuel continued on with God and became the prophet counseling a whole nation, drawing them back to God, correcting their new king in his error, and putting God first, no matter what. If we put too much importance on measuring up to another person, or deifying them regardless of their actions, we can set ourselves (and them!) up for a fall. The higher we elevate other people, the greater the fall when they fail us – often times just by being human.

Beth Moore has included something neat in a couple of her teachings - an anagram for EASTER: Every Alternate Savior Takes Early Retirement! If anyone you are looking to as a mentor is promoted (in your estimation) to the position of being your "savior", they will flat out disappoint you. It's inevitable. Human beings were built for encouragement and friendship, helping to bear our burdens with us for short periods of time, not as saviors – that job is already filled! Substituting anyone human for that role spells disaster.

As a direct result of a Bible study I did recently called "Idol Lies" by Dee Brestin, I discovered I have a tendency to *continually* elevate one or two key relationships in my life to this status, without realizing it. My parents, a couple of my friends, my husband, and my children – even a pastor or two - have all been elevated to unhealthy heights in my life! Additionally, I discovered that it came in succession – when one deeply disappointed or hurt me, I built a wall in my heart to protect myself from re-wounding there and inadvertently substituted a different relationship to that level, beginning the cycle of the fall for someone else.

It's not easy to recognize sometimes. It's not like you're bowing down and worshipping them openly, like most people think of idolatry. But I know now that when I gave their opinions, emotional approval or comfort, too much weight in my decisions, it was a sign of misplaced priority. I handled different situations poorly, sometimes contrary to my moral code, just to "keep the peace". I pray to God He keeps me from this now! Anyone we place in the position Jesus designed for Himself as Savior is sure to fail. And I don't want that kind of pain for them, or for me! There are things only God can do for us and in us. Shoulder to shoulder, we can encourage one another and bring everything to God in faith. Letting God be our only God allows our relationships with people to flourish.

Relationships can be potent without being controlling. We all have things we're good at and things we need help with. We need to keep our relationships in proper context – offering from our strengths to them and being willing to accept help from others from their strengths for our weaknesses. No one has everything they need in their own package – that's the way it works, so we will be dependent on God and be able to help people through mutual cooperation. Jesus clearly says: "My grace is sufficient for you, for my power is made perfect in weakness."[12] to which Paul answers, "Therefore I will boast all the more gladly about my weaknesses, so that Christ's power may rest on me."[13]

Being too prideful to let other people know when we're hurting or feeling weakened isolates us and depreciates opportunities for the good we can do for each other in that sharing process. Being "real" about what you are going through can be the very thing that leap frogs you to the next victory – and enables you the privilege of taking others along with you! Beth Moore said something on Life Today one day that I love! "People aren't looking for you to have it all together. They're looking to see how we act when we don't." [14]

At a Women of Faith conference in Hartford, Connecticut this fall I heard some wonderful teaching about this exact thing. Any and all of the speakers from these conferences exemplify this concept beautifully. Marilyn Meberg, Patsy Clairmont, Luci Swindoll, Sheila Walsh, and Thelma Wells have been doing this for years. Each and every story they can tell you is filled with the Grace that was more than enough to carry them through their excruciating experiences. The next generation is following in their footsteps, standing on their shoulders and reaching great heights. I highly recommend digging into all of their resources for anything you may be going through! Glennon Doyle Melton's book "Carry On Warrior – The Power of Embracing Your Messy, Beautiful Life" and Jen Hatmaker's book "For the Love – Fighting for Grace in a World of Impossible Standards" can give you a heart-full of examples on how amazingly powerful being "real" with one another can be.

Be willing to be vulnerable with one another – without elevating people beyond reasonable expectations - it is a potent mixture that produces hope for everyone around you.

Adjust the Goal with Godly Counsel

"Hope deferred makes the heart sick, but when the desire is fulfilled it is a tree of life."[15] It's true. We want what we want; we don't want to have to wait – and we definitely don't want to suffer while we wait. We want to avoid being heart-sick. The end goal for most people is to see our desires fulfilled, so we can be happy. The problem is we have limited vision. Sometimes the things we think will make us happy are empty shadows that are distracting us from our true direction. We need godly Wisdom to see the difference.

We can wait for God to bring us to the places of fulfillment, or we can push through on our own. If we choose not to wait for God to bring His direction, forcing our own solutions can boomerang in very short order. In our finite perspective, we can do even more damage (and we are capable of doing some pretty messed up things to fulfill our own desires sometimes!) Often the solutions we come up with are based on the previously discussed comparisons or our limited perceptions of the current situation.

In light of my "orphan mentality", when I compared how I felt and what I was thought I was missing in my childhood to the movies, the songs, and the people around me, I got more depressed. It didn't match up. I felt abandoned in my childhood by the disparity in the "Disney dads" and my dad (orphaned once), and then after my parents died, the hope of having that kind of storybook relationship with both of them happening "someday", died with them and left me feeling orphaned again.

But realizing that mindset put me at a disadvantage was not sufficient to break its hold on my emotions. What was my problem? That all happened over 20 years ago! It didn't make sense to me. Why was the pain of the loss compounding instead of easing with time? I was a grown woman! I was supposed to be beyond all that kind of stuff! I had people depending on me, I needed to be solid. Who had time and money to go to counseling to get all that stuff straightened out when there was wash and homework to do and life to be living!?

I could be going along "just fine" and then a situation would come up that made me feel like a scared, uncertain little girl all over again who needed to get a smile, a wink - any indication that someone else noticed, that they approved of me, that I had no reason to feel so insecure.

I was going to church and was reading the Bible almost every day, but for some reason I didn't make the connection that seems so obvious to me now - God Himself wanted to BE my security. Up to this point I wanted to hear from people with skin on them, people I could see and look up to and connect with. But their (and my) vision was often obscured by our humanity. But that didn't stop me from trying.

I had gone to counseling earlier in my life. I have talked with people who really had a heart for others and their input has been very helpful. Some were more effective than others but sometimes applying their advice made certain situations worse. Their counsel was based on what I was able to relate to them in the limited time we had. The absence of crucial bits of information - things I didn't think to share or details I didn't know about - made a difference in the application of their recommendations.

God can absolutely use other people who can ask just the right questions for you to work through barriers in a protected atmosphere full of godly intentions. But we need to keep our common humanity in the forefront. We all have our own baggage and our own blind spots. Whether it is intentional or not – putting excess value in another *person*'s opinion of your situation can lead to more trouble. Yes, it's a risk, but sometimes the results of taking that risk are astounding! Let God lead you through your options together.

Nothing can compare to the direction I have gotten from The "Wonderful Counselor"[16]! When I got so desperate to have the ache removed, to address the pain that was holding me back, Jesus was there. I didn't need to make an appointment. I didn't need to explain the "back story" or fill in the family history. He met me in the pages of His Word, in my heart and in the pages of other people's writings in humor, experience, encouragement and persistence. He kept plugging away, gently teaching and proving Himself to me each day. I am so grateful for God's understanding, patience and faithfulness in meeting my needs in Him! Whether I had 5 minutes or two hours, I sat and read and wrote and poured my heart out to God, trying so hard to make it all make sense. The piece I seemed to be missing was then resting in His care.

During one of my quiet times, God used Isaiah to show me how desperately He wanted me to rest in and trust Him! It even came with a musical score that still runs in my head! "In repentance and rest is your salvation, in quietness and trust is your strength, but you would have none of it. You said, 'No, we will flee on horses.' Therefore you will flee! You said, 'We will ride off on swift horses.' Therefore your pursuers will be swift! A thousand will flee at the threat of one; at the threat of five you will all flee away till you are left like a flagstaff on a mountaintop, like a banner on a hill. Yet the LORD longs to be gracious to you; therefore he will rise up to show you compassion. For the LORD is a God of justice. Blessed are all who wait for him!" [17]

How could I miss it? Why did I keep insisting on doing it in my own effort when He was waiting for me so patiently to *let Him take care of me*? It was the deepest longing of my heart, but I seemed blinded to it. He was waiting for me to stop putting my trust in all my "horses" of self-provision, self-protection and self-promotion – and I didn't "get it". Like a toddler insisting "I do it myself!" I ended up with my clothes on backwards and my hair sticking up in all the wrong places. I had dirt on my face that was easy for others to see, but I wouldn't look in the Biblical mirror and let Him gently wash it off me. He didn't give up; He tenderly and repeatedly showed me my error until I understood. He is such a loving, gentle Daddy!

Anyone who has known me for any length of time will confirm I tend to think things to death. I reason things through, turning over the details one by one until I think I have all the factors I need to understand a given situation. But I'm also impatient. I want to be DOING something about the situation, solving it, getting rid of the discomfort of it. Sometimes I jumped ahead and did the wrong things.

Sometimes I lagged behind to make sure I was making the right choices when I should have acted. We all can say the same thing, I guess. Over time, the choices I made built walls that gave me the illusion of security – but those barriers also doubled as insulation that became a prison from which I couldn't seem to break free. God by-passed all those walls in my head and went right to the healing I needed in my heart. He met me exactly where I was in each moment and showed me His love and care for me.

The reassurances of His rest, care and blessed quiet in those moments lightened my heart in ways I can't even describe. This is not the only time this has happened, but what I felt right then was far greater than anything I had or ever will be able to finagle into existence on my own, no matter how hard I try. I need to remember to repent, rest, listen quietly and trust Him to keep from building more walls. No matter how intelligent we think we are, when we spend time with Him in His Word, He surprises us with amazing options that had never occurred to us before. A bunch of pieces all come together, a "devine epiphany" and we are set free from obstacles we didn't know were there!

Free Indeed

Case in point: In my early 30's, during a quiet time one morning, I re-read Psalm 139. This time it penetrated the fog farther than it had previously and God applied it directly to one of the darkest places in my soul, a monument to very specific lies I picked up earlier in my life. As I was reading "For You did form my inward parts; You knit me together in my mother's womb…my frame was not hidden from You when I was being formed in secret [and] intricately and curiously wrought in the depths of the earth, Your eyes saw my unformed substance, and in Your Book all the days of my life were written before ever they took shape, when there was yet none of them."[18] for some reason only known to God Himself, He connected that with another passage I had read earlier: "…who owe their birth neither to bloods nor to the will of the flesh [that of a physical impulse], nor to the will of man [that of a natural father], but to God. [They are born of God!]"[19]

I started bawling like a baby, tears streaming down my face as I realized that a very distinct and suffocating weight I had been carrying was suddenly gone. The accuser and father of lies had used a specific bit of misinformation to create a wall in my mind that would keep me from understanding how precious I truly was to God for many years. This "thought block" had taken up residence years ago and had locked me into a pain-filled pit. As it disintegrated and shattered into tiny pieces, God's healing expanded my heart beyond the bounds of its former prison, and I was able to see it for the first time as the jumble of lies it truly was. I saw how my perceptions of so many things were poisoned by this insidious and destructive belief for so long. And now I was free of it!

Anyone sitting there at the time would have thought I was having a nervous breakdown as I just kept saying "Thank you God!" over and over again. I was a grown woman with two children of my own, seemingly well adjusted. But God knew this lie was there and it needed to go. Being very careful not to hurt me in the process, God had been chipping away at this deception in me for a *long time*! This wasn't a dynamite job, it required precision. He needed to release something deep in me for us to proceed from there together. It was time. Several months before my 9th birthday, my mom got pregnant with my second brother. It was a great opportunity to learn about how babies grow inside and are born and we had lots of fun looking at baby name books together. My dad had recently become born again. Things had gotten strained between my mom and dad even back then, but this new beginning seemed to have a renewing effect on their relationship. To all of us, the anticipation of our new little one in the house was exciting.

As we were learning the (age-appropriate) details about the pregnancy and birthing process, I did the math and realized that I was born only six months after my parents' wedding day. When I questioned my mom about it, she let me know that "although they had not done things in the right order", she and my dad loved each other and that I was not "the reason they got married". She explained that they were going to get married anyway, even if it would have been a little later in the year. Subject addressed. A new perspective on relationships was initiated - and new ammunition for the enemy to use was introduced to my young heart. Later on when my parents' marriage was failing amid communication and financial stresses, I was primed for taking the blame for all of it as the first-born.

Side note: Dr. Kevin Leman's books on birth order give a wonderful insight to the personality characteristics inherent to the place of your birth order in your biological family. Some of these characteristics are beneficial and some are harmful – and he has a book for all of them. The one I am applying to my own life is "The First-Born Advantage". It is a resource targeted for me to mitigate the destructive tendencies I developed as the first-born and take full opportunity in the advantages of the same. It shares perspectives that help me recognize both the detriments and benefits of these tendencies and increase my ability to grow through it.

One of these characteristics is the tendency to feel responsible for others' actions and situations because of things you have done or said – and ultimately because you are. So it was with me at that point. It became my fault that my parents were having so much trouble. "They would have found mates that they could truly be happy with if it wasn't for me being born". (Isn't it sickening what lies and underhandedness evil uses to destroy us from the inside out?) I internalized all that junk and buried it deep inside, trying to make my parents' marriage work, trying to interpret their communications with one another so they could hear what the other one *meant to say* instead of the lop-sided way they said it.

For most of the time before they died, before and after their divorce, I was the self-appointed ambassador between them, trying to reconcile between two hurt, fearful and angry adults. My mom realized part of this and tried to keep me out of it, but I was desperate for them to resolve things. I kept substituting my own translations between them, trying to interpret each of their responses to the other to take the harshness out and convey how they "should have said it" to each other. It didn't work.

So into my own marriage I brought that pain, hidden down deep that I was the cause of it all. Both that it happened at all and that it was my failure to fix it. I should never have been born. I should have done things differently. Maybe if I tried something else, it would have worked out. God had taken many, many opportunities to point out the lies imbedded in these thoughts. Even though I had heard things like this before, and I realized that these thoughts are shared by many people all over the world, it took this final keystone being knocked out for me to be free of its weight.

I saw how my thoughts were poisoned by the belief that I was a "mistake". All the pain that all of us had gone through, all the dysfunction, all the unacceptable behavior of everyone in the family I believed was somehow my fault for being conceived "by accident". Now, God specifically told me point blank that I was *not* born due to "a natural father's impulse" or my parents' lack of self-control, but I was specifically and purposefully created by God Himself "intricately and curiously wrought" intentionally and lovingly for a reason!

I was finally able to understand I was "set up" by the enemy as a 9-year-old girl. I was interpreting my surroundings in my young mind with the only framework I had at the time, and he was using my immaturity and innocence against me to cast a sense of false blame over my heart. Satan used this faulty foundation to build fences and curtains that shrouded my true value and identity very effectively for much of my life. And now those curtains were torn apart and the fences were broken off their hinges and flung out of my way - I was free of that lie!

How many people come to believe that the world would be better off without them? How many people fall prey to believing that they don't have a purpose and don't make a real difference to anyone else? Is it any wonder that one of the best Christmas movies of all time is Frank Capra's "It's a Wonderful Life"? A man named George, who had given up so many of the things he thought he wanted in life for other people, seemingly without reward or recognition, gives up on life itself, believing others would be better off if he had never been born. He gets the opportunity to see for himself all the people who would have been hurt, or even destroyed, if he had not been there to intercede. So many realizations come to a joyful ending when he sees what a difference for good he made. The implication is we often look in the wrong direction for validation and miss how much our lives mean to others.

We DO matter. We are here for a reason. We are created on purpose and we are a blessing to lots of people around us – sometimes when we are completely unaware of our impact! This new perspective gives us validation and purpose. We need to realize these truths. We need the loving perspective of God to reveal the lies in the whisperings we so easily believe about it somehow "all being our fault".

At the reading of these verses, God unequivocally put all the puzzle pieces together in front of my face and shined His bright Light of Truth and Redemption and said, "You were not born because of a few moments of a lack of propriety and self-control by two young people at one point in time (physical impulse). You were not born because they decided to keep you instead of seeking an abortion (will of a natural man or woman). You were not an accident! You were born because I wanted you to be born. I formed you. I knew every day of your life before your mom knew she was going to miss her period. I created you with brown eyes and brown hair and a talkative, curious, exuberant personality before your dad's heart skipped a beat and was wondering what he was going to do about any of it." (God also made **you** with your eye color, your hair, your personality, your tenderness in some areas and your strengths in others, so we can each take our place in His plan and help one another and accomplish AMAZING things together!) God spoke directly to my heart, insistent and aching for me to get His point: "I made you all on purpose." The release of tears and gratitude I felt when I found out and truly believed that I was NOT a mistake was monumental. But this was not the only thing God wanted me to understand in all this.

An Orphan No More!

By the time these revelations got through to me, more insidious accusations had been added to the previous lies and had whispered, "You're an orphan". Now, even though I was an adult, there were times that allegation pounded in my chest. No matter how old you are, there is a child inside that needs parental assurance. With my parents gone, I thought I had no way of getting that. God had a far different perspective and wanted to *make certain* I understood the joy of it: He added to His declaration "**I made you**" and said "I am your **Father**, you will *never* be an orphan!" The verses I read in John 14:18 and the Psalms assured me over and over again of these truths. Hebrews 13:5 assured me He would *never* forsake me; all of the book of the Song of Solomon told me that I am His beloved – the belonging, the security, the protection, the provision, the freedom and peace that passes all understanding wrapped me up tight and showed me in that moment that I *NEVER WAS* an orphan – and neither are you!

I am the princess daughter of the King of the universe! *You* are the cherished princess or prince of the King of Kings!

He made you and me on purpose. He has a plan for you and me to follow (Jer. 29:11) and assignments for us to fulfill down here that He predetermined long ago (Eph 2:10) - before we go back Home to rule and reign with Him (Rev 22:5). He wants you to be with Him forever (1 Thess. 4:17)! Say it to yourself as many times as it takes to sink in from your head to your heart: "God made me on purpose!"

With everything you've done and with every way you've been abused or debased by others you still have immense value and are dearly loved by God and other people! Someone shared a wonderful illustration that helped me with my doubts in this area: Someone holds up a $100.00 bill, crisp and clean and new, and asks "who wants this?" EVERYONE! They can't fall over one another fast enough to get it. But, what happens if I crumple it up? What if it's wrinkled? Do you still want it? Of Course! It's still a hundred dollar bill! What if it gets thrown on the ground and stepped on? And dirty, and muddy? Do you still want it? YES! It doesn't lose its value because it has dirt on it. It can be washed and dried and fulfill the purpose for which it was created. No matter how dog-eared it gets, it still holds its value because that's what it was made for. The same principle applies to us – only much more so – for we are worth far more than paper money created by any country's government!

God created us with intrinsic value. He knows we are not going to stay crisp and clean and unused in this life. We have our flesh, other hurting, damaged people, and the enemy of our souls to deal with. We make choices and other people make choices that hurt us and wrinkle us and muddy us up – but we are still priceless and eternally precious because God created us and then redeemed us Himself!

The miracle of God's restoration of us is that in His All-knowing-ness He even works into our purpose and plans that the very things that we think make us valueless and worthless – the wrinkles and mud and gravel ground into us in our path of life - are part of what HE USES to help us fulfill our hearts' desires and greatest joy! We can allow the Holy Spirit to help us find the treasure God placed in us, no matter how deeply buried we think it is!

I will probably never get over the joy, the relief and the gratitude I felt when, after 32 years of regret and shame, God healed me and I truly accepted His forgiveness for aborting my first child at the age of 16. I realized that the pain and remorse I was holding onto was actually blocking the purpose He created me for! God flat out tells us that He comforts us "...so that we may also be able to comfort (console and encourage) those who are in any kind of trouble or distress, with the comfort (consolation and encouragement) *with which we ourselves are comforted* (consoled and encouraged) by God."[20] (emphasis mine) The double-barreled freedom I received in the moment that I accepted that I was both His child, on purpose, and completely forgiven from the guilt and shame of my abortion was exhilarating! There is no doubt in my mind - I can't keep it to myself and I will forever run to that particular battle line to help comfort and show the way to other women who are still trapped in the same remorseful deception.

The very thing that had caused me the most pain in my life is now being used by God to bring freedom to others. As I share the same comfort He showed me when I thought I was "as adjusted to it as I could get", I delight in watching as the Grace of God releases this same weight in others. Pain healed, purpose revealed.

God tells us "It is the glory of God to conceal a thing, but the glory of kings is to search out a thing."[21] - and God calls *us* "kings"![22] If we view this life as a treasure hunt – to seek out the purpose God created us for, and view the trials we go through merely as obstacles to overcome in the adventure during the search - we can and will rise to the challenge with the encouragement of other believers along the way!

Now instead of wasting time trying to find belonging, I can face each day not distracted by the tyranny of the immediate. I don't have to miss my opportunities to find out what that purpose looks like. He made me. That thought alone is enough for me to lift my head high and anticipate life. It takes daily grace to re-focus on that thought with all that we are subjected to here. And sometimes I get side-tracked by distractions. But I can regain my proper perspective anytime I choose to.

Amid all the junk that life can throw at us, we can thrive! As a daughter and wife and mother and sister and friend, I can explore fulfilling my individual purpose from the perspective of what being God's Princess looks like. He shows us different things we may face along the way and how not to let them overwhelm us. We can find the jewel and treasure hidden by God in each situation just for us.

In a woman's conference I attended, Beth Moore taught on "The Lost Art of Treasure" and showed us important steps on not missing out on those gems in our lives.[23] (I don't see it on the website yet, but it could be included any time http://www.lifeway.com/article/160695/) Based on Luke chapter 2, Beth pointed out 8 things we need to understand about the Lost Art of Treasure. This is only a brief synopsis, but this was the icing on the cake for the awareness I needed to make permanent these realizations with which God balmed my heart in this area:

1) There are Treasures out there! Believe it, look for them in every moment, be ready for it.

2) They are not *my* treasures until they make it past my defenses. All those "coping mechanisms", deception and self-protective filters in our perspective need to be breached for us to *own* these gifts of God to the point where nothing can take them away from us.

3) Treasures strung together can bring healing. Learn to hold onto the treasures from earlier times in our life, because, gathered together here and there, just like a string of pearls, they can add up to deep healing - a treasure indeed!

4) Most people will miss the treasure entirely. Don't stop at just being amazed at what is happening, make the effort to mull it over, meditate on it, and hide it in your heart. Allow God to show you how the puzzle pieces fit together. Like Mary "treasured up all these things and pondered them in her heart,"[24] holding in our hearts times when special things happen and being able to refer back to them later is a gift in itself. Treasure what God is showing you along the way before running off to the next thing. Beth said, "Eat it before you tweet it!"

5) The Fine Art of Treasuring got lost in the same trash as our Time. Go get it. Put margin back in your life. She

illustrated this point by showing us part of Dr. Richard A. Swensen's book "Margin" and the bell curve showing peak productivity drops off to fatigue and exhaustion when we fail to incorporate off-time and recreation in our lives (sounds familiar from Genesis and Exodus: "6 days you shall work, but the 7th you shall *rest*") take the time to *enjoy* the fruit of your labors.

6) Where there is one treasure, there may be many. Not all the treasures laid up for us are out in the open. "Seek and you shall find"[25] - slow down enough to look around for other things that are not so obvious.

7) We'll minimize our Treasure if we overlook past hardship and pain. If our highest goal is to get out of the pain we are feeling right now, we might be in danger of missing the treasures that are wrapped up for us in those moments. Feel around in the darkness if you have to, but realize that God doesn't permit pain in our lives without a purpose. Beth said there are treasures in your difficulties, waiting for you to find them. Take the time to discover them, even in the dark. And

8) When you feel you've lost your treasure, look to Jesus (not for the treasure you lost). Beth points out beautifully that in Christ "...are hidden all the treasures of wisdom and knowledge."[26] Anything and everything we need to know, need to have, need to see – *everything* is hidden in Him. Instead of trying to find the treasure as a separate thing, make it a priority to find Jesus Himself – all the treasures you could ever hope to find in 10 lifetimes are already in His hand, held specifically by Him waiting for you. (It was a great conference! I hope it gets turned into a Bible study and released in written form!)

Understand this my friend: Your healing, your purpose, your true identity, your reason for living, the beauty of the heart and life God created for you and created you for, is found in Him. You never were a mistake, you never were an orphan; you just couldn't see your palace and King from where you were standing with all that junk in the way!

"If God is for us, who can be against us? ...who graciously gives us all things... who justifies... Christ Jesus who died – more than that, who was raised to life – is at the right hand of God and is also interceding for us...in all these things we are more than conquerors through him who loved us"[27]! And He promised "To him who overcomes I will give to eat from the tree of life"[28] "...and the manna that is hidden."[29].

I will spend the rest of my life discovering what that purpose is. I will explore all the ways I can use the gifts and talents He built into me to build up someone else who is having a hard time. I will be a grateful recipient of others' help toward me when I am having times of struggle - keeping focus on My Daddy and King on the throne. I have a wonderful part to play in a role He designed specifically for me. And so do you! By sharing my part, and encouraging you to share yours, we can show the world that yes, this truly is a Wonderful Life! From "orphan" to royalty – may we all embrace this Truth!

Footnotes

[1] Psalm 3:3 (amp)

[2] "My Fair Lady" 1964 Alan Lerner, Lerner and Lowe/ Warner Bros.

[3] Ibid

[4] Ibid

[5] "Cinderella" 1965 Joseph Shrank/ Rodgers and Hammerstein

[6] http://thinkexist.com/quotation/music_hath_charms_to_ soothe_a_savage_breast-to/151217.html

[7] Mic. 7:19 (amp)

[8] Phil. 4:8 (amp)

[9] Ibid

[10] Phil. 3:13-14 (amp)

[11] Jimmy Evans teaching "Overcoming Comparison" – ourdreammarriage.com Marriage Today copyright 2011

[12] 2 Cor. 12:9 (NIV)

[13] ibid

[14] Beth Moore on Wednesdays with Beth on Life Today

[15] Prov. 13:12 (amp)

[16] Isa. 9:6 (NIV)

[17] Isa. 30:15-18 (NIV)

[18] Ps. 139:13-16 (amp)

[19] John 1:13 (amp)

[20] 2 Cor. 1:4 (amp)

[21] Prov. 25:2 (amp)

[22] Rev 5:9-10 (amp)

[23] Beth Moore's Living Proof Live women's conference from Lowell Mass. 2010

[24] Luke 2:19 (NIV)

[25] Matt 7:7 (NIV)

[26] Col. 2:3 (NIV)

[27] Rom. 8:31-37 (NIV)

[28] Rev. 2:7 (NIV)

[29] Rev 2:17 (amp)

Suggested Resources

"Hind's Feet in High Places" by Hannah Hurnard copyright 1975 by Tyndale House publishers

"Keeping a Princess Heart In a Not-So-Fairy-Tale World" by Nicole Johnson copyright 2003 by W Publishing Group

Jimmy Evans' teaching on the Orphan Spirit – https://www.youtube.com/watch?v=q8zudEvjD10

"The Root of Rejection" by Joyce Meyer © 2002

"The First Born Advantage – Making Your Birth Order Work for You" by Kevin Leman copyright 2008 by Revell Publishing

"Keeping a Princess Heart in a Not-So-Fairy-Tale World" by Nicole Johnson, video www.freshbrewedlife.com

"God's Leading Lady" T. D. Jakes 2003 Berkley Trade

"Boundaries" by Dr Henry Cloud and Dr John Townsend © 1992

"Confronting Without Offending" by Deborah Smith Pegues © 2009

"Seven Things That Steal Your Joy" by Joyce Meyer © 2004

"Margin" by Dr. Richard A. Swensen

http://yourmove.is/ "Breathing Room" Andy Stanley's teaching from North Point Church in Atlanta, GA http://yourmove.is/episode/ep4-choosing-to-cheat-2/

Chapter 9

Trusting the Captain and the Anchor

"[Now] we have this [hope] as a sure and steadfast anchor of the soul [it cannot slip and it cannot break down under whoever steps out upon it – a hope] that reaches farther and enters into [the very certainty of the Presence] within the veil." Hebrews 6:19

It still and repeatedly amazes me the things that God uses to make a point, teach a lesson and just wrap my heart in His Grace! So it is right now in this very unexpected time in my life.

When my brother and I were little, my father's parents owned a cottage on Lake Winnipesaukee in New Hampshire. Because we were early risers, my Nana would leave breakfast out for us the night before and tell us we needed to stay inside, eat breakfast and watch TV until she woke up, *then* we could go do stuff together.

I don't know how many times we ignored this directive but I have memories of walking down the narrow, winding, pine-canopied path with my younger brother, picking and eating wild strawberries as small as the size of pencil erasers – but oh! So sweet! – and making our way down to the lake-front, that was open to those who owned or rented cottages there. It had a dock off to the left where everyone who had one, docked their boats. Crayfish skittered around the sand in the water and under the dock; the beach was fairly small, but very peaceful. Of course it was - it couldn't have been more than 6:30 in the morning! The sand became pretty boring very quickly, not having brought our shovels and buckets with us to mold anything close to a sand castle so inevitably, we would end up playing tetherball on the far right side of this area.

You can't play tetherball quietly. We'd be batting that thing back and forth, oblivious to the people still sleeping, not very far from the beach. Not having to go to their regular jobs for however long their vacations allowed, the adults had stayed up way past our bedtimes and were now trying to make the most of their ability to sleep in. What did we know about that? We were 7 or 8 years old! Anyway...

The thing you find out quickly about tetherball is that the ball doesn't really go anywhere. For those of you who may not know what tetherball is: a volleyball-sized ball is formed with a grommet in it which attaches to a thin nylon rope (tether) that is itself attached to the top of a tall, metal pole. The rope hangs about 2/3 of the way down the pole - when not in use. The object of the game is to bat the ball in one direction until the tether is wound around the pole to the end.

The problem is the other person is also trying to bat the thing around the other way so they wind the ball all the way to the end of the rope in *their* direction. The taller you are, or the more you can punch down on the ball and make the ball upswing when it winds around to the other person's side, out of their reach, the better your chances of winning. First one person seems to be making progress and then it starts winding around the other way. This can go on for a long time!

"Sneaking" out of the cottage and just enjoying these times in the early morning is a great memory for me – I don't remember getting in trouble for doing this, although I know I must have at the time! I know the neighbors must have called my Nana and she must have come to get us – but I really don't remember that part! (As I write this, I am doing a Bible study with Beth Moore called Living Beyond Yourself and got to the part this morning about "godly sorrow" bringing "repentance that leads to salvation"[1], with Beth's focus on not harboring "cherished sins"[2]. I had asked God to show me what sins I was cherishing - and this came up. I now ask God to help me repent from the rebellion and disobedience that I was romanticizing, and to be able to cherish the childhood memory, without cherishing the sin associated with it! He is faithful!)

Fast forward to July 2009: My husband and I are celebrating our 25th wedding anniversary having booked a 6-day windjammer cruise on a pinky schooner, sailing around in Penobscot Bay, off the Maine coast. We've never done anything like this before. We are two of 8 people including the crew on this boat. Learning about jibs and halyards and tacking and all kinds of terms and just really enjoying the break from the "work-a-day" world with teen children, time clocks, and work reports. We also had just moved into the dream-house we recently finished building – overseeing, really, with different contractors doing each thing how we pictured it should be – not really turning out that way, but that's another chapter! We really needed a break!

It was the first time in a very long time that I was truly happy. For an entire week, Steve and I had time together, sharing quiet talks here and there. The boat was only 58 feet long, so we got to know the other passengers and crew pretty well, talking about our families, jobs, spending time reading the books we brought, writing in notebooks, sharing stories, helping with the dishes and the meal preparation - on a woodstove in the galley on a wooden boat. (http://schoonersummertime.com/smrship.html check it out!) It was great!

But two days back from the trip, I was once again getting in frustration mode with the day-to-day details that make the house run smoothly. Unsuccessfully. VERY unsuccessfully! My husband, missing the smile that practically never left my face on vacation, took my face in his hands and said (almost pleading with me), "Please, Tracy! You were happy for a whole week. Don't lose it!" With that plea, I began taking – or *making* - opportunities to have fun (loading up the Nerf suction cup gun and hiding it in the cabinet, so that later that day, when I came home for lunch, I could surprise my home-bound teens with an ambush "strike and run" in the hallway! (After all, they had met us in the driveway with water balloons after our 6 hour trip back from Maine!) I got my smile back again and worked not to lose it, trying to find ways to lighten up and not take things so seriously again. The "course adjustments" that week went pretty well overall. Until Saturday.

My daughter, son-in-law and grandkids came over for lunch, to pick up a few things and spend time with us for the day. Being oblivious to the emotional undercurrent, I was running around, attending the grill and making side dishes for us all to enjoy the first sit down dinner since we came back from our trip. When grace was said and I put a burger in my mouth, my daughter said, "We are moving to Oregon on August 29th".

This was way worse than laundry and dishes not being done!

All week, my early morning quiet times with God had been filled with reminders about His Peace not being like the world, teaching me to let Him gently wash away the shortcomings of other people in His own time (without my enthusiastic help!), while we all cooperate with Him to just love one another without finger pointing and condemnation. We are (or can be!) far too busy paying attention to the process WE are involved in while He cleans US just as gently and patiently as He does with others, knowing that He is doing this as our Loving Daddy. All this was great preparation. Of course it was - **He** knew it was coming, even when I am clueless! And He was getting me ready to lean into His arms for the stability He would give me when my world was rocked again by things I couldn't foresee!

This news hit me like a ton of bricks. I sat there with my 2-year-old grandson on my lap, who was eating his lunch; tears were streaming down my face, and I couldn't stop. I didn't want to give free-reign to my emotions because I didn't want to scare Jason (it is very unnerving for little ones to see their parents and grandparent crying. It scares them, shaking their security), so I stuffed it, swallowing hard and trying not to react. While we sat there, I was thinking through all the implications for how would we be able to travel that far with my husband's health issues (thirteen hours one way, including airport layovers and driving time). Fears and emotions were running high with thoughts of "I'll never see them again". (I was remembering the terms "photographic-" and "prophetic thinking" from a teaching by Jimmy Evans called "How to Think When Life Stinks"; seeing the words "never" or "always" are clues you are falling for deception and in need of a thought adjustment!) And although I could easily see it happening in her thought processes, I didn't recognize it in mine until much later.

My daughter talked through all the reasons why she needed to leave and why it was the best and only solution to their situation while all these other things were running through my head. Then she turned to me and asked, "So, what do you think?" My head was swimming with the surprise of it all and although I knew logical reasons and alternative solutions to their problems this move was intended to solve, none of them came out of my mouth. All I had screaming in my head was an overwhelming sense of loss with the words "It's not our decision to make", "they have their own life to live". The Bible says we need to "always be prepared to give an answer to everyone who asks you ..."³, but the answer failed me at that moment. The next day I had the presence of mind to be able to vocalize the concept of "geographic cures" not being an answer to inner issues. I tried to tell her of the other consequences of relocation: the costs associated with a move and the lack of day-to-day support of family and church they were used to, etc. "knowing" that they hadn't taken these considerations into account. When I tried to answer her question from the previous afternoon, I was told the plane tickets had already been purchased and the decision was made. They had their minds set and the time for "feedback" had passed. The emotional separation process had begun (the inner building of protective walls to lessen the pain you know is coming with impending distance). I felt cut off. I knew better in my head, but my heart was breaking and that didn't leave much focus on what my head "knew".

I cried for 4 days. I was frantic to spend as much time with them before they left as possible, but their looming departure was stealing the joy from the time we had left. During one of the conversations, my daughter said "For cryin' out loud Mom, we're not dying, we're moving!" It all felt the same to me. When I looked at them I couldn't stop the tears for the thoughts of losing them to the move – it was hard enough to make it a point to work within everyone's schedule to get together for Sunday dinner when they were a half hour away. How could we make the time now when we had to consider taking time off of work, include the travel time and not make it a blinding rush of activity? I was trying not to "guilt" my daughter, but wanting her to change her decision. It surprised me that I had to fight another emotion: anger. I found myself trying not to be angry about them pursuing this option in the first place. There were so many things my husband and I could clearly see that were going to happen that they hadn't anticipated, but the door for acceptance of other solutions was closed. I struggled back and forth whether this was a situation that God had initiated or if it was a mistake that He would be redeeming later on – in all honesty, I still don't know. What matters is it was a reality I did not want to be dealing with. More on that later...

My emotions were not stable and the surgery I'd had two years earlier for endometriosis left my hormones on a roller coaster that just added to the feeling of unbalance - like trying to get your "sea legs" after not being on the water for a while. My son's girl friend said "Mom, you have a whole month to enjoy time with them, don't miss out on the fun by being miserable about the move now!" My husband repeated the same sentiment in different words a few days later. I was trying. Wise words from people who loved me were trying to reposition my perspective. I was grateful for the effort, but my emotions still had too much sway at that point.

A Change in Focus

I decided to be proactive. Once I accepted the fact they were moving, I went to the next logical step. I began thinking about solutions to the problems the distance would create in keeping in touch, taking into account my grandchildren's ages – 1 and 2 years old.

The phone doesn't work with kids that young - their attention span is so tiny and there's no visual aspect to go with it! What could we do? Letters are a waste for that age, they can't read. Friends of ours were in a similar situation – their son and daughter-in-law moved to Japan just after the wedding. They have Skype set up with webcams and microphones. Great! If I have to deal with a reality I didn't have any part in deciding, then I would make the best of it by finding alternative ways of communicating with them.

When I did try to be reasonable about the whole thing, I realized my husband was taking it harder than I was. He was just more silent about it all. He was trying to be strong for me and then silently trying to deal with his own thoughts on the subject. I tried to get him to talk about it with me when we were alone.

I told Steve later, "You told me so tenderly last week, 'you were happy for a whole week, don't lose it!' What happened to that idea?" He said, "That was before my grandson was being taken 3,000 miles away!" (Proverbs says "Children's children are the crown of old men"[4] – he ain't just whistling Dixie! Jason and Steve have a special bond I love to see!) We were both thinking of all the activities we could finally get to do with Jason and Emily now that they were getting older. ("You see, we are different; but we are not so different" comes to mind from a line in a comedy routine!)

We also struggled with losing Jennifer. In 23 years, we had never spent a holiday apart. We always had at least one meal a week together – even after she got married and had her own family. This would be her first birthday since I had her that I couldn't hold her! Why was my objection to this loss so incomprehensible to her?

When I went to my counseling session that week (I had just begun seeing someone two months before, after *talking about it* for years – talk about the provision of God!) I was inconsolable, fearful and overwrought. On the way over there, I started to build my own self-protective walls to insulate my heart from the pain I was feeling. I was thinking through the tears, "yeah, it's probably better that they move on their own for a while so they can grow together and depend on each other – instead of me stepping in all the time. They are so young (then the "hard wall" interjection) - and *they* still have a *lot* to learn!"

I kid you not! SO clearly in my thoughts at that very moment, Word for word, I heard in my heart: "Uh, Tracy? They're not the *only* ones that have a *lot to learn*." Gentle but pointed, I knew God's voice, warning me, that I had just crossed the line into self-righteousness again. He wasn't condemning me, just shining a warning light and calling me back to the main road. After a mental "oops!" and regretful acknowledgement that that line of thought was not going to help my situation at all (!), I thought, "well, I am on my way to the counselor's office, now is the best time to start!" I told her about our "conversation" as soon as I walked in the door.

We got updated since our last visit and then she asked, out of what felt like left field to me, "What does being a grandmother mean to you?" What? I just told her my heart was breaking about losing my daughter, son-in-law and grandkids to a 3,000 mile move. What does that have to do with anything?

Change of topic, but ok, let's go with that. Well, I was off and running, talking about all the wonderful things my Nana and Grandpa had done with us and for us: buying our bikes and swing set, having us set up with twin beds in a room of our own in their house, bringing us to the neatest places we would never have seen on our own.

There were so many things I hadn't thought of in such a long time – things that I had just accepted as everyday life for Grandparents that I learned much later no one else I knew got to enjoy. My grandparents had a soda delivery service that brought all kinds of soda right to their house – my favorite was birch beer! It was such a treat to be able to choose from a neat variety of flavors, our own old-fashioned soda bottles from wooden crates on the breezeway porch! We did so many things together: gardening, cooking, playing, reading - they were awesome to us! Until...

My heart felt the drop even now...they moved to Florida when I was ten. Not just as a vacation place like before, not just traveling to Arizona and bringing me and my brother turquoise jewelry and those bolo neckties that

464

looked like a road runner, or to New Hampshire to the cottage where we could visit for a couple weeks, but moved to Florida to live permanently.

I know we had other times with them after that, we have pictures to prove it, but in my flawed 10 year-old mind, I never saw them again. It wasn't the same as seeing them any time we wanted during the week and on weekends. Within two years after that, my grandfather found out he had cancer. I was his princess, but I couldn't do anything about that one. I remember my parents talking about a trip to Mexico for Laetrile treatments that worked really well, but after several months it came back. The memories about how the chemotherapy he tried later on just drained the life out of him are still hard to take. I never saw him again. He died when I was 12.

My Nana and I exchanged cards and letters for years after that. But by the time she came up for my wedding when I was in my 20's, she didn't look like I had remembered; the daily intimate contact was gone. We enjoyed the memories of what we had from before, but I was too busy with last minute wedding preparations to really catch up with everything. I had all I could do at that point just getting up the decorations for the reception. But even then she was there for me. With me standing on a ladder, she handed up crepe paper streamers to me for the walls and the basketball hoop. ☺

A few years later, as a young wife and mom, she sent me tickets to come down to see her. I was thrilled! She was still in the same house she had gotten with my Grandpa all those years before. We shared pictures and memories, stayed up late talking, and visiting with some of her friends, introducing me to people I had only heard about in her letters. She brought me out to my first Benny Hanna's - knives and food flying – it was so much fun!

We had recaptured part of the relationship we had so enjoyed years before. A few years after that, we visited again, but this time was for my dad (her son). He now had cancer and she came for a visit with my uncle. A few months later, the visit was for his funeral. Then it was her turn. She got sick, moved away from the house she had gotten with my grandfather in Florida to move into an assisted living facility in Michigan to be closer to my uncle. I went to see her there and shared some good hugging time, another good restaurant and more memories. I am grateful for the trip but it was really a final good-by – a chance to see one another face to face one more time. Twenty seven years after losing her husband, she joined him again. The sadness I dealt with combining past and present losses was hard to take.

Now, talking about it, all this pain was fresh on my heart all over again, only stronger, multiplied by the threat of a repeat performance - but this time with a change of roles. Thoughts I never suspected weren't mine, told me the cycle would repeat again. Only this time, I would be the grandmother. The lie of that chain reaction happened so quickly, I was completely oblivious to its origin! It was *not* a done deal, it was photographic thinking – but I hadn't put that together yet. I just believed the lie that once they were gone, that was it, they wouldn't move back, I'd never see them again and nothing about that could ever change. Once I saw the breakdown of the thought process that interjected the hopelessness I was feeling, my attitude completely changed.

Instead of pain and loss being the predominant feeling, now I was just plain ticked off! How could I be so foolishly unaware of the sneakiness of intruding, lying thoughts and just accept them as inevitable! Thinking about this, I remembered two things: When the thief is discovered, "he must restore seven times [what he stole]"[5] and "The thief comes only to steal, kill and destroy; I have come that they may have life, and have it to the full"[6] There is nothing in what I know of God that says my family situation couldn't change! God is a God of redemption, connection, and relationship. The Bible clearly says He makes a way (in reality) where there is no way (to our earthly eyes for it to happen). God, Who "makes a way through the sea and a path through the mighty waters"[7] could and would make a way for me through this difficult situation. Why had I so easily fallen for the dark prophesies of heartache and separation?

In a moment in time, sitting there in the counselor's office, all this stuff came back to my mind. I realized the real reason I was so devastated by the news of my daughter's family leaving was the fear that history would repeat and I would never be able to do and go and have the experiences and memories like that with Jason and Emily like my grandparents had with me. It also brought back the grief and loss over my Nana and Grandpa's moving and subsequent deaths that were buried and fermenting in there, unseen for years of busyness and doing things in my own life.

The emotions were now brought fresh and too quickly to the surface for me to handle by myself – but of course, I didn't have to. Thank God for His provision! My counselor helped me walk through the conclusions I had made about how this current move would turn out in the present, looked at it as **F**alse **E**vidence **A**ppearing **R**eal (I love that anagram for fear – it gives assurance that the future doesn't have to be what you dread, but what you can anticipate God working out for you in His Loving Favor!).

She shared with me ways to ensure that distance doesn't have to be so big a factor in relationships now – with email, post cards, little packages, pictures, skyping etc. I can have and do everything from home – only without the hugs – and those I can still get with visits to and from them, and see the parts of the country I've never seen and have wanted to for a long time! My past grief over earlier family losses could now be separated from the present and be put in its proper place and healed as a natural part of life. I could now process, as an adult, the events that I lacked the maturity to understand as a pre-teen. It was a good realization to make.

As the week progressed, my quiet times with God in the morning when everyone else was sleeping, brought up both the past and the present in lots of things God has been building and removing as part of a bigger process – all lessons I am learning again and again, incorporating more details along the way. Verses of promise and trusting God's heart lift my thoughts from darkness.

One morning, before my daughter's family even left, my brother had sent me an email to read something in Jeremiah. But I almost never read just one verse. I read the whole chapter to get the context of what was being said. So, with tears streaming down my eyes, trying to read while asking God to please help me block out my sadness and help me concentrate on Him before my day started, I got half-way through the chapter and read: "Thus says the Lord: Restrain your voice from weeping and your eyes from tears..." (*do I have your attention? I kid you not! It was right there in black and white! But it got even better...*) "...for your work will be rewarded, says the Lord; and [your children] shall return from the enemy's land. And there is hope for your future, says the Lord, your children shall come back to their own country."[8]

God couldn't have been more direct with me if He had manifested in the flesh, put His arm around my shoulder and dried my face Himself! No, I didn't stop crying right then, in fact, I cried even harder! But this time my tears had hope in them.

God then used very specific verses to remind me of Truth that combated the dark fears of my heart: "Man's steps are ordered by the Lord. How then can a man understand his way?"[9] and, "O Lord, I know the way of a man is not in himself, it is not in man to direct his own steps."[10] I grabbed onto these verses, memorizing them on the spot, and held on for dear life. My daughter would be coming back. I just didn't know how or when – and God gave me these assurances before she even left! Isaiah 22:22 and Revelation 3:7 tells us that God opens doors no man can shut and closes doors no man can open. I needed to trust Him with all of it. If God wanted this door open, nothing I could do would close it, and I did not want to add fighting against God to my frustration! (see Acts 5:34-39!) I had already experienced that when we bought the pickup truck. I didn't want to take that road again. I truly believe today that God had multiple reasons for moving my daughter's family out to Oregon.

The tenderness He took in giving this broken-hearted mother the precious gift of acceptance, while He continues to work out what He needs to work in all of us, is so priceless to me! Whether this geographical separation was to be measured in months or years, I was assured that it would indeed be a temporary situation with divine purpose.

 A lot happened in those months as a direct result. In my grief over losing the day-to-day contact with them, my perspective on how little control we really do have over our own lives deepened. My faith in why we need to depend on God so completely for our direction and decisions was tested and grew stronger. We can make plans until Christmas, but if those plans are not built on what God wants to happen in our lives, our plans will not succeed - and I am much quicker to realize that's not a bad thing.

"A man plan his way, but the Lord directs his steps and makes them sure"[11] This verse makes me step back and breathe deeply to clear the fear-fog and trust in the only God worth following – the One Who loves me and all my family, and has the ability to bring tangles of different threads and jumbled colors to His throne and weave the beautiful tapestry of our lives, joined together with others, for our good and redemption, just like He promises.

When I was in an Easter musical a few years back, I learned a song that can still steady me if I revert back to a doubting heart. Jesus' mother Mary is singing through tears at the cross: "God is too wise to be mistaken; God is too good to be unkind. So when you don't understand, when you don't see His plan, when you can't see His Hand, trust His Heart!"[12]

God isn't done yet. There is still an on-going unfolding of things He still wanted and wants me to understand. One of the things I am very grateful for as He leads me in Bible study, with the help of some pretty amazing people, is the revelation in the Word in the words He uses. Perfection isn't used as an end result. Maturity isn't a finish line. It's a **process**. The words used in places like Ephesians 4:12: "His intention was the *perfecting* and the full *equipping* of the saints, His consecrated people, that they should do the work of *ministering toward building* up Christ's body, the church" (emphasis mine) and Philippians 1:6: "...He Who began a good work in you *will continue* until the Day of Jesus Christ, right up to the Day of His return, *developing* that good work and *bringing it to full completion* in you" (emphasis mine), shows that progression. Translated from the Greek, these "-ing" words are what scholars call the "present active participle" and (I am told) that "denotes continuous and ongoing action."[13]

No matter how old we get, no matter how "experienced" we are, we are all a work in progress and He's not going to be finished working and developing us until we are at His side in heaven! That can be discouraging for those of us with perfectionist tendencies that want to get it right and be done with it! But that's not how it works. If it could be completed that way, then we wouldn't need Jesus as the "author and finisher of our faith"[14]! Each thing we go through, each pleasant and unpleasant thing we experience, teaches us something valuable. And NOTHING is wasted! He uses everything, past, present and future to teach us and comfort us and encourage us - to keep us pressing forward.

Mother Theresa is quoted as saying "I know that God never gives us more than we can handle – sometimes I just wish He didn't trust me so much!"[15] I can put both hands and a foot in the air and testify to that one! But when it comes down to it, it is a great comfort to know the Truth of that reality in God – He promises to "never leave you nor forsake you"[16] and bring us along the paths He has "prepared"[17] for us. He helps and guides us all along the way, and says He will not to let any harm overtake us[18] When I am not looking at the waves of the storms around me and keep my eyes on His Face, I can walk on water and so much more[19]! Holding His Hand, "I can do all things through Christ Who strengthens me"[20] -and I love Him all the more for it!

I am finding He *delights* in "show[ing] Himself strong" to and *for* those who seek Him![21], our Hero, the Giving God[22] Who comes to us while we are holding onto our scraped knees and cradles our tearful faces, holding us tenderly, inviting us to curl up into His lap and just be comforted by Him! Like a song by Casting Crowns – "Just Be Held" He doesn't need us to hold on – we are being held. (I love that!)

We have times of comfort and we have times of unexpected rewards – just because we are His children! He encourages us to look through His pockets to see what He has put there just for us! I can't work hard enough to earn that kind of favor and acceptance in ten lifetimes! That's the point – we don't have to! He loves us and cares for us because we *can't* do it for ourselves! And He is always using new ways to show us He loves us – individually tailored for our own experiences, personalities, wounds, expectations, and desires. Out of left field sometimes, in ways that don't make sense sometimes to my legalistic, "holy" verses "secular" separation-of-religion-from-the-rest-of-life tendencies, He throws in a quote from a movie or song that encourages me in the unexpected events and adventures we don't anticipate having or experiencing.

472

In "The Pagemaster", a partially animated movie from 1994, a young boy who is afraid of everything experiences some things that terrify him in a world he has little control over. With the help of some living books he meets along the way, he finds the fear that has imprisoned him in his young life is worth fighting against. Part of the journey includes how he meets his companions Adventure, Fantasy and Horror and how they help him find his new confidence.[23]

As this story progresses, the books help their young charge to face his fears, lighten up a little from being so serious, and take some risks for the sake of friendship that bring rewards beyond any of his expectations, transforming him into a more confident young man. In their journey together to find the exit, the boy realizes that even though things are hard at the time, the satisfaction of getting through to the other side of each battle and the things you learn along the way are permanently yours from then on, to keep. Sounds a LOT like Beth Moore's points last chapter about the Treasures....

God teaches us much the same way. Your companions along the way are given as help to encourage you and see you through! They help us navigate life a little easier with the things we will face in future "adventures"! Galatians chapter 6 is as good a navigation of this process in interpersonal relationship as it gets! "Let us not become weary in doing good, for at the proper time we will reap a harvest if we do not give up"[24] As God leads us in difficult places to show us these secret things about us, we grow. Those are the very things that bring purified gold and silver out of, for and in us. God *does* lead us into scary places sometimes, but He NEVER leaves us alone in them. He is worthy of our trust, even if we don't know what He's going to do next. Would God be worth trusting and following if He was "small" enough for us to be able to understand? Most assuredly not!

Sometimes the sure knowledge of His Overpowering and Never-ending Love is the handrail we can to hold onto when the rollercoaster turns of life get *really* unnerving! In "The Chronicles of Narnia: The Lion, The Witch and The Wardrobe", based on CS Lewis's 1950's book: when the children ask the Beavers to describe Aslan, "Is He a tame lion?" They laugh incredulously and tenderly at the same time – "No, He is *not* tame, but He is good!"[25] I heartily agree! He has proven Himself to me over and over again – God is absolutely *not* tame – He has taken me on some of the wildest rides of my life – and not all of them were pleasant! But He NEVER left me alone or stopped drawing me close to Him. Despite the destructive, arrogant, rebellious, horrible and down-right stupid things I've done in my life, He NEVER stopped loving me! He is *GOOD*! I have learned to remember that when my emotions lead me to doubt the Truth of that some days. And in teaching me, He leads me to share what I am learning with others.

Lots of previous situations where He has rescued and brought blessing out of difficult circumstances fill my mind – and an object lesson coordinates with this from our trip to Maine that July -

God brought up my sailing trip: The captain who owned the boat was the one who set the course each day. He was up before we were, instructing the crew, charting the course, and making preparations for the events that day, all before we weighed anchor. If the weather was not optimum, he made adjustments in the course and speed of the boat to bring us to a lee shore (sheltered from the wind that blew on the open water), either dropping anchor or mooring in a harbor, putting up a special "rain fly" for shelter on deck, and letting us know what was available on shore. We were able to help with the rigging, raising and lowering sails, helping with the dishes and meal preparation – he even allowed us to take turns steering the ship, while he told us the direction to aim for and showed us the buoys to avoid rocks and shoals that would be a problem for us. But it was always his boat. It was always he that decided when meals would be served - on deck or below, he that charted the course and decided when we set sail and when we dropped the anchor for the night, always allowing time before the darkness came to prepare the ship, and us, for a peaceful night's sleep. The anchor was going to keep us from drifting during the night. Even with the currents and tides pushing on the boat and lulling us to sleep, we would still be where we needed to be in the morning at which point we would weigh anchor and begin cruising for the day all over again.

God combined the memories of the distant past and this anniversary trip to comfort my heart over Jennifer's impending departure to tell me: "When she was little, your relationship was like your beachside game of tetherball. It was exciting, up close, sometimes tiring and right there - on the beach. Now the season has changed and she's on a boat of her own – along with her husband and her children. She has the same Captain you have in charge of her ship. (Amid music swelling and refrains of "My Anchor Holds" ringing in my ears) She has the same Anchor to keep her from drifting when she's asleep or in the dark.

Her Captain sets her course as He does for you. He will let her steer in some places, navigating around rocks and shoals by keeping an eye on the lighthouses and buoys that warn her away from danger and tell her where the channels are that are safe to travel. There will be times when she finds herself sailing right alongside of other boats, enjoying the same currents and sunshine. And there will be days she'll feel like she's the only boat out there. And if she does take the boat too close to some reef or rocks, and do damage to the boat, the Captain is still faithful and capable. He will gently lay her boat over on the beach and do the repairs that need doing between the falling and return of the tide, restoring her to sea-worthiness and with a little more awareness of the dangers that can be lurking just under the surface of the waters we all travel!

As for you, as her Mom (and you too, Dad) you still have a very important role to play: you are now Home Port. It is written on the side of her boat. Her launching place, the place she was commissioned. And periodically she will return to home port. Sails open to the wind taking her into familiar waters for a restful homecoming. Sometimes it will be for a day, sometimes for a week or more. But she will return. Remember My promise to you and hold on to it no matter what things look like on the surface: "Thus says the LORD, Refrain your voice from weeping and your eyes from tears for your work will be rewarded says the LORD and [your children] shall return from the enemy's land. And there is hope for your future, says the LORD; Your children shall come back to their own country."[26]

I am so grateful for the times when God knows how badly I need to hear reassurances and encouragement (despite my first-born, independent, get-it-done self) as He reminds me of His Power and Grace and Goodness all at once toward my heart. I cherish those promised assurances for my children. I can <u>choose </u>to trust Him.

 I was not as frantic and overwrought by her departure as I was the first few days I heard the news. I still didn't like the idea, and I knew there were more tears to follow but my heart was not in a panic in desperation and grief over a combination of loss, past and present. God healed a breach in there somewhere and helped me reach an acceptance and peace at the same time. Even before they left, I had an anticipation of their return to Home Port for visits – and maybe relocation near us later on when other things got settled. It also came with a firm confidence in our financial ability to make whatever adjustments were needed (not in my strength, or by forcing things in my timing, but in God's provision). I didn't have to accept the sneaking lies that say we or they would never be able to afford a change – what God calls for, He pays for – and sometimes in some pretty inventive ways!

I was also able to look forward to opportunities to expand our horizons - to see things out there we had not seen yet when we visited them. We had more immediate reasons to take trips now beyond our "bucket list" wanting to see all the places we saw on the Travel Channel!

"I know the plans I have for you declares the LORD, plans to prosper you and not to harm you, plans to give you hope and a future."[27] I don't want to miss it by wrapping myself in the "never" and "always" lies that keep me bemoaning something I can't change in the moment! I need to lean into a deeper appreciation that God is trustworthy and faithful. This situation definitely gave me the opportunity to learn that!

God brought me through a lot of personal business that had little to do with my daughter in those first few years - relationship building and conflict resolution opportunities, my post-abortion recovery program, financial stewardship instruction, lessons on boundaries! – all things I had put on the back burner in lieu of spending time with them. My priorities needed adjusting and evidently I hadn't been allowing God to adjust them while they were here.

It took time to get from the panic over the separation to *full* acceptance that when God was done doing what He intended in this break, that He was fully capable of fulfilling the promise He made to me in my loft that morning. And the process developed a deeper reliance on Him in my heart. Patience while I was waiting for all this to unfold was harder.

It was 14 months after they moved before we got Skype. The computer connection cut out on us sometimes, and the three-hour time difference and our varied work schedules limited the number of times we talked per week, but we *could* see one another. We also went cross country a couple times, which was something my husband and I had talked about doing when we were first dating. We went out for a visit for Jason's third birthday, and then for Jenn and Ralph's anniversary that first year. The year after, we were only able to go once – for Emily's third birthday. We had to reconcile our longing to see them with the reality of financial limitations sometimes. We talked on the phone when we could, enjoying longer conversations when possible. It was hard to be content with the distance.

We were all learning some pretty important lessons along the way – some easier and more pleasant than others. I hoped we were making the most of a situation we couldn't change...months had passed and other people told me I was hoping in something that wouldn't happen – that I needed to accept their relocation as permanent and move on with that new reality. A couple times, I began to question whether her return would be figurative or literal. But those temptations to doubt what I knew in my heart so clearly that morning just made me tighten my grip on His promise to me. God told us we were supposed to look at all the witnesses of faith in Hebrews chapter 11! 20 years went by between the time that Abraham was told Sarah would bear him a son and the time Isaac was born – but it did happen[28]. All the others listed in this "Hall of Faith" would not let go of their assurances for what God promised. The timing for this promise's fulfillment was no more in my power than that it had been in theirs. But my faith was. I would not let go of what I heard that morning in my loft – no matter how long it took.

Two years, 3 months and 24 days after she told me they were leaving, I got a phone call. "Mom, you know how we were supposed to be coming out for a week-long visit in February?" My heart stopped (No! Please God!...) "Yeah?" "Well, when we get to Connecticut, we're not leaving." I was in a side room, off a hallway, in the middle of a training seminar, talking to her on a cell phone. I wanted to cheer at the top of my lungs! I kept my voice low and told her I was thrilled.

"Can we stay with you and Dad for a while till we get jobs again?" "Of course! Your Dad and I decided that *before you left*." I had to get off the phone and return to the seminar. But you know as soon as the lunch break started, the last thing on my mind was food! THEN I could cheer as loud as I wanted to: I called her back "HOORAY!!!! I am sooo excited!" We talked about details and made arrangements over the course of the next two weeks.

It has been over three years since my daughter moved – back home! After 2 ½ years of living in Oregon, they came back to home port - relocating for three years with us, and then getting their own place in the same town! The tears and the anxious thoughts I had for so long were natural, but such an unnecessary torment! Looking back on the progression of my grief, it was classic textbook: denial, anger, bargaining, depression and acceptance[29]. When it all started, I was big-time ticked off and fought hard not to blame others for the situations that "made them leave" (sometimes unsuccessfully). When I reached the point that God had a purpose in this separation, I made up my mind to learn what those things were, holding onto the previously mentioned verses as incentive and hope that, maybe once I completed the treasure hunt, they would return.

We've all had opportunities to learn many more lessons. Yes, God is Good. Yes, He is Faithful. He is ALWAYS true to His Word. And He will help you get the barnacles off your boat while you're waiting in dry dock, looking forward to navigating familiar waters again!

I will never be able to put God in a box - thank Goodness! If I could put Him in a box, He would be too small to be the

God Who is in Sovereign control of my life! I can't figure out all the why's and wherefore's of what His plan is in any given situation. There are times I don't agree (at least at first) with some of the courses He's charted for me. I may not understand the purpose behind the storms He decided to take me through instead of weathering it out in a lee shore harbor. He is not tame. But He <u>is</u> good. And I can trust Him to bring me – and the ones I love - safely Home. Until then, we have a continuing process unfolding, adding to the journey, to the adventure as He builds and grows in us the things He created us to be and do. And I will be content in that knowledge.

I will follow My Captain and see the sights He has planned for me. I will rest in the cabin He prepared for me here, while I anticipate the eternal mansion on that beautiful shore! With all my heart, I pray you will too. I pray that you will see the futility of keeping offenses in your heart. That you will experience the joy of release from self-condemnation for regret-filled choices in your past, as I continually am learning to do in mine. I pray that you will look forward to the unexpected bends in the road with anticipation instead of dread, holding tight to the handrail of His Love. He is absolutely worthy of your deepest Trust. You can count on it!

Footnotes

[1] 2 Cor. 7:14 (NIV)

[2] "Living Beyond Yourself – Exploring the Fruit of the Spirit" By Beth Moore p. 158 LifeWay Press 1998

[3] 1 Pet. 3:15 (NIV)

[4] Prov 17:6 (amp)

[5] Prov. 6:31 (amp)

[6] John 10:10 (NIV)

[7] Isa. 43:16 (amp)

[8] Jer. 31:16-17 (amp)

[9] Prov. 20:24 (amp)

[10] Jer. 10:23 (NKJV)

[11] Prov. 16:9 (amp)

[12] "Trust His Heart" Babbie Mason

[13] http://kcusers.com/faithassembly/GreekFiles/Lessons/Greek102-35.pdf

[14] Heb. 12:2 (NKJV)

[15] http://www.goodreads.com/author/quotes/838305.Mother_Teresa

[16] Heb 13:5b (NKJV)

[17] Ps. 85:13 (NIV)

[18] Ps. 91 (NIV)

[19] Matt. 14:25-30, John 14:12 (NIV)

[20] Phil 4:13 (NKJV)

[21] 2 Chron. 16:9 (NKJV)

[22] Jas. 1:5 (amp)

[23] "The Pagemaster" 1994 Joe Johnson/20th Century Fox

[24] Gal. 6:9 (NIV)

[25] "The Chronicles of Narnia: The Lion, The Witch and the Wardrobe" 2005 Walden Media/Walt Disney Pictures based on CS Lewis book "The Lion, The Witch and The Wardrobe" © 1950

[26] Jer. 31:16-17 (amp)

[27] Jer. 29:11 (NIV)

[28] Gen. ch. 17 - 18

[29] Stages of Grief, Kübler-Ross, E. (1969) *On Death and Dying*, Routledge, ISBN 0415040159

Suggested Resources

"Personal Holiness in Times of Temptation" by Bruce Wilkinson © 1998

"From Dream to Destiny" by Robert Morris © 2005

"Living Free" by Robert Morris and James Robison © 2010

Chapter 10

The Ultimate Deception v. Eternal Reality

"He hath made everything beautiful in its time: also he
hath set eternity in their heart, yet so that man cannot
find out the work that God hath done from the beginning
even to the end."
Ecclesiastes 3:11 (ASV)

I've read this verse dozens of times - in various
translations, during different times of my life. It's never
had the impact – the raw emotional awareness – or
understanding that it had one night recently. I know that I
naturally have more of a sense of mortality as I get older.
And I've known that there is most definitely something
greater than li'l ol' me in this world for a long time. But so
do lots of people. There's an inner knowing somehow that
everything around us - nature, space, biology, philosophy,
literature,   language,   incidents,   "accidents",
"coincidences", EVERYTHING – points to something Bigger
and Greater than just what one man can do or impact in
his or her lifetime.

Sure, I've had things happen that have triggered more
thought on this than others. Going to a funeral of a loved
one has this effect on most people – suddenly being faced
with the "What's next?" up close and personal lends itself
to contemplating things beyond our physical existence. In
my experience, contemplating the brevity of life with

mindfulness to "make it count" can help prioritize what's truly important and identify what is merely "pressing". There is a distinct difference, and I have not always been able to see that. Reflecting on how some have left their mark on history despite various challenges can be very motivating. Encouraging accounts of great feats from people who have become every day heroes – sometimes unawares – is inspiring.

Sometimes it's not a person, but a natural occurrence that triggers this contemplation. Things like sunsets and sunrises, especially during particularly trying times in life, have that impact on me when I take the time to just sit quietly.

One day quite some time ago now, I was in one of those seasons that everything seemed to be caving in on me. I woke up before anyone else and went to sit in my rocking chair in the living room. I was completely engulfed in the darkness, tears streaming down my face as I sat, praying almost silently for I don't know how long. I poured out my heart to God, asking Him to help me, to somehow show me what I needed to do. As I began to calm down, turning one thing after another over to Him, I finally opened my eyes. What I saw could easily be explained by natural phenomena. But I knew it was much more than that. My Daddy gave me a gift that morning: the complete assurance of His care. His Peace and the certain knowledge He'd not only heard my cries to Him, but He was promising me that every one of those things I had laid in His lap would be taken care of by Him for his little girl.

The entire room was filled with rainbows. The same symbol He had used centuries before to assure Noah that he could be sure of God's care after the flood, was now shining on everything in the room, including me. The sunrise was shining through the cut glass edges of my front door windows. Each cut, each angled piece of glass, was refracting the streams of light into distinct assurances from Him to me. Some of them were a foot long, some only inches long, but the entire room sparkled with the little signs of promise. They each and all conveyed His message to me in the stillness of this morning: "I will never leave you nor forsake you." "I am with you always." "Nothing will in any ways harm you." I just needed to open my eyes to see His care over me.

The tears that came then were tears of gratitude and acknowledgement of the assurances He had given me in that moment. In two more minutes they slowly faded as the sun rose higher and the angle changed, but I had seen them dancing on the walls, I had seen the love all around me, promising me that at His direction everything would indeed work out for my good. And He has been faithful (as always) to His promise. What if I had kept my eyes closed a few minutes longer? What if instead of relinquishing each care I had simply cried in complaint and sadness and missed His Peace? I am grateful – very, very grateful that wasn't the case!

We no longer live in that house, but my "promise door" moment still reminds me of His tender care when I feel dark and isolated. Feelings can lie to us, but God never does. And I can tell you He has taken many more opportunities since then to assure me of His watchful care over the years.

Sometimes it's through a documentary about things I wouldn't know about without others who use their talents to share information about things around us. There's an appropriate sense of humility and wonder I've felt watching things like "The Miracle of Life" that chronicle the incomparable development of a human being. Two distinct cells come together at conception and in 40 very short weeks become an intricate, vocal and growing testimony to a caring, detail-oriented Designer and Maker without equal.

Sometimes it takes on bigger proportions. Consider volcanoes, earthquakes or other things that gives a glimpse into the magnitude of His power. Or investigate the oceans, teeming with so many different kinds of life! The layers of different habitats, the currents circulating water all over the globe – all are a testament to His grandeur and amazing genius.

So many intricate details that need to fit exactly in place for any of it to work, from tear ducts to tectonic plates. The distance and relation between the planet, sun and moon determining the tides from over eight hundred thousand miles away is awe-inspiring! The complexity of a Swiss watch cannot compare to the elaborateness found in grand scale in the universe and in tiny microcosms all around us. We are still learning more and more about so much every day. Realizations of the intricacy of the physical world clearly declare the existence of the unseen eternal one. It's so inter-dependent; it simply isn't possible it just "happened".

We are compelled to acknowledge the Mind that could set all these specifications in such perfect order just by speaking them into existence. "For since the creation of the world His invisible attributes are clearly seen, being understood by the things that are made, even His eternal power and Godhead, so that they are without excuse"[1].

The steady stream of evidence coming to us from our senses, our environment, the situations we find ourselves in – and the circumstances we escape from! - shape who we become and these things cannot be explained by merely physical existence. There is something else, something invisible, intangible and eternal we long to know more about. This is not happenstance; it is purposeful and pointed.

He communicates His love for us, He makes provision for every need and sets the ability in our hearts and minds to understand various parts of it. This knowledge is only enhanced by the ultimate invitation: He wants us to *know Him personally*. How magnificent is that?

Like I've shared previously, so many things have imparted to me an awareness of struggles between good and evil, Light and darkness, victory and utter defeat. Everywhere at every time throughout history people have testified to this truth in so many cultures, in so many ways, using so many different means, it is inescapable. C.S. Lewis, J.R.R. Tolkien, Hannah Hurnard, and thousands of others have exercised a wonderful ability to help us see what they've envisioned – and encourage us to peek into something bigger than ourselves by what they've written in black and white on a page.

Others have used their gifts and talents in the areas of engineering, physics and various trades to convey these truths. The building of the great cathedrals in Europe is a perfect example - a declaration of the dedication and tenacity of so many thousands of people who each put decades of skilled workmanship into these amazing structures, some of them knowing they would never see it completed in their lifetimes. Yet the integrity of each one of them who put so much excellence into their particular tasks in the project, parts of which would never been seen by human eyes when it was completed, speaks to their faith in the unseen eternal realm.

With the advent of more recent media, cinema, CGI and so on, others have digitally formatted their thoughts of what else might be out there – in character, condition, and concept. And they build on one another in amazing ways. Thoughts contemplated about what effect one event or one decision has on others around them, and what would happen if we had the opportunity to change those decisions, has long been a recurring theme. Tear-jerker, feel good movies like "It's a Wonderful Life" and fun trips through possibilities like "Back to the Future" serve to pique our curiosity.

Time travel described by H.G. Wells, characters and situations on off-world locations by Gene Roddenberry, J Michael Straczynski, George Lucas and Stephen Spielberg, and multiple dimensions posed from different perspectives from comic books to movies like "The Butterfly Effect", have all added pieces of thoughts and concepts that came together like a giant puzzle, each piece fitting perfectly into others all around us. It's a wonderful exploration of the possibilities.

But there are times I've experienced a perspective on this "more-than-I-can see" realm that, and instead of comforting me or putting me in a general sense of awe, can – and have – rocked me to my core. With the world in more and more chaos, many people have been made aware that we are being bombarded by warnings; a constant stream of admonishment from so many sources that we need to be prepared for something big coming sooner than we think. Each occurrence tries to break through the false sense of normalcy and routine that lulls us to sleep. Not a physical sleep, but a spiritual lethargy that seems to gloss over what we can't see as being unimportant for the moment. We think: It'll wait until I get this next thing done.

The problem with this lethargy is that there is always one more thing...one moment multiplies into others and soon you realize – like a modern-day Rip Van Winkle - that the moments of sleep piled together have become years. Time can be a slowly-creeping and determined thief that robs the passion, the purpose and the pursuit of what we are supposed to be focusing on: the real reason we exist at all.

God is not trying to keep this all a secret from us. He tells us repeatedly in myriad ways: "Wake up!..." in fact He uses these words and tells us why. "Therefore He says, Awake, O sleeper, and arise from the dead, and Christ shall shine (make day dawn) upon you *and* give you light. Look carefully then how you walk! Live purposefully *and* worthily *and* accurately, not as the unwise *and* witless, but as wise (sensible, intelligent people)..."[2]

The clarion calls that wake us come in different forms to rouse us from our slumber. With each awakening, we jump with a start that brings an urgency, a heightened awareness and a spiritual "ok, I see it, I'm up, I'm on it...". But if we're not careful – and I have not been as careful as I believe I should be – the routine and present day-to-day responsibilities take their former place and the lull creeps in again. Like drifting back to nap for "just 5 more minutes", we succumb to the nothing that silently threatens engagement in our life's purpose.

It seems ironic that one way God shakes me from my spiritual snooze button is through dreams. We can get the most amazing messages through dreams, when our guard is down and the physical effort we expend during the day gives way to exhaustion and we can't help but put the responsibilities of this life down for a few hours.

I have intense dreams. I always have. The scenery in my dreamscape is vivid as anything I ever saw on a movie screen. And I remember. Sometimes for a few moments and sometimes for days, but I remember the details, the colors, and the emotions on a level I have not heard from others I've talked to about this. Sometimes it's a wonderful gift, other times it is deeply disturbing and I have to seriously battle with trying to dissipate the images from my head.

One night several years ago, I got one of these clarion calls through a dream that heightened my awareness of urgency that, although it was disturbing, I knew it was something I did NOT want to forget. It was a message about something much bigger, much more important than some random romp through a land of not-quite-real images in my head. It was a continuation of a lesson I had been learning during my quiet times about becoming aware of and guarding our spiritual access. It even seemed to have a title –

Doors and Windows

Doors and windows are interesting things. They both provide and block access. They provide access for light, heat, vision and visitors and allow us passage we cannot access through solid walls. They act as gateways of a sort, blocking casual entrance. And because of this, they also function on a more serious note as a means of defense. More than a few westerns show the good guys locked in mortal battle inside their homes with the bad guys attacking from outside, guns blazing, with the inhabitants ducking down behind the walls and shooting out of the windows or cross-shaped holes in the shutters to withstand the attack.

This is not just a physical truth, but a metaphor for internal access. We not only have physical doors and windows in buildings we inhabit, we have unseen doors and windows in our lives: invisible attributes of our mind and wills that have direct impact on how we interact in the physical world. These points of access are no less important simply because they are not visible. In many ways, they are more important because they give access to something much more valuable than a physical building. Poets have written for centuries about our eyes being the windows of our soul and more than one of us have had the emotional doors of our hearts slammed shut or broken, so this is not a new concept.

We are specifically told in Scripture that it is our responsibility to guard these doors and windows, and often the direction given adds the imperative and urgency of "above all else". Referring to us as soldiers, we are told directly and in parable form that we need to prepare, fight and conquer to defend and guard these access points over our hearts, minds, thoughts and attitudes as they determine our actions and therefore our direction in life. Most of the time, our day-to-day lives of waking up, going to work, coming home to eat, and getting the sleep we need to do it all again the next day, dims the urgency of these directives. But then we get a call. This dream was one of mine.

This dream was the strangest, most convoluted dream I have had in a very long time! Part of it was in a marina area near the water, part of it was in an Asian restaurant that seemed to be in the middle of a city and looked like one of those pagodas with the fancy roofs. It involved kidnapping and subplots and betrayal of alliances and fighting against enemies, but through most of it, it was a game. Almost like we were merely following a movie script and if anything went wrong, we just picked up from the last place that was done right, and started again to make the next cut. Most of the people involved in it – some of whom I know personally - all were acting like it was a game and the stakes were merely the playing out of this particular exercise. They (and we) weren't putting much effort into winning because it didn't matter too much in the end.

Toward the end of the dream, the scenery changed again and we were in a large sprawling house in the middle of an open field. It looked like a farm house with a large open-rail porch out front. It was a single-floor dwelling with lots of connecting rooms and windows with thin, white curtains covering each one. When I turned to look out one of the windows at the other side advancing toward us, I was able to see and hear them.

Suddenly the tone of the whole thing changed and they weren't acting like it was a game anymore. They were dressed in military uniforms. They picked up guns with bayonets attached to them. They started talking strategy saying, "We are going to stick them in the guts first and (making motions in circles with the guns) gut them, then we'll shoot them when they're on the floor unable to stop us, and finish them." I was horrified! Everything had changed drastically and no one else knew this!

As they started going around toward the side of the house, I started yelling to the others on "my team", rallying them to pick up things that they could use as weapons and prepare for the attack "Lock the doors! Throw the deadbolts! They're coming!" As I made my way frantically around the inside of the house, each time I got to a door (and each room I went into had a door to the outside wall), I would just barely be throwing the deadbolt into the lock as they were reaching the door. As I would breathe a sigh of relief, they would calmly advance to the next room and go for that door, which I would just make it to, sometimes just milliseconds before they would be pushing against the door and trying the lock!

My heart was pounding, I was yelling for the others to get the other doors, but they weren't there. When I made it around to the last side of the house, the rest of my "team" were sitting in chairs, lounging on the open porch. As I looked around, I realized there was not only no deadbolt here – there was not even a door! The porch opened up into the rest of the house with no enclosure whatsoever; there was no heavy area to hide behind. As various members of my side started to walk away in their false sense of security (after I told them breathlessly that I had gotten all the doors secured) I called out to them, "you don't understand! This isn't a game to them anymore! They are serious about gutting and killing us!"

My husband reached up and said, "No Problem, this will keep them out." As he pulled down a freshly-painted, thin rolling metal shade (similar to ones some buildings have as a security shield over the doors to keep would-be burglars from breaking through at night). But it wasn't secure, and it wasn't made of metal; it was almost cork-like in its construction and the fresh paint, that deep rust color that is so popular in home décor, was still damp. It wasn't strong enough to stop anything and it didn't cover the whole area. There were gaping spaces on both sides of it leading right into the house.

The others all walked away, still with no sense of urgency or imminent danger, some into the house and others around the outside. They simply refused to accept what I told them. I wasn't going to go down without a fight. I decided that with everything else blocked off, this was where I needed to make my stand. I was in a panic as I looked around for some kind of weapon I could use. I found a brass fireplace tool handle sticking out from a corner in the foyer and was hoping it was one of those pokers, but when I took hold of it and pulled it out, I found it was a hearth shovel like my grandmother used to clear the ash out of the fireplace. It was narrow and flared out a little at the scooping end. It wasn't what I had expected, but it would have to do. I picked it up and thought, "It needs a longer handle than that …"

Thinking of the bayonets, as I lifted it up to see how far it would reach, I swished it around a couple times and the handle was suddenly 6 feet long. Reassured that even though it was no match for what they had, at least I could give them a fight for it. As I turned toward the door – I didn't have long to wait - a couple of them came around the house, one out in front and coming up onto the porch.

(Even though I have no idea who this man is really, I knew him in the dream) I said, "I'm sorry Billy, I can't let you in. I am going to defend my home even if I have to use this to do it." He didn't seem worried but came right up to me, pushing his chest against the shovel, and stopped. There was no anger or sense of urgency in his face; no defiance, no vitriol, not acting like a zombie or anything, just a matter-of-fact advance, confident in the success of his campaign.

I heard a noise behind me and turned to see the rest of the enemy's side coming around through the room off to the left – *from inside my house*! They were already inside and I had no chance of escape. They had won.

I turned to their leader, remembering how I had dead-bolted each one of the doors so frantically, my mind was racing...I *knew* I hadn't missed one. I dropped my arm to my side, knowing what was coming, I had, after all, heard their plan. I knew I didn't have the ability to defend myself against so many. Still holding onto the shovel, but feeling defeated and numb to what was going to happen, I had to know – I asked him how they got in. Before he could answer, a little blond girl, maybe 9 - 10 years old, I know I've never seen, calmly stepped around the corner and said, "You hadn't done anything with the windows, they just lifted me up and let me in." (Just then I remembered the kitchen window above the sink) I had done my best to bolt the doors by myself, but without help from the others, the enemy had no difficulty finding an opening somewhere else.

No one else on my side was left. I was alone and thinking "if only the others had helped me – one of them could have gotten the windows..." My thoughts trailed off as I stood there defeated, and I knew it was over. I was outnumbered and there was nothing I could do to save myself at that point.

I woke up at that moment, no blood and guts, no last minute bayonet or scary movement from the other side, it just ended right there, as I woke up with an unfolding recap of events - a "debriefing" of sorts - to see what I could learn from the experience. It translated to "real life" immediately as God applied it to my own battles. As I became more aware of the surroundings in my bedroom, without actually hearing the phrase "the moral of the story is:" I realized what it was: it doesn't matter how many doors you dead-bolt and how many other things are covered if you leave the windows unlocked and the porch is indefensible.

I ran to my computer and started journaling the whole thing and everything I was being made aware of through it. It was an intense time of realization and it created a sense of renewed purpose and determination not to forget, not to let the lull take over again. I needed to remember. I needed to share this. They needed to know – just like in the dream. You need to know! The stakes are too high to let trivial things take precedence day after day.

The realizations were flowing freely from my head to the page. As I typed it in, I ramped up my determination and kept asking how can I apply this awareness to my own life? I wanted to translate the lessons I learned in this very strange manner to personal action, not just let it fade with the dream.

War Games

Your life is like your house. There are rooms of challenges and conflict, and rooms of attitudes and actions. They all have windows of vision and doors of access – what you can see from the inside looking out and who can get in from the outside. Some barriers we put up for decoration and some we need to put up for protection. You can put up barriers that decorate like curtains, to obscure some of the view from the outside world. People will not be able to see some of what you have on the inside if they haven't spent some time in the rooms with you. But the barriers meant for protection need to be more substantial and are essential to keep destructive influences out of our hearts.

That is the way it is in life. It doesn't matter how frantically you lock the doors in one room or one area of your life, if other areas leave you open to attack. No one person can defend the whole house by themselves. That is the purpose of fellowship. Spending time and sharing encouragement with other Christians is vital for consistent and sustained victory in life. It takes teamwork and other people with common goals and understanding of what the real stakes are to advance and grow spiritually. If we are not seeing the enemy for what he really is and realizing his true intentions, if we don't practice how to win our battles, we have no chance of a worthy defense. We do well to beware of apathy and complacency.

It's like the military doing practice drills, "war games", playing out different scenarios, challenging ourselves on how to win against different strategies so we are not taken by surprise when we are faced with various obstacles. We need to take this seriously.

We need to realize the enemy is not playing - fair or otherwise. Jesus warned us: "The thief comes only in order to steal, kill and destroy..."[3] Let the meaning of that word truly sink in: destroy. Our enemy's goal is not merely to delay us, or put a detour or two in front of us. His goal is our complete and utter destruction. Not one good thing left standing.

Life is not a game. Yes, there are parts of it that are very enjoyable and we can have a lot of fun. But our enemy is serious in his intention and seeks any opening he can to get through. He wants nothing more than to gut us and watch us writhe in pain before he finishes us off. He will use everything he has at his disposal to win – even using seemingly innocent things to gain advantage over us. "Harmless" indulgences, secret sins, questionable relationships, time-consuming past times. He doesn't have to use overtly evil things to deter us from defending our position; he can also use good things that are simply not what needs to be done right then to distract us from the God-things we need to be engaged in at that moment. Our enemy pities no one; young or old, innocent child or seasoned senior. He is merciless.

But the Good News is we CAN succeed against him! And thankfully, we are not alone in our defense. Our enemy is not omnipotent, all-powerful or infallible. But our God is!

And in the verse previous to His warning about the enemy's intent, Jesus tells us: "I am the Door; anyone who enters through Me will be saved (will live). He will come in and he will go out [freely], and will find pasture."[4] The houses we build may have gaps and open areas that are indefensible, but Jesus is secure. "Trust in the LORD forever, for the LORD, the LORD himself, is the Rock eternal."[5] He invites us to build our lives on Him as our Foundation, tells us He is the Door, and that He "came so they may have and enjoy life, and have it in abundance (to the full, till it overflows)."[6]

So why the sense of urgency? What's the big deal? Because His defense, His security, His Life expressed in our lives is not automatic for everyone. It is an offer that needs to be accepted.

Jesus did His part. He came to us. He lived among us. He taught, healed and shared knowledge of His connection with the Father with us, and told us we could have this same connection. And then He gave His life for us. His sacrifice stands as an offer "for whosoever will". We have a part to complete. "For whosoever shall **call upon** the name of the Lord shall be saved."[7](emphasis mine)[7] *If we* enter Him as the Door...*if we* call on His name... "if we.." shows the conditions that need to be met before the results we are looking for can be reached. But what "if we" ...*don't*? Jesus is not trying to hide anything. He tells us clearly:

"Whoever comes to Me, and hears My sayings and does them, I will show you whom he is like: He is like a man building a house, who dug deep and laid the foundation on the rock. And when the flood arose, the stream beat vehemently against that house, and could not shake it, for it was founded on the rock. But he who heard and did nothing is like a man who built a house on the earth without a foundation, against which the stream beat vehemently; and immediately it fell. And the ruin of that house was great."[8]

If we come, if we hear, if we do...then we will be on a solid foundation when the storms advance on us. If we do not come, if we do not hear, if we do not do, then we are refusing the offer of the Solid Foundation and our ruin will be great. This is not an emotionless dismissal. This is the plea of a tender-hearted Father warning of the consequences of being outside His impenetrable shelter when the enemy comes. We can avoid these consequences by our own free-will; it is our choice to accept – or reject - the invitation! We can be one of "whosoever will". He wants to help us, He wants to give us access to His full arsenal of weapons against the enemy of our souls. But He is a Gentleman and will not force His Will – or His Protection - on us.

Without His protection we are out in the open field with no cover. We need to choose to walk through the Door, the protective Gate to the walled city. Once inside the gate, the protection, the connection, the relationship is

504

secure. But that's not the end of the story. It's the first step of the journey. Then comes the growing - the training in righteousness – the "preparation of the Gospel of Peace"[9]. One of the things we do in preparation is cooperating with the Holy Spirit in closing off unguarded access to the enemy.

"Nevertheless, God's solid foundation stands firm, sealed with this inscription: 'The Lord knows those who are his,' and, 'Everyone who confesses the name of the Lord must turn away from wickedness.'"[10] Wickedness (the state of being or doing things we know are wrong) in any area of your life is an opening the enemy will take advantage of. It's not a one-shot deal. Turning away from wickedness is an on-going process that continually advances from one hindrance to another. Just like the enemy in my dream, he tries to get access at each door.

But God tells us all His solution to this in 2 Chronicles 7:14: "If my people, who are called by my name, will humble themselves and pray and seek my face and turn from their wicked ways, then I will hear from heaven, and I will forgive their sin and will heal their land." Each sin or "wicked way" we leave unconfessed becomes a door the enemy can use to gain access to our hearts. If we humbly admit our need, turn away from and confess those sins, praying to God, seeking His will for us, He promises He will hear us, forgive us, and heal – not only our lives, but "our land" – others around us, the places we are, our families. If we…

But if we busy ourselves with pointing out others' shortcomings, declaring it's their fault we were left defenseless, and fail to address our own weaknesses, we don't get to experience freedom from sin's hold on us. When we do begin to address our own flaws, we find no shortage of material to turn to God with! ☺ As soon as we close off access to one form of temptation, we discover others that were previously masked by the more obvious faults. Roll up your sleeves and get ready for the on-going process of confession and relinquishing. But don't let it discourage you. Keep your eyes on the prize! The writer of Hebrews told us, "No discipline seems pleasant at the time, but painful. Later on, however, it produces a harvest of righteousness and peace for those who have been trained by it."[11] Remember, it really doesn't matter how well you bolt the doors in your house (in this case, the more obvious sins (like murder), if you have left some windows (like pride, lying, and sowing discord) wide open. Celebrate your victories, but don't get cocky. A false sense of security can be deadly.

Are you especially generous? Are you a good money manager? Do you make it a priority to take care of what you already have? Do you work a full day's work for a full day's pay – even when no one is looking? Did you throw the dead bolt of gratitude? Did you lock the door against greed? Are you basically a forgiving person and realize that holding onto grudges hurts you as much as (or even more than) the person you're staying mad at? Have you addressed your anger problem? There are lots of doors to lock and many ways the enemy can get in. Addressing these and many other issues in your life will help you better defend yourself against attack.

But no matter how good you are at locking some of those doors, no matter how self-satisfied you are that you are better than the next guy at trustworthiness, fidelity, work ethics, stewardship, or even meal preparation, if you leave windows open in other areas, the enemy will use these weaknesses to breach your perimeter and gain access to your home and your life.

Overcoming smoking, swearing or drinking is not going to close off the access the enemy has through resentment, food- and approval-addiction. (OUCH! I know, right?) It's like in the dream, when you lock one door, the enemy doesn't freak out, he just moves to the next door. The minute you become aware that something is an issue in your life, attack it, get rid of it in God's Grace and with every bit of help the Holy Spirit gives you. Don't lose your sense of urgency.

Reviewing the things God has given me victory over through the years enforces the gratitude over His faithfulness to me. That's a good thing. But I needed to see there is still much to be done. I don't want to lose the zeal of my "first love" and begin coasting through my faith walk. I can't afford to keep justifying lingering spiritual weaknesses by pointing out things I no longer have a problem with. No amount of self-congratulation on how good a job I did some areas in the past is going to make a difference when I'm face-to-face with a bayonet and someone who wants to use it against me because I left other areas unguarded in my present. I don't need to do it out a sense of panic or doom. Instead of dreading each issue, treat it like a really good shower after a long day!

Allow God to wash away all the things that hurt us from the inside – our personal hindrances and "cherished sins" - in order to gain victory. Keep cooperating with the Holy Spirit to clean out the whole thing. That is spiritual growth. There is "pre" in preparation that must be done, and it can't be done at the last minute if you want to win. A newborn cannot wield a broadsword. A toddler can't defend against a terrorist. We need to grow in our Faith, choose to ditch the weights that pull us backward. Learn how to use the weapons in the arsenal, increase in skill and develop the talents He's placed inside each one of us for the position He's prepared for us in the battle.

King David was VERY aware of this; acknowledging in two different Psalms (18:34 and 144:1), God "teaches my hands to war". We are responsible for reporting for "war game" training as He equips us with everything we need to stand against the attack. We need to develop proficiency. It takes time. And repetition. Without daily trips to the quartermaster, we will not have what we need in times of adversity. We need to become familiar with each weapon He gives us, what they are capable of, and how to use them most effectively. Just like swishing around that hearth shovel in my dream, the more we use the weapons we acquire, the stronger and more effective they become in our hands. We need to be personally aware of the fortress we run into that can shield us from attack.

When it comes right down to it, no matter how competent you are in your own abilities, you can't do it in your own strength. Neither can I. You can gather family and friends around to take some of the load off, but there will be times when they are busy with their own diversions or battles and will not be able to meet your need at that moment of attack. But God said His Grace is sufficient! In His empowerment, we become warriors who have a shared understanding of the real battle. We can purposefully advance against the enemies' plan of attack and WIN!

The Commander over us all - the One Who knows every bit of the enemy's strategy — has already defeated his poisonous plans through His own extreme obedience. The High Priest Who knows what you're going through and who you're up against, knows how to defeat each tactic the enemy uses against you. "For we do not have a high priest who is unable to empathize with our weaknesses, but we have one who has been tempted in every way, just as we are—yet he did not sin. Let us then approach God's throne of grace with confidence, so that we may receive mercy and find grace to help us in our time of need."[12]

"... there is a friend who sticks closer than a brother"[13], and He is never taken off-guard. Jesus, the living Word of God is sharper than any two-edged sword. And He laid down

His life for you and for me. He said, "Greater love has no one than this: to lay down one's life for one's friends. You are my friends if you do what I command. I no longer call you servants, because a servant does not know his master's business. Instead, I have called you friends, for everything that I learned from my Father I have made known to you."[14] These words are not the demands of some sadistic kill-joy who wants to pull all your strings, but those of an older brother whose already gone off to war and come back as the conquering hero – who wants to show you how to win when your battles come.

We are not alone: there are thousands who have gone before us who have fought the fight in faith. Hebrews 11 mentions many of those recorded in the Bible; some more familiar than others: Abel, Enoch, Noah, Abraham, Isaac, Jacob, and some lesser known heroes: Gideon, Barak, Samson and Jephthah."[15] Each of these men were listed in the "hall of faith" but were far from perfect. They each had times of fear, failure and defeat. But they didn't *stay* defeated. God points these heroes out to us for a reason. "Therefore, since we are surrounded by such a great cloud of witnesses, let us throw off everything that hinders and the sin that so easily entangles. And let us run with perseverance the race marked out for us, fixing our eyes on Jesus, the pioneer and perfecter of faith. For the joy set before him he endured the cross, scorning its shame, and sat down at the right hand of the throne of God. Consider him who endured such opposition from sinners, so that you will not grow weary and lose heart."[16]

We have allies. We have an ancient cloud of witnesses and modern day heroes we can be encouraged by when we feel weary so we don't lose heart. We have our own ancestors who answered the call to faith and lived in God's Grace to show the way for us. We have friends and family who seek God's counsel, direction and correction to make the most of each opportunity to take back stolen ground. Those who are trained by Him, who've been through instruction on identifying and defeating the enemy are great resources to hone your own battle skills. We become "mutual aid" for one another, the way it is meant to be – "As iron sharpens iron, so one person sharpens another."[17]

To put it in military terms again, think of the different levels in the chain of command. Maybe you're a private. Maybe you've had basic training and you can hold off for a while. Maybe you're a sergeant. Maybe you've been in a battle or two and know some things to help you defend your territory a little longer. Maybe you've experienced so many hard things in life that you're a lieutenant – or even a colonel. You've experienced the enemy's attacks before; you know some of his tactics and can prepare and give directions to the troops in your care. But even a colonel can't defend a house against an overwhelming enemy on his own. It takes an army, working together with a proven strategy with a leader who sees the big picture. A Leader that not only knows *our* weaknesses and vulnerabilities and knows what to do to correct them, but also knows *the enemy's* weaknesses and can mount an *offensive battle against him*, breaking his lines of communication and supply. As your successes add up, you begin making alliances with more people who have had these battles before and can share the confidence that these victories are attainable – we can succeed – and this is how to do it!

That Leader is more than a general or an admiral. He's bigger and more important than the commander-in-chief. He is not some distant officer in the safety of the C & C (Command and Control) tent to the rear of the war zone, who gives orders not knowing the dangers or the conditions in the trenches, while you're pinned down and helpless against the strafing fire and artillery bombardment of countless adversaries! He is the Lord of Hosts. He is the Lion of Judah. He is the Almighty God and Everlasting Father. He is Emmanuel – God <u>With</u> Us.

He is in the trenches with all of us, showing us the soldiers' manual for battle. He gives us rest times when others fight on the front lines and we get R & R (Rest and Relaxation) to rebuild our strength and refresh our tired souls. He equips us for each battle, He trains us for combat. Not only that, He BECAME the fortress, a hiding place for us to run into and be safe from danger: "The Lord is my Rock, my **Fortress**, and my Deliverer; my God, my keen and firm Strength in Whom I will trust and take refuge, my Shield, and the Horn of my salvation, my High Tower."[18] That sounds a lot more defensible than an open porch with a cork shade in front of it! God is there for us – if only we run to Him!

He knew it all "before the foundation of the world", He became everything you need and He waits for you to call on Him. He calls out to you and clearly says "Come to me all you who are weary, who labor and are heavy-laden and I will give you rest...learn from Me...and you will find rest for your souls"[19] and promises us a victorious outcome in His service: "He who dwells in the secret place of the Most High shall remain stable and fixed under the shadow of the Almighty [Whose power no foe can withstand]. I will say of the Lord He is my Refuge and my Fortress, my God; on Him I lean and rely and in Him I [confidently] trust...He will cover you with His pinions, and under His wings shall you trust and find refuge; His truth and His faithfulness are a shield and a buckler. You shall not be afraid...a thousand may fall at your side and ten thousand at your right hand, but it shall not come near you...(God says) He shall call upon Me and I will answer him in trouble; I will deliver him and honor him..."[20]

Understand that you have an enemy who will stop at nothing to gut you and watch you squirm! If you've lived any of life at all, look into your heart, look into your past and know the truth of it! But we are not left to fend for ourselves in this battle against this cruel enemy. When all you can see is the enemy and his advancing army, when you feel defeated before you even start, when you start seeing the people around you with suspicion and cynicism, wondering when they are going to turn on you, look "to the hills".

King David knew this prescription for life's challenges very well! In Psalm 121 he sings: "I will lift up my eyes to the hills ...From whence shall my help come? My help comes from the Lord, Who made heaven and earth."[21] He does not allow your foot to slip; He doesn't sleep or take a day off. He keeps and defends you when you have no way to do any of it in your own strength! and He never gives up – "The Lord will keep your going out and your coming in from this time forth and forevermore."[22] That kind of confidence is hard to defeat, no matter who the enemy is.

Even if we can't see it right away, we can KNOW that God is with us and is undoubtedly fighting for us! In 2 Kings, the Syrian army came by night and surrounded the town so Elisha would not escape them. They had been trying to take him out for months, and every time they had him in their sights, he "somehow" managed to escape. But now they had finally cornered him; there seemed no way out for the prophet of God this time. When Elisha's servant started freaking out, Elisha reminded him Who they were working for. "[Elisha] answered, 'Fear not; for those with us are more than those with them.' Then Elisha prayed, 'Lord, I pray You, open his eyes that he may see.'"[23] What he saw stunned him: the mountain was full of horses and chariots of fire all around them! The host of heaven was *encamped around the enemy*! As the enemy set up around Elisha during the night, his defenders – the very host of heaven! - had set themselves up around them. Please don't miss this! God will do the same for you! The Lord of Hosts will not let you fall. You just need someone to help you to see into the temporarily unseen reality sometimes. God has placed many "Elisha's" around us. He has many champions who can see the battle for what it really is — everyday, normal people that you work with, have lunch with, and sometimes just can't figure out. They are here for a reason — to help us see more than we can on our own.

You not only need to see our defenders and champions for who they are, you also need to see your enemy the way God sees them: not in fear, but in confident anticipation of the coming victory. Elisha's servant saw the enemy and was afraid. They were intent on destroying Elisha. But Elisha's reaction went beyond being fearless. His perspective was one of compassion for the people being deceived and used by the real, unseen foe. When he had the victory right in his hands, he opted for compassion toward them — which totally took me off-guard when I read it.

Weren't these people the enemy? They'd been trying to kill him! But Elisha didn't call on this fiery host that had surrounded the opposing army to kill them, wipe them out, or just make them cease to be — all of which they were indeed capable of doing! Instead, he prayed that they be struck with blindness. It seems a poor second choice, but okay, let's go with that for now. Self-reliant, self-dependent warriors used to having their way on the battle field, boasting of their victories, plundering one city after another and congratulating themselves for it, are suddenly as helpless as newborn kittens. This may have some promise in it after all. Elisha then tells them that he is not the one they seek and tells them he will bring them to whom they are looking for — and he leads them into Samaria! When they are inside the city, Elisha prays again for their eyes to be opened and they see where they are —

in front of the King of Israel – *their* enemy – delivered like sheep for the slaughter they had intended for Elisha!

The King of Israel, excited at this seeming deliverance of certain victory over this army without any effort on his part, stands drooling over the prospect, anticipating the next step: "My father, shall I slay them? Shall I slay them?"[24]This isn't a typo, the king repeated the question twice, excitedly asking permission from someone who was his spiritual intermediary with God Himself, to kill a previously ruthless and now helpless enemy in his gates. But the prophet questions the king about his emotional state: "...would you slay those you have taken captive with your sword and bow? Set bread and water before them, that they may eat and drink and return to their master." [25]

Compassion Wins Out Over Revenge

Adopting a different perspective can sometimes mean turning of the battle in your favor in ways you never thought possible. Sometimes we get so upset by the *people* we seem to be battling, that we forget who the real enemy is. Ephesians 6: 12 tells us we are NOT "battling against flesh and blood but against...forces of wickedness in high places." If we stop to view our enemies as pawns in the battle being used by the *real* enemy in their own ignorance, we need not take it personally when they hurt us. 2 Timothy clearly tells us that we must: "··· correct (our) opponents with courtesy and gentleness, in the hope that God may grant that they will repent and come to know the Truth [that they will perceive and recognize and become accurately acquainted with and acknowledge it], And that they may come to their senses [and] escape out of the snare of the devil, having been held captive by him, [henceforth] to do His [God's] will."[26]

As the result of Elisha's direction, and the king's response, the army of the enemy were refreshed in their physical need with a "great provision" of food and drink, released to return back to their own land, and their hearts were changed by the experience – "...and the bands of Syria came no more into the land of Israel."[27] They not only defeated the enemy, they were instrumental in releasing them from deception *they* were fighting under and in the process had one less enemy to battle against! It was a win-win for both sides!

Listening to Jesus' admonition to "pray for your enemies, bless those who spitefully use you"[28] sounds so opposite what we would think to do on our own! But it works! These enemies, who wanted nothing more than to drag Elisha back to their king as trophy of their victory and do whatever they chose to him, were fed, rescued and released at his word! As a result, they lost the will to fight against them anymore.

Contrary to how some today are characterizing it, Faith is not some wimpy way out of conflict and a crutch we use to get by in an unmanageable world! It is the only sure way to victory! In seeing our opponents in this light, we CAN see the real enemy and see the host of heaven ready to battle for us – time and time again God tells us the battle is not yours – "the battle is the Lord's!"[29] His way of fighting this battle may seem counter-productive and unorthodox sometimes – pray for your enemies, bless those who curse you – how can that possibly work?

Well, in Romans, Paul says, "Do not let yourself be overcome by evil, but overcome (master) evil with good."[30] God knows that as we begin to fight what we see as injustice and inequity in any relationship, we often stoop to a lower level. We gravitate toward the justification that what they did was wrong, so we are going to fight the same way they did. But when you fight evil with more evil, there is no escape from evil, rather it is contagious. BUT...if we chose to fight evil with good, if we take a position of protection and security in God and pray FOR the other person and treat them "like you would want to be treated", something snaps the strategy of the enemy in pieces. It's a two-pronged offensive that involves changing what we contribute to the battle and allowing God to disarm the enemy. He tells us He wants to be our "defender" and the "lifter of our heads"[31]. When we give Him the chance to do that, amazing things happen!

Part of what Jesus was teaching in Luke 6 is also found in Proverbs 25. When we read it in context, we get seemingly strange instructions and even stranger indications of the outcome: "If your enemy is hungry, give him bread to eat; and if he is thirsty, give him water to drink;[K] [22]For in doing so, you will [a]heap coals of fire upon his head, and the Lord will reward you."[32] Now when you are angry at someone or someone is hurtful and cruel to you and you read this, you can tend to start wringing your hands (just like the king of Israel in front of Elisha) saying, Yeah! Bring it on! (Shall we kill them!?) or, we can sound a little more spiritually mature than that and say, "Okay, I WILL pray for them and do good things for them – as long as God keeps

His bargain and burns them up with His coals of fire on their heads!"

But did you notice that little (k) and between verse 21 and 22 and the [a] in front of the word "heap" imbedded in this passage? It gives a footnote in my amplified Bible that may disappoint someone in that state of mind – or you can allow it to lift your hope to something far better than revenge. You can defeat the real enemy who is holding *them* captive. The footnote states: "This is not to be understood as a revengeful act intended to embarrass its victim, but just the opposite. The picture is that of the high priest (Lev. 16:12) who, on the Day of Atonement, took his censer and filled it with 'coals of fire' from off the altar of burnt offering, and then put incense on the coals to create a pleasing, sweet-smelling fragrance. The cloud or smoke of the incense covered the mercy seat and was acceptable to God for atonement. Samuel Wesley wrote: 'So artists melt the sullen ore of lead, By heaping coals of fire upon its head; In the kind warmth the metal learns to glow, And pure from dross the silver runs below.' 1"[33]

Dross is the junk that is stuck inside a precious metal that decreases its purity. Carefully melting the metal – at a controlled temperature - and removing the dross is part of the process that increases its value. This is what the Holy Spirit does in your life and in mine. Stepping out of the way and allowing the Holy Spirit to be the one administering heat (instead of us letting loose with some fire of our own) is what is being called for here. When the Holy Spirit administers the heat in controlled times and amounts, He removes the junk in all of us that makes us not as attractive as we will be when He's done.

We don't like the heat when the melting process is happening to us – but we sure do like the results on the other end! That's the difference between "life" and "Life".

The little "l", life hurts so deeply sometimes it is almost too hard to bear. But the big "L", Life is the ultimate fortress of Healing. No matter how battered you feel, you can begin to see and experience the Life you were created for – even *during* the battles you are facing. We may feel surrounded by adversaries and troubles, but there is great opportunity behind every door – we only need spiritual eyes to see it in the positive light it can become: "For a wide door of opportunity for effectual [service] has opened to me [there, a great and promising one], and [there are] many adversaries."[34]

So praying for our enemies, feeding them, giving them a drink, meeting evil actions with good, understanding that you're not alone in the battle, and cooperating with the host of heaven around you, releases the people you thought of as the enemy from the real enemy's grip of deception, destruction and death to that big "L"; Life that is a joy to share and explore!

Yes it takes effort, and, no, it is not comfortable or easy, but in the end it is the only real way to lasting peace and joy that is not dependent on your own efforts. We *can* stop struggling and frantically slamming windows and doors against continuous attack in fear and frustration! We can be victorious. We just need to heed the instructions we are getting all around us – listen to the conversation coming from heaven:

1) Focus on the Door, not the adversaries. Remember, Jesus said, "I am the Door; anyone who enters in through Me will be saved (will live). He will come in and he will go out [freely], and will find pasture."[35] Get to know the Voice of your Savior. Don't be caught off guard by the lull in the battle. "Behold, I send an Angel before you to keep and guard you on the way and to bring you to the place I have prepared."[36] We have a part in this: "Keep and guard your heart with all vigilance and above all that you guard, for out of it flow the springs of life."[37] Begin to ask God for His instruction – set aside time for a Quiet Time for the two of you to get to know one another ☺ He already knows you! Get to know Him! See what He has for you.

2) Prepare. "David prepared iron in abundance for nails for the doors of the gates and for the couplings, and bronze in abundance without weighing,..."[38] David had set aside literally tons of supplies for the building of the Temple. Although God told him it was good that he had in his heart to do this, and appreciated David's devotion toward Him, it was not God's intention for David to build it, but He reserved that task for Solomon. What if David hadn't set aside all those things? Sometimes the preparations we make are for future generations to fulfill. Prepare anyway – it is in our preparations that we position our children and

those we mentor for the greatness they are destined to step into. And WE are better off for it too!

Don't put it off these crucial times of preparations - or think 'that may be fine and good for you, but it doesn't really have an impact on me, it just doesn't work for me'. "If you [profess ignorance and] say, Behold, we did not know this, does not He Who weighs and ponders the heart perceive and consider it? And He Who guards your life, does not He know it? And shall not He render to [you and] every man according to his works?[39] Sitting apathetically – or defiantly - on the porch, taking the good things life has to give without getting to know the One Who is the Provider and Protector of your life, is dangerous! "But take heed to yourselves and be on your guard, lest your hearts be overburdened and depressed (weighed down) with the giddiness and headache and nausea of self-indulgence, drunkenness, and worldly worries and cares pertaining to [the business of] this life, and [lest] that day come upon you suddenly like a trap or a noose;"[40]

Life is not a singular exercise – you don't do it in a bubble by yourself. Warn others, train your children and show your family and your friends to see it for what it is. Help them prepare their defenses against the enemy. "Only take heed, and guard your life diligently, lest you forget the things which your eyes have seen and lest they depart from your [mind and] heart all the days of your life.

Teach them to your children and your children's children –"[41]

3) Strengthen yourself. Use the time we have to prepare for the time not yet here. Some people may trivialize the importance of preparation. This is not a new concept. Aesop wrote "The Grasshopper and the Ants" long before any of us were born. God takes the time to warn us. Heed the warnings. "All your fortresses are fig trees with early figs; if they are shaken they will fall into the mouth of the eater. Behold, your troops in the midst of you are [as weak and helpless as] women; the gates of your land are set wide open to your enemies [without effort]; fire consumes your bars. Draw for yourself the water [necessary] for a [long continued] siege, make strong your fortresses! Go down into the clay pits and trample the mortar; make ready the brick kiln [to burn bricks for the bulwarks]!"[42] Sounds a little too medieval for you? How about something more recent:

At a women's conference, Lisa Bevere was teaching on this from a very unlikely source ☺ She pointed out, that sometimes we, like Sarah Connor in Terminator 1, are totally taken off-guard by the vicious attacks of an enemy. She had no knowledge of its existence, but she needed to realize something crucial. The enemy won't stop just because you think, "...but I haven't done anything!"[43] Sometimes the enemy can see what's ahead before you become aware of it. Your current ignorance of your future mission does not deter him from preemptive attacks. The guy who was sent back in time to save Sarah revealed the enemy's destructive purpose is not in what we have done so far, or are currently aware of, but against what is going to happen in the future. At her insistence that she hadn't done anything to anyone, he tells her (and I got chills!), "No, but you will."[44]

Preparation may be difficult and seem like you are making too much of suppositions with no concrete proof. Looking at things like Doomsday Preppers may cause some people to laugh. Others take it very seriously. Some people can take things to extremes; and those crying out like the children's book "Chicken Little" – "the sky is falling!" when it doesn't happen, tends to dull others' ears to the certainty that one day, it will.

The fact is that God already told us an end of temporal things is coming. Revelation is the clearest picture of what some call the "end times", but it is by no means the only place God shares details of what will happen. In Matthew chapter 24, Jesus Himself gives a very clear picture of what the situations and events that will take place. He tells us that even though we won't know "the day and the hour"[45] He admonishes us not to be deceived or taken unaware.

Preparation is a good thing: ask any Boy Scout who's ever gone camping without going over the check list of needed supplies. At best it's inconvenient. At worst, you're up a creek with no paddle and shivering with hypothermia. However God leads you to, prepare. The pay-off for your efforts is immense! Look at others as examples of determination and perseverance: how about Noah? A flood? An ark? What will the neighbors think? But for over 100 years Noah was faithful is his preparations. It is a certainty that others laughed. He persevered. He started building the ark when he was 500 years old! He didn't let his age stop him; he prepared faithfully when God warned him of impending flood: "[Prompted] by faith Noah, being forewarned by God concerning events of which as yet there was no visible sign, took heed and diligently and reverently constructed and prepared an ark for the deliverance of his own family. By this [his faith which relied on God] he passed judgment and sentence on the world's unbelief and became an heir and possessor of righteousness..."[46]

What is the pay off? It's a lot of work to go through while others are sitting on the porch oblivious to what is coming. Why should we be any different? The payoff is Victory and Peace: "And God's peace [shall be yours, that tranquil state of a soul assured of its salvation through Christ, and so fearing nothing from God and being content with its earthly lot of whatever sort that is, that peace] which transcends all understanding shall garrison and mount guard over your hearts and minds in Christ Jesus."[47] That kind of peace attracts the attention of people around you who see you being calm under pressure. And opens doors of opportunity to "share the reason for your hope..."[48]

When the victory is won, you rest content – no fear, no doubt. "Violence shall no more be heard in your land, nor devastation or destruction within your borders, but you shall call your walls Salvation and your gates Praise."[49]

And when the people you are battling see that you are not treating them the way they intended to and had been treating you, when they see your response to their "unreasoning wrath"[50] is to rely more heavily on God for the Grace to be delivered, things can change dramatically. Instead of striking back on your own, and giving them something to retaliate for, we have higher options. IF we bless them, provide for their need, and return good for evil, they have no one left to point to, to justify their own junk. It may not happen all at once, it may not happen for months of trying. But if we stop to listen to God's timing and God's way of handling a situation, we may find the different choices we are called to make provide a much different outcome than we could have originally hoped for.

Now I want to bring balance to this from the beginning – notice when and how Elisha blesses and prays for his enemies. He doesn't walk out to them when they are surrounding him in Dothan, and bless them with freedom. He first waits for them to be aware of how far they have sunk, for them to be unsure of themselves. After having prayed for them to be as *physically* blinded as they were *spiritually* blind, he leads them to a place of awareness. He prays for their sight to be restored and reveals that they are indeed the ones who are in dire need. Their own blood-thirst has put them in a position of helplessness and defeat. From *this* position, where he is safe and provided for, he then provides mercy, provision and freedom for them.

When they realize they are at the mercy of their own enemy, and instead of dismemberment receive compassion, their hearts have no choice but see the deception of their previous mindset - to repent, turn from what they had done in the past, and live differently. What about the Israelites? What if they had not been willing to listen to Elisha's restraint? They had not had so obvious an opportunity for payback in their lifetimes! But by listening to the wisdom of their prophet, they gained much more than revenge; they gained peace – inside and out.

When circumstances seem so clearly to be an open door toward revenge laid in your lap to revel in, instead of giving into it, choose a higher road. Compassion and blessing (from a position of protection and awareness that God is our defender) disarms the people who were being used by our REAL enemy. By showing them the noose they themselves walked into in their deception, we show them the way to their own freedom! No one says that's an easy way to live; "turning the other cheek" can get pretty painful sometimes! But time and time again in both the Old and New Testaments, Jesus shows us the Truth of it. As a result of this higher path, Israel enjoyed the relief of one less enemy to fight, as they "came no more into the land of Israel"[51].

Another Call

Even knowing all this, reading through it, writing it down, being passionate about really walking in freedom during my morning quiet times can give way to the spiritual complacency when the things of this world and schedules and responsibilities loom larger than the unseen reality. Time marches surely on – the snooze button re-engages... Thankfully, God does not let us stay in snooze mode indefinitely – He calls again, and again to shake us from our slumber...

Understand that, as a result of everything I have previously written and so many more experiences that are not recorded in this book, I process things in a different way than I have in the past. More often than not, things that come up in my life trigger realizations of God working behind the scenes to get us to realize something He has already repeatedly tried to get us to understand. I know now that He is not angry at us for not "getting it" the first several (hundred) times He told us, but He is patient and tries again and again to coax us out of our stubborn, sometimes self-willed ignorance.

Knowing this about Him reminds me again that God can and does use anything He wants to to break through the distracted and preoccupied cocoons we shelter ourselves in sometimes – and He is not confined to our pre-conceived ideas of the separation of secular and holy. He doesn't need to stay within the boundaries of what we normally think of as religious or spiritual considerations. He can get his message across during a prayer in your rocking chair, walk in the park, a dream – and yes, a sci-fi action movie in the privacy of your living room.

Totally unaware that I had been "sleeping" again, I sat down with my husband one night. We watched the movie "Oblivion".

My reaction took me entirely off-guard. All the things God had been gathering for me over the years, all the little bits of information and experiences He'd woven into my life seemed to suddenly combine like vinegar and baking soda, and I became completely undone in the middle of my living room. I couldn't have held it together if I tried! It all came to a head – an epiphany if there ever was one – incorporating this verse about God "setting eternity in men's hearts" with intensity and depth.

When I watched this movie I was impacted by the behind-the-scenes, life application of characters and perspectives in a way I hadn't considered before.

When the story begins, Jack, the main character is narrating the back story. There's been a great battle. "We won the war, but lost the planet."[52] He details where he fits into the maintenance phase of the project and how he and his other team member, Victoria, are two weeks away from "going home" to Titan, one of Saturn's moons. But something happens. As Jack makes certain discoveries, meets other characters, begins to remember things, he fits them into his current circumstances. He — and we — discover he's being lied to. His very existence is called into question and it shatters his understanding of reality. He begins to reassess everything about his life.

We get to see how Victoria, his team member (and I assumed wife) responds to Jack's inner questions. At one point, trying to share part of his longing for the simpler life before their planet had been destroyed, Jack brings Victoria some flowers he's been growing on the surface. She quickly drops them from the balcony high over the scarred landscape, talking about the imminence of their return to Titan. She repeats her insistence they not do anything that jeopardizes that expectation. She wants nothing to do with his departure from her safe, sanitized existence.

The story follows him as he decides how to respond to inescapable proof of his newly altered reality. He chooses, with the help of some people who know what's *really* going on, to break regulations (something he's done in smaller ways here and there in the past) and to DO something to rectify the all-encompassing deception that has dominated his life.

Later in the story, when he tries to explain to Victoria what is really going on, she refuses to allow for any deviation from what she's been told. She is simply looking forward to the current task being over so she can get to where she really wants to be - completely unaware that this too is a lie. He tries desperately to tell her what's really happening, but she won't listen. When that deception is shattered for her, she doesn't respond well. Without giving anything away, it's a disaster!

In light of this outcome, when he has the opportunity to have a "do-over" of sorts, Jack gives her the option of coming away with him - away from the confines of the station to "see what's down there". Maybe if she saw for herself... She makes an appeal to him not to "go there again", calmly insisting on her original plan. Evidently, they've had this conversation before. This time, he simply walks away, allowing her to choose – without all the pertinent information – not to follow him away from her comfort zone. Disappointed with Victoria's choice, but resolved to what needs to be done, he goes on to fight the real battle without her.

By this time, I've already got a lump in my throat. And it's nowhere near the end of the movie.

He returns to the people who informed him of their real situation. Sally, who directs and monitors their every move on the station, is not what she appears to be. Staying within the confines of the deception she continually reinforces will prove to be deadly for them. When her real identity is revealed, it reminded me, "Satan himself masquerades as an angel of light"[53] Jack is driven by a new determination to do whatever it takes to save his world, at any cost. This is what my husband calls the "grand gesture".

Side note: One of my husband's roles in my life is to explain things from a male perspective that I would otherwise not have the benefit of understanding. He does this really well and sometimes puts together connections for me that make all the difference in the world. One such insight concerned some men's reticence to do simple things to endear themselves to their wives. ☺ He said they don't want to take out the garbage, clean the litter box, and other "little" things that hardly seem impressive or noteworthy; but "every man pictures himself climbing the highest mountain, crossing the raging river, slaying the dragon, saving the world, rescuing the girl, and receiving her admiration and gratitude in the process." A sentiment, by the way shared in dozens of examples by John and Stasi Eldredge in books like: "Love and War", "The Way of the Wild Heart", "Epic", "Captivating" and "You Have What It Takes".

The "grand gesture" refers to the sensational, dashing ways our heroes come to our rescue, defend us and repel danger for us against incredible odds. The action, the battles, and the rescues that happened in this movie definitely filled the bill on this front. But I was blubbering my head off at the end, seeing something completely different.

All I could think about was the heart-ache, the unbelievably wrenching heart-ache, of knowing the truth and not being able to tell someone you really care about. You know something that will set them free, save their lives, or make everything better, but because you already know (strongly suspect, deduce from previous encounters) what their reaction is going to be, you hesitate (or avoid telling them completely). It's distance where you don't want it. Even if it's only temporary, you desperately want it to be different. In some cases it would be just an inconvenient ruffling of someone's feathers so to speak and then it blows over. In other situations it will prevent you from accomplishing what you know is imperative.

Do you tell them anyway? Do you "risk the mission" trying to explain why they need to understand something pivotal, when there's a very real probability their response will end disastrously for both of you? Obviously there are differences in real life and a movie script and the analogy can only go so far, but it warrants consideration nonetheless. As we've seen earlier, there very definitely is a time to speak and a time to be silent. How do we determine when is which? Do we really *know* how someone will respond? Or is it all just based on fears and suppositions of how we **think** they will react? What if we're wrong?

Some information needs to be shared regardless of how it will impact others in some situations. Health diagnoses, interpersonal realities, warnings of imminent danger are all things we know are uncomfortable to bring up, but we have an understanding that emotional comfort levels are not the primary factor in deciding when we need to tell others hard realities. Truth can be uncomfortable sometimes, but there are times it needs to be spoken – even over the objections of others. But what about things that don't seem so pivotal?

An old saying about conversational taboos tells us never to talk about sex, politics or religion. But almost everyone talks about sex and politics – even in the public discourse. In fact, you can be called "out of touch" (or worse) if you *don't* engage in debate on those topics. The delivery can be rude, funny or insulting and it doesn't matter, you are told to lighten up or "get real". The one subject left out of "polite" conversation is religion. Unless you're saying that every path is equally valid and everyone can and does have the right to pursue their own form of spirituality, the conversation generally ends pretty quickly. And if you are expressing your opinion with any kind of affinity toward Christianity - you are labeled a bigot, exclusive, or a hypocrite for not living up to the perfect standard of what someone else thinks you believe, even by those who feel that belief is foolish. And the stakes have become increasingly higher. More and more people who simply profess belief in Jesus Christ have been tortured and executed in horrible ways.

It's a daunting obstacle to overcome, so most people shy away from the topic, afraid to rock the boat. Peer-pressure on steroids is the norm in this area. Even in "tolerant" societies, people who publically stand to share their Christian faith are (culturally speaking) marginalized, black- listed, thought to be a little kooky – or dreaded as the "Bible thumper". Conform to the rules of silence, don't cross that line, be safe, what difference will it really make? They won't listen anyway.

But what if they do? What if sharing what you know, or at least bringing it up in discussion, makes a major change in the outcome of what's happening? The decisions we make in being true to what we believe can be fearful and agonizing.

I think of the scene from "The Sound of Music" when Lisl's beau, faced with being a "good soldier" or choosing to look the other way and let her and her family escape, chooses to be a "good soldier". The von Trapps are heart-broken over Rolf's choice to betray them to the Nazi's but it was his choice to make and they had to go from there. They run to freedom, leaving him behind with his choice.

I think of historical accounts from "The Diary of Anne Frank" and Corrie Ten Boom's "The Hiding Place" (as well as the Underground Railroad and other times in world history where ordinary people have defied the powerful to help others in time of great distress) where good people risked their lives to hide and to save those whose fate was on the chopping block – and the whistle-blowers who, for promises of special consideration and immunity, turned them into authorities only to realize too late the weight of their choices. Some choices have a greater impact and have longer lasting consequences than we realize when we first decide. Relational betrayal – whether followed by self-righteousness or regret - is nothing new. Look at Cain and Abel, Sampson and Delilah, Judas and Jesus.

Modern-day examples flood us in the news: families divided on the basis of religious expression, genocide based on professions of certain faiths. Some are silenced while others demand unquestioning adherence. The stakes seem higher as each day passes.

I have never had as deep an awareness of the down-side of our God-given freedom to choose. The fear of rejection and the possibilities for great joy or great sorrow, sometimes irrevocably hang in the balance. The heart-break of those who are regarded as inconsequential, foolish or a waste of time by those they care deeply about is profound.

I only recently have begun to get deeper shades of understanding when considering this aspect of God's love for us. He knows what should be done, tells us how to do everything for our perfect peace, good and safety. And we refuse for various reasons - whether full-on disobedience or rebellion, or out of ignorance, distraction or fear. But God displays the appropriate response to this conundrum clearly in so many ways.

In giving us the freedom to choose – our "free will" – He puts Himself in a position to accept our choices, even if it goes against His heart's desire to see us fulfilled, happy, productive and blessed. He told Adam, "You are free to eat from any tree… but you must not eat from [this] tree …for when you eat from it you will certainly die."[54] Clear as crystal in His instructions and the consequences. Adam and Eve chose to disobey. And God abided by their decision.

It broke His heart, but He knew it would. He prepared a solution "before the foundation of the world"[55] to the problem of bad choices. He couldn't keep the consequences from happening. He had already told them the consequences were coming before they disobeyed. He tells us very clearly, we "reap what [we] sow."[56] But His "plans are higher than" ours.[57] Instead of canceling the harvest they sowed, He took it on Himself. He became redemption from our consequences through His self-sacrifice. But even that is not forced on us. When Jesus was hanging on the cross, one man railed at Him, the other repented. Both were guilty; only one chose the redemption. The other did not. Only one was assured of his place in paradise.

Even in this, God gives us the freedom to choose. However, He is anything but a disinterested, apathetic observer to the decision process. The Bible shows He is not unmoved by our reluctance to choose the better path. All over Scriptures, we see God longing for us, pleading and interceding for us, and yes, being patient with our repeated refusals: "The Lord is not slow in keeping his promise, as some understand slowness. Instead he is patient with you, not wanting anyone to perish, but everyone to come to repentance."[58] His heart breaks for some of our choices, knowing all too well how much our wayward or defiant decisions will hurt us. But He allows us to make those choices. And then He offers us a better way: "Jesus said to him, I am the Way and the Truth and the Life; no one comes to the Father except through Me."[59]

Is it any wonder God calls Himself our Father? I don't think anyone on the planet knows the pain of other's wayward choices more deeply than a parent. Think about it. God is completely omniscient. He knows everything, before during and after any of it happens. He knows what we will do, when we will do it, why we will do it and when we won't follow Him, regardless of His desire and instruction for us to do otherwise. The pain involved in watching each of us go through the heart-wrenching torment we sometimes choose for ourselves, or that other people choose for us by their actions, must be geometrically multiplied for Him! As He constrains Himself to allow some of those consequences to shape and motivate us to choose the right path, He also intercedes when He knows it will be too much for us to bear. In my estimation, that agony is a huge downside to omniscience!

It hurts me even on a greatly reduced scale of human experience! There are times when our earthly understanding alone tells us which way our kids should go in certain situations. We want to be able to save them the difficulties we had to go through. We hope that if we share what we know from mistakes we've made that their lives will be less complicated. Will it really? Sometimes yes - sometimes no.

How do we compassionately warn, help without enabling, and still give them the dignity and respect to make choices for themselves even when it pains us to sit back and watch? The fact that we are far from omniscient just adds more pain and fear to our deliberations!

Do we choose to speak, to warn and teach our children – even grown children – what we believe they should do or not do for their own good? Sometimes it's easier to stay quiet. Sometimes we would rather not "rattle that cage". And sometimes we end up in "I told you so mode" which doesn't help build goodwill into the relationship, even if we did try to warn them. What if they "never speak to us again?" What if they stay mad at us and our relationship is affected for years? We're human beings with all the foibles that come with our humanity. If we truly care, we pray that comes through. We don't stop loving them when they choose differently than we hoped they would. Sometimes their choices surprise us and we are proven wrong – sometimes we hope they do prove us wrong!

These spoken and unspoken fears stir up deep emotions, but our reticence is not to be a deterrent to speak. We shouldn't allow ourselves to be silent just because we don't feel comfortable. Our emotional burden is to be a call to prayer. God is to be our guidance in the when, where, how and if to speak in every situation. God does tell us when we are to be silent and when we are to speak. And when the instruction to speak is clearly known, speak you must. The responsibility level born by those who know to tell others is dramatically proclaimed in the Bible in several places.

"Son of man, I have made you a watchman for the people of Israel, so hear the word I **speak and give them warning from me. When** I say to the wicked, 'You wicked person, you will surely die,' and **you do not speak out to dissuade them from their ways**, that wicked person will die for their sin, and **I will hold you accountable for their blood**. But **if you do warn the wicked person to turn from their ways and they do not do so**, they will die for their sin, though **you yourself will be saved**."[60] (emphasis mine). Responsibility is clear here. But so are the rewards! The passage also goes on to say that if you warn them and they do turn away from their wickedness,...hurray! Both you and they are saved. (Tracy paraphrase LOL ☺)

Think this is a little too drastic to apply to your life? Try looking up the word "tell" on Biblegateway.com or in your concordance sometime. How many times do you see someone being instructed to tell someone else about something a tad off-norm that was crucial to an upcoming event.

I mean, think about it: what if, when God told Moses about the first Passover, he thought to himself, "They're gonna think I'm nuts! '...strike the lintel and the two doorposts with the [lamb's] blood. And none of you shall go out of the door of his house until morning' [61] no matter what you hear during the night? Really? That's gonna save them? ...save them from what? "...all the firstborn in the land of Egypt shall die"[62] Yeah, that's gonna go over really big! They'd already told Moses to leave them alone after Pharaoh took away their straw to make bricks.[63] Thanks for nothin' Moses! But what if he hadn't told them? What if they hadn't listened?

And what about Jeremiah? Tell them if they don't repent and change their ways, they are going to be defeated by foreigners and Jerusalem will be destroyed.[64] Are you serious? Yeah! It happened just like he said it would when they discounted the warning as empty prattle. They thought no one could possibly destroy their city! And after they were carried off, he tried to comfort them by telling them, don't worry about it, make the best of this situation 'cause it's gonna be okay, "settle down, plant gardens,...marry,...do not decrease" and when "seventy years are completed... I will" bring you back home.[65] Really? Will you make up your mind? But the historical facts verify all of what Jeremiah told them long before it happened.

The ones who didn't listen to him and tried to fight (including their king) were wiped out, but the ones who were taken to Babylon, who learned what they could, made the best of their situation and still held onto their faith, are held up as heroes hundreds of generations later: Daniel, Shadrach, Meshach, and Abednego, are legendary for their interaction with several kings in the face of foreign conquest. And 70 years later, a group of Israelites returned to their homeland and rebuilt the city.[66]

Even people who do not identify themselves as Christians have heard of these four men. What about Jonah, John the Baptist, Paul, and others? They all had uncomfortable things to tell people - things that went against the grain of conversational protocols. What if they hadn't shared what they were told? Nineveh would have been flattened like Sodom and Gomorrah, there would be no disciples who repented and followed Jesus, the early church would have died when Jesus ascended into heaven and you would not have access to God's Word in print, airwaves and computers all over the world.

We need to be ready; we need to be prepared so that when the opportunity arises we can share with others: "Preach the word; be prepared in season and out of season; correct, rebuke and encourage—with great patience and careful instruction."[67]

Tell them. Prayerfully and humbly. In love and gentleness. Not sure when or how to broach the subject? "If any of you is deficient in wisdom, let him ask of the giving God

[Who gives] to everyone liberally *and* ungrudgingly, without reproaching *or* faultfinding, and it will be given him."[68]

Need a little more reassurance and encouragement? Check out Paul's solution: ask for help from others in prayer! "And [pray] also for me, that [freedom of] utterance may be given me, that I may open my mouth to proclaim boldly the mystery of the good news (the Gospel), For which I am an ambassador in a coupling chain [in prison. Pray] that I may declare it boldly *and* courageously, as I ought to do"[69]

It's not always going to be convenient or comfortable, but we can step forward in faith for the strength to do what needs doing: "Let us then fearlessly *and* confidently *and* boldly draw near to the throne of grace (the throne of God's unmerited favor to us sinners), that we may receive mercy [for our failures] and find grace to help in good time for every need [appropriate help and well-timed help, coming just when we need it]."[70]

We are not responsible for others' reactions, but we are responsible to share, to tell, to admonish and teach, training the younger... bear one another's burdens. "So we take comfort *and* are encouraged *and* confidently *and* boldly say, The Lord is my Helper; I will not be seized with alarm [I will not fear or dread or be terrified]. What can man do to me?"[71]

Paul experienced a break in relationship with some believers who resisted what he had to share with them. It happens. But it worked out better in the long run for all of them!

 Paul had a difficult thing to address with the Corinthian church. It involved not only someone who had committed incest[72], but the fact that the others had not confronted him with it or responded to correct it. In fact, they seemed to have ignored that it was a problem at all[73]. Their silence on the matter translated to acceptance of the behavior. Their reluctance to bring it up allowed it to continue and that was harmful to each of them individually and to the church as a whole. Paul certainly had emotional reservations about not offending these new believers. "For I wrote you out of great sorrow and deep distress [with mental torture and anxiety] of heart, [yes, and] with many tears, not to cause you pain but in order to make you realize the overflowing love that I continue increasingly to have for you."[74] They were "like beloved children"[75] to him.

But Paul had a bigger goal in mind than their acceptance of him and relational equilibrium. Paul flat out told them to expel the offender from their fellowship for his actions.[76] When they did finally reprimand him, it was direct and painful. But then Paul taught them something else. By pressing through his own reluctance in teaching them the first lesson on accountability, it opened the door to the follow-up instruction on living in Grace. He was able to restore an entire town!

"For even though I did grieve you with my letter, I do not regret [it now], though I did regret it; for I see that that letter did pain you, though only for a little while; Yet I am glad now, not because you were pained, but because you were pained into repentance [and so turned back to God]; for you felt a grief such as God meant you to feel, so that in nothing you might suffer loss through us *or* harm for what we did. For godly grief *and* the pain God is permitted to direct, produce a repentance that leads *and* contributes to salvation *and* deliverance from evil, and it never brings regret; but worldly grief (the hopeless sorrow that is characteristic of the pagan world) is deadly [breeding and ending in death]. For [you can look back now and] observe what this same godly sorrow has done for you *and* has produced in you..."[77]

Paul's instruction to them epitomized Grace, the model of what God calls each of us to do toward one another as He has done and continually does for us following repentance – forgiveness and restoration. "The punishment inflicted on him by the majority is sufficient. Now instead, you ought to forgive and comfort him, so that he will not be overwhelmed by excessive sorrow. I urge you, therefore, to reaffirm your love for him. Another reason I wrote you was to see if you would stand the test and be obedient in everything. Anyone you forgive, I also forgive. And what I have forgiven—if there was anything to forgive—I have forgiven in the sight of Christ for your sake, in order that Satan might not outwit us. For we are not unaware of his schemes."[78] Our deceptive enemy schemes and distracts us from truth and love to outwit us and to use our own emotions against us and those we love. When we follow God's prescription for these maladies, we are healed and become powerful through the One Who is always for us.

Godly sorrow leads to repentance and more than just restoration of relationship – much more! Pray for people! There is much more at stake than the day-to-day work, home, playtime, sleep illusion around us!

Pray "[That you may really come] to know [practically, through experience for yourselves] the love of Christ, which far surpasses mere knowledge [without experience]; that you may be filled [through all your being] unto all the fullness of God [may have the richest measure of the divine Presence, and become a body wholly filled and flooded with God Himself]! Now to Him Who, by (in consequence of) the [action of His] power that is at work within us, is able to [carry out His purpose and] do superabundantly, far over *and* above all that we [dare] ask or think [infinitely beyond our highest prayers, desires, thoughts, hopes, or dreams]—To Him be glory in the church and in Christ Jesus throughout all generations forever and ever. Amen (so be it)."[79]

And so it happens today. People like Billy Graham (and all his children!), speaking to millions of people warning and evangelizing on faith have changed lives and influenced the course of history for generations. Ray Comfort and Kirk Cameron through "Way of the Master", Ravi Zacharias, Luis Palau and many others, each in their own arena, are warning and sharing personal testimony and the demonstrable empowerment of Christ in our lifetime. But some don't want to hear. Some don't want to ruffle feathers. Some – including me – sometimes shy away from telling what we've experienced because we don't want to risk the possible strain in relationships that "telling" can cause. Again, the question tries to silence us: What if they won't speak to me again?

But God has an answer to that too. What if it saves? What if it's exactly what they need to hear to pull them out of the mess they're in? What if... Speak the truth in love. Not with condemnation and judgmentalism, but in Grace, in gentleness, in humility, empowerment for good, to dispel fear, lies and division. In Love. Not in fear... (Now that's the rub...)

Oblivion. Even the word brings on dread. The end of it all. What good can come of it? All the behind the scenes wrangling the enemy has used to create the deceptive illusion of "reality" came to a head and overwhelmed my heart during that movie. I WAS afraid, and that fear dominated what I was experiencing in that moment. The fear of those I love not accepting the Truth of the eternal and refusing to finding out what their part of the real "mission" is while we're here drew only panic from my heart. I knew I didn't want to leave unsaid what I was thinking, but how was I going to communicate the thoughts that were crushing me from the inside?

I tried through my sobs to answer my husband's questions as to why this movie had affected me so unexpectedly. He hates to see me unhappy and if tears are involved, he wants to fix it as quickly as possible. The disjointed phrases I was able to get out weren't helping to ease his increasing discomfort.

All I could manage to squeak out at the time was "God has set eternity in men's hearts and we just don't get it!" and "Don't be a Victoria!" The images of books and movies and personal experiences, realizations of the differences between this life that we live in the here and now, being so full of distraction with jobs, paying bills, playing games, raising children, growing older, having hobbies, traveling and so many other things we get to do all filled my head at the same time. I was equating Victoria's insistence on staying in the station to all of us succumbing to the illusion that this physical world is all there is, so-let's-make-the-most-of-it mindset. The spiritual slumber...willfully held on to regardless of the evidence.

I felt like I was trying to explain a reservoir of information through a garden hose. I'm still not sure I was able to communicate, even after I calmed down, what had me so fearful and so desperate to share the importance of the realization I had that night. I am praying God deciphered what I seemed so unable to relay to my husband – and later my children.

I realized that all of it – everything here, no matter how enjoyable or agonizing – is all vanity, just like Solomon said repeatedly in Ecclesiastes. It's all a grand illusion, a smoke screen for what's really happening around us - the eternal us. We are not alone. There is so much more to life than what we see. It can be a comforting thought or an unqualified dread!

Frank Peretti's novels "This Present Darkness" and "Piercing the Darkness" were a clear relay for me, illustrating the "other-ness" with a glimpse into what kind of "others" he perceived working behind the scenes. The visual characterizations of the seen and unseen personalities were so descriptive I could practically see them for myself. Reading these books was not my introduction to this concept, but gave a visual representation to a confirmation of what I already knew to be true. Not everything that impacts us is visible.

God truly _has_ set eternity in men's hearts. The Amplified Bible gives explanation with the statement: "He has made everything beautiful in its time. He also has planted eternity in men's hearts _and_ minds [a divinely implanted sense of a purpose working through the ages which nothing under the sun but God alone can satisfy], yet so that men cannot find out what God has done from the beginning to the end."[80] We have an internal "knowing" that there is something grander, something bigger, more immense than we can possible take in with five senses in ten lifetimes.

Repeated in different ways, in different media throughout history, that sense of eternity, of something bigger and infinite is communicated to us; there truly is "no new thing under the sun"[81] Finite man cannot comprehend everything out there from beginning to end. None of us gets the whole picture - but we all get pieces of the whole. Divinely chosen and custom-fitted pieces specifically designed for us. *Out of necessity*, none of us get the same set of pieces! We need each other. We need to communicate with one another. The pieces fit together; we can't afford to keep them apart. We need to share and interact with one another. And we need to use this opportunity wisely. There's so much at stake!

I woke up one morning a few months ago after a very difficult couple of days. There were several things happening that were definitely NOT comfortable. No matter where I was, there was one of three major situations that were commandeering my peace of mind and had me in knots emotionally. I asked for prayer. I decided to take a deep breath and leave the junk off to one side and just do what I needed to get done in that moment. I tuned the radio to a local Christian station to listen to music on my way to get some groceries. My focus was successfully deflected from the problems, even temporarily, as I reminded myself to trust God in all of it. When I came home, the problems were still very much in play, but I had set them aside. I put the groceries away, said my nighttime prayers and went to bed.

I woke up with a Chris Tomlin song running through my head reminding me that Jesus not only loves me completely, He is for me, He is faithful and He is fully present. With that blanket of peace wrapped around me a verse popped into my head with it – "...in Him all things consist (cohere, are held together)."[82] and the comfort saturated me, bathing my heart in Grace. Everything is under God's complete control, nothing happens without His permission. The transient nature of what we have here in this time-bound existence is evident in bits and pieces of the "bigger-ness" we each feel in our hearts.

A line from a movie, part of what we've seen on You Tube, a familiar saying from a family member, can bring forth laughter or nods of understanding even when you don't quite have the time or the words to relay everything you want to say at that moment. There's something Greater than us.

In a comedy album (yes, it's vinyl and plays on a turntable!) we have of "The Two Thousand Year Old Man", Carl Reiner interviews Mel Brooks as if he had lived for thousands of years and was sharing some deep insights into life. When asked if he believes in an all-knowing being, God, or Yahweh, Mel's character tells of how the cavemen used to bow to Phil, the local bully. When Phil was beating them up one day, lightning came down out of heaven and struck Phil dead. And THAT, he said, was beginning of faith. They all looked up and said (in a sing-song-y kind of voice), "There's something bigger than Phil!"[83]

Let me assure you that there absolutely is something bigger than Phil. And your mortgage. And the current political situation. And the petty disagreements that keep us separated over inconsequential topics of discussion. There is a bigger reality happening all around us that involves a battle with and between unseen forces. We do not have the luxury of not taking sides and sitting this one out. We need to choose. We DO choose. Even not choosing – or choosing not to talk about it – is a choice.

The power of choice has been given to us. And our free-will carries with it an incredible power. The weight of everything we will ever experience here and now (and in our eternal future) depends on some of the choices we make right now. Some choices we get to have a do-over with – others we don't. Sometimes the choices have permanent effects and consequences. Not everyone knows this - and some get upset when you try to tell them. If we're honest enough to admit it, we get upset when others try to tell us too.

But it is increasingly more obvious and less and less deniable that what we can perceive with our natural senses is not our complete reality. There's MORE - much, much more. And our comfort level – or lack of it – with the discussion is not the determining factor of its existence. We don't want to talk about certain subjects. We want to stay within the confines of our own little station. It's safer. It's familiar. But it's not real. We've been deceived by the distraction of the here and now, by what is visible and imminent and tangible. Don't be a Victoria. Don't turn away from the discussion of the unseen. Refusal to dialog doesn't make it less real. It just keeps us out of a vital loop of information.

We need discernment. We're not just supposed to accept anything every Tom, Dick and Harriett says to us, no matter how passionate they are when they say it. But we need to listen to one another. To share this awareness, our experiences, the things that give us strength, and the things that open up new possibilities. Some will be merely amusing, a way to enjoy one another's company. Some will be helpful, a way to ease someone else's journey by sharing with others in similar situations. Some will rock your world and it will never be the same. That's the way it is. Don't shy away from it.

We are relational, eternal and powerful. The direction we choose with those attributes is critical. Fear tries to twist the direction we choose or choose not to take.

Jesus said we are to reject fear – "Do not let your hearts be troubled (distressed, agitated). You believe in *and* adhere to *and* trust in *and* rely on God; believe in *and* adhere to *and* trust in *and* rely also on Me...Peace I leave with you; My [own] peace I now give *and* bequeath to you. Not as the world gives do I give to you. Do not let your hearts be troubled, neither let them be afraid. [Stop allowing yourselves to be agitated and disturbed; and do not permit yourselves to be fearful and intimidated and cowardly and unsettled.]"[84]

Why would He be so insistent about not letting fear get in the way? Because we affect one another more than we know. "For as the body is one and has many members, but all the members of that one body, being many, are one body, so also *is* Christ... For in fact the body is not one member but many. .. But now God has set the members, each one of them, in the body just as He pleased... And the eye cannot say to the hand, "I have no need of you"; nor again the head to the feet, "I have no need of you." No, much rather, those members of the body which seem to be weaker are necessary. And those *members* of the body which we think to be less honorable, on these we bestow greater honor; "[85] We truly are one part in a bigger body, each with our own part to play, function to perform, reason for existence. In Him. He holds all of us and it together!

"For it was in Him that all things were created, in heaven and on earth, things seen and things unseen, whether thrones, dominions, rulers, or authorities; all things were created *and* exist through Him [by His service, intervention] and in *and* for Him. And He Himself existed before all things, and in Him all things consist (cohere, are held together). He also is the Head of [His] body, the church; seeing He is the Beginning, the Firstborn from among the dead, so that He alone in everything *and* in every respect might occupy the chief place [stand first and be preeminent]." [86]

Not sure about the concept of being part of a bigger body? Not sure any of this really makes a difference in the choices you make in the privacy or your own home? in your own life? With you own time?

I went to my second March For Life in Washington DC in January 2015. It was an amazing thing to see a sea of people all gathered for the same purpose – one large body of people gathered to stand for something bigger than themselves, their jobs, their families, the day-to-day considerations. But the big group was made up of dozens of smaller groups and individuals from all over the country. Hundreds of busloads of people, each from their own denominations and churches, Knights of Columbus, Youth For Life, Stand True, advocacy groups like Keep Infants with Down Syndrome (KIDS), National Pro-Life Alliance, Concerned Women for America, and schools like Shanley High School who got to carry the banner out in front of the parade – for Life.

They were gathered to defend, to protect and to loudly proclaim the Truth that Every Life is a Gift. They were standing in the gap to protect unborn lives from one of most dangerous deceptions the enemy uses: that one life doesn't matter that much, that that one life, if it's somehow "damaged" or the "wrong" gender or simply inconvenient is not worth enough time to grow, live, breathe, learn and contribute something to this life, to experience their place in history.

In the panic and uncertainty of those moments when these choices are made, what difference can we very finite, very temporal-minded, very self-centered beings truly fathom about the potential importance that someone we haven't met yet could possibly have on the entire world? It's just one life. It can't possibly be worth the agony and angst I'm going through right now, right?

Check out the Silent No More crew holding their signs, women who made that fearful choice, or had that choice sometimes forcibly thrust upon them for any number of reasons or sources. Their presence and testimonies on the steps of the Supreme Court building in the heart of our capitol year after year attests loudly to the fact that abortion does hurt – and not only that, but this pain can just as assuredly be healed! Consider how many multiplied millions of women with stories similar to mine in that respect are standing there and in different cities in different situations all over the world, since 1974 when 5 people decided that there was no way to legally determine when life begins. They decided that as long as these lives were snuffed out before we could prove their sentient viability, it was legal to terminate their initial growth process.

5 people determined the fate of millions of people with the stroke of a pen. It's not just one life. It's not just the loss of one inconvenient, random chance of an egg or a sperm coming together to set your heart aflutter for a couple weeks or months and then with the help of a facility or a doctor or another broken-hearted, deceived human being determining that one life is more deserving of more time here than another. It's so much bigger than that!

One person deciding the other way would have changed the outcome for millions of people that are no longer here. Due to Roe V. Wade we're missing millions of people on this planet. People that were formed deliberately by God with a specific purpose. People who were supposed to live and grow and face the challenges that developed the unique gifts and characteristics and talents and attitudes and passions for things they cared so deeply about that they would have changed the face of the planet in their specific realm and sphere of influence. And without them, we are less. Not merely in numbers, but in quality of life for all of us! Without them we still suffer cancer. Without them, we miss the teacher that could have encouraged that one difficult kid to greatness. Without them, we miss the firefighter that would have saved that one person in a burning building. Without them we miss the one piece of music that would have triggered a thought that keeps us pressing on in our own difficulties to fulfill part of our purpose. In History.

And it's one, and one and one...added together for 44 years. Multiplied millions who never got to take their place, to do their part, to become the person who did that thing who changed the world. Not for any other reason than some people fell for the ultimate deception that this is all there is: "eat, drink and be merry for tomorrow we die" [87]. The lies are constantly barraging us from inside and out: Get what you can, when you can, before someone else takes it away from you. You are not worth anything more than what you can do in this moment and if my

557

current moment is more important than the moments that may happen for someone else on the other side of right now, then so be it. Those other moments that don't matter to me right now aren't worth the uncomfortability I could experience if I choose a different path.

We are so blinded by the "now" - the eating to work to play to eat to work to play to eat to work mentality - that those who have more money or more influence, or more time or more physical prowess, or more of anything are more valuable than someone who is not born yet, or that are less _____ than you (you fill in the blank) that we miss the incalculable value of one life.

You are treasured. There is no way in God's eyes to put a price tag, a monetary value on how much you mean to Him in the "big picture". You are an irreplaceable, unique thread in the middle of an enormous tapestry that needs to be there in your own place, in your part of the design, to catch the links and the threads of those other strings and threads around you in different parts of the tapestry. Without the connections to the other threads in the tapestry, the weave is weaker, unraveling in critical spots that change the integrity and the strength of this piece.

You matter. And You matter. And He matters. And She matters. And they matter. And when they are missing, We are less.

It's not just a matter of numbers of people, but of choices we make within our own lives. When we take the "easy way out" of any challenge, we affect everyone around us as well. What difference does it make if I over eat, if I drink, if I smoke, if I don't take the initiative to address that anger problem, if I don't get a handle on my personal spending habits, if I open myself up to multiple sexual partners, if I don't reach out to others who are hurting, if I don't make the effort to get to know God personally, if I procrastinate my life away in addictions to video or computer games, TV programs, social media, pornography, or other "harmless" indulgences, "what difference does it make, I'm not hurting anyone". Really?

If we indulge that habit that makes us weaker, or sicker, or distracted, or isolated, we fail to make the contributions to the weave we were designed to make. If we indulge emotional subjugation to destructive tendencies, we not only miss out on what we could accomplish when we are finally free of that bondage, but we also debilitate others who are on the receiving end of our outbursts, teaching them by our actions - and passing on the reliance on – these same tendencies and thereby encouraging them to remain enslaved by the same emotional captivity. And so goes the generational influence of the indebtedness to sin.

God offers a better way, a freedom from subjugation to these temporal roadblocks that elevates us and gets us to look higher than our immediate circumstances. A perspective that gives us encouragement in the immediate dimness of any situation to rise above and see something bigger, something more permanent, something that matters and will continue to exist long after the present situation is nothing more than a blink or an afterthought in life itself.

"The Word became flesh and dwelt among us"[88] for a reason. And the maker of words, the linguist supreme behind language itself shows Himself at every step to encourage us, to teach us, to invite us into relationship with Him. It all involves us so intricately, but it's not about us. It's so much bigger than us – it's about Him. The One - the Alpha and Omega - the Beginning and the End. The One Who is and was and is to come.[89] History – His Story. And we are each and all important because of the individual parts we are called to be in His Story. No one is inconsequential. No one is below consideration, or above another. We each have our contribution to make. Whether we make a 90 or 100 year contribution, or a 30 second contribution that triggers a perspective, a bit of knowledge, and experience that deepens understanding. It's all just as important in the tapestry.

He is calling to you. He is asking you to see the Person behind the reason to surrender, the Purpose behind the struggle with an addiction, the Strength behind the sacrifice that "[that lifts me] out from among the dead [even while in the body]."[90] So we can take our un-encumbered, unhindered, un-enslaved, *victorious* place in His Story.

We are finite. We have no idea how long the thread of our lives is. We don't really know from one day to the next if our plans or expectations for what, when, how or if we will spend the next day, month, or year of our lives will happen. That is one reason David prayed so fervently: "So teach *us* to number our days, That we may gain a heart of wisdom."[91] He will answer your prayer!

We need Wisdom to persevere. We need Wisdom to live in Grace. We need Wisdom to have patience with others – especially when they are doing the same things we do! ☺ I used to challenge the thought that the things that upset us the most are the very things we do in our own lives. I don't do that! I *wouldn't* do those things! But God is not a liar. He said, "You therefore have no excuse…because you who judge are habitually practicing the very same things [that you censure and denounce]."[92] So I asked Him to show me. And He answered that prayer too. I was embarrassed in some cases and mortified in others. It was true. It's just the consequences of me doing it to others didn't have the harmful impact on me that my actions had on them. Acknowledging this reality was a great motivator to get up from the sidelines and cooperate with Him in the process of change!

One of my pet peeves is procrastination. It drives me crazy when someone else's lack of planning, preparation or action in a certain task delays what I need to do or impacts me in some way that I see as harmful. But what if I change my focus? When I use the enemy's accusation of others of their moments of procrastination, as a call to examine my own delays, it gives me the opportunity to cooperate with God on my issues and pass Grace on to others for theirs.

How often has my lack of action, preparation or planning impacted someone else for the worse? How long have I allowed fear of rejection to stop me from contributing my part to the bigger picture of someone else's life? How long have I allowed my reticence for confrontation to keep me from righting a wrong, correcting an error or teaching others what I know? How long will I keep pointing fingers at others to deflect blame as I hold on to "cherished sins"? How much harm did my selfishness and rebellious wandering from age 15 – 24 do to others that I did not consider in my youth? In the here and now: How long will I view others with prideful disdain? How long will I succumb to compulsive eating to satisfy emotional discomfort? How long before I care more about what God thinks and less about other's rejection – and demonstrate those priorities by my actions, or inaction? And what about procrastination: How long did it take me to finish this book? ☺ How long will it take me to get my first book in audio book form? How long will it be before I make the arrangements to get the song God gave me over a decade ago onto paper and in music form to share with others? Well?

I don't know all of it, though I am aware of some of the answers to these ponderings. And it humbles me to repentance and brings me to my knees in prayerful gratitude when I consider His Amazing Grace at each of these steps. God is truly in complete control. There is Grace and forgiveness for our sins, missteps, and delays. God does not bring anything to our attention to condemn us but to encourage us and call us to action. And His perspective is far grander than we have the capacity to grasp. Sometimes things that we see as delays were the necessary waiting periods for all the other threads to be woven into place for His intended impact to happen. "But when the fullness of the time was come, God sent forth his Son..."[93] When all those necessary events and situations had taken place, then He came, "once for all."[94] He was patiently waiting for all the other conditions to be in place. And so it is with us. We are not the same people we were a year ago. Much has happened and we are in a different place than we were. So there is no condemnation for the past. And there is a call forward. "Brothers and sisters, I do not consider myself yet to have taken hold of it. But one thing I do: Forgetting what is behind and straining toward what is ahead, I press on toward the goal to win the prize for which God has called me heavenward in Christ Jesus."[95]

Don't be a Victoria, content with the illusion of business as usual in spite of the evidence. Open your eyes, look to the hills. It's not a game – it *is* war. But it is winnable and worth the effort in the wonderful outcome!

We need to foster a sense of urgency within a peaceful heart that calls out knowing God is in complete control. I must do my part because others are counting on my threads of the tapestry and my pieces of the puzzle to complete their part! "Therefore He says, Awake, O sleeper, and arise from the dead, and Christ shall shine (make day dawn) upon you *and* give you light."[96] Shine your light, sing your song, write your book, take your place, rid yourself of that hindrance, learn what you are lacking, share in others' stories, help someone who is distressed, repent from your defeats and leave them behind, celebrate all the victories, seek the face of the One Who has your answers. Don't procrastinate! It matters; you matter! Prayerfully take your story and make it part of His Story. ☺

It doesn't matter where you start. But it absolutely matters that you do start now. There is little time left - and much to do. Begin today. It is amazing what God does with a very imperfect, but willing heart! I am living proof - and so are you! You have not gotten this far by accident. You are not where you are right now by chance, but by divine providence. I am certain God has been, is and will continue to redeem everything for His glory and our good. In this truth I find peace in the storms, from accusation, self-condemnation and guilt. Let Him take your thread and weave it where He wants it to go. Let Him take the puzzle pieces that seem so jumbled all around you and show you were they fit. Once a vessel is broken and then mended, it is stronger than it was at first because of the mending process – and so it can be with you. Let Him take all the broken pieces you feel your life is and make the most amazing mosaic the world has ever seen. Beautiful, strong and re-purposed to shine!   May this become your prayer as it has become mine:

My Daddy, Father God,
Enlighten what is dark in me...
Strengthen what is weak in me...
Mend what is broken in me...
Heal what is sick in me...
And lastly,
Revive whatever peace and love has died in me.
In the Name of Your Precious Son, Jesus
My Savior, my Redeemer, my Brother,
Amen.

***

Footnotes

[1] Rom. 1:20 (NKJV)

[2] Eph. 5:14-15

[3] John 10:10a (amp)

[4] John 10:9 (amp)

[5] Isa. 26:4 (NIV)

[6] John 10:10b (amp)

[7] Rom 10:13(KJV)

[8] Matt. 7:24-27

[9] Eph. 6:15

[10] 2 Tim. 2:19

[11] Heb. 12:11

[12] Heb. 4:15-16

[13] Prov. 18:24

[14] John 15:13-15 (NIV)

[15] Heb. 11:32

[16] Heb 12:1-3

[17] Prov. 27:17

[18] Ps. 14:2

[19] Matt. 11:28

[20] Ps. 91 (amp)

[21] Ps. 121:1-2

[22] Ps. 121:8

[23] 2 Kings 6:16-18

[24] ibid v. 21

[25] ibid. v. 22

[26] 2 Tim 2:25-26 (amp)

[27] 2 Kings 6:23 (amp)

[28] Luke 6:27-28

[29] 1 Sam 17:47, 1 Sam 25:28, 2 Chron. 20:15, Prov. 21:31, Isa. 13:14, Zeph. 1:14

[30] Rom. 12:21 (amp)

[31] Ps. 3:3

[32] Prov. 25:21-22

[33] footnote from Proverbs 25:21-23, pg. 726 The Amplified Bible, Zondervan Expanded Edition, copyright 1954, 1958, 1962, 1964, 1965, 1987 by The Lockman Foundation

[34] 1 Cor. 16:9 (amp)

[35] John 10:9 (amp)

[36] Exo. 23:20 (amp)

[37] Prov. 4:23(amp)

[38] 1 Chron. 22:3(amp)

[39] Prov. 24:12 (amp)

[40] Luke 21:34(amp)

[41] Deut. 4:9(amp)

[42] Nah. 3:12-14(amp)

[43] "Terminator" 1984 James Cameron/Gale Ann Hurd, Orion Pictures

[44] ibid

[45] Matt. 24:36, Mark 13:32

[46] Heb 11:7(amp)

[47] Phil. 4:7(amp)

[48] 1 Pet. 3:15(NIV)

[49] Isa. 60:18 (amp)

[50] Prov. 27:3 (amp)

[51] 2Kin. 6:23

[52] "Oblivion" 2013 Joseph Kosinski

[53] 2 Cor. 11:14 (NIV)

[54] Gen. 2:16-17 (NIV)

[55] 1 Pet. 1:20 (amp)

[56] Gal. 6:7 (amp)

[57] Isa. 55:9 (NIV)

⁵⁸ 2 Pet. 3:9 (NIV)

⁵⁹ John 14:6 (NIV)

⁶⁰ Ezek. 33:7-9 (NIV)

⁶¹ Exod. 12:22 (NKJV)

⁶² Exod. 11:5 (NKJV)

⁶³ Exod. 5:21 (NKJV)

⁶⁴ Jer. 21:4-10 (NIV)

⁶⁵ Jer. 29:5, 6, 10 (NKJV)

⁶⁶ Ezra 9:9, Neh. 7-8

⁶⁷ 2 Tim. 4:2 (NIV)

⁶⁸ Jas. 1:5 (amp)

⁶⁹ Eph. 6:19 (amp)

⁷⁰ Heb. 4:16 (amp)

⁷¹ Heb. 13:6 (amp)

⁷² 1 Cor. 5:5, 2 Cor. 2:5 (amp)

⁷³ 1 Cor. 5:1-2 (NIV)

[74] 2 Cor. 2:4 (amp)

[75] 1 Cor. 4:14 (NIV)

[76] 1 Cor. 5:12 (NIV)

[77] 2 Cor. 7:8-11 (amp)

[78] 2 Cor. 2:6-11 (NIV)

[79] Eph. 3:19-21 (amp)

[80] Eccl. 3:11 (amp)

[81] Eccl. 1:9 (amp)

[82] Col. 1:17 (amp)

[83] "Two Thousand and Thirteen" 1973 Carl Reiner/Mel Brooks, Warner Bros.

[84] John 14:1, 27 (amp)

[85] 1 Cor. 12:12, 14, 18, 22-23 (NIV)

[86] Col 1:16-18 (amp)

[87] Isa. 22:13

[88] John 1:4a (NKJV)

[89] Rev. 1:8 (amp)

[90]Phil. 3:11b (amp)

[91] Ps. 90:12 (NIV)

[92] Rom. 2:1 (amp)

[93] Gal 4:4 (NKJV)

[94] Heb 9:12 (NKJV)

[95] Phil 3:13-14 (NIV)

[96] Eph. 5:14 (amp)

Suggested Resources

"This Present Darkness" by Frank Piretti

"Piercing the Darkness" by Frank Piretti

"Love and War" by John and Stasi Eldgredge

"Captivating" by John and Stasi Eldgredge

"So Long Insecurty" by Beth Moore

"Idol Lies" by Dee Brestin

"Bondage Breaker" by Neil Anderson

"Victory Over the Darkness" by Neil Anderson

"Reclaiming Surrendered Ground" by Jim Logan

The Book of Ecclesiastes!

The Book of Proverbs!

Epilogue

This book has been my sharing of some of the battles with, for and against several of the invisible foes I have faced. Some of them come from within me: pride, fear, anger, rebellion. Some battles I am grateful to have lost – because in losing what I thought I was fighting for, I gained so much more in the process. In other battles, I forced my way and my will and won what I fought for - and lost more than I thought possible. The deceptions I have believed in the past have cost me dearly. I so much want to spare others the weight of those defeats. But ironically, as a result of God's redemption in each one of those defeats, I have been made over, stronger, less fearful, and more aware of the cunning foe and his schemes to distract, discourage and destroy anything good, anything praiseworthy, anything that would draw us closer to the One Who loved us so much He gave His all for us. For me. And for you.

The "unseen" Hero of my story saved me from myself, from my sin, and wrapped His royal robe around my shoulders, calling me Beautiful and gave me the ability and confidence to believe it. He can do the same for you. Romans chapter 8 has some amazing words of encouragement. Here are some highlights, and I pray you'll read all of it for yourself: "Therefore there is now no condemnation for those who are in Christ Jesus...the law of the Spirit of life in Christ Jesus has freed us from the law of sin and death...For the Spirit which you have received is...the Spirit of adoption by which we cry, 'Abba! Father!'...we are children of God...I consider the sufferings of this present time are not worth being compared with the glory that is about to be revealed...so too, the Holy Spirit comes to our aid and bears us up in our weakness...the Spirit intercedes in behalf of the saints in harmony with God's will. And we know that all things work together for good for those who love God and are called according to [His] design and purpose...If God be for us, who can be against us?...Amid all these things we are more than conquerors and gain a surpassing victory through Him Who loved us. For I am persuaded beyond doubt that neither death nor life, nor angels, nor principalities, nor things impending and threatening, nor things to come nor powers, nor height nor depth nor anything else in all creation will be able to separate us from the love of God in Christ Jesus our Lord."

Nothing. Not a hard childhood, not a divorce, not an abortion, not misunderstandings, not your own sin, not other people's decisions, not a bully, not drugs, not rape, not murder, not wealth, not poverty, not fame, not popularity, not shame. Nothing in all creation can ever separate you from the Love of God in Christ Jesus.

You can read the most amazing words of comfort and encouragement and never appropriate them for yourself. It took me years to get it. And I hope you get it sooner than I did. I hope you grab on for dear life and never lose sight of the unseen reality His Word can open up to you. I pray my Stories from this well - my personal experiences - have opened up possibilities and opportunities you've never taken notice of before. They are there. They are for "whosoever will". "Whosoever shall call upon the name of the Lord shall be saved"[1]. Not might, not could, not maybe in the by and by, but suck it up for now, live in fear of not quite making it and continually trying in your own strength to keep pulling yourself up by your own bootstraps. Everyone who calls on His name will be saved. Attempting life any other way will only trip you up and lead to disappointment and frustration. Reach up. Look up. His arm is not too short to reach you no matter where you are – He said so. He promised. And He is faithful to keep His promises. Always.

I'd like to share something else with you. Powerful words I found on the website for Casting Crowns about a song I first heard when I was half-way through writing this book.

"...When Jesus met the woman at the well, he talked to her about spiritual water, symbolic of eternal life in him. She did what lost people do. She related everything to the physical, to the here and now. When he offered living water, she hoped he meant providing her a shortcut to the daily chore of drawing water, and she likely was a little cynical in her response. Jesus said, "I'll give you water and you'll never thirst again." The Samaritan woman was like, "Oh, yeah? Well, give me some of that water so I won't have to come back to this well anymore." This woman thought she was standing by a well and talking to a man, but really she was standing by a hole in the ground and talking to the Well. [*my note: I LOVE that part!*] We're all like this woman. We come to Jesus and we think we already have our wells that sustain us. Our wells are called control or power or approval or talent or even entitlement. When we already have what we think is going to fulfill us, we usually just come to Jesus only to ask him to sprinkle blessings on our thing so our thing will work even better. But Jesus isn't life enhancement. Jesus is life. All he asks is that we take what we think are our wells, realize that they are nothing but dry holes in the ground, and leave it all behind. He asks us to come to the one true Well."[2]

The song that was written by Matthew West and Mark Hall on this topic could not possibly summarize the theme of this book better if I tried a hundred years. With their permission, I'd like to share it with you:

The Well

I have what you need, But you keep on searchin,
I've done all the work, But you keep on workin,
When you're runnin on empty, And you can't find the remedy,
Just come to the well.

You can spend your whole life, Chasin what's missing,
But that empty inside, It just ain't gonna listen.

When nothing can satisfy, And the world leaves you high and dry,
Just come to the well

And all who thirst will thirst no more,
And all who search will find what their souls long for,
The world will try, but it can never fill,
So leave it all behind, and come to the well

So bring me your heart No matter how broken,
Just come as you are, When your last prayer is spoken,
Just rest in my arms a while, You'll feel the change my child,
When you come to the well

And all who thirst will thirst no more,
And all who search will find what their souls long for,
The world will try, but it can never fill,
So leave it all behind, and come to the well

Yeah
Leave it all behind

The world will try, but it can never fill... leave it all behind

And now that you're full,
Of love beyond measure,
Your joy's gonna flow,
Like a stream in the desert,
Soon all the world will see that living water is found in Me,
Cuz you came to the well

And all who thirst will thirst no more,
And all who search will find what their souls long for,
The world will try, but it can never fill,
So leave it all behind, and come to the well[3]

Leave it all behind. Everything you thought was giving you what you desperately needed: personal perfection, avoiding rejection, comfort, addiction, even religion! Drink deeply from the well of refreshment, encouragement and Truth. It will set you free from all that the world promises and can never deliver. And when you're enjoying that water, go back for the others. Share your own stories; you have at least one that bears repeating! Let God redeem your story His Way. It will amaze you what happens!

We never walk this path alone. In addition to Jesus, the Living Water and the Holy Spirit to comfort and convict us to repentance, God gives us many tutors, many mentors, many opportunities to help us along the Way. Please use the references and resource lists at the end of each chapter - and the people God divinely placed in your path - to learn from some godly men and women, to mentor others and do your part to help the Body of Christ work together better. So many people have had a part in my journey and I am grateful for their courage and willingness to live their lives out in the open for me to learn from their successes and mistakes!

I pray that you will take the time to share your life stories with the ones you love instead of allowing distractions and modern appliances to tell you what you need, drawing you into ever-enclosing circles around the TV, video games, cell phones and social media that don't require any real personal contact – engage fully in the journey of the heart.

That is exactly what God intended when James penned "confess to one another therefore your faults (your slips, your false steps, your offenses, your sins) and pray [also] for one another, that you may be healed and restored [to a spiritual tone of mind and heart]...."[4] We can avoid many pitfalls that we need not attend; if we only seek God's perfect Wisdom to perceive the traps the enemy has set along our path. We can stand strong and not fall for them! When your house is built on a sure foundation, the winds can blow and not blow you over! The Living Word will lead the Way to Wisdom worth holding onto.

May God bless and keep you in His perfect Peace. May you know the height and depth and length and breadth of the love God has for you. May you always be enraptured with His beauty, as He is in yours. May you truly come to believe that you were created in and with special purpose, designed and knit together by God Himself, each detail thought out well in advance so you can allow Him to maximize your potential AND dependence on Him as your Source. Live as if each person around you were Jesus, and one day when He is, we will have no cause for embarrassment! Until we meet in the air...I will see you at the Well! God Bless you~

Footnotes

[1] Rom. 10:13 (KJV)

[2] https://www.castingcrowns.com/music/lyrics/well

[3] "The Well" Words and Music by Mark Hall and Matthew West

Copyright © 2011 Sony/ATV Music Publishing LLC, My Refuge

Music, Songs of Southside Independent Music Publishing LLC,

External Combustion Music and Songs for Delaney.

[4] Jas. 5:17 (amp)

About the Author

Tracy is a Connecticut native, happily married for 32 years to her husband, Stephen. She is the mother of two and grandmother of three. In addition to her present position as Postmaster in her local post office, she enjoys gardening, cooking and traveling.

She has been a member of Christian Fellowship Church in Scotland CT for 24 years. Her first publication, "The Power of Choices", released in 2010, is her testimony concerning her abortion experience. She shares a candid look at the unintended consequences and unexpected devastation of post-abortion distress - and the healing she never dreamed was possible.

This second book, "Stories From the Well", shares her personal journey through issues prevalent in our society, including questioning God's existence and character, the cultural inclination toward divorce, how to successfully address anger issues, the need for encouragement, learning to trust and the absolute necessity of personal faith and preparation for difficulty. It also includes an updated version of her post-abortion testimony.

Tracy wants to maximize her gifts of writing, singing and teaching to impact others by sharing her own experiences and the lessons she is learning along the way, speaking at schools, churches and events. She also facilitates the post-abortion Bible study "Forgiven and Set Free" by Linda Cochrane for others who are struggling with accepting God's forgiveness in the aftermath of abortion through her local Pregnancy Resource Centers.

www.ingramcontent.com/pod-product-compliance
Lightning Source LLC
Chambersburg PA
CBHW060231100426
42742CB00011B/1508